THE CANADIAN MILITIA

THE CANADIAN MILITIA

From 1855
An Historical Summary

by
David A. Morris, CD, QOR
with a foreword by
C.P. Stacey, OC, OBE, CD, PhD
former Director, Historical Section, General Staff, Ottawa

THE BOSTON MILLS PRESS

This book could never have been completed without the help and encouragement of my wife.

Canadian Cataloguing in Publication Data

Morris, David A. (David Adley), 1946-
   The Canadian Militia, From 1855
ISBN 0-919822-51-7
1. Canada.   Canadian Army — History.   I. Title.

UA600.M67 1983   355.3'1'0971   C83-090128-0

Published in Canada by:
   The Boston Mills Press
   98 Main Street, Erin, Ontario N0B 1T0

We gratefully acknowledge the financial assistance of the Canada Council, the Ontario Arts Council and the Office of the Secretary of State.

Winners of the
Heritage Canada
Communications Award

American Association
for State and Local History
Award Winner

Canada: from the Huron-Iroquoian "kennata", "a collection of huts" (village)

In 1534, Jacques Cartier (the French explorer who was the first European to penetrate the interior of North America) encountered Iroquois tribesmen who told of "kennata" further up from where the "great river" (St. Lawrence) emptied into the gulf near where they had met. Cartier was directed upriver to "Stadacona" and "Hochelaga" (Indian villages on the sites of present-day Quebec City and Montreal, respectively). These place-names were to re-appear much later in the "Hochelaga Fusiliers" and "Stadacona Rifles" of the "Volunteer Militia of Canada". "Kennata" was understood by Jacques Cartier to be the name of the "country" in which these settlements were found rather than a general term for the settlements themselves. His journals thereafter referred to the land he had discovered as "Canada".

Foreword

It is a pleasure to introduce this valuable volume by David Morris on the Canadian Militia. This book is the product of tremendous research and has clearly been a true labour of love. We should be grateful to the author for the years of patient and dedicated effort he has devoted to eliciting the historical details of the many units that have served Canada in peace and war since the early days of Queen Victoria's reign. The military organizations whose story is encapsulated herein have helped to make Canadian history; many of them are still making it! Service and sacrifice in many quarters of the world are recorded in the battle honours which have been too numerous to list in their entirety. It is worth recalling that the militia units which have been chronicled by Mr. Morris were kept alive through the years by the unselfish efforts of innumerable Canadians whose only rewards were the pleasures of comradeship and the consciousness of service. This is what Burke called "the cheap defence of nations". Even the "reformers" who in recent years have done so much harm to Canada's military forces have not been so foolish as to lay hands on the regimental system which is the great strength of the army. This historical record of our regiments recalls the encouraging fact that behind the flimsy facade of "unification", Canada still possesses in essentials a Navy, an Army and an Air Force which are ready to serve, as they have before, in an hour of need.

C. P. Stacey

INTRODUCTION

The writer has not attempted a comprehensive history of Canada's militia; rather, a chronology of the development and organization of that force in readiness upon which our country has based its' substantial contribution to victory in all conflicts forced upon it.

NOTE

The designation "militia" may be applied to all military units (excepting, that is, those of the Royal Canadian Navy and the Royal Canadian Air Force) for prior to the authorization of a "Canadian Army" in 1940, there was in existence a "Permanent Active Militia" (more commonly referred to as the "Permanent Force") and a "Non-Permanent Active Militia" (more commonly referred to as the "Militia"). With the advent of the "Canadian Army", the "Permanent Active Militia" was re-designated the "Active Force" and the "Non-Permanent Active Militia" was re-designated the "Reserve Force". These elements were further re-designated in 1954 as the "Regular" and "Militia" components of the "Canadian Army".

Canadian militia tradition may be considered as having originated in the "militia companies", one (or more) of which was associated with each parish in New France (Quebec). As early as 1651, the "captain of the inhabitants of Three Rivers" had been instructed to require that his settlers maintain arms and take turns at guard duty as a result of the almost-constant marauding of the Iroquois. During the attack by the New Englanders on Quebec City in 1690, the majority of the defenders were drawn from the "militia". These French-speaking Canadian "militiamen", who fought in defence of their settlements in New France, were spread throughout the regular battalions during the last campaigns of the French regime in Canada. Following the capitulation of New France in 1760, the existing system of "militia companies" was incorporated within the British administration of their new "Province of Quebec". A battalion of "Canadians" (as His Majesty's new subjects in Quebec were referred to) was organized in 1764 for service during the Pontiac rising. This battalion, which accompanied British regular troops in the relief of Detroit, did not engage in any fighting but did receive praise for its efficient service.

During the American Revolution/War of Independence (1775-1783), there was in existence an "American Establishment" of the British Army, one regiment of which may be considered as being perpetuated by a Canadian militia regiment. This establishment included the following units:

The "Queen's Rangers" or "1st American Regiment", which had been formed by the amalgamation of the "Queen's Loyal Virginians" and the "King's Rangers", may be considered as being perpetuated by "The Queen's York Rangers (1st American Regiment) (R.C.A.C.) (Militia)".

The "Volunteers of Ireland" or "2nd American Regiment"

The "New York Volunteers" or "3rd American Regiment"

The "King's American Regiment" or "4th American Regiment"

The "British Legion" or "5th American Regiment"

The Constitutional Act of 1791 had re-organized the "Province of Quebec" (which had consisted of much of present-day Ontario and Quebec) as the separate colonies of Upper Canada (Ontario) and Lower Canada (Quebec). On 31 March 1793, during the second session of the first parliament of Upper Canada which was held at Newark (now Niagara-on-the-Lake), legislation introducing the first "militia act" was passed, the governing principle being universal liability for military service of the entire male population (between the ages of 16 and 50) who were obliged to enroll in the militia (neglect of which resulted in a fine of $4.00). This "Sedentary Milita" was divided into "regiments", the "companies" of which were mustered and inspected twice annually by their appointed captains. Muster parades were lated reduced to an annual debacle in celebration of the King's birthday. It must be emphasized that this "militia", which numbered approximately 4,000 men in 1793, was neither armed, nor uniformed, nor paid! The militia act was later amended to include men of up to 60 in the annual muster.

The "Queen's Rangers", a locally-recruited regiment under command of the Lieutenant-Governor, was formed in Upper Canada in 1792 and employed in the construction of fortifications and public roads until disbanded in 1802. Due to the withdrawal of British troops from North America as a result of the Napoleonic Wars, authorization was given for "provincial" regiments to be formed in their respective colonies. The "Royal New Brunswick Regiment" and the "Royal Nova Scotia Regiment" thereby came into existence in 1793. Both regiments were subsequently elevated in status to that of "fencibles" whose members were liable for general service in North America. The "Newfoundland Regiment of Fencible Infantry" was formed in 1795.

In 1796, the "Royal Canadian Volunteer Regiment" was formed in Lower Canada. Between 1796 and 1799, detachments of the regiment were involved in the construction of Fort St. Joseph (on that island in the channel connecting Lake Huron with Lake Superior) and Fort Malden (near Amherstburg on the Detroit River). The three "fencible" regiments and the "Royal Canadian Volunteer Regiment" were disbanded in 1802 as a result of the Treaty of Amiens which had restored peace to the warring powers of Europe. Upon the outbreak of further hostilities in Europe in 1803, "fencible" regiments were again formed in New Brunswick, Nova Scotia and Newfoundland. In 1810, the "New Brunswick Regiment of Fencible Infantry" was elevated in status to that of a "regiment of the line" and re-designated the "104th (New Brunswick) Regiment of Foot".

Prior to the Anglo-American War of 1812 to 1814, Major-General Sir Isaac Brock (Commander-in-Chief of British Forces in Upper Canada) had proposed that two companies be selected from each regiment of the "Sedentary Militia" and designated "flank companies" which were to be trained six times per month until properly trained and then once monthly. The remaining "service companies" were to be "embodied" for active service only when necessary as a last resort. The "flank companies", which provided a trained nucleus that could be depended upon in time of emergency, were the core of the militia in Upper Canada and, numbering approximately 800 men upon the outbreak of war in 1812, were "called out" to concentrate on the Niagara frontier. At the Battle of Queenston Heights (1812), one "flank company" from each of the "5th Regiment, Lincoln Militia" and the "2nd Regiment, York Militia" and both companies from the "3rd Regiment, York Militia" were in action. In February of 1813, the legislature of Upper Canada authorized the formation of a "Volunteer Incorporated Militia Battalion" for service during the war and offered a bounty of $8.00 to each man upon enlistment. The majority of volunteers had already seen service as members of the "flank companies".

The "104th (New Brunswick) Regiment of Foot", which had been transferred to Upper Canada in 1813, fought at both Fort George and the Battle of Beaver Dams in 1813 and at both the Battle of Lundy's Lane and Fort Erie in 1814. The regiment was awarded the battle-honour "NIAGARA" for its' service in that campaign. The "Nova Scotia Fencible Infantry" remained on garrison duty in the maritime colonies throughout the Anglo-American War of 1812 to 1814. The "Royal Newfoundland Fencible Infantry", detachments of which fought at Fort Detroit in 1812, both Fort York and Fort George in 1813 and at Fort Michilimackinac in 1814, may be considered as being peprpetuated by "The Royal Newfoundland Regiment (Militia)". The "Glengarry Fencible Light Infantry", which may be considered as being perpetuated by "The Stormont, Dundas and Glengarry Highlanders (Militia)", was awarded the battle-honour "NIAGARA" for its' service at the Battle of Lundy's Lane in 1814. Detachments of the regiment fought at both Fort York and Fort George in 1813 and at both Fort Ontario (Oswego, New York) and Fort Erie in 1814.

The "Select Embodied Militia", which had been formed in Lower Canada from men of the "Sedentary Militia", fought at the Battle of Chateauguay (near Montreal) in Lower Canada. A "Canadian Fencible Infantry Regiment", which had been formed in Lower Canada prior to the Anglo-American War of 1812 to 1814, fought at Chateauguay (near Montreal) in Lower Canada and at Chrysler's Farm (near Morrisburg) in Upper Canada. Both of these battles were fought in 1813. The "Provincial Corps of Light Infantry" (or "Canadian Voltigeurs") fought at both Chateauguay and Chrysler's Farm and may be considered as being perpetuated by "Les Voltigeurs de Quebec (Milice)".

The "Volunteer Incorporated Militia Battalion" concentrated at York (now Toronto) for training prior to its' move in July of 1814 to the Niagara frontier where, with a strength of approximately 300, it went into action at the Battle of Lundy's Lane and suffered casualties of 142 all ranks killed, wounded, taken prisoner or missing. Lieutenant-General Sir Gordon Drummond, in his official despatch, referred to "the very creditable and excellent defence made by the Incorporated Militia Battalion". In recognition of its' service, the battalion was presented regimental colours upon which was inscribed the battle-honour "NIAGARA".

The "Provincial Dragoons", which served on the lines of communication between Montreal and the Niagara frontier, may be considered as being perpetuated by "57 Field Regiment (2nd/10th Dragoons), R.C.A. (Militia)". An "incorporated artillery company" and the "Corps of Provisional Artillery Drivers" were formed in Lower Canada to assist the regular artillerymen during the war.

Thus was a strong military tradition established in Canada. It must be emphasized that regular British troops ("the scum of the earth . . . enlisted for drink", according to the Duke of Wellington) bore the brunt of battle in defence of Canada during the Anglo-American War of 1812 to 1814.

Subsequently, a "Montreal Rifle Corps" and the "Royal Montreal Cavalry" were in existence at various times. The "1st Toronto Artillery Company" and the "Royal Montreal Artillery" both were "called out" for active service during the "rebellion in the Canadas" (1837) which led to the eventual establishment of responsible government for the British colonies in North America. A battalion of "incorporated militia", the personnel of which were provided by the counties of Durham, Northumberland, Prince Edward and Simcoe and the towns of Kingston and Perth, garrisoned the "military establishment" at Penetanguishene from 1840 until 1843. This establishment had been organized as a result of the terms of peace ending the War of 1812 to 1814 which required that British forces vacate their bases on the upper lakes.

In 1840, the "Royal Canadian Rifle Regiment", a regular regiment of the British Army to be recruited in Canada from veterans having not less than seven years of service in a "regiment of the line", was organized for garrison service along the Canadian-American border. This regiment served at Penetanguishene from 1846 until 1851. The strain upon the resources of the British Army owing to the Crimean War (1854-1856) was such that the colonies were asked to assume a greater share in their own defence. As a result, the combined legislature (which had been established due to the union in 1841 of the colonies of Upper and Lower Canada following the rebellions of 1837) passed a new "militia act" in 1855. This act authorized the formation of the "Volunteer Militia" from which is descended the present "Canadian Militia". The first units of this armed, uniformed and paid "Volunteer Militia of Canada" were organized as follows:

The "First Volunteer Militia Rifle Company of Montreal" (authorized on 31 August 1855) is still in existence as "A" Company of "The Canadian Grenadier Guards (6th Battalion, The Canadian Guards) (Militia)".

The "First Volunteer Militia Rifle Company of Quebec City" (authorized on 31 August 1855) was disbanded in 1861.

The "Volunteer Militia Field Battery of Quebec City" (authorized on 31 August 1855) is still in existence as "57 Field Battery, R.C.A.".

The "Volunteer Militia Company of Foot Artillery of Quebec City" (authorized on 31 August 1855) was disbanded in 1874.

The "First Troop of Volunteer Militia Cavalry of the County of Frontenac" (authorized on 20 September 1855) was incorporated within the "4th Regiment of Cavalry" which, after subsequent re-organizations and re-designations, was disbanded in 1965 as the "4th Princess Louise Dragoon Guards (Militia)".

The "2nd Volunteer Militia Rifle Company of Montreal (authorized on 27 September 1855) is still in existence as "B" Company of "The Canadian Grenadier Guards (6th Battalion, The Canadian Guards (Militia)".

The "Volunteer Militia Rifle Company of Brockville" (authorized on 27 September 1855) is still in existence as "A" Company of "The Brockville Rifles (Militia)".

The "1st Volunteer Militia Rifle Company of St. Catharines" (authorized on 27 September 1855) is still in existence as "A" Company of "The Lincoln and Welland Regiment (Militia)".

The "Volunteer Militia Troop of Cavalry of St. Catharines" (authorized on 27 September 1855) was incorporated within the "2nd Regiment of Cavalry" which, after subsequent re-organizations and re-designations, was disbanded in 1970 as "57 Field Regiment (2nd/10th Dragoons), R.C.A. (Militia)".

The "1st Volunteer Militia Troop of Cavalry of Montreal" (authorized on 27 September 1855) is still in existence as "A" Squadron of "The Royal Canadian Hussars (Montreal) (Militia)".

The "Volunteer Militia Field Battery of Ottawa" (authorized on 27 September 1855) is still in existence as "2 Field Battery, R.C.A.".

The "Volunteer Militia Field Battery of Montreal" (authorized on 27 September 1855) is still in existence as "7 Field Battery, R.C.A.".

The "1st Volunteer Militia Rifle Company of Kingston" (authorized on 14 November 1855) is still in existence as "A" Company of "The Princess of Wales' Own Regiment (Militia)".

The "Volunteer Militia Company of Foot Artillery of Kingston" (authorized on 14 November 1855) was re-organized in 1856 as a field battery which after subsequent re-organization and re-designation as "32 Anti-Tank Battery, R.C.A." was incorporated within "The Brockville Rifles (Militia)".

The "Volunteer Militia Field Battery of Hamilton" (authorized on 6 December 1855) is still in existence as "11 Field Battery, R.C.A.".

The "1st Volunteer Militia Troop of Cavalry of the County of Wentworth" (authorized on 20 December 1855) was disbanded in 1865.

The "1st Volunteer Militia Rifle Company of Hamilton" (authorized on 27 December 1885) is still in existence as "A" Company of "The Royal Hamilton Light Infantry (Wentworth Regiment) (Militia)".

The "2nd Volunteer Militia Rifle Company of Hamilton" (authorized on 27 December 1855) is still in existence as "B" Company of "The Royal Hamilton Light Infantry (Wentworth Regiment) (Militia)".

The "2nd Volunteer Militia Rifle Company of Kingston" (authorized on 27 December 1855) is still in existence as "B" Company of "The Princess of Wales' Own Regiment (Militia)".

The "Volunteer Militia Rifle Company of Barrie" (authorized on 27 December 1885) is still in existence as 'B" Company of "The Grey and Simcoe Foresters (Militia)".

The "1st Troop of Volunteer Militia Cavalry of the County of York" (authorized on 27 December 1855) is still in existence as "A" Squadron of "The Governor-General's Horse Guards (Militia)".

The "2nd Troop of Volunteer Militia Cavalry of the County of York" (authorized on 27 December 1855) is still in existence as "B" Squadron of "The Governor-General's Horse Guards (Militia)".

Due to the further strain placed upon the British Army as a result of the Indian Mutiny (1857-1858), the British government, with the concurrence of the government of the united Province of Canada, authorized the recruiting in Canada of a regular British regiment to be designated the "100th (Prince of Wales' Royal Canadian) Regiment of Foot". This regiment was permitted to carry the battle-honour "NIAGARA" that had been awarded to the previous "100th Regiment of Foot" which participated in the capture of the American fort at the mouth of the Niagara River in 1813 during the Anglo-American War of 1812 to 1814. Recruiting for the "100th (Prince of Wales' Royal Canadian) Regiment of Foot" was carried out at London, Toronto, Kingston, Montreal and Quebec City. The regiment mustered at the Citadel in Quebec City and was later in garrison at Gibraltar, Malta and in the United Kingdom. In 1881, the regiment was re-designated

"1st Battalion, The Prince of Wales' Leinster Regiment (Royal Canadians)" which was later in garrison at Halifax immediately prior to serving in South Africa during the "Boer" War.

In 1859, authorization was given for the independent "companies of rifles" to be formed into "regiments" according to the preference of the members of the particular units. The following regiments were thus formed between 1859 and 1863:

The "First 'Prince of Wales' Rifles'" (authorized in 1859 as the "First Battalion, Volunteer Militia Rifles of Canada") was amalgamated with the "6th 'Hochelaga Fusiliers'" in 1898 and is still in existence as "The Canadian Grenadier Guards (6th Battalion, The Canadian Guards) (Militia)".

The "2nd 'Queen's Own Rifles'" (authorized in 1860 as the "2nd Battalion, Volunteer Militia Rifles of Canada") is still in existence as "The Queen's Own Rifles of Canada (Militia)".

The "3rd 'Victoria Rifles'" (authorized in 1862 as the "3rd Battalion, Volunteer Militia Rifles of Canada") was disbanded in 1965 as "The Victoria Rifles of Canada (Militia)".

The "4th 'Chasseurs Canadiens'" (authorized in 1862 as the "4th Battalion, Volunteer Militia Rifles of Canada") was disbanded in 1936 as "Les Chasseurs Canadians (Non-Permanent Active Militia)".

The "5th 'Royal Light Infantry'" (authorized in 1862 as the "5th Battalion, Volunteer Militia Rifles of Canada") is still in existence as "The Black Watch (Royal Highland Regiment) of Canada (Militia)".

The "6th 'Hochelaga Fusiliers'" (authorized in 1862 as the "6th Battalion, Volunteer Militia Rifles of Canada") was amalgamated with the "First 'Prince of Wales' Rifles'" in 1898 and is still in existence as "The Canadian Grenadier Guards (6th Battalion, The Canadian Guards) (Militia)".

The "7th Battalion, Volunteer Militia Rifles of Canada" (authorized in 1862) was disbanded in 1864 and its' numerical designation in the "militia list" allocated to the "London Light Infantry" (authorized in 1866) which is still in existence as "4th Battalion, The Royal Canadian Regiment (London and Oxford Fusiliers) (Militia)".

The "8th 'Stadacona Rifles'" (authorized in 1862 as the "8th Battalion, Volunteer Militia Rifles of Canada") was disbanded in 1966 as "The Royal Rifles of Canada (Militia)".

The "9th 'Voltigeurs de Quebec'" (authorized in 1862 as the "9th Battalion, Volunteer Militia Rifles of Canada") is still in existence as "Les Voltigeurs de Quebec (Milice)".

The "10th 'Royal Grenadiers'" (authorized in 1862 as the "10th Battalion, Volunteer Militia Rifles of Canada") is still in existence as "The Royal Regiment of Canada (Militia)".

The "11th 'Argentuil Rangers'" (authorized in 1862 as the "11th Battalion, Volunteer Militia Rifles of Canada") was disbanded in 1912.

The "12th Battalion, Volunteer Militia Rifles of Canada" (authorized in 1862) was disbanded in 1864 and its' numerical designation in the "militia list" allocated to the "York Rangers" (authorized in 1866) which is still in existence as "The Queen's York Rangers (1st American Regiment) (R.C.A.C.) (Militia)".

The "13th Battalion, Volunteer Militia Infantry of Canada" (authorized in 1862) is still in existence as "The Royal Hamilton Light Infantry (Wentworth Regiment) (Militia)".

The "14th 'Princess of Wales' Own Rifles'" (authorized in 1863 as the "14th Battalion, Volunteer Militia Rifles of Canada") is still in existence as "The Princess of Wales' Own Regiment (Militia)".

The "15th 'Argyll Light Infantry'" (authorized in 1863 as the "15th Battalion, Volunteer Militia Infantry of Canada") was, after subsequent re-organization and re-designation, incorporated within "The Hastings and Prince Edward Regiment (Militia)" which is still in existence.

Most, if not all, units of the "Volunteer Militia of Canada" were "called out" in whole or in part for local defence at various times during the Fenian Raids (1866 and 1870). The "First 'Prince of Wales' Rifles'" was called out for service on the Canadian-American border during both Fenian Raids. The "2nd 'Queens's Own Rifles'" first saw action at Ridgeway (near Fort Erie) during the Fenian Raids of 1866. The "3rd 'Victoria Rifles'" first saw action at Eccles Hill on the Quebec-Vermont border during the Fenian Raids of 1870. "Volunteer Militia Naval Companies" at Dunnville, Hamilton and Toronto were placed on active service during the Fenian Raids of 1866.

Two rifle battalions (the "1st 'Ontario' Rifles" and the "2nd 'Quebec' Rifles"), consisting of men who had been enrolled for a period of one year and a further year at the discretion of the government, were mobilized at Toronto in 1870 and served at Fort Garry (now Winnipeg) upon the outbreak of rebellion in the Red River Colony. Following the withdrawal of most British troops from Canada in 1871, the Dominion Government authorized the formation of permanent "batteries of garrison artillery" which were to "maintain warlike stores" necessary for the defence of the new nation. These batteries are still in existence as "A" and "B" Batteries of "1 Regiment, Royal Canadian Horse Artillery (Regular)". Specified units were mobilized for active service in Saskatchewan during the "Riel" Rebellion and were awarded the battle-honour "NORTH-WEST CANADA, 1885".

Militia units provided most of the volunteers for the "2nd (Special Service) Battalion, Royal Canadian Regiment of Infantry" which was formed for service in South Africa during the "Boer" War and gained particular distinction through its' action at the Battle of Paardeberg in 1900. Militia cavalry units provided volunteers for the "Canadian Mounted Rifles" which fought in South Africa. A battle-honour for "SOUTH AFRICA" was awarded to all militia units that provided a substantial number of volunteers for service in South Africa during the "Boer" War. Thus, at the dawn of a new century, the "Canadian Militia" had established a tradition of service that was to contribute much in the coming global conflicts.

CONTENTS

THE ROYAL CANADIAN INFANTRY CORPS

Corps Motto: *"ACER"* / *("THE MAPLE")*
The Royal Canadian School of Infantry: CAMP BORDEN, Ontario

NOTE (1)
Armoured regiments (sub-designated "R.C.A.C.") which originated as battalions of infantry have been included in this section.

NOTE (2)
Battle honours, where listed, are those of a general nature which have been included in order to properly define the service of a particular infantry battalion (or are those which are unique to that unit). A battle honour for *"THE GREAT WAR"* indicates that the unit recruited one or more battalions which served in the United Kingdom during the Great War for the period specified by the accompanying year-date. These battalions, although they did not serve in France, were integral to the Canadian Expeditionary Force in that they proved the administrative structure through which personnel were recruited in Canada and forwarded to the United Kingdom for advanced training in the "reserve battalions" prior to their being posted to France as reinforcements for battalions of the "Canadian Corps" in the field. The reader is advised to refer to specific regimental histories for a complete list of the battle honours awarded to a particular infantry battalion.

THE CANADIAN GUARDS (REGULAR)

The "Regiment of Canadian Guards" was formed in 1953.

Regimental March: *"THE STANDARD OF ST. GEORGE"*
Regimental Motto: *"A MARI USQUE AD MARE"*
   ("FROM SEA UNTO SEA")
Regimental Depot: CAMP PETAWAWA, Ontario

1st Battalion — CAMP PICTON, Ontario
The battalion, which had been formed in 1953, was disbanded in 1968.

2nd Battalion — CAMP PETAWAWA, Ontario
The battalion, which had been formed in 1953, was disbanded in 1970.

3rd Battalion — CAMP VALCARTIER, Quebec
The battalion, which had been formed in 1951 as the "1st Canadian Infantry Battalion" for service with the "27th Canadian Infantry Brigade Group" in West Germany, was disbanded in 1957.

4th Battalion — CAMP IPPERWASH, Ontario
The battalion, which had been formed in 1952 as the "2nd Canadian Infantry Battalion" for "rotation" with the "1st Canadian Infantry Battalion", served in Korea subsequent to the armistice and was disbanded in 1957.

Affiliated British Units:
THE GRENADIER GUARDS
THE COLDSTREAM GUARDS
THE SCOTS GUARDS
THE IRISH GUARDS
THE WELSH GUARDS

THE GOVERNOR-GENERAL'S FOOT GUARDS
(5th Battalion, CANADIAN GUARDS) (MILITIA)

The battalion, which originated in 1872 and incorported the "Civil Service Rifle Regiment" which had been formed in 1866, provided the "Guards Company of Sharpshooters" which served in Saskatchewan during the "Riel" Rebellion (1885).

Regimental March: *"MILANOLLO"*
Regimental Motto: *"CIVITAS ET PRINCEPT CURA NOSTRA"*
     ("COUNTRY AND RULER ARE OUR CONCERN")
Major Battle Honours:
NORTH-WEST CANADA, 1885 — SOUTH AFRICA, 1899-1900 — VIMY RIDGE — PURSUIT TO MONS — FRANCE AND FLANDERS, 1915-1918 — THE RHINELAND — NORTH-WEST EUROPE, 1944-1945
Headquarters — The Drill Hall, Cartier Square, OTTAWA, Ontario
Number "1" Company originated in 1869 as a company of "Civil Service Rifles".
Number "2" Company originated in 1872 as a company of "Civil Service Rifles".
Number "3" Company
Number "4" Company was disbanded in 1970.

Affiliated British Unit:
THE COLDSTREAM GUARDS

THE CANADIAN GRENADIER GUARDS
(6th Battalion, CANADIAN GUARDS) (MILITIA)

The battalion originated in 1859 as the "First Battalion, Volunteer Militia Rifles of Canada" (First "Prince of Wales' Rifles").

Regimental March: *"THE BRITISH GRENADIERS"*
Regimental Motto: *"NULLI SECUNDUS"* / (*"SECOND TO NONE"*)
Major Battle Honours:
SOUTH AFRICA, 1899-1900 — VIMY RIDGE — FRANCE AND FLANDERS, 1916-1918 — THE RHINELAND — NORTH-WEST EUROPE, 1944-45

A "divisional tank battalion" sub-designated "Canadian Grenadier Guards" was formed in Canada in 1945 for allocation to the "Canadian Army (Pacific Force)" for the projected assault on the Japanese home islands. This battalion was disbanded in 1945.

Headquarters — MONTREAL, QUEBEC
Number "1" Company originated in 1855 as the "First Volunteer Militia Rifle Company of Montreal".
Number "2" Company originated in 1855 as the "2nd Volunteer Militia Rifle Company of Montreal".
Number "3" Company was disbanded in 1970.
Number "4" Company was disbanded in 1970.

Affiliated British Unit:
THE GRENADIER GUARDS

THE ROYAL CANADIAN REGIMENT (REGULAR)

The Regiment originated in 1883 as the "Infantry School Corps"

Regimental March: *"THE ROYAL CANADIAN REGIMENT"*
Regimental Motto: *"PRO PATRIA"* / (*"FOR COUNTRY"*)
Major Battle Honours:
SASKATCHEWAN — NORTH-WEST CANADA, 1885 — PAARDEBERG — SOUTH AFRICA, 1899-1900 — VIMY RIDGE — PURSUIT TO MONS — FRANCE AND FLANDERS, 1915-1918 — LANDING IN SICILY — ITALY, 1943-1945 —NORTH-WEST EUROPE, 1945 — KOREA, 1951-1953

The "1st Battalion (Royal Canadian Regiment), 1st Canadian Infantry Regiment", which had been formed in Canada in 1945 for allocation to the "Canadian Army (Pacific Force)" for the projected assault on the Japanese home islands, was later re-designated "The Royal Canadian Regiment (Active Force)"

Home Station: Wolseley Barracks, LONDON, Ontario

"A" Company, 1st Battalion — Wolseley Barracks, LONDON, Ontario
"A" Company of the "Infantry School Corps" was formed in 1883 at Fredericton, New Brunswick. "A" Company of the "2nd (Special Service) Battalion, Royal Canadian Regiment of Infantry" was recuited in Manitoba and British Columbia in 1899 for service in South Africa.
"B" Company, 1st Battalion — Wolseley Barracks, LONDON, Ontario
"B" Company of the "Infantry School Corps" was formed in 1883 at St. John's, Quebec. "B" Company of the "2nd (Special Service) Battalion, Royal Canadian Regiment of Infantry" was recruited at London in 1899 for service in South Africa.
"C" Company, 1st Battalion — Wolseley Barracks, LONDON, Ontario
"C" Company of the "Infantry School Corps" was formed in 1883 at Toronto and served in Saskatchewan during the "Riel" Rebellion (1885). "C" Company of the "2nd (Special Service) Battalion, Royal Canadian Regiment of Infantry" was recruited at Toronto in 1899 for service in South Africa.
"D" Company, 1st Battalion — Wolseley Barracks, LONDON, Ontario
"D" Company of the "Infantry School Corps" was formed in 1887 at London. "D" Company of the "2nd (Special Service) Battalion, Royal Canadian Regiment of Infantry" was recruited at Kingston and Ottawa in 1899 for service in South Africa.
"E" (Combat Support) Company, 1st Battalion
— Wolseley Barracks, LONDON, Ontario
"E" Company of the "2nd (Special Service) Battalion, Royal Canadian Regiment of Infantry" was recruited at Montreal in 1899 for service in South Africa.
"F" (Administrative Support) Company, 1st Battalion
— Wolseley Barracks, LONDON, Ontario
"F" Company of the "2nd (Special Service) Battalion, Royal Canadian Regiment of Infantry" was recruited at Quebec City in 1899 for service in South Africa.

The "1st Battalion" is a unit of the "Special Service Force".

"G" Company, 2nd Battalion — CAMP GAGETOWN, New Brunswick
"G" Company of the "2nd (Special Service) Battalion, Royal Canadian Regiment of Infantry" was recruited in New Brunswick and Prince Edward Island in 1899 for service in South Africa.
"H" Company, 2nd Battalion — CAMP GAGETOWN, New Brunswick
"H" Company of the "2nd (Special Service) Battalion, Royal Canadian Regiment of Infantry" was recruited in Nova Scotia in 1899 for service in South Africa.
"I" Company, 2nd Battalion — CAMP GAGETOWN, New Brunswick

"J" Company, 2nd Battalion — CAMP GAGETOWN, New Brunswick
"K" (Combat Support) Company, 2nd Battalion — CAMP GAGETOWN, New Brunswick
"L" (Administrative Support) Company, 2nd Battalion — CAMP GAGETOWN, N.B.

The "2nd Battalion", a unit of "5ieme Groupe-Brigade du Canada", was formed in 1970 from personnel of both battalions of "The Black Watch (Royal Highland Regiment) of Canada (Regular)" and replaced the original "2nd Battalion, The Royal Canadian Regiment (Regular)" which, having been formed in 1950, was re-designated "3 (Mechanized) Commando, Canadian Airborne Regiment" upon re-organization in 1970.
The "2nd (Special Service) Battalion, Royal Canadian Regiment of Infantry" served in South Africa during the "Boer" War.

"M" Company, 3rd Battalion — BADEN, West Germany
"N" Company, 3rd Battalion — BADEN, West Germany
"O" Company, 3rd Battalion — BADEN, West Germany
"P" Company, 3rd Battalion — BADEN, West Germany
"Q" (Combat Support) Company, 3rd Battalion —BADEN, West Germany
"R" (Administrative Support) Company, 3rd Battalion — BADEN, West Germany

The "3rd Battalion", a unit of "4 Canadian Mechanized Brigade Group", was relocated from Camp Petawawa in 1977, having been formed in 1970 from personnel of "2nd Battalion, The Canadian Guards (Regular)", and replaced the original "3rd Battalion, The Royal Canadian Regiment" which had been formed in 1950 and disbanded in 1954.
The "3rd (Special Service) Battalion, Royal Canadian Regiment of Infantry" was formed in 1900 to garrison the Citadel at Halifax, and served until 1902, thereby releasing British troops for service in South Africa.

Affiliated British Units:
THE ROYAL REGIMENT OF FUSILIERS
THE GLOUCESTERSHIRE REGIMENT

THE ROYAL CANADIAN REGIMENT (LONDON AND OXFORD FUSILIERS) (MILITIA)

The battalion was formed in 1954 by the amalgamation of "The Oxford Rifles" which had originated in 1863 as the "Oxford Battalion of Rifles" and "The Canadian Fusiliers" which had originated in 1866 as the "7th 'London Light Infantry'"

Regimental March: *"THE ROYAL CANADIAN REGIMENT"*
Regimental Motto: *"PRO PATRIA"* / *"FOR COUNTRY")*
Major Battle Honours:
NORTH-WEST CANADA, 1885 — SOUTH AFRICA, 1899-1900 — VIMY RIDGE — PURSUIT TO MONS — FRANCE AND FLANDERS, 1915-1918

The "Canadian Fusiliers" served on Kiska in the Aleutian Islands in 1943 as a unit of the "13th Canadian Infantry Brigade Group".

"S" Company, 4th Battalion — Prevost Armoury, LONDON, Ontario
This (formerly "A") company was relocated from Woodstock in 1970.
"T" Company, 4th Battalion — STRATFORD, Ontario
This (formerly "B") company was relocated from Woodstock in 1965 thereby continuing a militia presence subsequent to the disbandment of "The Perth Regiment".
"U" Company, 4th Battalion — Prevost Armoury, LONDON, Ontario
This company was formed in 1970 by the re-organization of the headquarters element of the battalion.
"C" Company was disbanded in 1970 at London.
"D" Company was disbanded in 1970 at London.
"Support" Company was disbanded in 1970 at London.

Affiliated British Unit:
THE ROYAL REGIMENT OF FUSILIERS

PRINCESS PATRICIA'S CANADIAN LIGHT INFANTRY (REGULAR)

The Regiment was formed in 1914 and fought in France as a unit of the British Expeditionary Force prior to being transferred to the Canadian Expeditionary Force in 1915.

Regimental March: *"TIPPERARY"*
Major Battle Honours:
VIMY RIDGE — PURSUIT TO MONS — FRANCE AND FLANDERS, 1914-1918 — LANDING IN SICILY — ITALY, 1943-1945 — NORTH-WEST EUROPE, 1945 — KAPYONG — KOREA, 1950-1953

The "1st Battalion (P.P.C.L.I.), 2nd Canadian Infantry Regiment", which had been formed in Canada in 1945 for allocation to the "Canadian Army (Pacific Force)" for the projected assault on the Japanese home islands, was later re-designated "Princess Patricia's Canadian Light Infantry (Active Force)".

Home Station: Currie Barracks, CALGARY, Alberta

1st Battalion — Currie Barracks, CALGARY, Alberta
The battalion is a unit of "1 Canadian Brigade Group".

2nd Battalion — Kapyong Barracks, WINNIPEG, Manitoba
The battalion, which was formed in 1950, is a unit of "1 Canadian Brigade Group".

3rd Battalion — Work Point Barracks, ESQUIMALT (VICTORIA), British Columbia
The battalion, a unit of "1 Canadian Brigade Group", was formed in 1970 by the re-designation of "1st Battalion, The Queen's Own Rifles of Canada (Regular)" and replaced the original "3rd Battalion, P.P.C.L.I." which had been formed in 1950 and disbanded in 1954.

Affiliated British Unit:
THE ROYAL GREEN JACKETS

THE LOYAL EDMONTON REGIMENT (4th Battalion, P.P.C.L.I.) (MILITIA)

The battalion originated in 1908 as the "Edmonton Fusiliers".

Regimental March: *"BONNIE DUNDEE"*
Major Battle Honours:
VIMY RIDGE — PURSUIT TO MONS — FRANCE AND FLANDERS, 1915-1918 —
LANDING IN SICILY — ITALY, 1943-1945 — NORTH-WEST EUROPE, 1945

The "3rd Battalion (Loyal Edmonton Regiment), 2nd Canadian Infantry Regiment", which had been formed in Canada in 1945 for allocation to the "Canadian Army (Pacific Force)" for the projected assault on the Japanese home islands, was disbanded in 1945.

Headquarters — Griesbach Barracks, EDMONTON, Alberta
"A" Company, which maintained a detached platoon at Vegreville from 1954 until 1965, was relocated at Edmonton from Vermillion in 1965.
"B" Company was relocated at Edmonton from Vegreville in 1954.
"C" Company, after relocation from Ross Creek in 1954, was disbanded in 1970 at Edmonton.
"D" Company, after relocation from Grande Prairie in 1965, was disbanded in 1970 at the Prince of Wales' Armoury in Edmonton. (Note that "D" Company of "The Edmonton Regiment" landed on Spitsbergen during the raid on that Norwegian island in the Barents Sea in 1941.)
"E" Company was disbanded in 1965 at Fort Smith in the North-West Territories. (Note that a previous "E" Company was formed in 1951 to recruit for the "1st Canadian Infantry Battalion" which was re-designated "3rd Battalion, The Canadian Guards (Regular)" in 1953.)
"F" Company was formed in 1952 to recruit for the "2nd Canadian Infantry Battalion" which was re-designated "4th Battalion, The Canadian Guards (Regular)" in 1953.
The Machine-Gun Platoon, after relocation from Dawson Creek in 1965, was disbanded in 1970 at Edmonton.
The Mortar Platoon, after relocation from Stony Plain in 1965, was disbanded in 1970 at Edmonton.
The Anti-Tank Platoon, after relocation from Peace River in 1965, was disbanded in 1970 at Edmonton.

Affiliated British Unit:
THE QUEEN'S LANCASHIRE REGIMENT

ROYAL VINGT-DEUXIEME REGIMENT (REGULIER)

The Regiment was formed in 1920 and perpetuates the "22nd (Canadien-Francais) Infantry Battalion, C.E.F." which fought in France as a unit of the "Canadian Corps" during the Great War.

Regimental March: *"VIVE LA CANADIENNE"*
Regimental Motto: *"JE ME SOUVIENS"* / *("I REMEMBER")*
Major Battle Honours:
VIMY RIDGE — PURSUIT TO MONS — FRANCE AND FLANDERS, 1915-1918 — LANDING IN SICILY — ITALY, 1943-1945 — NORTH-WEST EUROPE, 1945 — KOREA, 1951-1953

The "1st Battalion (Royal 22ieme Regiment), 3rd Canadian Infantry Regiment", which had been formed in Canada in 1945 for allocation to the "Canadian Army (Pacific Force)" for the projected assault on the Japanese home islands, was later re-designated "Royal Vingt-Deuxieme Regiment (Active Force)".

Quartier General: La Citadelle, QUEBEC CITY

1iere Bataillon — LAHR, West Germany
Le bataillon est un unit de "4 Canadian Mechanized Brigade Group".

2ieme Bataillon — La Citadelle, QUEBEC CITY
Le bataillon, qui est forme en 1950, est un unit de "5ieme Groupe-Brigade du Canada".

3ieme Bataillon — CAMP VALCARTIER, Quebec
Le bataillon, qui est forme en 1950, est un unit de "5ieme Groupe-Brigade du Canada".

Affiliated British Unit:
THE ROYAL WELCH FUSILIERS

4ieme Bataillon, ROYAL VINGT-DEUXIEME REGIMENT (MILICE)

The battalion was formed in 1954 by the re-designation of "Le Regiment de Chateauguay" which had been formed in 1901 by the amalgamation of the "Voltigeurs de Beauharnois" which had originated in 1869 and the "Voltigeurs de Chateauguay" which had originated in 1872.

Regimental March: *"VIVE LA CANADIENNE"*
Regimental Motto: *"JE ME SOUVIENS"* / (*"I REMEMBER"*)
Headquarters — MONTREAL, Quebec
"A" Company was relocated at Montreal from St-Jean in 1965
"B" Company was relocated at St-Jerome from Montreal in 1965 thereby continuing a militia presence subsequent to the disbandment of "Le Regiment de Joliette".
"C" Company was disbanded in 1970 at Montreal.
"D" Company, after relocation from Valleyfield in 1968, was disbanded in 1970 at Montreal.
"Support" Company was disbanded in 1970 at Montreal.

Affiliated British Unit:
THE STAFFORDSHIRE REGIMENT

LES FUSILIERS DU ST-LAURENT (MILICE)

The battalion, which originated in 1869 as the "Provisional Battalion of Rimouski", incorporated "Le Regiment de Montmagny" and was sub-designated "5ieme Bataillon, Royal Vingt-Deuxieme Regiment" in 1954.

Regimental March: *"VIVE LA CANADIENNE"*
Regimental Motto: *"J'Y SUIS EN GARDE / ("I AM ON GUARD")*
Battle Honour: THE GREAT WAR, 1916
Headquarters — RIMOUSKI, Quebec
"A" Company — RIVIERE DU LOUP, Quebec
"B" Company was relocated at Rimouski from Montmagny in 1965.
"C" Company — MATANE, Quebec
"D" Company was disbanded in 1970 at Cabano.
"Support" Company was disbanded in 1970 at Rimouski.

Affiliated British Unit:
THE ROYAL REGIMENT OF FUSILIERS

6ieme Bataillon, ROYAL VINGT-DEUXIEME REGIMENT (MILICE)

The battalion, which originated in 1871 as the "Provisional Battalion of St. Hyacinthe", received its present designation in 1954.

Regimental March: *"VIVE LA CANADIENNE"*
Regimental Motto: *"JE ME SOUVIENS"* / *("I REMEMBER")*
Headquarters — ST-HYACINTHE, Quebec
"A" Company was relocated at St-Hyacinthe from Acton Vale in 1965.
"B" Company was relocated at Drummondville from St-Hyacinthe in 1968 thereby continuing a militia presence subsequent to the disbandment of "74 Field Battery, R.C.A.".
"C" Company was disbanded in 1970 at St-Hyacinthe.
"D" Company, after relocation from Tracy in 1965, was disbanded in 1970 at St-Hyacinthe.
"Support" Company was disbanded in 1970 at St-Hyacinthe.

Affiliated British Unit:
THE ROYAL WELCH FUSILIERS

THE QUEEN'S OWN RIFLES OF CANADA (REGULAR)

The regiment was formed in 1953.

Regimental March: *"THE BUFFS"*
Regimental Motto: *"IN PACE PARATUS"* / *("IN PEACE PREPARED")*
Regimental Depot: Currie Barracks, CALGARY, Alberta

1st Battalion — Work Point Barracks, ESQUIMALT (VICTORIA), B.C.
The battalion, which had been formed in 1951 as the "1st Canadian Rifle Battalion" for service with the "27th Canadian Infantry Brigade Group" in West Germany, was re-designated "3rd Battalion, Princess Patricia's Canadian Light Infantry" in 1970.

2nd Battalion — Currie Barracks, CALGARY, Alberta
The battalion, which had been formed in 1951 as the "2nd Canadian Rifle Battalion" for "rotation" with the "1st Canadian Rifle Battalion", served in Korea subsequent to the armistice and was disbanded in 1968.

Affiliated British Units:
THE QUEEN'S REGIMENT
THE ROYAL GREEN JACKETS

THE QUEEN'S OWN RIFLES OF CANADA (MILITIA)

The battalion originated in 1860 as the "2nd Battalion, Volunteer Militia Rifles of Canada (2nd "Queen's Own Rifles") which had been organized as follows:

"1" Company, which had originated in 1855 as the "Volunteer Militia Rifle Company of Barrie, was removed from the battalion in 1866 and re-designated "1" Company of the "Simcoe Battalion of Infantry" (now "The Grey and Simcoe Foresters").

"2" Company originated in 1856 as the "1st Volunteer Militia Rifle Company of Toronto".

"3" Company originated in 1856 as the "3rd Volunteer Militia Rifle Company of Toronto".

"4" Company originated in 1856 as the "Volunteer Militia Highland Rifle Company of Toronto".

"5" Company originated in 1856 as the "Volunteer Militia Company of Foot Artillery of Toronto".

"6" Company, which had originated in 1858 as the "Volunteer Militia Highland Rifle Company of Whitby", was removed from the battalion in 1866 and re-designated "1" Company of the "Ontario Battalion of Infantry" (now "The Ontario Regiment (R.C.A.C.)").

Regimental March: *"THE BUFFS"*
Regimental Double-Past: *"MONEY MUSK"*
Regimental Motto: *"IN PACE PARATUS"* / (*"IN PEACE PREPARED"*)
Major Battle Honours:
NORTH-WEST CANADA, 1885 — SOUTH AFRICA, 1899-1900 — VIMY RIDGE — PURSUIT TO MONS — FRANCE AND FLANDERS, 1915-1918 — NORMANDY LANDING — THE RHINELAND — NORTH-WEST EUROPE, 1944-1945
Headquarters — Moss Park Armoury, TORONTO, Ontario
"Buffs" Company — Moss Park Armoury, TORONTO, Ontario
This (formely "A") company commemorates the battalion's affiliation with "The Queen's Own Buffs (The Royal Kent Regiment)" (now "2nd Battalion, The Queen's Regiment").
"60th" Company — NORTH TORONTO, Ontario
This (formerly "B") company commemorates the battalion's affiliation with "The King's Royal Rifle Corps" (now "2nd Battalion, The Royal Green Jackets").
"Victoria" Company — Moss Park Armoury, TORONTO, Ontario
This (formerly "C") company perpetuates the title of "The Victoria Rifles of Canada".
"D" Company was disbanded in 1970 at Toronto.
"E" Company was formed in 1951 to recruit for the "1st Canadian Rifle Battalion" which was re-designated "1st Battalion, The Queen's Own Rifles of Canada (Regular)" in 1953.
"F" Company was formed in 1952 to recruit for the "2nd Canadian Rifle Battalion" which was re-designated "2nd Battalion, The Queen's Own Rifles of Canada (Regular)" in 1953.
"Gurkha" Company — Moss Park Armoury, TORONTO, Ontario
This company, which commemorates the battalion's affiliation with the "Brigade of Gurkhas", comprises the regimental "pioneers" and "skirmishers" who perform nineteenth-century foot drill and musketry.
"Support" Company was disbanded in 1970 at Toronto.

Affiliated British Units:
THE QUEEN'S REGIMENT
THE ROYAL GREEN JACKETS
THE BRIGADE OF GURKHAS

THE VICTORIA RIFLES OF CANADA (MILITIA)

The battalion, which had originated in 1862 as the "3rd Battalion, Volunteer Militia Rifles of Canada" (3rd "Victoria Rifles"), was disbanded in 1965.

Regimental March: *"LUTZOW'S WILD HUNT"*
Regimental Motto: *"PRO ARIS ET FOCIS"*
      (*"FOR OUR ALTARS AND OUR HEARTHS"*)
Major Battle Honours:
ECCLES HILL (1870) — SOUTH AFRICA, 1899-1900 — VIMY RIDGE — PURSUIT TO MONS — FRANCE AND FLANDERS, 1915-1918
Headquarters — MONTREAL, Quebec
"A" Company
"B" Company
"C" Company
"D" Company
"E" Company was formed in 1951 to recruit for the "1st Canadian Rifle Battalion" which was re-designated "1st Battalion, The Queen's Own Rifles of Canada (Regular)" in 1953.
"F" Company was formed in 1952 to recruit for the "2nd Canadian Rifle Battalion" which was re-designated "2nd Battalion, The Queen's Own Rifles of Canada (Regular)" in 1953.
"Support" Company

Affiliated British Unit:
THE ROYAL GREEN JACKETS

THE BLACK WATCH (ROYAL HIGHLAND REGIMENT) OF CANADA (REGULAR)

The Regiment was formed in 1953.

Regimental March: *"THE HIGHLAND LADDIE"*
Regimental Motto: *"NEMO ME IMPUNE LACESSIT"*
   ("NONE PROVOKE ME WITH IMPUNITY")
Regimental Depot: St. Andrew's Barracks, CAMP GAGETOWN, New Brunswick

1st Battalion — St. Andrew's Barracks, CAMP GAGETOWN, New Brunswick
The battalion, which had been formed in 1951 as the "1st Canadian Highland Battalion" for service with the "27th Canadian Infantry Brigade Group" in West Germany, was disbanded in 1970.

2nd Battalion — St. Andrew's Barracks, CAMP GAGETOWN, New Brunswick
The battalion, which had been formed in 1951 as the "2nd Canadian Highland Battalion" for "rotation" with the "1st Canadian Highland Battalion", served in Korea subsequent to the armistice and was disbanded in 1970.

Affiliated British Unit:
THE BLACK WATCH (ROYAL HIGHLAND REGIMENT)

THE BLACK WATCH (ROYAL HIGHLAND REGIMENT) OF CANADA (MILITIA)

The battalion originated in 1862 as the "5th Battalion, Volunteer Militia Rifles of Canada" (5th "Royal Light Infantry").

Regimental March: *"THE HIGHLAND LADDIE"*
Regimental Motto: *"NEMO ME IMPUNE LACESSIT"*
      ("NONE PROVOKE ME WITH IMPUNITY")
Major Battle Honours:
SOUTH AFRICA, 1899-1900 — VIMY RIDGE — PURSUIT TO MONS — FRANCE AND FLANDERS, 1915-1918 — THE RHINELAND — NORTH-WEST EUROPE, 1944-45
Headquarters — MONTREAL, Quebec
"A" Company
"B" Company
"C" Company was disbanded in 1970.
"D" Company was disbanded in 1970.
"E" Company was formed in 1951 to recruit for the "1st Canadian Highland Battalion" which was re-designated "1st Battalion, The Black Watch (Royal Highland Regiment) of Canada (Regular)" in 1953.
"F" Company was formed in 1952 to recruit for the "2nd Canadian Highland Battalion" which was re-designated "2nd Battalion, The Black Watch (Royal Highland Regiment) of Canada (Regular)" in 1953.
"Support" Company was disbanded in 1970.

Affiliated British Unit:
THE BLACK WATCH (ROYAL HIGHLAND REGIMENT)

THE ROYAL RIFLES OF CANADA (MILITIA)

The battalion, which had originated in 1862 as the "8th Battalion, Volunteer Militia Rifles of Canada (8th "Stadacona Rifles"), was disbanded in 1966.

Regimental March: *"I'M NINETY-FIVE"*
Regimental Motto: *"VOLENS ET VALENS"*
    ("WILLING AND STRONG")
Major Battle Hounours:
SOUTH AFRICA, 1899-1900 — THE GREAT WAR, 1916 — HONG KONG — SOUTH-EAST ASIA, 1941
Headquarters — QUEBEC CITY
"A" Company
"B" Company
"C" Company
"D" Company
"Support" Company

Affiliated British Unit:
THE ROYAL GREEN JACKETS

LES VOLTIGEURS DE QUEBEC (MILICE)

The battalion, which originated in 1862 as the "9th Battalion, Volunteer Militia Rifles of Canada" (9th "Voltigeurs de Quebec"), incorporated "Le Regiment de Quebec" in 1954. "Les Voltigeurs de Quebec (Milice)" may be considered as perpetuating the "Provincial Corps of Light Infantry" (or "Canadian Voltigeurs") which fought at Chateauquay (near Montreal) in Lower Canada and at Chrysler's farm (near Morrisburg) in Upper Canada during the Anglo-American War of 1812 to 1814.

Regimental March: *"LES VOLTIGEURS DE QUEBEC"*
Regimental Motto: *"FORCE A SUPERBE, MERCY A FOIBLE"*
    ("VIOLENCE TO THE MIGHTY, MERCY TO THE WEAK")
Major Battle Honours:
NORTH-WEST CANADA, 1885 — THE GREAT WAR, 1916
Headquarters —Manege Grande-Allee, QUEBEC CITY
"A" Company
"B" Company
"C" Company
"D" Company was disbanded in 1970.
"Support" Company was disbanded in 1970.

Affiliated British Unit:
THE LIGHT INFANTRY

THE ROYAL REGIMENT OF CANADA (MILITIA)

The battalion was formed in 1936 by the amalgamation of "The Royal Grenadiers" which had originated in 1862 as the "10th Battalion, Volunteer Militia Rifles of Canada" (10th "Royal Grenadiers") and "The Toronto Regiment" which had originated in 1920 in perpetuation of the "3rd Infantry Battalion (The Toronto Regiment), C.E.F." which fought in France as a unit of the "Canadian Corps" during the Great War.

Regimental March: *"THE BRITISH GRENADIERS"*
Regimental Motto: *"NEC ASPERA TERRENT"*
　　　("NOR DO DIFFICULTIES DETER US")
Major Battle Honours:
FISH CREEK — NORTH-WEST CANADA, 1885 — SOUTH AFRICA, 1899-1900 — VIMY RIDGE — PURSUIT TO MONS — FRANCE AND FLANDERS, 1915-1918 — DIEPPE — THE RHINELAND — NORTH-WEST EUROPE, 1942, 1944-1945
Headquarters — Fort York Armoury, TORONTO, Ontario
"Grenadier" (formerly "A") Company commemorates "The Royal Grenadiers" with which "The Toronto Regiment" was amalgamated in 1936 to form "The Royal Regiment of Toronto Grenadiers" which was re-designated "The Royal Regiment of Canada" in 1939.
"Toronto" (formerly "B") Company commemorates "The Toronto Regiment" with which "The Royal Grenadiers" was amalgamated in 1936 to form "The Royal Regiment of Toronto Grenadiers" which was re-designated "The Royal Regiment of Canada" in 1939.
"123rd" (formerly "C") Company commemorates the "123rd Infantry Battalion, C.E.F." which fought in France during the Great War as a unit of the "Canadian Corps".
"D" Company was disbanded in 1970.
"Support" Company was disbanded in 1970.

Affiliated British Unit:
THE KING'S REGIMENT (MANCHESTER AND LIVERPOOL)
Prior to the Great War, the "Royal Grenadiers" had been affiliated with "The Prince of Wales' Leinster Regiment (Royal Canadians)" which, having been recruited in Canada in 1858, had been in garrison at Halifax prior to serving in South Africa during the "Boer" War.

THE ROYAL HAMILTON LIGHT INFANTRY (WENTWORTH REGIMENT) (MILITIA)

The battalion was formed in 1936 by the amalgamation of "The Royal Hamilton Light Infantry" which had originated in 1862 as the "13th Battalion, Volunteer Militia Infantry of Canada" and "The Wentworth Regiment" which had originated in 1872 as the "Wentworth Battalion of Infantry".

Regimental March: *"THE MOUNTAIN ROSE"*
Regimental Motto: *"SEMPER PARATUS"* / *("ALWAYS READY")*
Major Battle Honours:
SOUTH AFRICA, 1900 — VIMY RIDGE — PURSUIT TO MONS — FRANCE AND FLANDERS, 1915-1918 — DIEPPE — THE RHINELAND — NORTH-WEST EUROPE, 1942, 1944-1945
Headquarters — HAMILTON, Ontario
"A" Company, which originated in 1855 as the "1st Volunteer Militia Rifle Company of Hamilton", was relocated at Hamilton from Ancaster in 1965.
"B" Company, which originated in 1855 as the "2nd Volunteer Militia Rifle Company of Hamilton", was relocated at Hamilton from Waterdown in 1965.
"C" Company — HAMILTON, Ontario
"D" Company was disbanded in 1970 at Hamilton.
"E" Company was formed in 1951 to recruit for the "1st Canadian Rifle Battalion" which was re-designated "1st Battalion, The Queen's Own Rifles of Canada (Regular)" in 1953.
"F" Company was formed in 1952 to recruit for the "2nd Canadian Rifle Battalion" which was re-designated "2nd Battalion, The Queen's Own Rifles of Canada (Regular)" in 1953.
"Support" Company was disbanded in 1970 at Hamilton.

Affiliated British Unit:
THE LIGHT INFANTRY

THE PRINCESS OF WALES' OWN REGIMENT (MILITIA)

The battalion originated in 1863 as the "14th Battalion, Volunteer Militia Rifles of Canada" (14th "Princess of Wales' Own Rifles").

Regimental March: *"THE BUFFS"*
Regimental Motto: *"NUMQUAM CEDE"* / (*"YIELD TO NONE"*)
Major Battle Honours:
SOUTH AFRICA, 1900 — VIMY RIDGE — PURSUIT TO MONS — FRANCE AND FLANDERS, 1915-1918
Headquarters — KINGSTON, Ontario
"A" Company originated in 1855 as the "1st Volunteer Militia Rifle Company of Kingston".
"B" Company originated in 1855 as the "2nd Volunteer Militia Rifle Company of Kingston".
"C" Company was disbanded in 1970 at Kingston.
"D" Company was disbanded in 1970 at Kingston.
"Support" Company was disbanded in 1970 at Kingston.

Affiliated British Unit:
THE QUEEN'S LANCASHIRE REGIMENT

THE ALGONQUIN REGIMENT (MILITIA)

The battalion was formed in 1936 by the amalgamation of "B", "C" and "D" Companies of the existing "Algonquin Regiment" which had originated in 1900 as the "Algonquin Rifles" and "The Northern Pioneers" which had originated in 1903 as the "Northern Fusiliers". (Note that "A" Company of the existing "Algonquin Regiment" was amalgamated with "The Sault Ste. Marie Regiment" which had originated in 1913 as the "Soo Rifles" to form "The Sault Ste. Marie and Sudbury Regiment (Non-Permanent Active Militia)" which was converted in 1946 and re-organized as "49 (Sault Ste. Marie) Heavy Anti-Aircraft Regiment, R.C.A. (Reserve Force)" and "58 (Sudbury) LIght Anti-Aircraft Regiment, R.C.A. (Reserve Force)".)

Regimental March: *"WE LEAD, OTHERS FOLLOW"*
Regimental Motto: *"NE-KAH-NE-TAH"*
      (*"WE LEAD, OTHERS FOLLOW"*)
Major Battle Honours:
FRANCE AND FLANDERS, 1917-1918 — THE RHINELAND — NORTH-WEST EUROPE, 1944-1945
Headquarters — Chippewa Barracks, NORTH BAY, Ontario
"A" Company was relocated at North Bay from Kapuskasing in 1970.
"B" Company was relocated at Timmins from Virginiatown in 1965.
"C" Company was disbanded in 1970 at Haileybury.
"D" Company, after relocation from Timmins in 1965, was disbanded in 1970 at Kirkland Lake.
"E" Company was formed in 1951 to recruit for the "1st Canadian Infantry Battalion" which was re-designated "3rd Battalion, The Canadian Guards (Regular)" in 1953.
"F" Company was formed in 1952 to recruit for the "2nd Canadian Infantry Battalion" which was re-designated "4th Battalion, The Canadian Guards (Regular)" in 1953.
"Support" Company was disbanded in 1970 at North Bay.

Affiliated British Unit:
THE DUKE OF EDINBURGH'S ROYAL REGIMENT

THE CAMERON HIGHLANDERS OF OTTAWA (MILITIA)

The battalion originated in 1866 as the "Carleton Battalion of Infantry".

Regimental March: "MARCH OF THE CAMERON MEN"
Regimental Motto: "ADVANCE"
Major Battle Honours:
SOUTH AFRICA, 1899-1900 — VIMY RIDGE — FRANCE AND FLANDERS, 1916-1918 —
NORMANDY LANDING — THE RHINELAND — NORTH-WEST EUROPE, 1944-1945
Headquarters — The Drill Hall, Cartier Square, OTTAWA, Ontario
"A" Company
"B" Company
"C" Company was disbanded in 1970.
"D" Company was disbanded in 1970.
"Support" Company was disbanded in 1970.

Affiliated British Unit:
THE QUEEN'S OWN HIGHLANDERS

THE ELGIN REGIMENT (R.C.A.C.) (MILITIA)

The Regiment, which was converted to armour in 1954, originated in 1866 as the "Elgin Battalion of Infantry" and provided the "1st Canadian Tank Delivery Squadron" which landed in Sicily as a unit of the "1st Canadian Corps" during the Second World War.

Regimental March: *"I'M NINETY-FIVE"*
Regimental Motto: *"OFFICIUM PRIMUM"* / *("DUTY FIRST")*
Major Battle Honours:
THE GREAT WAR, 1916 — ITALY, 1943-1945 — NORTH-WEST EUROPE, 1944-1945
Headquarters — ST. THOMAS, Ontario
"A" Squadron
"B" Squadron
"C" Squadron was disbanded in 1970.

Affiliated British Unit:
THE ROYAL REGIMENT OF FUSILIERS

1st Battalion, THE ESSEX AND KENT SCOTTISH REGIMENT (MILITIA)

The battalion was formed in 1954 by the re-designation of "The Essex Scottish Regiment", which had originated as the "Essex Battalion of Infantry", upon amalgamation with "The Kent Regiment".

Regimental March: *"THE HIGHLAND LADDIE"*
Regimental Motto: *"SEMPER PARATUS"* / (*"ALWAYS READY"*)
Major Battle Honours:
VIMY RIDGE — PURSUIT TO MONS — FRANCE AND FLANDERS, 1915-1918 — DIEPPE — THE RHINELAND — NORTH-WEST EUROPE, 1942, 1944-1945
Headquarters — WINDSOR, Ontario
"Headquarters" was re-organized in 1965 as a sub-unit of "The Essex and Kent Scottish Regiment" which was formed by the amalgamation of "1st Battalion, The Essex and Kent Scottish Regiment" and "2nd Battalion, The Essex and Kent Scottish Regiment".
"A" Company — WINDSOR, Ontario
This company was re-organized in 1965 as a sub-unit of "The Essex and Kent Scottish Regiment".
"B" Company — WINDSOR, Ontario
This company was re-organized in 1965 as a sub-unit of "The Essex and Kent Scottish Regiment".
"C" Company was disbanded in 1965 at Windsor.
"D" Company was disbanded in 1965 at Leamington.
"Support" Company — WINDSOR, Ontario
This company was re-organized in 1965 as a sub-unit of "The Essex and Kent Scottish Regiment".

Affiliated British Unit:
THE QUEEN'S REGIMENT

2nd Battalion, THE ESSEX AND KENT SCOTTISH REGIMENT (MILITIA)

The battalion was formed in 1954 by the re-designation of "The Kent Regiment", which had originated in 1866 as the "Kent Battalion of Infantry", upon amalgamation with "The Essex Scottish Regiment".

Regimental March: *"A HUNDRED PIPERS"*
Regimental Motto: *"SEMPER PARATUS"* / *("ALWAYS READY")*
Battle Honour: THE GREAT WAR, 1917
Headquarters— CHATHAM, Ontario
"Headquarters" was disbanded in 1965 upon the amalgamation of "1st Battalion, The Essex and Kent Scottish Regiment" and "2nd Battalion, The Essex and Kent Scottish Regiment".
"A" Company was disbanded in 1965 at Chatham.
"B" Company was disbanded in 1965 at Chatham.
"C" Company —CHATHAM, Ontario
This company was re-organized in 1965 as a sub-unit of "The Essex and Kent Scottish Regiment".
"D" Company — WALLACEBURG, Ontario
This company was relocated at Chatham in 1965 and re-organized as a sub-unit of "The Essex and Kent Scottish Regiment".
"Support" Company was disbanded in 1965 at Chatham.

Affiliated British Unit:
THE QUEEN'S REGIMENT

THE ESSEX AND KENT SCOTTISH REGIMENT (MILITIA)

The battalion was formed in 1965 by the amalgamation of "1st Battalion, The Essex and Kent Scottish Regiment" and "2nd Battalion, The Essex and Kent Scottish Regiment".

Regimental Marches: *"THE HIGHLAND LADDIE"* and *"A HUNDRED PIPERS"*
Regimental Motto: *"SEMPER PARATUS"* / *("ALWAYS READY")*
Major Battle Honours:
VIMY RIDGE — PURSUIT TO MONS — FRANCE AND FLANDERS, 1915-1918 — DIEPPE — THE RHINELAND — NORTH-WEST EUROPE, 1942, 1944-1945
Headquarters — WINDSOR, Ontario
"A" Company — WINDSOR, Ontario
"B" Company — WINDSOR, Ontario
"C" Company — CHATHAM, Ontario
"D" Company was disbanded in 1970 at Chatham.
"Support" Company was disbanded in 1970 at Windsor.

Affiliated British Unit:
THE QUEEN'S REGIMENT

THE GREY AND SIMCOE FORESTERS (MILITIA)

The battalion was formed in 1936 by the amalgamation of "The Grey Regiment" and "The Simcoe Foresters", both of which had originated in 1866. The "Simcoe Foresters" provided four companies for service with the "York and Simcoe Provisional Battalion" in Saskatchewan during the "Riel" Rebellion (1885).

Regimental March: *"THE GREYS"*
Major Battle Honours:
NORTH-WEST CANADA, 1885 — THE GREAT WAR, 1916-1917
Headquarters — OWEN SOUND, Ontario
"A" Company — OWEN SOUND, Ontario
"B" Company — BARRIE, Ontario
This company originated in 1855 as the "Volunteer Militia Rifle Company of Barrie" which, from 1860 until 1866, had been "1" Company of the "2nd Battalion, Volunteer Militia Rifles of Canada" (now "The Queen's Own Rifles of Canada (Militia)").
The following sub-units of "The Grey and Simcoe Foresters (R.C.A.C.)" were disposed of as follows:
"C" Squadron, which maintained a detached troop at Orillia until 1965, was, upon conversion of the regiment to infantry in 1970, disbanded at Midland.
"D" Squadron — ORILLIA, Ontario
The squadron was re-organized in 1959 as a detached troop of "C" Squadron.

Affiliated British Unit:
THE WORCESTERSHIRE AND SHERWOOD FORESTERS

THE HASTINGS AND PRINCE EDWARD REGIMENT (MILITIA)

The battalion was formed in 1920 by the amalgamation of "The Prince Edward Regiment" which had originated in 1863 as the "Prince Edward Battalion of Infantry" and "The Hastings Rifles" which had originated in 1866 as the "Hastings Battalion of Infantry" which provided one company for service with the "Midland Provisional Battalion" in Saskatchewan during the "Riel" Rebellion (1885).

Regimental March: *"I'M NINETY-FIVE"*
Regimental Motto: *"PARATUS" / ("READY")*
Major Battle Honours:
NORTH-WEST CANADA, 1885 — THE GREAT WAR, 1915-1917 — LANDING IN SICILY — ITALY, 1943-1945 — NORTH-WEST EUROPE, 1945

The "2nd Battalion (Hastings and Prince Edward Regiment), 1st Canadian Infantry Regiment", which had been formed in Canada in 1945 for allocation to the "Canadian Army (Pacific Force)" for the projected assault on the Japanese home islands, was disbanded in 1945.

"Headquarters" was relocated at Belleville from Madoc in 1954 upon the incorporation within "The Hastings and Prince Edward Regiment" of "Headquarters, 9 Anti-Tank Regiment (The Argyll Light Infantry), R.C.A. (Reserve Force)" This regiment was formed in 1946 by the conversion and re-designation of "The Argyll Light Infantry (Tank) (Non-Permanent Active Militia)" which had originated in 1863 as the "15th Battalion, Volunteer Militia Infantry of Canada" (15th "Argyll Light Infantry") which provided one company for service with the "Midland Provisional Battalion" in Saskatchewan during the "Riel" Rebellion (1885).

"A" Company, which originated as the "Volunteer Militia Rifle Company of Belleville", was relocated at Belleville from Trenton in 1965.
"B" Company, which maintained a detached platoon at Norwood from 1954 until 1965, was, after relocation at Belleville from Madoc in 1965, relocated at Peterborough in 1970 thereby continuing a militia presence subsequent to the disbandment of "50 Field Regiment (The Prince of Wales' Rangers), R.C.A.".
"C" Company, which maintained a detached platoon at Millbrook from 1954 until 1965, was, after relocation at Port Hope from Belleville in 1954, relocated at Belleville in 1965 and disbanded in 1970. The company had been relocated at Port Hope thereby continuing a militia presence subsequent to the disbandment of "The Midland Regiment (Reserve Force)" which originated in 1866 as the "Northumberland" and "East Durham" battalions of infantry which provided three companies for service with the "Midland Provisional Battalion" in Saskatchewan during the "Riel" Rebellion (1885).
"D" Company, after relocation from Picton in 1965, was disbanded in 1970 at Belleville.
"E" Company was formed in 1951 to recruit for the "1st Canadian Infantry Battalion" which was re-designated "3rd Battalion, The Canadian Guards (Regular)" in 1953.
"F" Company was formed in 1952 to recruit for the "2nd Canadian Infantry Battlion" which was re-designated "4th Battalion, The Canadian Guards (Regular)" in 1953.
"Support" Company was disbanded in 1970 at Belleville.

Affiliated British Unit:
THE QUEEN'S REGIMENT

THE LAKE SUPERIOR SCOTTISH REGIMENT (MILITIA)

The battalion originated in 1905.

Regimental March: *"THE HIGHLAND LADDIE"*
Regimental Motto: *"INTER PERICULA INTREPIDI"*
      (*"INTO BATTLE UNAFRAID"*)
Major Battle Honours:
VIMY RIDGE — FRANCE AND FLANDERS, 1916-1918 — THE RHINELAND — NORTH-WEST EUROPE, 1944-1945
Headquarters — THUNDER BAY, Ontario
"A" Company — THUNDER BAY, Ontario
This company maintains detached platoons at Marathon and Geraldton.
"B" Company — THUNDER BAY, Ontario
"C" Company, after relocation from Atikokan in 1965, was disbanded in 1970 at Thunder Bay.
"D" Company, after relocation from Terrace Bay in 1965, was disbanded in 1970 at Thunder Bay.
"Support" Company was disbanded in 1970 at Thunder Bay.

Affiliated British Unit:
THE ROYAL ANGLIAN REGIMENT

THE LANARK AND RENFREW SCOTTISH REGIMENT (MILITIA)

The battalion originated in 1866 as the "Brockville Battalion of Infantry".

Regimental March: *"THE HIGHLAND LADDIE"*
Regimental Motto: *"FAC ET SPERA"* / *("DO AND HOPE")*
Major Battle Honours:
THE GREAT WAR, 1916-1917 — ITALY, 1944-1945
Headquarters — PEMBROKE, Ontario
"A" Company was relocated at Pembroke from Renfrew in 1970.
"B" Company — PEMBROKE, Ontario
"C" Company was disbanded in 1970 at Carleton Place.
"D" Company, after relocation from Perth in 1965, was disbanded in 1970 at Pembroke.
"Support" Company was disbanded in 1970 at Pembroke.

Affiliated British Unit:
THE BLACK WATCH (ROYAL HIGHLAND REGIMENT)

THE BROCKVILLE RIFLES (MILITIA)

The battalion originated in 1866 as the "Brockville Battalion of Rifles".

Regimental March: *"BONNIE DUNDEE"*
Regimental Motto: *"SEMPER PARATUS"* / (*"ALWAYS READY"*)
Battle Honour: THE GREAT WAR, 1916-1918
Headquarters — BROCKVILLE, Ontario
"A" Company originated in 1855 as the "Volunteer Militia Rifle Company of Brockville".
"B" Company
"C" Company was disbanded in 1970.
"D" Company was disbanded in 1970.
"Support" Company was disbanded in 1970.

Affiliated British Unit:
THE ROYAL GREEN JACKETS

THE LINCOLN AND WELLAND REGIMENT (MILITIA)

The battalion originated in 1863 as the "Lincoln Battalion of Infantry".

Regimental March: *"THE LINCOLNSHIRE POACHER"*
Regimental Motto: "NON NOBIS SED PATRIAE"
     ("NOT FOR OURSELVES BUT OUR COUNTRY")
Major Battle Honours:
THE GREAT WAR, 1916-1917 — THE RHINELAND — NORTH-WEST EUROPE, 1944-1945
Headquarters — ST. CATHARINES, Ontario
"A" Company, — ST. CATHARINES, Ontario
This company originated in 1855 as the "1st Volunteer Militia Rifle Company of St. Catharines".
"B" Company, after relocation in 1965 from Butler's Barracks in Niagara-on-the-Lake, was disbanded in 1970 at St. Catharines.
"C" Company, after relocation from Fort Erie in 1965, was disbanded in 1970 at St. Catharines.
"D" Company — NIAGARA FALLS, Ontario
"Support" Company was disbanded in 1970 at St. Catharines.

Affiliated British Unit:
THE ROYAL ANGLIAN REGIMENT

THE ONTARIO REGIMENT (R.C.A.C.) (MILITIA)

The Regiment, which originated in 1866 as the "Ontario Battalion of Infantry", was converted to armour in 1946.

Regimental March: *"JOHN PEEL"*
Regimental Motto: *"FIDELIS ET PARATUS"* / *("FAITHFUL AND READY")*
Major Battle Honours:
VIMY RIDGE — FRANCE AND FLANDERS, 1917-1918 — ADVANCE TO FLORENCE — ITALY, 1943-1945 — ARNHEM (1945) — NORTH-WEST EUROPE, 1945
Headquarters — Colonel R. S. McLaughlin Armoury, OSHAWA, Ontario
"A" Squadron originated in 1858 as the "Volunteer Militia Highland Rifle Company of Whitby" which, from 1860 until 1866, had been "6" Company of the "2nd Battalion, Volunteer Militia Rifles of Canada" (now "The Queen's Own Rifles of Canada (Militia)").
"B" Squadron originated as the "Volunteer Militia Infantry Company of Oshawa".
"C" Squadron originated as the "Volunteer Militia Rifle Company of Oshawa".

Affiliated British Unit:
THE ROYAL REGIMENT OF WALES

THE LORNE SCOTS (PEEL, DUFFERIN AND HALTON REGIMENT) (MILITIA)

The battalion was formed in 1936 by the amalgamation of "The Lorne Rifles" which had originated in 1866 as the "Halton Battalion of Infantry" and "The Peel and Dufferin Regiment" which had originated in 1866 as the "Peel Battalion of Infantry".

Regimental March: *"THE CAMPBELLS ARE COMING"*
Regimental Motto: *"AIR SON AR DUTHCHAIS"*
    (*"FOR OUR ALTARS AND OUR HOMES"*)
Major Battle Honours:
THE GREAT WAR, 1915-1918 — ITALY, 1943-1945 — NORTH-WEST EUROPE, 1944-1945
Headquarters — BRAMPTON, Ontario
"A" Company was relocated at Oakville from Port Credit in 1965.
"B" Company, which maintained a detached platoon at Burlington from 1946 until 1954, was relocated at Brampton from Oakville in 1970.
"C" Company — GEORGETOWN, Ontario
This company maintained a detached platoon at Milton until 1965.
"D" Company, after relocation from Orangeville in 1965, was disbanded in 1970 at Brampton.
"Support" Company was disbanded in 1970 at Brampton.

Affiliated British Unit:
THE ROYAL REGIMENT OF FUSILIERS

THE PERTH REGIMENT (MILITIA)

The battalion, which had originated in 1866 as the "Perth Battalion of Infantry", was disbanded in 1965.

Regimental March: *"KENMURE'S ON AND AWA"*
Regimental Motto: *"AUDAX ET CAUTUS"*
      ("DARING AND CAUTION")
Major Battle Honours:
THE GREAT WAR, 1916-1917 — ITALY, 1944-1945 — DELFZIJL POCKET — NORTH-WEST EUROPE, 1945
"Headquarters" — STRATFORD, Ontario
"A" Company originated as the "Volunteer Militia Rifle Company of Stratford".
"B" Company originated as the "Volunteer Militia Infantry Company of Straford".
"C" Company
"D" Company
"Support" Company

Affiliated British Unit:
THE CAMERONIANS (SCOTTISH RIFLES)

THE STORMONT, DUNDAS AND GLENGARRY HIGHLANDERS (MILITIA)

The battalion, which originated in 1868 as the "Stormont and Glengarry Battalion of Infantry", may be considered as perpetuating the "Glengarry Fencible Light Infantry" which fought on the Niagara frontier in Upper Canada (Ontario) during the Anglo-American War of 1812 to 1814.

Regimental March: *"BONNIE DUNDEE"*
Regimental Motto: *"DILEAS GU BAS"*
     ("FAITHFUL UNTO DEATH")
Major Battle Honours:
THE GREAT WAR, 1916-1917 — NORMANDY LANDING — THE RHINELAND — NORTH-WEST EUROPE, 1944-1945
Headquarters — CORNWALL, Ontario
"A" Company, which originated as the "1st Volunteer Militia Rifle Company of Cornwall", was relocated at Cornwall from Morrisburg in 1954.
"B" Company — CORNWALL, Ontario
This company originated as the "2nd Volunteer Militia Rifle Company of Cornwall".
"C" Company, after relocation from Maxville in 1954, was disbanded in 1970 at Cornwall.
"D" Company, after relocation from Alexandria in 1965, was disbanded in 1970 at Cornwall.
"Support" Company was disbanded in 1970 at Cornwall.

THE HIGHLAND FUSILIERS OF CANADA (MILITIA)

The battalion was formed in 1965 by the amalgamation of "The Highland Light Infantry of Canada" which had originated in 1866 as the "Waterloo Battalion of Infantry" and "The Scots Fusiliers of Canada" which had originated in 1914 as "The North Waterloo Regiment".

Regimental March: *"THE HIGHLAND LADDIE"*
Regimental Motto: *"DEFENCE NOT DEFIANCE"*
Major Battle Honours:
THE GREAT WAR, 1915-1917 — NORMANDY LANDING — THE RHINELAND — NORTH-WEST EUROPE, 1944-1945
Headquarters — CAMBRIDGE, Ontario
"A" Company — CAMBRIDGE, Ontario
"B" Company — KITCHENER, Ontario
"C" Company was disbanded in 1970 at Cambridge.
"D" Company was disbanded in 1970 at Cambridge.
"Support" Company was disbanded in 1970 at Kitchener.

Affiliated British Unit:
THE ROYAL HIGHLAND FUSILIERS

THE QUEEN'S YORK RANGERS (1st AMERICAN REGIMENT) (R.C.A.C.) (MILITIA)

The Regiment originated in 1866 as the "York Battalion of Infantry" which provided four companies for service with the "York and Simcoe Provisional Battalion" in Saskatchewan during the "Riel" Rebellion (1885).

Regimental March: *"BRAGANZA"*
Regimental Motto: *"REMEMBERING THEIR GALLANTRY IN FORMER DAYS"*
Major Battle Honours:
NORTH-WEST CANADA, 1885 — VIMY RIDGE — POLYGON WOOD — PURSUIT TO MONS — FRANCE AND FLANDERS, 1915-1918
Headquarters — Fort York Armoury, TORONTO, Ontario
"A" Squadron — AURORA, Ontario
This squadron originated as the "Volunteer Militia Infantry Company of Aurora".
"B" Squadron was relocated at Toronto from Newmarket in 1970.
"C" Squadron was disbanded in 1970 at Toronto.

Affiliated British Units:
THE QUEEN'S REGIMENT
THE GREEN HOWARDS

LE REGIMENT DE MAISONNEUVE (MILICE)

The battalion originated in 1880.

Regimental March: "SAMBRE ET MEUSE"
Regimental Motto: "BON COEUR ET BON BRAS"
    ("GOOD HEART AND STRONG ARM")
Major Battle Honours:
THE GREAT WAR, 1915-1916 — THE RHINELAND — NORTH-WEST EUROPE, 1944-1945
Headquarters — MONTREAL, Quebec
"A" Company
"B" Company
"C" Company was disbanded in 1970.
"D" Company was disbanded in 1970.
"Support Company was disbanded in 1970.

Affiliated British Unit:
THE LIGHT INFANTRY

LE REGIMENT DE LA CHAUDIERE (MILICE)

The battalion, which originated in 1869 as the "Provisional Battalion of Dorchester", incorporated "Le Regiment de Levis" in 1954.

Regimental March: *"SAMBRE ET MEUSE"*
Regimental Motto: *"AERE PERENNIUS"* / (*"TRUER THAN STEEL"*)
Major Battle Honours:
NORMANDY LANDING — THE RHINELAND — NORTH-WEST EUROPE, 1944-1945
Headquarters — LEVIS, Quebec
"A" Company — BEAUCEVILLE, Quebec
"B" Company — LAC MEGANTIC, Quebec
"C" Company — LEVIS, Quebec
"D" Company was disbanded in 1970 at Levis.
"Support" Company, after relocation from Quebec City in 1954, was disbanded in 1970 at Levis.

LE REGIMENT DE HULL (R.C.A.C.) (MILICE)

The Regiment originated in 1914 and was converted to armour in 1946.

Regimental March: *"LA MARCHE DE LA VICTOIRE"*
Regimental Motto: *"ON NE PASSE PAS"* / (*"NONE SHALL PASS"*)
Battle Honour: THE GREAT WAR, 1917

The "Regiment de Hull" served on Kiska in the Aleutian Islands in 1943 as a unit of the "13th Canadian Infantry Brigade Group".

Headquarters — Manege de Salaberry, HULL, Quebec
"A" Squadron
"B" Squadron
"C" Squadron was disbanded in 1970.

LE REGIMENT DE JOLIETTE (MILICE)

The battalion, which had originated in 1871 as the "Provisional Battalion of Joliette", was disbanded in 1965.

Regimental March: *"LE REGIMENT DE JOLIETTE"*
Regimental Motto: *"QUEM TIMEBO"* / (*"WHO SHALL I FEAR?"*)
Headquarters — JOLIETTE, Quebec
"A" Company, after relocation from Lachute in 1954, was disbanded in 1965 at Joliette.
"B" Company was disbanded in 1965 at Joliette.
"C" Company, after relocation from Shawinigan Falls in 1954, was disbanded in 1965 at Joliette.
"D" Company was disbanded in 1965 at St-Jerome.
"Support" Company was disbanded in 1965 at Joliette.

Affiliated British Unit:
THE ROYAL GREEN JACKETS

THE ROYAL MONTREAL REGIMENT (MILITIA)

The battalion, which originated as the "Westmount Rifles", provided the "headquarters defence battalion" for the "First Canadian Army" during the Second World War.

Regimental March: "CA IRA"
Major Battle Honours:
VIMY RIDGE — PURSUIT TO MONS — FRANCE AND FLANDERS, 1915-1918 —
NORTH-WEST EUROPE, 1944-1945

A "divisional reconnaissance troop" sub-designated "Royal Montreal Regiment" was formed in Canada in 1945 for allocation to the "Canadian Army (Pacific Force)" for the projected assault on the Japanese home islands. This "troop" was disbanded in 1945.

Headquarters — WESTMOUNT (MONTREAL), Quebec
"A" Company
"B" Company
"C" Company was disbanded in 1970.
"D" Company was disbanded in 1970.
"Support" Company was disbanded in 1970.

Affiliated British Unit:
THE PRINCE OF WALES' OWN REGIMENT OF YORKSHIRE

LES FUSILIERS MONT-ROYAL (MILICE)

The battalion originated in 1869 as the "Mount Royal Rifles".

Regimental March: *"THE JOCKEY OF YORK"*
Regimental Motto: *"NUMQUAM RETRORSUM"*
        ("NONE SHALL CAUSE OUR RETREAT")
Major Battle Honours:
NORTH-WEST CANADA, 1885 — THE GREAT WAR, 1916-1918 — DIEPPE — THE RHINELAND — NORTH-WEST EUROPE, 1942, 1944-1945
Headquarters — MONTREAL, Quebec
"A" Company
"B" Company
"C" Company was disbanded in 1970.
"D" Company was disbanded in 1970.
"E" Company was formed in 1951 to recruit for the "1st Canadian Infantry Battalion" which was re-designated "3rd Battalion, The Canadian Guards (Regular)" in 1953.
"F" Company was formed in 1952 to recruit for the "2nd Canadian Infantry Battalion" which was re-designated "4th Battalion, The Canadian Guards (Regular)" in 1953.
"Support" Company was disbanded in 1970.

Affiliated British Unit:
THE YORK AND LANCASTER REGIMENT

LE REGIMENT DU SAGUENAY (MILICE)

The battalion originated in 1900.

Regimental March: *"LE REGIMENT DU SAGUENAY"*
Regimental Motto: *"DIEU ET PATRIE"* / *("GOD AND COUNTRY")*
Headquarters — CHICOUTIMI, Quebec
"A" Company was relocated at Chicoutimi from Arvida in 1970.
"B" Company was relocated at Chicoutimi from Bagotville in 1965.
"C" Company, which had been relocated in 1965 at Jonquiere from Chicoutimi thereby continuing a militia presence subsequent to the disbandment of "25 Technical Squadron, R.C.E.M.E.", was relocated at Arvida in 1968.
"D" Company was disbanded in 1970 at Chicoutimi.
"Support" Company was disbanded in 1970 at Chicoutimi.

LES FUSILIERS DE SHERBROOKE (MILICE)

The battalion originated in 1867.

Regimental March: *"THE BRITISH GRENADIERS"*
Regimental Motto: *"DROIT AU BUT"*
 ("STRAIGHT TO THE POINT")
Major Battle Honours:
THE GREAT WAR, 1916-1917 — NORMANDY LANDING — THE RHINELAND — NORTH-WEST EUROPE, 1944-1945
Headquarters — SHERBROOKE, Quebec
"A" Company — SHERBROOKE, Quebec
"B" Company — SHERBROOKE, Quebec
"C" Company — SHERBROOKE, Quebec
"D" Company, after relocation in 1965 from Magog where it had continued a militia presence subsequent to the relocation of "73 Field Battery, R.C.A.", was disbanded in 1970 at Sherbrooke. "Support" Company was disbanded in 1970 at Sherbrooke.

12ieme REGIMENT BLINDE DU CANADA (MILICE)

The Regiment was formed in 1970 by the re-designation of "Le Regiment de Trois-Rivieres (R.C.A.C.) (Militia)" which had originated in 1871 as the "Provisional Battalion of Three Rivers".

Regimental March: *"MY BOY WILLIE"*
Regimental Motto: *"ADSUM"* / ("I AM PRESENT")
Major Battle Honours:
THE GREAT WAR, 1917 — LANDING IN SICILY — ADVANCE TO FLORENCE — ITALY, 1943-1945 — NORTH-WEST EUROPE, 1945
Headquarters — TROIS-RIVIERES, Quebec
"A" Squadron
"B" Squadron
"C" Squadron was disbanded in 1970.

1st Battalion, THE ROYAL NEW BRUNSWICK REGIMENT (MILITIA)

The battalion was formed in 1954 by the amalgamation of "The Carleton and York Regiment" which had originated in 1869 as the "Carleton" battalions of infantry and "The New Brunswick Scottish Regiment" which had been formed in 1946 by the amalgamation of "The New Brunswick Rangers" and "The Saint John Fusiliers".

Regimental March: "A HUNDRED PIPERS"
Regimental Motto: "SPEM REDUXIT" / ("SHE LEADS TO HOPE")
Major Battle Honours:
SOUTH AFRICA, 1899-1900, 1902 — VIMY RIDGE — FRANCE AND FLANDERS, 1915-1918 — LANDING IN SICILY — ITALY, 1943-1945 — THE RHINELAND — NORTH-WEST EUROPE, 1944-1945

The "2nd Battalion (Carleton and York Regiment), 3rd Canadian Infantry Regiment", which had been formed in Canada in 1945 for allocation to the "Canadian Army (Pacfic Force)" for the projected assault on the Japanese home islands, was disbanded in 1945.

"Headquarters" was relocated at Fredericton from Saint John in 1970.
"A" Company —EDMUNDSTON, New Brunswick
"B" Company — FREDERICTON, New Brunswick
"C" Company was relocated at Fredericton from Grand Falls in 1970.
"D" Company was disbanded in 1970 at Saint John.
"E" Company of "The Carleton and York Regiment" was formed in 1951 to recruit for the "1st Canadian Infantry Battalion" which was re-designated "3rd Battalion, The Canadian Guards (Regular)" in 1953.
"F" Company of "The Carleton and York Regiment" was formed in 1952 to recruit for the "2nd Canadian Infantry Battalion" which was re-designated "4th Battalion, The Canadian Guards (Regular)" in 1953.
"Support" Company was disbanded in 1970 at Saint John.

Affiliated British Unit:
THE QUEEN'S REGIMENT

2nd Battalion, THE ROYAL NEW BRUNSWICK REGIMENT (MILITIA)

The battalion was formed in 1954 by the re-designation of "The North Shore (New Brunswick) Regiment" which had originated in 1870 as the "Northumberland (New Brunswick) Battalion of Infantry", upon amalgamation with "The Carleton and York Regiment".

Regimental March: *"THE OLD NORTH SHORE"*
Regimental Motto: *"SPEM REDUXIT"* / (*"SHE LEADS TO HOPE"*)
Major Battle Honours:
THE GREAT WAR, 1916-1917 — NORMANDY LANDING — THE RHINELAND — NORTH-WEST EUROPE, 1944-1945
Headquarters — BATHURST, New Brunswick
"A" Company was relocated at Newcastle from Chatham in 1965.
"B" Company — BATHURST, New Brunswick
"C" Company — CAMPBELLTON, New Brunswick
"D" Company, after relocation from Dalhousie in 1965, was disbanded in 1970 at Campbellton.
"Support" Company was disbanded in 1970 at Newcastle.

Affiliated British Unit:
THE QUEEN'S REGIMENT

THE HALIFAX RIFLES (R.C.A.C.) (MILITIA)

The Regiment, which was disbanded in 1965, originated in 1860 as the "Halifax Volunteer Battalion of Rifles" which provided three companies for service with the "Halifax Provisional Battalion" in Saskatchewan during the "Riel" Rebellion (1885). The "Halifax Volunteer Battalion of Rifles" had incorporated the following independent companies:

The "Scottish Rifles"
The "Chebucto Greys"
The "Mayflower Rifles"
The "Halifax Rifles"
The "Irish Rifles"
The "Dartmouth Rifles"

Regimental March: *"LUTZOW'S WILD HUNT"*
Regimental Motto: *"CEDE NULLIS"* / *("YIELD TO NONE")*
Major Battle Honours:
NORTH-WEST CANADA, 1885 — SOUTH AFRICA, 1899-1900 — THE GREAT WAR, 1915-1917
Headquarters — HALIFAX, Nova Scotia
"A" Squadron
"B" Squadron
"C" Squadron

Affiliated British Unit:
THE ROYAL GREEN JACKETS

THE PRINCESS LOUISE FUSILIERS (MILITIA)

The battalion, which originated in 1869, provided three companies for service with the "Halifax Provisional Battalion" in Saskatchewan during the "Riel" Rebellion (1885).

Regimental March: *"THE BRITISH GRENADIERS"*
Regimental Motto: *"FIDELITER"* / *("FAITHFULLY")*
Major Battle Honours:
NORTH-WEST CANADA, 1885 — SOUTH AFRICA, 1899-1900 — THE GREAT WAR, 1916-1917 — ITALY, 1944-1945 — DELFZIJL POCKET — NORTH-WEST EUROPE, 1945
Headquarters — HALIFAX, Nova Scotia
"A" Company — HALIFAX, Nova Scotia
"B" Company was relocated at Halifax from Bedford in 1954.
"C" Company, after relocation from Dartmouth in 1954, was disbanded in 1970 at Halifax.
"D" Company, after relocation from Imperoyal in 1954, was disbanded in 1970 at Halifax.
"Support" Company was disbanded in 1970 at Halifax.

Affiliated British Unit:
THE ROYAL IRISH RANGERS

1st Battalion, THE NOVA SCOTIA HIGHLANDERS (MILITIA)

The battalion was formed in 1954 by the amalgamation of "The North Nova Scotia Highlanders" and "The Pictou Highlanders", both of which had originated in 1871 as "provisional" battalions of infantry, upon amalgamation with "The Cape Breton Highlanders".

Regimental March: *"THE ATHOLL HIGHLANDERS"*
Regimental Motto: *"SOL NA FEAR FEARAIL"*
    (*"BREED OF MANLY MEN"*)
Major Battle Honours:
SOUTH AFRICA, 1899-1900 — VIMY RIDGE — FRANCE AND FLANDERS, 1915-1918 —
NORMANDY LANDING — THE RHINELAND — NORTH-WEST EUROPE, 1944-1945
Headquarters — NEW GLASGOW, Nova Scotia
"A" Company — NEW GLASGOW, Nova Scotia
"B" Company — SPRINGHILL, Nova Scotia
"C" Company — TRURO, Nova Scotia
"D" Company — AMHERST, Nova Scotia
"E" Company — PICTOU, Nova Scotia
(Note that "E" Company of "The North Nova Scotia Highlanders" was formed in 1951 to recruit for the "1st Canadian Highland Battalion" which was re-designated "1st Battalion, The Black Watch (Royal Highland Regiment) of Canada (Regular)" in 1953.)
"F" Company of "The North Nova Scotia Highlanders" was formed in 1952 to recruit for the "2nd Canadian Highland Battalion" which was re-designated "2nd Battalion, The Black Watch (Royal Highland Regiment) of Canada (Regular)" in 1953.

Affiliated British Unit:
THE QUEEN'S OWN HIGHLANDERS

2nd Battalion, THE NOVA SCOTIA HIGHLANDERS (MILITIA)

The battalion was formed in 1954 by the re-designation of "The Cape Breton Highlanders" which had originated in 1871 as a "provisional" battalion of infantry, upon amalgamation with both "The North Nova Scotia Highlanders" and "The Pictou Highlanders".

Regimental March: *"THE HIGHLAND LADDIE"*
Regimental Motto: *"SIOL NA FEAR FEARAIL"*
    ("BREED OF MANLY MEN")
Major Battle Honours:
VIMY RIDGE — FRANCE AND FLANDERS, 1917-1918 — ITALY, 1944-1945 — DELFZIJL POCKET — NORTH-WEST EUROPE, 1945
Headquarters — Victoria Park Armoury, SYDNEY, Nova Scotia
"A" Company — NORTH SYDNEY, Nova Scotia
"B" Company — GLACE BAY, Nova Scotia
"C" Company — Victoria Park Armoury, SYDNEY, Nova Scotia
"D" Company, after relocation from New Waterford in 1965, was disbanded in 1970 at Sydney.
"Support" Company was disbanded in 1970 at Sydney.

Affiliated British Unit:
THE QUEEN'S OWN HIGHLANDERS

THE WEST NOVA SCOTIA REGIMENT (MILITIA)

The battalion was formed in 1936 by the amalgamation of "The Annapolis Regiment" which had originated in 1869 as the "First Regiment of Annapolis County" and "The Lunenburg Regiment" which had originated in 1870 as a "provisional" battalion of infantry.

Regimental March: *"GOD BLESS THE PRINCE OF WALES"*
Regimental Motto: *"SEMPER FIDELIS"* / *("ALWAYS FAITHFUL")*
Major Battle Honours:
THE GREAT WAR, 1916-1917 — LANDING IN SICILY — ITALY, 1943-1945 — NORTH-WEST EUROPE, 1945

The "3rd Battalion (West Nova Scotia Regiment), 3rd Canadian Infantry Regiment", which had been formed in Canada in 1945 for allocation to the "Canadian Army (Pacific Force)" for the projected assault on the Japanese home islands, was disbanded in 1945.

Headquarters — ALDERSHOT, Nova Scotia
"A" Company — was relocated at Aldershot from Lunenburg in 1970.
This company originated as the "1st Volunteer Militia Infantry Company of Lunenburg".
"B" Company — KENTVILLE, Nova Scotia
"C" Company — WINDSOR, Nova Scotia
"D" Company — MIDDLETON, Nova Scotia
"Support" Company was disbanded in 1970 at Aldershot.

Affiliated British Unit:
THE QUEEN'S LANCASHIRE REGIMENT

THE PRINCE EDWARD ISLAND REGIMENT (R.C.A.C.) (MILITIA)

The Regiment was formed in 1946 by the amalgamation of "The Prince Edward Island Highlanders" which had originated in 1875 as the "Queen's County Provisional Battalion of Infantry" and "The Prince Edward Island Light Horse" which had originated in 1901 as "The Prince Edward Island Mounted Rifles".

Regimental March: *"OLD SOLOMON LEVI"*
Regimental Motto: *"PARVA SUB INGENTI"*
      (*"THE SMALL UNDER PROTECTION OF THE GREAT"*)
Major Battle Honours:
SOUTH AFRICA, 1900 — THE GREAT WAR, 1916-1917 — NORTH-WEST EUROPE, 1945
Headquarters — Queen Charlotte Armoury, CHARLOTTETOWN, P.E.I.
"A" Squadron — Queen Charlotte Armoury, CHARLOTTETOWN, P.E.I.
"B" Squadron was relocated at Charlottetown in 1970 from Montague where it had continued a militia presence subsequent to the disbandment of "204 Light Anti-Aircraft Battery, R.C.A. (Reserve Force)".
"C" Squadron — SUMMERSIDE, Prince Edward Island

Affiliated British Unit:
9th/12th QUEEN'S ROYAL LANCERS

THE ROYAL WINNIPEG RIFLES (MILITIA)

The battalion, which originated in 1883 as the "90th 'Winnipeg' Battalion of Rifles", incorporated "The Winnipeg Light Infantry" in 1955.

Regimental March: *"OLD SOLOMON LEVI"*
Regimental Motto: *"HOSTIE ACIE NOMINATI"*
        ("NAMED BY THE ENEMY")
Major Battle Honours:
FISH CREEK — NORTH-WEST CANADA, 1885 — SOUTH AFRICA, 1899-1900 — VIMY RIDGE — PURSUIT TO MONS — FRANCE AND FLANDERS, 1915-1918 — NORMANDY LANDING — THE RHINELAND — NORTH-WEST EUROPE, 1944-1945
Headquarters — Minto Armoury, WINNIPEG, Manitoba
"A" Company
"B" Company
"C" Company was disbanded in 1970.
"D" Company was disbanded in 1970.
"E" Company was formed in 1951 to recruit for the "1st Canadian Rifle Battalion" which was re-designated "1st Battalion, The Queen's Own Rifles of Canada (Regular)" in 1953.
"F" Company was formed in 1952 to recruit for the "2nd Canadian Rifle Battalion" which was re-designated "2nd Battalion, The Queen's Own Rifles of Canada (Regular)" in 1953.
"Support" Company was disbanded in 1970.

Affiliated British Unit:
THE ROYAL GREEN JACKETS

THE WINNIPEG GRENADIERS (MILITIA)

The battalion, which had originated in 1908 as the "100th Regiment", was disbanded in 1965.

Regimental March: *"THE BRITISH GRENADIERS"*
Regimental Motto: *"ADSUM"* / *("I AM PRESENT")*
Major Battle Honours:
VIMY RIDGE — FRANCE AND FLANDERS, 1916-1918 — HONG KONG — SOUTH-EAST
ASIA, 1941

The battalion, having been destroyed while fighting in the defence of Hong Kong, was re-formed in Canada in 1942 and served on Kiska in the Aleutian Islands in 1943 as a unit of the "13th Canadian Infantry Brigade Group".

Headquarters — WINNIPEG, MANITOBA
"A" Company
"B" Company
"C" Company
"D" Company
"Support" Company

Affiliated British Unit:
THE SCOTS GUARDS

THE REGINA RIFLE REGIMENT (MILITIA)

The battalion originated in 1905 as an element of the "Saskatchewan Rifles".

Regimental March: *"LUTZOW'S WILD HUNT"*
Major Battle Honours:
VIMY RIDGE — PURSUIT TO MONS — FRANCE AND FLANDERS, 1915-1918 —
NORMANDY LANDING — THE RHINELAND — NORTH-WEST EUROPE, 1944-1945
Headquarters — REGINA, Saskatchewan
"A" Company — REGINA, Saskatchewan
"B" Company was relocated at Regina from Fort Qu'Appelle in 1965.
"C" Company was disbanded in 1970 at Regina.
"D" Company was disbanded in 1970 at Regina.
"E" Company was formed in 1951 to recruit for the "1st Canadian Rifle Battalion" which was re-designated "1st Battalion, The Queen's Own Rifles of Canada (Regular)" in 1953.
"F" Company was formed in 1952 to recruit for the "2nd Canadian Rifle Battalion" which was re-designated "2nd Battalion, The Queen's Own Rifles of Canada (Regular)" in 1953.
"Support" Company was disbanded in 1965 at Regina.

Affiliated British Unit:
THE ROYAL GREEN JACKETS

1st Battalion, THE NORTH SASKATCHEWAN REGIMENT (MILITIA)

The battalion, which was formed in 1955 by the re-designation of "The Prince Albert and Battleford Volunteers" upon amalgamation with "The Saskatoon Light Infantry", perpetuates the "Battleford Infantry Company" and the "Moose Mountain Scouts", both of which were raised for service in Saskatchewan during the "Riel" Rebellion (1885).

Regimental March: *"THE MOUNTAIN ROSE"*
Major Battle Honours:
NORTH-WEST CANADA, 1885 — VIMY RIDGE — FRANCE AND FLANDERS, 1915-1918
"Headquarters" was disbanded in 1970 at Prince Albert.
"A" Company was disbanded in 1970 at North Battleford.
"B" Company — PRINCE ALBERT, Saskatchewan
This company was re-organized as a sub-unit of "The North Saskatchewan Regiment" which was formed in 1970 by the amalgamation of "1st Battalion, The North Saskatchewan Regiment" and "2nd Battalion, The North Saskatchewan Regiment".
"C" Company was disbanded in 1970 at Lloydminster.
"D" Company, after relocation from Melfort in 1965, was disbanded in 1970 at Prince Albert.
"Support" Company was disbanded in 1970 at Prince Albert.

Affiliated British Unit:
THE LIGHT INFANTRY

2nd Battalion, THE NORTH SASKATCHEWAN REGIMENT (MILITIA)

The battalion was formed in 1955 by the re-designation of "The Saskatoon Light Infantry", which had originated in 1912 as the "Saskatoon Fusiliers", upon amalgamation with "The Prince Albert and Battleford Volunteers" which had originated in 1913.

Regimental March: *"THE MOUNTAIN ROSE"*
Major Battle Honours:
VIMY RIDGE — FRANCE AND FLANDERS, 1915-1918 — LANDING IN SICILY — ITALY, 1943-1945 — NORTH-WEST EUROPE, 1945

The "Saskatoon Light Infantry" provided a machine-gun detachment which landed on Spitsbergen during the raid on that Norwegian island in the Barents Sea in 1941. Three "cannon" (machine-gun) companies sub-designated "Saskatoon Light Infantry" were formed in Canada in 1945 for allocation to the "Canadian Army (Pacific Force)" for the projected assault on the Japanese home islands. These companies were disbanded in 1945.

Headquarters — Sergeant Hugh Cairns Armoury, SASKATOON, Saskatchewan
"Headquarters" was re-organized as a sub-unit of "The North Saskatchewan Regiment" which was formed in 1970 by the amalgamation of "1st Battalion, The North Saskatchewan Regiment" and "2nd Battalion, The North Sasketchewan Regiment".
"A" Company — SASKATOON, Saskatchewan
This company was re-organized in 1970 as a sub-unit of "The North Saskatchewan Regiment".
"B" Company was disbanded in 1970 at Saskatoon.
"C" Company, after relocation at Saskatoon from Rosetown in 1965, was re-organized in 1970 as a sub-unit of "The North Saskatchewan Regiment".
"D" Company, after relocation from Kindersley in 1965, was disbanded in 1970 at Saskatoon.
"Support" Company was disbanded in 1970 at Saskatoon.

Affiliated British Unit:
THE LIGHT INFANTRY

THE NORTH SASKATCHEWAN REGIMENT (MILITIA)

The battalion was formed in 1970 by the amalgamation of "1st Battalion, The North Saskatchewan Regiment" and "2nd Battalion, The North Saskatchewan Regiment".

Regimental March: *"THE MOUNTAIN ROSE"*
Major Battle Honours:
NORTH-WEST CANADA, 1885 — VIMY RIDGE — FRANCE AND FLANDERS, 1915-1918 — LANDING IN SICILY — ITALY, 1943-1945 — NORTH-WEST EUROPE, 1945
Headquarters — Sergeant Hugh Cairns Armoury, SASKATOON, Saskatchewan
"A" Company — Sergeant Hugh Cairns Armoury, SASKATOON, Saskatchewan
"B" Company — PRINCE ALBERT, Saskatchewan
"C" Company — Sergeant Hugh Cairns Armoury, SASKATOON, Saskatchewan

Affiliated British Unit:
THE LIGHT INFANTRY

THE SOUTH SASKATCHEWAN REGIMENT (MILITIA)

The battalion, which was disbanded in 1968, had been formed in 1936 by the amalgamation of "The Weyburn Regiment" and "The Saskatchewan Border Regiment", both of which had originated in 1905 as elements of the "Saskatchewan Rifles".

Regimental March: *"THE WARWICKSHIRE LADS"*
Regimental Motto: *"PRO PATRIA"* / *("FOR COUNTRY")*
Major Battle Honours:
THE GREAT WAR, 1916 — DIEPPE — THE RHINELAND — NORTH-WEST EUROPE, 1942, 1944-1945
"Headquarters", after relocation from Weyburn in 1954, was disbanded in 1968 at Estevan.
"A" Company, after relocation from Weyburn in 1965, was disbanded in 1968 at Estevan.
"B" Company was disbanded in 1968 at Estevan.
"C" Company, after relocation from Assiniboia in 1954, was disbanded in 1968 at Estevan.
"D" Company, after relocation from Oxbow in 1954, was disbanded in 1968 at Esteven.
"Support" Company was disbanded in 1968 at Estevan.

Affiliated British Unit:
THE ROYAL REGIMENT OF FUSILIERS

THE CALGARY HIGHLANDERS (MILITIA)

The battalion originated in 1910 as an element of the "Calgary Rifles".

Regimental March: *"THE HIGHLAND LADDIE"*
Major Battle Honours:
VIMY RIDGE — PURSUIT TO MONS — FRANCE AND FLANDERS, 1915-1918 — THE RHINELAND — NORTH-WEST EUROPE, 1944-1945
Headquarters — Mewata Armoury, CALGARY, Alberta
"A" Company was relocated at Calgary from Vulcan in 1965.
"B" Company was relocated at Calgary from Banff in 1954.
"C" Company was disbanded in 1970 at Drumheller.
"D" Company was disbanded in 1970 at Calgary.
"Support" Company was disbanded in 1970 at Calgary.

Affiliated British Unit:
THE ARGYLL AND SUTHERLAND HIGHLANDERS

THE KING'S OWN CALGARY REGIMENT (R.C.A.C.) (MILITIA)

The Regiment originated in 1910 as an element of the "Calgary Rifles".

Regimental March: "COLONEL BOGEY"
Regimental Motto: "ONWARD"
Major Battle Honours:
VIMY RIDGE — FRANCE AND FLANDERS, 1916-1918 — DIEPPE — NORTH-WEST
EUROPE, 1942 — ADVANCE TO FLORENCE — ITALY, 1943-1945 — NORTH-WEST
EUROPE, 1945
Headquarters — Mewata Armoury, CALGARY, Alberta
"A" Squardon was relocated at Calgary from Strathmore in 1965.
"B" Squadron — Mewata Armoury, CALGARY, Alberta
"C" Squadron, after relocation from Red Deer in 1965, was disbanded in 1970 at Calgary.

Affiliated British Unit:
THE KING'S OWN ROYAL BORDER REGIMENT

THE BRITISH COLUMBIA REGIMENT (R.C.A.C.) (MILITIA)

The Regiment, which originated in 1896 as the "2nd Battalion, 5th 'British Columbia' Regiment of Garrison Artillery" which was converted in 1899 and re-designated "The Duke of Connaught's Own Rifles" in 1900, was converted to armour in 1946.

Regimental March: *"I'M NINETY-FIVE"*
Major Battle Honours:
SOUTH AFRICA, 1899-1900 — VIMY RIDGE — PURSUIT TO MONS — FRANCE AND FLANDERS, 1915-1918 — THE RHINELAND — NORTH-WEST EUROPE, 1944-1945
Headquarters — VANCOUVER, British Columbia
"A" Squadron — VANCOUVER, British Columbia
"B" Squadron — VANCOUVER, British Columbia
"C" Squadron, after relocation from Nanaimo in 1965, was disbanded in 1970 at Vancouver.

Affiliated British Unit:
THE ROYAL GREEN JACKETS

THE ROCKY MOUNTAIN RANGERS (MILITIA)

Independent companies of "Rocky Mountain Rangers" had been in existence since 1898.

Regimental March: *"THE BLUE CANADIAN ROCKIES"*
Regimental Motto: *"KLOSHE NANITCHE"*
    (*"KEEP A GOOD LOOKOUT"*)
Battle Honour: THE GREAT WAR, 1916-1917

The battalion served on Kiska in the Aleutian Islands in 1943 as a unit of the "13th Canadian Infantry Brigade Group".

Headquarters — KAMLOOPS, British Columbia
"A" Company was relocated at Kamloops from Prince George in 1970.
"B" Company, which maintained a detached platoon at Quesnel until 1965, was relocated at Revelstoke from Kamloops in 1970. This company was further relocated at Salmon Arm in 1977.
"C" Company, which maintainted a detached platoon at Armstrong until 1965, was disbanded in 1970 at Salmon Arm.
"D" Company was disbanded in 1970 at Revelstoke.
"Support" Company, after relocation from Merritt in 1968, was disbanded in 1970 at Kamloops.

THE IRISH FUSILIERS OF CANADA (VANCOUVER REGIMENT) (MILITIA)

The battalion was disbanded in 1965.

Regimental March: "GARRY OWEN"
Regimental Motto: "FAUGH A BALLAGH" / ("CLEAR THE WAY")
Major Battle Honours:
VIMY RIDGE — FRANCE AND FLANDERS, 1915-1918
Headquarters — VANCOUVER, British Columbia
"A" Company was disbanded at Vancouver.
"B" Company was disbanded at Vancouver.
"C" Company was disbanded at Powell River.
"D" Company, which had been formed in 1958 by the conversion and re-designation of "120 (Independent) Field Battery, R.C.A. (Militia)", was disbanded at Prince Rupert.
"Support" Company was disbanded at Vancouver.

Affiliated British Unit:
THE ROYAL IRISH RANGERS

THE ROYAL WESTMINSTER REGIMENT (MILITIA)

The battalion originated as the "Westminster Fusiliers" which had been formed by the reorganization of those companies of "The Duke of Connaught's Own Rifles" located in New Westminster.

Regimental March: *"THE WARWICKSHIRE LADS"*
Regimental Motto: *"PRO REGE ET PATRIA"*
        ("FOR OUR KING AND COUNTRY")
Major Battle Honours:
VIMY RIDGE — FRANCE AND FLANDERS, 1916-1918 — ITALY, 1944-1945 — DELFZIJL POCKET — NORTH-WEST EUROPE, 1945
Headquarters — NEW WESTMINSTER, British Columbia
"A" Company was relocated at New Westminster in 1970 from Abbotsford where it had continued a militia presence subsequent to the disbandment of "152 Transport Company, R.C.A.S.C.".
"B" Company was relocated at New Westminster from Mission in 1965.
"C" Company was disbanded in 1970 at New Westminster.
"D" Company was disbanded in 1970 at New Westminster.
"Support" Company was disbanded in 1970 at New Westminster.

Affiliated British Unit:
THE ROYAL REGIMENT OF FUSILIERS

48th HIGHLANDERS OF CANADA (MILITIA)

The battalion was formed in 1891.

Regimental March: *"THE HIGHLAND LADDIE"*
Regimental Motto: *"DILEAS GU BRATH"* / *("FAITHFUL FOREVER")*
Major Battle Honours:
SOUTH AFRICA, 1899-1900 — VIMY RIDGE — PURSUIT TO MONS — FRANCE AND
FLANDERS, 1915-1918 — LANDING IN SICILY — ITALY, 1943-1945 — NORTH-WEST
EUROPE, 1945

The "3rd Battalion (48th Highlanders), 1st Canadian Infantry Regiment". which had been formed
in Canada in 1945 for allocation to the "Canadian Army (Pacific Force)" for the projected assault
on the Japanese home islands, was disbanded in 1945.

Headquarters — Moss Park Armoury, TORONTO, Ontario
"A" Company
"B" Company
"C" Company
"D" Company was disbanded in 1970.
"E" Company was formed in 1951 to recruit for the "1st Canadian Highland Battalion" which was
re-designated "1st Battalion, The Black Watch (Royal Highland Regiment) of Canada (Regular)"
in 1953.
"F" Company was formed in 1952 to recruit for the "2nd Canadian Highland Battalion" which
was re-designated "2nd Battalion, The Black Watch (Royal Highland Regiment) of Canada
(Regular)" in 1953.
"Support" Company was disbanded in 1970.

Affiliated British Unit:
THE GORDON HIGHLANDERS

THE ARGYLL AND SUTHERLAND HIGHLANDERS OF CANADA (MILITIA)

The battalion was formed in 1903.

Regimental March: *"THE CAMPBELLS ARE COMING"*
Regimental Motto: *"ALBAINN GU BRATH"*
  ("SCOTLAND FOREVER")
Major Battle Honours:
VIMY RIDGE — PURSUIT TO MONS — FRANCE AND FLANDERS, 1915-1918 — THE RHINELAND — NORTH-WEST EUROPE, 1944-1945
Headquarters — HAMILTON, Ontario
"A" Company — HAMILTON, Ontario
"B" Company — HAMILTON, Ontario
"C" Company — HAMILTON, Ontario
"D" Company, after relocation from Grimsby in 1965, was disbanded in 1970 at Hamilton.
"Support" Company was disbanded in 1970 at Hamilton.

Affiliated British Unit:
THE ARGYLL AND SUTHERLAND HIGHLANDERS

THE QUEEN'S OWN CAMERON HIGHLANDERS OF CANADA (MILITIA)

The battalion was formed in 1910.

Regimental March: *"MARCH OF THE CAMERON MEN"*
Major Battle Honours:
VIMY RIDGE — PURSUIT TO MONS — FRANCE AND FLANDERS, 1916-1918 — DIEPPE
— THE RHINELAND — NORTH-WEST EUROPE, 1942, 1944-1945
Headquarters — Minto Armoury, WINNIPEG, Manitoba
"A" Company
"B" Company
"C" Company was disbanded in 1970.
"D" Company was disbanded in 1970.
"Support" Company was disbanded in 1970.

Affiliated British Unit:
THE QUEEN'S OWN HIGHLANDERS

THE SEAFORTH HIGHLANDERS OF CANADA (MILITIA)

The battalion was formed in 1910.

Regimental March: *"BLUE BONNETS OVER THE BORDER"*
Regimental Motto: *"CUIDICH'N RIGH"* / *("HELP THE KING")*
Major Battle Honours:
VIMY RIDGE — FRANCE AND FLANDERS, 1916-1918 — LANDING IN SICILY — ITALY, 1943-1945 — NORTH-WEST EUROPE, 1945

The "2nd Battalion (Seaforth Highlanders), 2nd Canadian Infantry Regiment", which had been formed in Canada in 1945 for allocation to the "Canadian Army (Pacific Force)" for the projected assault on the Japanese home islands, was disbanded in 1945.

Headquarters — VANCOUVER, British Columbia
"A" Company
"B" Company
"C" Company
"D" Company was disbanded in 1970.
"E" Company was formed in 1951 to recruit for the "1st Canadian Highland Battalion" which was re-designated "1st Battalion, The Black Watch (Royal Highland Regiment) of Canada (Regular)" in 1953.
"F" Company was formed in 1952 to recruit for the "2nd Canadian Highland Battalion" which was re-designated "2nd Battalion, The Black Watch (Royal Highland Regiment) of Canada (Regular)" in 1953.
"Support" Company was disbanded in 1970.

Affiliated British Unit:
THE QUEEN'S OWN HIGHLANDERS

THE CANADIAN SCOTTISH REGIMENT (MILITIA)

The battalion originated in 1912 as the "Victoria Fusiliers".

Regimental March: *"BLUE BONNETS OVER THE BORDER"*
Regimental Motto: *"DEAS GU GATH"* / (*"READY TO STING"*)
Major Battle Honours:
VIMY RIDGE — PURSUIT TO MONS — FRANCE AND FLANDERS, 1915-1918 —
NORMANDY LANDING — THE RHINELAND — NORTH-WEST EUROPE, 1944-1945
Headquarters — VICTORIA, British Columbia
"A" Company — VICTORIA, British Columbia
"B" Company — NANAIMO, British Columbia
"C" Company was relocated at Victoria from Courtenay in 1965.
"D" Company, after relocation from Port Alberni in 1965, was disbanded in 1970 at Victoria.
"E" Company, was formed in 1951 to recruit for the "1st Canadian Highland Battalion" which was re-designated "1st Battalion, The Black Watch (Royal Highland Regiment) of Canada (Regular)" in 1953.
"F" Company was formed in 1952 to recruit for the "2nd Canadian Highland Battalion" which was re-designated "2nd Battalion, The Black Watch (Royal Highland Regiment) of Canada (Regular)" in 1953.
"Support" Company was disbanded in 1970 at Victoria.

Affiliated British Unit:
THE ROYAL SCOTS

THE IRISH REGIMENT OF CANADA (MILITIA)

The battalion, which had originated in 1915 as the "110th 'Irish' Regiment", was disbanded in 1965.

Regimental March: "GARRY OWEN"
Regimental Motto: "FIOR GO BAS" / ("FAITHFUL UNTO DEATH")
Major Battle Honours:
PURSUIT TO MONS — FRANCE AND FLANDERS, 1917-1918 — ITALY, 1943-1945 — DELFZIJL POCKET — NORTH-WEST EUROPE, 1945
"Headquarters" was disbanded at Fort York Armoury in Toronto.
"A" Company was disbanded at Fort York Armoury in Toronto.
"B" Company was disbanded at Fort York Armoury in Toronto.
"C" Company was disbanded at Fort York Armoury in Toronto.
"D" Company was disbanded at Coriano Barracks in North York (Toronto).
"Support" Company was disbanded at Fort York Armoury in Toronto.

Affiliated British Unit:
THE ROYAL IRISH RANGERS

2nd Battalion, THE IRISH REGIMENT OF CANADA (MILITIA)

The battalion was formed in 1965 by the conversion and re-designation of "58 (Sudbury) Field Regiment, R.C.A. (Militia)" which had originated in 1946 as "58 (Sudbury) Light Anti-Aircraft Regiment, R.C.A. (Reserve Force)" by the conversion and re-designation of the Sudbury element of "The Ste. Marie and Sudbury Regiment (Non-Permanent Active Militia)". (Note that the Sault Ste. Marie element of "The Sault Ste. Marie and Sudbury Regiment" was converted in 1946 and re-designated "49 (Sault Ste. Marie) Heavy Anti-Aircraft Regiment, R.C.A. (Reserve Force)".)

Regimental March: "GARRY OWEN"
Regimental Motto: "FIOR GO BAS" / ("FAITHFUL UNTO DEATH")
Headquarters — SUDBURY, Ontario
"A" Company
"B" Company
"C" Company was disbanded in 1970.
"D" Company was disbanded in 1970.
"Support" Company was disbanded in 1970.

Affiliated British Unit:
THE ROYAL IRISH RANGERS

THE TORONTO SCOTTISH REGIMENT (MILITIA)

The battalion originated in 1920 in perpetuation of the "75th (Mississauga) Infantry Battalion, C.E.F." which fought in France as a unit of the "Canadian Corps" during the Great War.

Regimental March: *"BLUE BONNETS OVER THE BORDER"*
Regimental Motto: *"CARRY ON"*
Major Battle Honours:
VIMY RIDGE — FRANCE AND FLANDERS, 1916-1918 — DIEPPE — THE RHINELAND —
NORTH-WEST EUROPE, 1942, 1944-1945
Headquarters — Fort York Armoury, TORONTO, Ontario
"A" Company
"B" Company
"C" Company was disbanded in 1970.
"D" Company was disbanded in 1970.
"Support" Company was disbanded in 1970.

Affiliated British Unit:
THE 51st HIGHLANDER VOLUNTEERS

THE ROYAL NEWFOUNDLAND REGIMENT (MILITIA)

The battalion, which was formed in 1949 upon the entry into Confederation of the former British colony of Newfoundland, perpetuates the "Royal Newfoundland Regiment" that served in the British Army during the Great War and may be considered as perpetuating the "Royal Newfoundland Fencible Infantry" which fought in various actions along the Canadian-American border during the Anglo-American War of 1812 to 1814.

Regimental March: *"THE BANKS OF NEWFOUNDLAND"*
Major Battle Honours:
EGYPT, 1915-1916 — GALLIPOLI, 1915-1916 — FRANCE AND FLANDERS, 1916-1918
Headquarters — ST. JOHN'S, Newfoundland
"A" Company — Gallipoli Armoury, CORNER BROOK, Newfoundland
This company was re-organized in 1974 as a sub-unit of "2nd Battalion, The Royal Newfoundland Regiment".
"B" Company — GRAND FALLS, Newfoundland
This company was re-organized in 1974 as a sub-unit of "2nd Battalion, The Royal Newfoundland Regiment".
"C" Company — BELL ISLAND, Newfoundland
This company was re-organized in 1974 as a sub-unit of "1st Battalion, The Royal Newfoundland Regiment".
"D" Company — ST. JOHN'S, Newfoundland
This company was re-organized in 1974 as a sub-unit of "1st Battalion, The Royal Newfoundland Regiment".
"E" Company — ST. JOHN'S, Newfoundland
This company was re-organized in 1974 as a sub-unit of "1st Battalion, The Royal Newfoundland Regiment".

Affiliated British Unit:
THE ROYAL SCOTS

1st Battalion, THE ROYAL NEWFOUNDLAND REGIMENT (MILITIA)

Regimental March: *"THE BANKS OF NEWFOUNDLAND"*
Major Battle Honours:
EGYPT, 1915-1916 — GALLIPOLI, 1915-1916 — FRANCE AND FLANDERS, 1916-1918
Headquarters — ST. JOHN'S, Newfoundland
Logistical support for the battalion is provided by "36 (Newfoundland) Service Battalion".
"A" Company — ST. JOHN'S, Newfoundland
"B" Company — ST. JOHN'S, Newfoundland
"C" Company — BELL ISLAND, Newfoundland

Affiliated British Unit:
THE ROYAL SCOTS

2nd Battalion, THE ROYAL NEWFOUNDLAND REGIMENT (MILITIA)

Regimental March: "THE BANKS OF NEWFOUNDLAND"
Major Battle Honours:
EGYPT, 1915-1916 — GALLIPOLI, 1915-1916 — FRANCE AND FLANDERS, 1916-1918
Headquarters — Gallipoli Armoury, CORNER BROOK, Newfoundland
"A" Company — Gallipoli Armoury, CORNER BROOK, Newfoundland
Logistical support for the company is provided by a local platoon detached from "36 (Newfoundland) Service Battalion".
"B" Company — GRAND FALLS, Newfoundland
Logistical support for the company is provided by a local platoon detached from "36 (Newfoundland) Service Battalion".
"C" Company — STEPHENVILLE, Newfoundland
Logistical support for the company is provided by a local platoon detached from "36 (Newfoundland) Service Battalion".

Affiliated British Unit:
THE ROYAL SCOTS

THE YUKON REGIMENT (MILITIA)

The battalion, which had been formed in 1962, was disbanded in 1968.

Regimental March: *"THE YUKON REGIMENT"*
Headquarters — WHITEHORSE, Yukon Territory
"A" Company
"B" Company
"C" Company
"D" Company
"Support" Company

THE CANADIAN AIRBORNE REGIMENT (REGULAR)

The Regiment, which was formed in 1968, replaced the "Defence of Canada Force" that had been organized in 1958 and to which were allocated individual parachute-trained companies from within the establishments of the "Royal Canadian Regiment", "Princess Patricia's Canadian Light Infantry" and the "Royal Vingt-Deuxieme Regiment". From 1948 until 1958, one battalion from each of the "Royal Canadian Regiment", "Princess Patricia's Canadian Light Infantry" and the "Royal Vingt-Deuxieme Regiment" was allocated to a "Mobile Striking Force".

Regimental Motto: *"EX COELIS"* / *("OUT OF THE CLOUDS")*
"Regimental Headquarters", the "Airborne Headquarters and Signal Squadron" and the "Airborne Service Commando" were relocated in 1977 at Camp Petawawa from the "Canadian Airborne Centre" at Edmonton.
"1 Airborne Battery" was disbanded in 1977 upon replacement by "E" Battery of "2 Regiment, Royal Canadian Horse Artillery (Regular)".
"1 Airborne Field Squadron" was disbanded in 1977 upon replacement by an "airborne field squadron" within the establishment of "2 Combat Engineer Regiment (Regular)".

The "1iere Commando (Aeroporte)", which had been relocated from Camp Valcartier in 1970, was relocated at Camp Petawawa from the "Canadian Airborne Centre" at Edmonton in 1977 and perpetuates the "1st Canadian Parachute Battalion" which landed at Normandy and fought in North-West Europe as a unit of the British "6th Airborne Division" during the Second World War. The "1iere Commando (Aeroporte)", which receives personnel from the "Royal Vingt-Deuxieme Regiment", has served in Cyprus as a unit of the "United Nations Force".
Major Battle Honours:
NORMANDY LANDING — THE RHINE — NORTH-WEST EUROPE, 1944-1945

Affiliated British Unit:
1st Battalion, THE PARACHUTE REGIMENT

The "2nd (Airborne) Commando", which was relocated in 1977 at Camp Petawawa from the "Canadian Airborne Centre" at Edmonton, receives personnel from "Princess Patricia's Canadian Light Infantry" and perpetuates the "2nd Canadian Parachute Battalion" which was re-designated "1st Canadian Special Service Battalion" and fought in both Italy and Southern France as a unit of the joint Canadian/American "First Special Service Force" (the "Devil's Brigade") during the Second World War. The "2nd (Airborne) Commando" has served in Cyprus as a unit of the "United Nations Force".
Major Battle Honours:
ADVANCE TO THE TIBER — ITALY, 1943-1944 — SOUTHERN FRANCE, 1944

Affiliated British Unit:
2nd Battalion, THE PARACHUTE REGIMENT

The "3rd (Airborne) Commando" was formed in 1977 at Camp Petawawa by the re-organization of the "3rd (Mechanized) Commando" which had originated in 1970 at Lahr by the re-organization of "2nd Battalion, The Royal Canadian Regiment (Regular)". The unit receives personnel from "The Royal Canadian Regiment".

Affiliated British Unit:
3rd Battalion, THE PARACHUTE REGIMENT

INFANTRY BATTALIONS (1939-1945)

The Canadian Training School (United Kingdom)
"1" Wing was responsible for the training of officer candidates.
"2" Wing was responsible for the training of drivers and vehicle mechanics.
"3" Wing was responsible for the training of infantrymen in the handling of small arms.
"4" Wing was responsible for the training of company and platoon commanders.
"5" Wing was responsible for the training of infantrymen in basic military tactics.
"6" Wing was responsible for the training of infantrymen in chemical warfare.

THE ROYAL CANADIAN REGIMENT
The battalion fought in both Italy and North-West Europe.

PRINCESS PATRICIA'S CANADIAN LIGHT INFANTRY
The battalion fought in both Italy and North-West Europe.

LE ROYAL VINGT-DEUXIEME REGIMENT
The battalion fought in both Italy and North-West Europe.

THE GOVERNOR-GENERAL'S FOOT GUARDS
The "Governor-General's Foot Guards, C.A.S.F." fought as an armoured regiment in North-West Europe.
The "2nd Battalion" served in the Reserve Army.

THE CANADIAN GRENADIER GUARDS
The "Canadian Grenadier Guards, C.A.S.F." fought as an armoured regiment in North-West Europe.
The "2nd Battalion" served in the Reserve Army.

THE QUEEN'S OWN RIFLES OF CANADA
The "Queen's Own Rifles of Canada, C.A.S.F." fought in North-West Europe.
The "2nd Battalion" served in the Reserve Army.
The "3rd (Active) Battalion" served in Canada.
The 4th (Active) Battalion" was formed in North-West Europe for service with the "Canadian Army (Occupation Force)".

THE VICTORIA RIFLES OF CANADA
The "Victoria Rifles of Canada, C.A.S.F." served in Canada.
The "2nd Battalion" served in the Reserve Army.

THE BLACK WATCH (ROYAL HIGHLAND REGIMENT) OF CANADA
The "Black Watch (Royal Regiment) of Canada, C.A.S.F." fought in North-West Europe.
The "2nd (Active) Battalion" served in Canada.
The "3rd Battalion" served in the Reserve Army.
The "4th Battalion" served in the Reserve Army.

THE CANADIAN FUSILIERS
The "Canadian Fusiliers, C.A.S.F." served in Canada, the Aleutian Islands and the United Kingdom.
The "2nd Battalion" served in the Reserve Army.

THE ROYAL RIFLES OF CANADA
The "Royal Rifles of Canada, C.A.S.F." fought at Hong Kong.
The "2nd Battalion" served in the Reserve Army.

LES VOLTIGEURS DE QUEBEC
The "Voltigeurs de Quebec, C.A.S.F" served in Canada and the United Kingdom.
The "2nd Battalion" served in the Reserve Army.

THE ROYAL REGIMENT OF CANADA
The "Royal Regiment of Canada, C.A.S.F." fought in North-West Europe.
The "2nd Battalion" served in the Reserve Army.

THE ROYAL HAMILTON LIGHT INFANTRY (WENTWORTH REGIMENT)
The "Royal Hamilton Light Infantry (Wentworth Regiment), C.A.S.F." fought in North-West Europe.
The "2nd Battalion" served in the Reserve Army.

THE PRINCESS OF WALES' OWN REGIMENT
The "Princess of Wales' Own Regiment, C.A.S.F." served in Canada.
The "2nd Battalion" served in the Reserve Army.

THE ARGYLL LIGHT INFANTRY (TANK)
The battalion served in the Reserve Army.

THE ALGONQUIN REGIMENT
The "Algonquin Regiment, C.A.S.F." fought in North-West Europe.
The "2nd Battalion" served in the Reserve Army.

THE CAMERON HIGHLANDERS OF OTTAWA
The "Cameron Highlanders of Ottawa, C.A.S.F." fought in North-West Europe.
The "2nd Battalion" served in the Reserve Army.
The '3rd (Active) Battalion" was formed in North-West Europe for service with the "Canadian Army (Occupation Force)".

THE DUFFERIN AND HALDIMAND RIFLES OF CANADA
The "Dufferin and Haldimand Rifles of Canada, C.A.S.F." served in Canada.
The "2nd Battalion" served in the Reserve Army.

THE ELGIN REGIMENT
The "Elgin Regiment, C.A.S.F." fought as an armoured regiment in both Italy and North-West Europe.
The "2nd Battalion" served in the Reserve Army.

THE ESSEX REGIMENT (TANK)
The "Essex Regiment, C.A.S.F." served in Canada and the United Kingdom.
The "2nd Battalion" served in the Reserve Army.

THE ESSEX SCOTTISH REGIMENT
The "Essex Scottish Regiment, C.A.S.F" fought in North-West Europe.
The "2nd Battalion" served in the Reserve Army.

THE GREY AND SIMCOE FORESTERS
The "Grey and Simcoe Foresters, C.A.S.F." served in Canada.
The "2nd Battalion" served in the Reserve Army.

THE HASTINGS AND PRINCE EDWARD REGIMENT
The "Hastings and Prince Edward Regiment, C.A.S.F." fought in both Italy and North-West Europe.
The "2nd Battalion" served in the Reserve Army.

THE KENT REGIMENT
The "Kent Regiment, C.A.S.F" served in Canada.
The "2nd Battalion" served in the Reserve Army.

THE LAKE SUPERIOR REGIMENT
The "Lake Superior Regiment, C.A.S.F." fought in North-West Europe.
The "2nd Battalion" served in the Reserve Army.

THE LANARK AND RENFREW SCOTTISH REGIMENT
The "Lanark and Renfrew Scottish Regiment, C.A.S.F." fought in Italy.
The "2nd Battalion" served in the Reserve Army.

THE BROCKVILLE RIFLES
The "Brockville Rifles, C.A.S.F." served in Canada and Jamaica.
The "2nd Battalion" served in the Reserve Army.

THE LINCOLN AND WELLAND REGIMENT
The "Lincoln and Welland Regiment, C.A.S.F." fought in North-West Europe.
The "2nd Battalion" served in the Reserve Army.

THE MIDDLESEX AND HURON REGIMENT
The battalion served in the Reserve Army.

THE MIDLAND REGIMENT (NORTHUMBERLAND AND DURHAM)
The "Midland Regiment, C.A.S.F." served in Canada.
The "2nd Battalion" served in the Reserve Army.

THE ONTARIO REGIMENT (TANK)
The "Ontario Regiment, C.A.S.F." fought as an armoured regiment in both Italy and North-West Europe.
The "2nd Battalion" served in the Reserve Army.

THE OXFORD RIFLES
The "Oxford Rifles, C.A.S.F." served in Canada.
The "2nd Battalion" served in the Reserve Army.

THE LORNE SCOTS (PEEL, DUFFERIN AND HALTON REGIMENT)
The "Lorne Scots (Peel, Dufferin and Halton Regiment), C.A.S.F." provided a platoon for the "ground defence" of each brigade and divisional headquarters in both Italy and North-West Europe.
The "2nd Battalion" served in the Reserve Army.

THE PERTH REGIMENT
The "Perth Regiment, C.A.S.F." fought in both Italy and North-West Europe.
The "2nd Battalion" served in the Reserve Army.

THE PRINCE OF WALES' RANGERS (PETERBOROUGH REGIMENT)
The "Prince of Wales' Rangers (Peterborough Regiment), C.A.S.F." served in Canada.
The "2nd Battalion" served in the Reserve Army.

THE STORMONT, DUNDAS AND GLENGARRY HIGHLANDERS
The "Stormont, Dundas and Glengarry Highlanders, C.A.S.F." fought in North-West Europe.
The "2nd Battalion" served in the Reserve Army.
The "3rd (Active) Battalion" was formed in North-West Europe for service with the "Canadian Army (Occupation Force)".

THE HIGHLAND LIGHT INFANTRY OF CANADA
The "Highland Light Infantry of Canada, C.A.S.F." fought in North-West Europe.
The "2nd Battalion" served in the Reserve Army.
The "3rd (Active) Battalion" was formed in North-West Europe for service with the "Canadian Army (Occupation Force)".

THE SCOTS FUSILIERS OF CANADA
The "Scots Fusiliers of Canada, C.A.S.F." served in Canada.
The "2nd Battalion" served in the Reserve Army.

THE QUEEN'S YORK RANGERS (1st AMERICAN REGIMENT)
The "Queen's York Rangers (1st American Regiment), C.A.S.F." served in Canada.
The "2nd Battalion" served in the Reserve Army.

LE REGIMENT DE MAISONNEUVE
Le "Regiment de Maisonneuve, C.A.S.F." fought in North-West Europe.
The "2nd Battalion" served in the Reserve Army.
The "3rd (Active) Battalion" served in Canada.

LE REGIMENT DE CHATEAUGUAY
The "Regiment de Chateauguay, C.A.S.F." served in Canada.
The "2nd Battalion" served in the Reserve Army.

LE REGIMENT DE LA CHAUDIERE
The "Regiment de la Chaudiere, C.A.S.F." fought in North-West Europe.
The "2nd Battalion" served in the Reserve Army.
The "3rd (Active) Battalion" was formed in North-West Europe for service with the "Canadian Army (Occupation Force)".

LE REGIMENT DE HULL
The "Regiment de Hull, C.A.S.F." served in Canada, the Aleutian Islands and the United Kingdom.
The "2nd Battalion" served in the Reserve Army.

LE REGIMENT DE JOLIETTE
The "Regiment de Joiliette, C.A.S.F." served in Canada.
The "2nd Battalion" served in the Reserve Army.

LE REGIMENT DE LEVIS
The "Regiment de Levis, C.A.S.F." served in Canada.
The "2nd Battalion" served in the Reserve Army.

LE REGIMENT DE MONTMAGNY
The "Regiment de Montmagny, C.A.S.F." served in Canada and the United Kingdom.
The "2nd Battalion" served in the Reserve Army.

THE ROYAL MONTREAL REGIMENT
The "Royal Montreal Regiment, C.A.S.F." fought in North-West Europe.
The "2nd Battalion" served in the Reserve Army.

LES FUSILIERS MONT-ROYAL
The "Fusiliers Mont-Royal, C.A.S.F." fought in North-West Europe.
The "2nd Battalion" served in the Reserve Army.
The "3rd (Active) Battalion" served in Canada.

LE REGIMENT DE QUEBEC
The "Regiment de Quebec, C.A.S.F." served in Canada.
The "2nd Battalion" served in the Reserve Army.

LE REGIMENT DU SAGUENAY
The battalion served in the Reserve Army.

LE REGIMENT DE SAINT-HYACINTHE
The "Regiment de St-Hyacinthe, C.A.S.F." served in Canada.
The "2nd Battalion" served in the Reserve Army.

LES FUSILIERS DU SAINT-LAURENT
The "Fusiliers du St-Laurent, C.A.S.F." served in Canada.
The "2nd Battalion" served in the Reserve Army.
The "3rd (Active) Battalion" served in the Reserve Army.

THE SHERBROOKE REGIMENT
The "Sherbrooke Regiment, C.A.S.F.", in conjunction with the "Fusiliers de Sherbrooke, C.A.S.F." fought in North-West Europe as an armoured regiment designated the "Sherbrooke Fusiliers".
The "2nd Battalion" served in the Reserve Army.

LES FUSILIERS DE SHERBROOKE
The "Fusiliers de Sherbrooke, C.A.S.F.", in conjunction with the "Sherbrooke Regiment, C.A.S.F.", fought in North-West Europe as an armoured regiment designated the "Sherbrooke Fusiliers".
The "2nd Battalion" served in the Reserve Army.

THE THREE RIVERS REGIMENT
The "Three Rivers Regiment, C.A.S.F." fought as an armoured regiment in both Italy and North-West Europe.
The "2nd Battalion" served in the Reserve Army.

THE CARLETON AND YORK REGIMENT
The "Carleton and York Regiment, C.A.S.F." fought in both Italy and North-West Europe.
The "2nd Battalion" served in the Reserve Army.

THE NEW BRUNSWICK RANGERS
The "New Brunswick Rangers, C.A.S.F." fought in North-West Europe.
The "2nd Battalion" served in the Reserve Army.

THE NEW BRUNSWICK REGIMENT (TANK)
The battalion served in the Reserve Army.

THE NORTH SHORE (NEW BRUNSWICK) REGIMENT
The "North Shore (New Brunswick) Regiment, C.A.S.F." fought in North-West Europe.
The "2nd Battalion" served in the Reserve Army.

THE SAINT JOHN FUSILIERS
The "Saint John Fusiliers, C.A.S.F." served in Canada.
The "2nd Battalion" served in the Reserve Army.

THE HALIFAX RIFLES
The "Halifax Rifles, C.A.S.F." served in Canada.
The "2nd Battalion" served in the Reserve Army.

THE PRINCESS LOUISE FUSILIERS
The "Princess Louise Fusiliers, C.A.S.F." fought in both Italy and North-West Europe.
The "2nd Battalion" served in the Reserve Army.

THE CAPE BRETON HIGHLANDERS
The "Cape Breton Highlanders, C.A.S.F." fought in both Italy and North-West Europe.
The "2nd Battalion" served in the Reserve Army.

THE NORTH NOVA SCOTIA HIGHLANDERS
The "North Nova Scotia Highlanders, C.A.S.F." fought in North-West Europe.
The "2nd Battalion" served in the Reserve Army.
The "3rd (Active) Battalion" was formed in North-West Europe for service with the "Canadian Army (Occupation Force)".

THE PICTOU HIGHLANDERS
The "Pictou Highlanders, C.A.S.F." served in Canada, Bermuda and the Bahama Islands.
The "2nd Battalion" served in the Reserve Army.

THE WEST NOVA SCOTIA REGIMENT
The "West Nova Scotia Regiment, C.A.S.F." fought in both Italy and North-West Europe.
The "2nd Battalion" served in the Reserve Army.

THE PRINCE EDWARD ISLAND HIGHLANDERS
The "Prince Edward Island Highlanders, C.A.S.F." served in Canada.
The "2nd Battalion" served in the Reserve Army.

THE ROYAL WINNIPEG RIFLES
The "Royal Winnipeg Rifles, C.A.S.F." fought in North-West Europe.
The "2nd Battalion" served in the Reserve Army.
The "3rd (Active) Battalion" served in Canada.
The "4th (Active) Battalion" was formed in North-West Europe for service with the "Canadian Army (Occupation Force)".

THE WINNIPEG GRENADIERS
The "Winnipeg Grenadiers, C.A.S.F." fought at Hong Kong.
The "2nd Battalion" served in the Reserve Army.

THE WINNIPEG LIGHT INFANTRY
The "Winnipeg Light Infantry, C.A.S.F." served in Canada.
The "2nd Battalion" served in the Reserve Army.

THE MANITOBA MOUNTED RIFLES
The battalion served in the Reserve Army.

THE KING'S OWN RIFLES IN CANADA
The "King's Own Rifles of Canada, C.A.S.F." served in Canada.
The "2nd Battalion" served in the Reserve Army.

THE PRINCE ALBERT AND BATTLEFORD VOLUNTEERS
The "Prince Albert Volunteers, C.A.S.F." served in Canada.
"2nd Battalion, The Prince Albert Volunteers" served in the Reserve Army.
The "Battleford Light Infantry (16th/22nd Saskatchewan Horse), C.A.S.F." served in Canada and the United Kingdom.
"2nd Battalion, The Battleford Light Infantry (16th/22nd Saskatchewan Horse)" served in the Reserve Army.

THE REGINA RIFLE REGIMENT
The "Regina Rifle Regiment, C.A.S.F." fought in North-West Europe.
The "2nd Battalion" served in the Reserve Army.
The "3rd (Active) Battalion" served in Canada.
The "4th (Active) Battalion" was formed in North-West Europe for service with the "Canadian Army (Occupation Force)".

THE SASKATOON LIGHT INFANTRY
The "Saskatoon Light Infantry, C.A.S.F." fought in both Italy and North-West Europe.
The "2nd Battalion" served in the Reserve Army.

THE SOUTH SASKATCHEWAN REGIMENT
The "South Saskatchewan Regiment, C.A.S.F." fought in North-West Europe.
The "2nd Battalion" served in the Reserve Army.

THE CALGARY HIGHLANDERS
The "Calgary Highlanders, C.A.S.F." fought in North-West Europe.
The "2nd Battalion" served in the Reserve Army.

THE CALGARY REGIMENT (TANK)
The "Calgary Regiment (Tank), C.A.S.F." fought as an armoured regiment in both Italy and North-West Europe.
The "2nd Battalion" served in the Reserve Army.

THE EDMONTON FUSILIERS
The "Edmonton Fusiliers, C.A.S.F." served in Canada.
The "2nd Battalion" served in the Reserve Army.
The "3rd (Active) Battalion" served in Canada.

THE LOYAL EDMONTON REGIMENT
The "Loyal Edmonton Regiment, C.A.S.F." fought in both Italy and North-West Europe.
The "2nd Battalion" served in the Reserve Army.

THE SOUTH ALBERTA REGIMENT
The "South Alberta Regiment, C.A.S.F." fought as an armoured regiment in North-West Europe.
The "2nd Battalion" served in the Reserve Army.

THE BRITISH COLUMBIA REGIMENT
The "British Columbia Regiment, C.A.S.F." fought as an armoured regiment in North-West Europe.
The "2nd Battalion" served in the Reserve Army.

THE ROCKY MOUNTAIN RANGERS
The "Rocky Mountain Rangers, C.A.S.F." served in Canada, the Aleutian Islands and the United Kingdom.
The "2nd Battalion" served in the Reserve Army.

THE PRINCE RUPERT REGIMENT
The "Prince Rupert Regiment, C.A.S.F." was formed for war-time service only and served in Canada.

THE IRISH FUSILIERS OF CANADA (VANCOUVER REGIMENT)
The "Irish Fusiliers of Canada (Vancouver Regiment), C.A.S.F." served in Canada and Jamaica.
The "2nd Battalion" served in the Reserve Army.
The "3rd (Active) Battalion" served in Canada.

THE WESTMINSTER REGIMENT
The "Westminster Regiment, C.A.S.F." fought in both Italy and North-West Europe.
The "2nd Battalion" served in the Reserve Army.

48th HIGHLANDERS OF CANADA
The "48th Highlanders of Canada, C.A.S.F." fought in both Italy and North-West Europe.
The "2nd Battalion" served in the Reserve Army.

THE ARGYLL AND SUTHERLAND HIGHLANDERS OF CANADA
The "Argyll and Sutherland Highlanders of Canada, C.A.S.F." served in Jamaica and fought in North-West Europe.
The "2nd Battalion" served in the Reserve Army.

THE QUEEN'S OWN CAMERON HIGHLANDERS OF CANADA
The "Queen's Own Cameron Highlanders of Canada, C.A.S.F." fought in North-West Europe.
The "2nd Battalion" served in the Reserve Army.

THE SEAFORTH HIGHLANDERS OF CANADA
The "Seaforth Highlanders of Canada, C.A.S.F." fought in both Italy and North-West Europe.
The "2nd Battalion" served in the Reserve Army.

THE CANADIAN SCOTTISH REGIMENT
The "Canadian Scottish Regiment, C.A.S.F." fought in North-West Europe.
The "2nd (Active) Battalion" served in Canada.
The "3rd Battalion" served in the Reserve Army.
The "4th (Active) Battalion" was formed in North-West Europe for service with the "Canadian Army (Occupation Force)".

THE SAULT STE. MARIE AND SUDBURY REGIMENT
The "Sault Ste. Marie and Sudbury Regiment, C.A.S.F." served in Canada.
The "2nd Battalion" served in the Reserve Army.

THE IRISH REGIMENT OF CANADA
The "Irish Regiment of Canada, C.A.S.F." fought in both Italy and North-West Europe.
The "2nd Battalion" served in the Reserve Army.

THE TORONTO SCOTTISH REGIMENT
The "Toronto Scottish Regiment, C.A.S.F." fought in North-West Europe.
The "2nd Battalion" served in the Reserve Army.

2nd/10th DRAGOONS, CANADIAN INFANTRY CORPS
The "2nd/10th Dragoons, C.A.S.F." served in Canada.

1st CANADIAN PARACHUTE BATTALION
The battalion fought in North-West Europe as a unit of the British "6th Airborne Division".

1st CANADIAN SPECIAL SERVICE BATTALION
The battalion fought in both Italy and southern France as a unit of the joint Canadian/American "First Special Service Force" (the "Devil's Brigade").

THE ROYAL CANADIAN ARMOURED CORPS

Corps March: "MY BOY WILLIE"
Corps School: CAMP BORDEN, Ontario

The "Canadian Armoured Fighting Vehicles School", which had originated in 1936 as the "Canadian Tank School", was disbanded in 1940 upon the formation of the "Canadian Armoured Corps Training Centre".

NOTE (1)

Armoured regiments (sub-designated "R.C.A.C.") which originated as battalions of infantry have been included in the section on the Royal Canadian Infantry Corps.

NOTE (2)

Battle honours, where listed, are those of a general nature which have been included in order to properly define the service of a particular armoured regiment (or are those which are unique to that unit). A battle honour for "THE GREAT WAR" indicates that the unit recruited one or more battalions which served in the United Kingdom during the Great War for the period specified by the accompanying year-date. These battalions, although they did not serve in France, were integral to the Canadian Expeditionary Force in that they provided the administrative structure through which personnel were recruited in Canada and forwarded to the United Kingdom for advanced training in the "reserve battalions" prior to their being posted to France as reinforcements for battalions of the "Canadian Corps" in the field. The reader is advised to refer to specific regimental histories for a complete list of the battle honours awarded to a particular armoured regiment.

THE ROYAL CANADIAN DRAGOONS (REGULAR)

The Regiment originated in 1883 as the "Cavalry School Corps" which, after amalgamation in 1892 with the "Canadian Mounted Rifle Corps" (which had been formed in 1885) and re-organization as a squadron of "Canadian Dragoons", received its' present designation in 1893.

Regimental March: *"MONSIEUR BEAUCAIRE"*
Major Battle Honours:
NORTH-WEST CANADA, 1885 — SOUTH AFRICA, 1900 — PURSUIT TO MONS — FRANCE AND FLANDERS, 1915-1918 — ITALY, 1944-1945 — NORTH-WEST EUROPE, 1945
Home Station: Carleton Barracks, CAMP GAGETOWN, New Brunswick
Headquarters — LAHR, West Germany
"A" Squadron — LAHR, West Germany
The squadron is a unit of "4 Canadian Mechanized Brigade Group".
"B" Squadron — LAHR, West Germany
The squadron is a unit of "4 Canadian Mechanized Brigade Group".
"C" Squadron — Carleton Barracks, CAMP GAGETOWN, New Brunswick
The squadron is a unit of the "Combat Training Centre".
"D" Squadron, which had been formed in 1951 for service with the "27th Canadian Infantry Brigade Group" in West Germany, served in Korea subsequent to the armistice.
The regiment provided a "reconnaissance squadron" for service with the "United Nations Emergency Force" in the Middle East at various times from 1956 until 1967.

Affiliated British Unit:
THE BLUES AND ROYALS

LORD STRATHCONA'S HORSE (ROYAL CANADIANS) (REGULAR)

The "Royal Canadian Mounted Rifles", which had originated in 1901 as "A" Squadron (Permanent Active Militia) of the "Canadian Mounted Rifles", was re-designated "Strathcona's Horse" in 1909 in perpetuation of the regiment of that name which had been raised by Donald Smith (Lord Strathcona) for service in South Africa during the "Boer" war.

Regimental March: *"SOLDIERS OF THE QUEEN"*
Regimental Motto: *"PERSEVERANCE"*
Major Battle Honours:
SOUTH AFRICA, 1900-1901 — PURSUIT TO MONS — FRANCE AND FLANDERS, 1915-1918 — ITALY, 1944-1945 — NORTH-WEST EUROPE, 1945 — KOREA, 1951-1953
Headquarters — Sarcee Barracks, CALGARY, Alberta
"A" Squadron fought in Korea in 1953.
"B" Squadron fought in Korea in 1952.
"C" Squadron fought in Korea in 1951.
"D" Squadron was removed from the Regiment in 1959 and re-organized as "B" Squadron of "The Fort Garry Horse (Regular)".
The Regiment, which provided a "reconnaissance squadron" for service with the "United Nations Emergency Force" in the Middle East at various times from 1956 until 1967, is presently a unit of "1 Canadian Brigade Group".

Affiliated British Unit:
17th/21st LANCERS

THE GOVERNOR-GENERAL'S HORSE GUARDS (MILITIA)

The Regiment was formed in 1936 by the amalgamation of "The Governor-General's Body Guard" which had originated in 1855 as the "1st Troop of Volunteer Militia Cavalry of the County of York" and the "Mississauga Horse" which had originated in 1903 as the "Toronto Light Horse". "The Governor-General's Body Guard" was "regimented" in 1889 by the incorporation of "2" and "3" Troops of the "provisional" regiment of cavalry which had been formed in 1872 to adminster the previously-independent troops of cavalry in "Military District 2".

"2nd Provisional Regiment of Cavalry"
Headquarters — OAK RIDGES, ONTARIO
"1" Troop — ST. CATHARINES, Ontario
This troop originated in 1855 as the "Volunteer Militia Troop of Cavalry of St. Catharines".
"2" Troop — OAK RIDGES, Ontario
This troop originated in 1855 as the "2nd Troop of Volunteer Militia Cavalry of the County of York".
"3" Troop — MARKHAM, Ontario
This troop originated in 1856 as the "Markham Troop of Volunteer Militia Cavalry of the County of York".
"4" Troop — GRIMSBY, Ontario
"5" Troop — BURFORD, Ontario
"6" Troop — QUEENSTON, Ontario

Regimental March: "MEN OF HARLECH"
Regimental Motto: "NULLI SECUNDUS" / ("NEVER SECOND")
Major Battle Honours:
NORTH-WEST CANADA, 1885 — SOUTH AFRICA, 1900 — VIMY RIDGE — FRANCE AND FLANDERS, 1915-1918 — ITALY, 1944-1945 — NORTH-WEST EUROPE, 1945
Headquarters — Denison Armoury, NORTH YORK (TORONTO), Ontario
"A" Squadron
"B" Squadron was relocated in 1954 at Toronto from Stouffville where it had been located since 1949.
"C" Squadron was disbanded in 1970.

Affiliated British Units:
THE BLUES AND ROYALS
THE QUEEN'S DRAGOON GUARDS

1st HUSSARS (MILITIA)

The Regiment originated in 1872 as a "provisional" regiment of cavalry and provided the "2nd Divisional Cavalry Squadron, C.E.F." which fought in France as a sub-unit of the "Canadian Light Horse" during the Great War.

The "1st Provisional Regiment of Cavalry" was formed to administer the previously-independent troops of cavalry in "Military District 1".
Headquarters — LONDON, Ontario
"1" Troop — ST. THOMAS, Ontario
This troop originated in 1856 as the "Volunteer Militia Troop of Cavalry of St. Thomas".
"2" Troop — LONDON, Ontario
This troop originated in 1856 as the "Volunteer Militia Troop of Cavalry of London".
"3" Troop — MOORETOWN, Ontario
This troop originated as a company of the "Lambton Battalion of Infantry".
"4" Troop — KINGSVILLE, Ontario

Regimental March: *"BONNIE DUNDEE"*
Regimental Motto: *"HODIE NON CRAS"*
　　　("TODAY NOT TOMORROW")
Major Battle Honours:
SOUTH AFRICA, 1900 — VIMY RIDGE — PURSUIT TO MONS — FRANCE AND FLANDERS, 1915-1918 — NORMANDY LANDING — THE RHINELAND — NORTH-WEST EUROPE, 1944-1945
Headquarters — Wolseley Barracks, LONDON, Ontario
"A" Squadron — Wolseley Barracks, LONDON, Ontario
"B" Squadron was disbanded in 1970 at London.
"C" Squadron was relocated at Sarnia from London in 1965 thereby continuing a militia presence subsequent to the disbandment of "26 Field Battery, R.C.A.".

Affiliated British Unit:
THE ROYAL HUSSARS

4th PRINCESS LOUISE DRAGOON GUARDS (MILITIA)

The Regiment, which was disbanded in 1965, had been formed in 1936 by the amalgamation of "The Princess Louise Dragoon Guards" which had originated in 1872 as the "Ottawa Troop of Cavalry" and the "4th Hussars of Canada" which had originated in 1875 as a "provisional" regiment of cavalry to administer the previously-independent troops of cavalry in "Military District 4".

"4th Provisional Regiment of Cavalry"
Headquarters — KINGSTON, Ontario
"1" Troop — KINGSTON, Ontario
This troop originated in 1855 as the "First Troop of Volunteer Militia Cavalry of the County of Frontenac".
"2" Troop — NAPANEE, Ontario
This troop originated in 1856 as the "Volunteer Militia Troop of Cavalry of Napanee".
"3" Troop — LOUGHBOROUGH, Ontario
This troop originated in 1856 as the "2nd Troop of Volunteer Militia Cavalry of the County of Frontenac".
"4" Troop — PRESCOTT, Ontario
"5" Troop — PICTON, Ontario

Regimental March: "MEN OF HARLECH"
Regimental Motto: "PRO ARIS ET FOCIS"
        ("FOR OUR ALTARS AND OUR HEARTHS")
Major Battle Honours:
SOUTH AFRICA, 1900 — THE GREAT WAR, 1916-1917 — ITALY, 1943-1945 — NORTH-WEST EUROPE, 1945
"Headquarters" was disbanded at Ottawa.
"A" Squadron was disbanded at Ottawa.
"B" Squadron, after relocation from Almonte in 1960, was disbanded at Ottawa.
"C" Squadron, which had been relocated from Ottawa in 1954 thereby continuing a militia presence subsequent to the disbandment of "180 Light Anti-Aircraft Battery, R.C.A." was disbanded at Prescott.
"D" Squadron, which had been relocated from Ottawa in 1959 thereby continuing a militia presence subsequent to the disbandment of "176 Light Anti-Aircraft Battery, R.C.A." was disbanded at Smith's Falls.

Affiliated British Unit:
THE ROYAL HUSSARS

THE ROYAL CANADIAN HUSSARS (MONTREAL) (MILITIA)

The Regiment was formed in 1954 by the amalgamation of the "6th Duke of Connaught's Royal Canadian Hussars" and the "17th Duke of York's Royal Canadian Hussars." The "Duke of Connaught's Hussars" had originated in 1855 as the "1st Volunteer Militia Troop of Cavalry of Montreal" which in 1879 was incorporated within the "provisional" regiment of cavalry that had been formed to administer the previously-independent troops of cavalry in "Military District 6". The "Duke of York's Hussars" had originated in 1897 as the "Montreal Hussars".

"6th Provisional Regiment of Cavalry"
Headquarters — MONTREAL, Quebec
"1" Troop — MONTREAL, Quebec
"2" Troop — ST. ANDREW'S, Quebec
"3" Troop — HAVELOCK, Quebec
"4" Troop — CLARENCEVILLE, Quebec

Regimental March: "ST. PATRICK'S DAY"
Regimental Motto: "NON NOBIS SED PATRIAE"
    ("NOT FOR OURSELVES BUT OUR COUNTRY")
Major Battle Honours:
SOUTH AFRICA, 1900 — VIMY RIDGE — FRANCE AND FLANDERS, 1915-1918 — THE RHINELAND — NORTH-WEST EUROPE, 1944-1945
Headquarters — MONTREAL, Quebec
"A" Squadron, after relocation at Longeuil from St-Jean in 1965, was relocated at Montreal in 1970.
"B" Squadron — LONGEUIL, Quebec
"C" Squadron was disbanded in 1970 at Montreal.

Affiliated British Unit:
13th/18th HUSSARS

THE SHERBROOKE HUSSARS (MILITIA)

The Regiment was formed in 1965 by the amalgamation of "The Sherbrooke Regiment (R.C.A.C.)" which had originated in 1866 as the "Sherbrooke Battalion of Infantry" and the "7th/11th Hussars" which had originated in 1867 as a "provisional" battalion of infantry that was converted to cavalry in 1903.

A "provisional" regiment of cavalry had been formed in 1872 to adminster the previously-independent troops of cavalry in "Military District 5".

"5th Provisional Regiment of Cavalry"
Headquarters — COOKSHIRE, Quebec
"1" Troop — COOKSHIRE, Quebec
"2" Troop — SHERBROOKE, Quebec
"3" Troop — STANSTEAD, Quebec
"4" Troop — COMPTON, Quebec
"5" Troop — SUTTON, Quebec

Regimental March: "MY BOY WILLIE"
Regimental Motto: "IN HOC SIGNO STABILITAS"
       ("STEADFAST IN THIS SIGN")
Major Battle Honors:
VIMY RIDGE — FRANCE AND FLANDERS, 1915-1918 — NORMANDY LANDING — THE RHINELAND — NORTH-WEST EUROPE, 1944-1945
Headquarters — SHERBROOKE, Quebec.
"A" Squadron originated as the "1st Volunteer Milita Rifle Company of Sherbrooke".
"B" Squadron originated as the "2nd Volunteer Militia Rifle Company of Sherbrooke".
"C" Squadron, which was disbanded in 1970 at Bury, had originated as the "Volunteer Militia Infantry Company of Bury".

Affiliated British Unit:
THE QUEEN'S OWN HUSSARS

8th CANADIAN HUSSARS (PRINCESS LOUISE'S) (REGULAR)

The Regiment was formed in 1957.
Regimental March: *"THE 8th HUSSARS"*
Regimental Motto: *"REGI PATRIAQUE FIDELIS"*
    ("FAITHFUL TO KING AND COUNTRY")
Headquarters — CAMP PETAWAWA, Ontario
"A" Squadron
"B" Squadron
"C" Squadron
The Regiment, which provided a "reconnaissance squadron" for service with the "United Nations Emergency Force" in the Middle East at various times from 1956 until 1967, is presently a unit of the "Special Service Force".

Affiliated British Unit:
THE QUEEN'S ROYAL IRISH HUSSARS

8th CANADIAN HUSSARS (PRINCESS LOUISE'S) (MILITIA)

The Regiment originated in 1866 as the "New Brunswick Regiment of Yeomanry Cavalry" which was re-organized in 1872 as a "provisional" regiment of cavalry to administer the previously-independent troops of cavalry in "Military District 8".

"8th Provisional Regiment of Cavalry"
Headquarters — APOHAQUI, New Brunswick
"1" Troop — HAMPTON, New Brunswick
"2" Troop — OSSEKEAG, New Brunswick
"3" Troop — APOHAQUI, New Brunswick
"4" Troop — HAMMOND, New Brunswick
"5" Troop — JOHNSTON, New Brunswick
"6" Troop — SHEDIAC, New Brunswick
"7" Troop — SPRINGFIELD, New Brunswick

Regimental March: *"THE 8th HUSSARS"*
Regimental Motto: *"REGI PATRIAQUE FIDELIS"*
    ("FAITHFUL TO KING AND COUNTRY")
Major Battle Honours:
FRANCE AND FLANDERS, 1915-1916 — ITALY, 1944-1945 — DELFZIJL POCKET — NORTH-WEST EUROPE, 1945
"Headquarters" was relocated at Moncton from Saint John in 1954.
"A" Squadron — MONCTON, New Brunswick
"B" Squadron — SUSSEX, New Brunswick
"C" Squadron was relocated at Sackville from Saint John in 1954.

Affiliated British Unit:
THE QUEEN'S ROYAL IRISH HUSSARS

12th MANITOBA DRAGOONS (MILITIA)

The Regiment, which was disbanded in 1965, perpetuates the "Winnipeg Battalion of Infantry" which had been formed in 1885 for service in Saskatchewan during the "Riel" Rebellion (1885).

Regimental March: *"COLONEL BOGEY"*
Regimental Motto: *"UBIQUE HONOUR ET EQUIS"*
    ("EVERYWHERE HONOUR AND EQUALITY")
Major Battle Honours:
NORTH-WEST CANADA, 1885 — SOUTH AFRICA, 1900 — THE GREAT WAR, 1914-1917 — THE RHINELAND — NORTH-WEST EUROPE, 1944-1945
"Headquarters" was disbanded at Virden.
"A" Squadron was disbanded at Minnedosa.
"B" Squadron was disbanded at Virden.
"C" Squadron was disbanded at Neepawa.
"D" Squadron was disbanded in 1954 at Shoal Lake.

Affiliated British Unit:
9th/12th ROYAL LANCERS

14th CANADIAN HUSSARS (MILITIA)

The Regiment, which had originated in 1910, was disbanded in 1968.

Regimental March: *"BONNIE DUNDEE"*
Regimental Motto: *"FREE AND FEARLESS"*
Major Battle Honours:
THE GREAT WAR, 1916 — THE RHINELAND — NORTH-WEST EUROPE, 1944-1945
"Headquarters" was disbanded at Swift Current, Saskatchewan.
"A" Squadron, which maintained a detached troop at Vanguard until 1954, was disbanded at Swift Current.
"B" Squadron, which maintained a detached troop at Gull Lake until 1954, was disbanded at Maple Creek.
"C" Squadron, which maintained a detached troop at Frontier until 1954, was, after relocation from Climax in 1954, disbanded at Shaunavon.

Affiliated British Unit:
14th/20th HUSSARS

THE SOUTH ALBERTA LIGHT HORSE (MILITIA)

The Regiment, which perpetuates the "Rocky Mountain Rangers" (1885), was formed in 1954 by the amalgamation of "Headquarters, 68 Light Anti-Aircraft Regiment (15th Alberta Light Horse), R.C.A. (Reserve Force)" which had originated in 1905 and "The South Alberta Regiment (R.C.A.C.) (Reserve Force)".

Regimental March: "A SOUTHERLY WIND AND A CLOUDY SKY"
Regimental Motto: "SEMPER ALACER" / "ALWAYS SWIFT")
Major Battle Honours:
NORTH-WEST CANADA, 1885 — VIMY RIDGE — PURSUIT TO MONS — FRANCE AND FLANDERS, 1915-1918 — THE RHINELAND — NORTH-WEST EUROPE, 1944-1945
"Headquarters" was relocated at Medicine Hat from Calgary in 1959.
"A" Squadron — MEDICINE HAT, Alberta
"B" Squadron, after relocation from Brooks in 1959, was relocated at Edmonton from Medicine Hat in 1977.
"C" Squadron, which maintained a detached troop at Bow Island until 1965, was, after relocation from Calgary in 1959, disbanded in 1970 at Medicine Hat.

Affiliated British Unit:
15th/19th HUSSARS

19th ALBERTA DRAGOONS (MILITIA)

The Regiment, which incorporated the "Edmonton Fusiliers" in 1946, originated in 1908 and provided the "1st Divisional Cavalry Squadron, C.E.F." which fought in France as a sub-unit of the "Canadian Light Horse" during the Great War.

Regimental March: *"JOHN PEEL"*
Major Battle Honours:
VIMY RIDGE — PURSUIT TO MONS — FRANCE AND FLANDERS, 1915-1918
"Headquarters" was disbanded in 1965 at Edmonton.
"A" Squadron was disbanded in 1965 at Edmonton.
"B" Squadron was disbanded in 1965 at Camrose.
"C" Squadron, after relocation in 1962 from Whitehorse in the Yukon Territory, was disbanded in 1965 at Fort Saskatchewan, Alberta.
"D" Squadron, which maintained a detached troop at Devon, was disbanded in 1965 at Wetaskiwin.

Affiliated British Unit:
15th/19th HUSSARS

THE BRITISH COLUMBIA DRAGOONS (MILITIA)

The Regiment originated in 1911 as the "British Columbia Horse".

Regimental March: *"FARE YE WELL INNISKILLING"*
Regimental Motto: *"QUANSEM ILEP"* / (*"ALWAYS FIRST"*)
Major Battle Honours:
VIMY RIDGE — PURSUIT TO MONS — FRANCE AND FLANDERS, 1915-1918 — ITALY, 1944-1945 — DELFZIJL POCKET — NORTH-WEST EUROPE, 1945
Headquarters — KELOWNA, British Columbia
"A" Squadron — VERNON, British Columbia
"B" Squadron — KELOWNA, British Columbia
"C" Squadron was disbanded in 1970 at Penticton.

Affiliated British Unit:
5th ROYAL INNISKILLING DRAGOON GUARDS

THE FORT GARRY HORSE (REGULAR)

The Regiment, which had been formed in 1958, was disbanded in 1970.

Regimental March: *"RED RIVER VALLEY"*
Regimental Motto: *"FACTA NON VERBA"* / (*"DEEDS NOT WORDS"*)
Headquarters — Sarcee Barracks, CALGARY, Alberta
"A" Squadron
"B" Squadron
"C" Squadron
The Regiment provided a "reconnaissance squadron" for service with the "United Nations Emergency Force" in the Middle East at various times from 1956 until 1967.

Affiliated British Unit:
4th/7th ROYAL DRAGOON GUARDS

THE FORT GARRY HORSE (MILITIA)

The Regiment, which originated in 1912, perpetuates "Boulton's Mounted Corps" which had been formed in 1885 for service in Saskatchewan during the "Riel" Rebellion (1885).

Regimental March: "RED RIVER VALLEY"
Regimental Motto: "FACTA NON VERBA" / ("DEEDS NOT WORDS")
Major Battle Honours:
FISH CREEK — NORTH-WEST CANADA, 1885 — PURSUIT TO MONS — FRANCE AND FLANDERS, 1916-1918 — NORMANDY LANDING — THE RHINELAND — NORTH-WEST EUROPE, 1944-1945
Headquarters — McGregor Armoury, WINNIPEG, Manitoba
"A" Squadron — McGregor Armoury, WINNIPEG, Manitoba
"B" Squadron was relocated at Winnipeg from Selkirk in 1954.
"C" Squadron was disbanded in 1970 at Winnipeg.

Affiliated British Unit:
4th/7th ROYAL DRAGOON GUARDS

THE SASKATCHEWAN DRAGOONS (MILITIA)

The Regiment was formed in 1946 by the conversion and re-designation of "The King's Own Rifles of Canada" which had originated in 1913 as the "60th Rifles of Canada".

Regimental March: *"PUNJAUB"*
Regimenyal Motto: *"ESPRIT D'INITIATIVE"*
        ("SPIRIT OF INITIATIVE")
Major Battle Honours: VIMY RIDGE — FRANCE AND FLANDERS, 1916-1918
Headquarters — MOOSE JAW, Saskatchewan
"A" Squadron — MOOSE JAW, Saskatchewan
This squadron was re-organized in 1970 as an "independent squadron".
"B" Squadron was disbanded in 1970 at Moose Jaw.
"C" Squadron, after relocation from Gravellbourgh in 1954, was disbanded in 1970 at Moose Jaw.

Affiliated British Unit:
THE ROYAL GREEN JACKETS

THE WINDSOR REGIMENT (R.C.A.C.) (MILITIA)

The Regiment originated in 1936 as "The Essex Regiment (Tank)".

Regimental March: "MY BOY WILLIE"
Regimental Motto: "SEMPER PARATUS" / ("ALWAYS READY")
Headquarters — WINDSOR, Ontario
"A" Squadron
"B" Squadron
"C" Squadron was disbanded in 1970.

Affiliated British Unit:
THE ROYAL SCOTS DRAGOON GUARDS

12ieme REGIMENT BLINDE DU CANADA (REGULIER)

Le regiment, qui a forme en 1970, est un unit de "5ieme Groupe-Brigade du Canada".

Regimental March: *"MY BOY WILLIE"*
Regimental Motto: *"ADSUM"* / (*"I AM PRESENT"*)
Quartier General — CAMP VALCARTIER, Quebec
Escadron "A"
Escadron "B"
Escadron "C"

TANK UNITS (1939-1945)

THE ROYAL CANADIAN DRAGOONS
The "1st Motorcycle Regiment (Royal Canadian Dragoons/Lord Strathcona's Horse)" served in Canada.
The "1st Armoured Car Regiment (Royal Canadian Dragoons)" fought in both Italy and North-West Europe.

LORD STRATHCONA'S HORSE (ROYAL CANADIANS)
The "1st Motorcycle Regiment (Royal Canadian Dragoons/Lord Strathcona's Horse)" served in Canada.
The "2nd Armoured Regiment (Lord Strathcona's Horse (Royal Canadians))" fought in both Italy and North-West Europe.

THE GOVERNOR-GENERAL'S HORSE GUARDS
The "2nd Motorcycle Regiment (Governor-General's Horse Guards)" served in Canada.
The "3rd Armoured Reconnaissance Regiment (Governor-General's Horse Guards)" fought in both Italy and North-West Europe.

4th PRINCESS LOUISE DRAGOON GUARDS
The "4th Reconnaissance Regiment (4th Princess Louise Dragoon Guards)" fought in both Italy and North-West Europe.

8th (PRINCESS LOUISE'S) NEW BRUNSWICK HUSSARS
The "4th Motorcycle Regiment (8th (Princess Louise's) New Brunswick Hussars)" served in Canada.
The "5th Armoured Regiment (8th (Princess Louise's) New Brunswick Hussars)" fought in both Italy and North-West Europe.

1st HUSSARS
The "6th Armoured Regiment (1st Hussars)" fought in North-West Europe.

17th DUKE OF YORK'S ROYAL CANADIAN HUSSARS
The "3rd Motorcycle Regiment (17th Duke of York's Royal Canadian Hussars)" served in Canada.
The "7th Reconnaissance Regiment (17th Duke of York's Royal Canadian Hussars)" fought in North-West Europe.

14th CANADIAN HUSSARS
The "8th Reconnaissance Regiment (14th Canadian Hussars)" fought in North-West Europe.

THE BRITISH COLUMBIA DRAGOONS
The "5th Motorcycle Regiment (British Columbia Dragoons)" served in Canada.
The "9th Armoured Regiment (British Columbia Dragoons)" fought in both Italy and North-West Europe.

THE FORT GARRY HORSE
The "10th Armoured Regiment (Fort Garry Horse)" fought in North-West Europe.

THE ONTARIO REGIMENT (TANK)
The "11th Armoured Regiment (Ontario Regiment)" fought in both Italy and North-West Europe.

THE THREE RIVERS REGIMENT (TANK)
The "12th Armoured Regiment (Three Rivers Regiment)" fought in both Italy and North-West Europe.

THE CALGARY REGIMENT (TANK)
The "14th Armoured Regiment (Calgary Regiment)" fought in both Italy and North-West Europe.

12th MANITOBA DRAGOONS
The "18th Armoured Car Regiment (12th Manitoba Dragoons)" fought in North-West Europe.

16th/22nd SASKATCHEWAN HORSE
The "20th Tank Battalion (16th/22nd Saskatchewan Horse)" served in both Canada and the United Kingdom.

THE GOVERNOR-GENERAL'S FOOT GUARDS
The "21st Armoured Regiment (Governor-General's Foot Guards)" fought in North-West Europe.

THE CANADIAN GRENADIER GUARDS
The "22nd Armoured Regiment (Canadian Grenadier Guards)" fought in North-West Europe. The "22nd Tank Battalion (Canadian Grenadier Guards)" was formed in Canada in 1945 for allocation to the "Canadian Army (Pacific Force)" for the projected assault on the Japanese home islands.

THE HALIFAX RIFLES
The "23rd Tank Battalion (Halifax Rifles)" served in both Canada and the United Kingdom.

LES VOLTIGEURS DE QUEBEC
The "24th Reconnaissance Regiment (Voltigeurs de Quebec)" served in Canada.

THE ELGIN REGIMENT
The "25th Armoured Delivery Regiment (Elgin Regiment)" fought in both Italy and North-West Europe.

THE GREY AND SIMCOE FORESTERS
The "26th Tank Battalion (Grey and Simcoe Foresters)" served in both Canada and the United Kingdom.

THE SHERBROOKE REGIMENT and LES FUSILIERS DE SHERBROOKE
The "27th Armoured Regiment (Sherbrooke Fusiliers)" fought in North-West Europe.

THE BRITISH COLUMBIA REGIMENT
The "28th Armoured Regiment (British Columbia Regiment)" fought in North-West Europe.

THE SOUTH ALBERTA REGIMENT
The "29th Armoured Reconnaissance Regiment (South Alberta Regiment)" fought in North-West Europe.

THE ESSEX REGIMENT (TANK)
The "30th Reconnaissance Regiment (Essex Regiment)" served in both Canada and the United Kingdom.

15th ALBERTA LIGHT HORSE
The "31st (Alberta) Reconnaissance Regiment" served in Canada.

THE ROYAL MONTREAL REGIMENT
The "32nd Reconnaissance Regiment (Royal Montreal Regiment)" served in the United Kingdom.

THE NEW BRUNSWICK REGIMENT (TANK)
The "1st Tank Brigade Headquarters Squadron (New Brunswick Regiment)" served in Canada.

THE PRINCE EDWARD ISLAND LIGHT HORSE
The "1st Armoured Brigade Headquarters Squadron (Prince Edward Island Light Horse)" served in both Canada and the United Kingdom.

7th/11th HUSSARS
The "2nd Armoured Brigade Headquarters Squadron (7th/11th Hussars)" served in both Canada and the United Kingdom.

6th DUKE OF CONNAUGHT'S ROYAL CANADIAN HUSSARS
The "5th Armoured Division Headquarters Squadron (6th Duke of Connaught's Royal Canadian Hussars)" served in both Canada and the United Kingdom.

1st CANADIAN ARMOURED PERSONNEL CARRIER REGIMENT
The regiment fought in North-West Europe as a unit of the British "79th Armoured Division".

THE ROYAL REGIMENT OF CANADIAN ARTILLERY

Regimental Quick March: *"THE BRITISH GRENADIERS"*
Regimental Slow March: *"THE ARTILLERY SLOW MARCH"*
Regimental Mottoes: *"UBIQUE"* / *("EVERYWHERE")*
    "QUO FAS ET GLORIA DUCUNT"
    ("WHITHER RIGHT AND GLORY LEAD")
The Royal Canadian School of Artillery: CAMP SHILO, Manitoba

NOTE

The current battery list originated with those batteries raised for overseas service during the Great War by the existing field batteries of the Non-Permanent Active Militia. Each battery is listed under its present designation or under that which was held at the time of disbandment. The entry for those batteries which originated by authorization of the Militia Act of 1855, or by conversion from subsequently-formed units of garrison artillery, includes a reference to the designation held at that time. During the Fenian Raids (1866 and 1870), militia field batteries were among those units which were placed on active service at vulnerable points along the border with the United States. Various artillery units of the Volunteer Militia served in Saskatchewan during the "Riel" Rebellion (1885). Militia field batteries did not serve in South Africa during the "Boer" War but did provide trained personnel for service with the three ("C", "D" and "E") batteries of Royal Canadian Field Artillery which were raised specifically for that conflict. During the Second World War, existing militia field batteries were the nucleus upon which field, anti-tank, light anti-aircraft and medium batteries were mobilized for active service. Subsequently, the Canadian Army (Reserve Force) (later the Canadian Army (Militia)) was called upon to recruit for the brigade group that was being formed for service in West Germany under the auspices of the North Atlantic Treaty Organization. As a result, the Royal Canadian Artillery raised six field batteries which provided for two field regiments that were to alternate between Europe and Canada. These regiments later served in Korea. Like-numbered British batteries, although not officially affiliated, have been linked with their Canadian counterparts along with a reference to the action in which they gained distinction. "Gunners" carry no battle honours but rather, upon their various badges and devices, bear the distinctions "UBIQUE" and "QUO FAS ET GLORIA DUCUNT".

1 Field Battery — Dow's Lake, OTTAWA, Ontatio
"1 Battery, C.F.A." fought in France during the Great War. "1 Light Anti-Aircraft Battery, R.C.A." fought in North-West Europe during the Second World War. "1 Field Battery" is presently a sub-unit of "30 Field Regiment, R.C.A." (The Bytown Gunners).
Affiliated British Unit:
1 Battery (The Blazers), R.A.

2 Field Battery — Dow's Lake, OTTAWA, Ontario
The "Volunteer Militia Field Battery of Ottawa" was formed in 1855. "2 Battery, C.F.A." fought in France during the Great War. "2 Field Battery, R.C.A.", which fought in North-West Europe during the Second World War, is presently a sub-unit of "30 Field Regiment, R.C.A." (The Bytown Gunners).
Affiliated British Unit:
2 Battery, R.A.

3 (Independent) Medium Battery — GANANOQUE, Ontario
"3 Battery, C.F.A." fought in France during the Great War. "3 Anti-Tank Battery, R.C.A." fought in North-West Europe during the Second World War. The battery also perpetuates "3 Medium Battery, R.C.A. (Permanent Force)" which fought in both Italy and North-West Europe during the Second World War. "3 (Independent) Medium Battery, R.C.A. (Militia)" was disbanded in 1965.
Affiliated British Unit:
3 Battery, R.A.

4 Field Battery —LINDSAY, Ontario
"4 Battery, C.F.A." fought in France during the Great War. "4 Anti-Tank Battery, R.C.A." fought in North-West Europe during the Second World War. "4 Field Battery", which had been relocated from Peterborough in 1946, was disbanded in 1954 as a sub-unit of "4 Field Regiment, R.C.A. (Reserve Force)". The battery's numerical designation was allocated to a locating battery that was formed in 1954 by the re-organization of "Headquarters, 60 Light Anti-Aircraft Regiment (The Brockville Rifles), R.C.A. (Reserve Force)". "4 Locating Battery (The Brockville Rifles), R.C.A. (Militia)" was later retroactively re-numbered in order to perpetuate "32 Anti-Tank Battery, R.C.A. (Reserve Force)" which had originated in 1855 as the "Volunteer Militia Company of Foot Artillery of Kingston".
Affiliated British Unit:
"4 (SPHINX) Battery, R.A." fought at Alexandria in Egypt in 1801 during the Napoleonic Wars.

5 (WESTMOUNT) Field Battery — MONTREAL, Quebec
"5 Battery, C.F.A." fought in France during the Great War. "5 Field Battery, R.C.A." fought in North-West Europe during the Second World War and subsequently recruited a battery for service with the "27th Canadian Infantry Brigade Group" in West Germany. This battery served in Korea subsequent to the armistice and was re-organized in 1953 as "G" Battery, R.C.H.A. which is presently a sub-unit of "3 Regiment, Royal Canadian Horse Artillery (Regular)". "5 Field Battery" was disbanded in 1965 as a sub-unit of "34 Field Regiment, R.C.A. (Militia)".
Affiliated British Unit:
"5 (GIBRALTAR) Battery, R.A.", which originated in Newfoundland in 1749, served at Gibraltar during the siege of 1779 to 1783.

6 (Independent) Field Battery — SYDNEY, Nova Scotia
"6 Battery, C.F.A." fought in France during the Great War. "6 Coast Battery, R.C.A." provided harbour defence for Sydney during the Second World War. "6(Independent) Field Battery, R.C.A. (Militia) was disbanded in 1965.
Affiliated British Unit:
6 Battery, R.A.

7 Field Battery — MONTREAL, Quebec

The "Volunteer Militia Field Battery of Montreal" was formed in 1855. "7 Battery, C.F.A." fought in France during the Great War. "7 Field Battery, R.C.A." fought in both Italy and North-West Europe during the Second World War. The battery also perpetuates "7 Medium Battery, R.C.A." which fought in both Italy and North-West Europe during the Second World War. "7 Field Battery" is presently a sub-unit of "2 Field Regiment, R.C.A.".

Affiliated British Unit:

"7 (SPHINX) Battery, R.A.", which fought at Alexandria in Egypt in 1801 during the Napoleonic Wars, fought in Borneo as a sub-unit of "95 Commando Regiment, R.A.", The battery was subsequently allocated to "29 Commando Regiment, R.A." which fought in support of "3 Commando Brigade, Royal Marines" in the Falkland Islands during the South Atlantic Campaign (1982).

8 Field Battery — MONCTON, New Brunswick

"8 Battery, C.F.A." fought in France during the Great War. "8 Field Battery, R.C.A.", which fought in both Italy and North-West Europe during the Second World War, was disbanded in 1954 as a sub-unit of "12 Field Regiment, R.C.A. (Reserve Force)".

Affiliated British Unit:

"8 (ALMA) Battery, R.A.", which fought at that battle in the Crimea in 1854 during the Anglo/French and Turkish war against the Russians (1854-1856), fought in Borneo as a sub-unit of "95 Commando Regiment, R.A.". The battery was subsequently allocated to "29 Commando Regiment, R.A." which fought in support of "3 Commando Brigade, Royal Marines" in the Falkland Islands during the South Atlantic Campaign (1982).

9 Field Battery — Moss Park Armoury, TORONTO, Ontario

The "Toronto Field Battery" originated in 1866 as a "Battery of Garrison Artillery". "9 Battery, C.F.A." fought in France during the Great War. "9 Field Battery, R.C.A." fought in both Italy and North-West Europe during the Second World War and subsequently recruited a battery for service with the "27th Canadian Infantry Brigade Group" in West Germany. This battery served in Korea subsequent to the armistice and was re-organized in 1953 as "H" Battery, R.C.H.A. which was disbanded in 1970 as a sub-unit of "3 Regiment, Royal Canadian Horse Artillery (Regular)". "9 Field Battery" is presently a sub-unit of "7 Toronto Regiment, R.C.A.".

Affiliated British Unit:

"9 (PLASSEY) Battery, R.A." fought at that battle in India in 1757.

10 Field Battery — ST. CATHARINES, Ontario

The "Welland Canal Field Battery" was formed in 1861. "10 Battery, C.F.A." fought in France during the Great War. "10 Field Battery, R.C.A.", which fought in both Italy and North-West Europe during the Second World War, is presently a sub-unit of "56 Field Regiment (The Dufferin and Haldimand Rifles of Canada), R.C.A.".

Affiliated British Unit:

"10 (ASSAYE) Battery, R.A." fought at that battle in India in 1803.

11 Field Battery — HAMILTON, Ontario

The "Volunteer Militia Field Battery of Hamilton" was formed in 1855. "11 Battery, C.F.A." fought in France during the Great War. "11 Field Battery, R.C.A., which landed at Normandy and fought in North-West Europe during the Second World War, is presently a sub-unit of "11 Field Regiment, R.C.A.".

Affiliated British Unit:

"11 (SPHINX) Battery, R.A." fought at Alexandria in Egypt in 1801 during the Napoleonic Wars.

12 Field Battery — LONDON, Ontario

"12 Battery, C.F.A." fought in France during the Great War. "12 Medium Battery, R.C.A." fought in North-West Europe during the Second World War. "12 Field Battery" was disbanded in 1965 as a sub-unit of "7 Field Regiment, R.C.A. (Militia)".

Affiliated British Unit:

"12 (MINDEN) Battery, R.A." fought at that battle in Germany in 1759 during the Seven-Years War (1756-1763).

13 Field Battery — PORTAGE LA PRAIRIE, Manitoba

The "Winnipeg Field Battery" served in Saskatchewan during the "Riel" Rebellion (1885). "13 Battery, C.F.A." fought in France during the Great War. "13 Field Battery, R.C.A." fought in North-West Europe during the Second World War and subsequently recruited a battery for service with the "27th Canadian Infantry Brigade Group" in West Germany. This battery served in Korea subsequent to the armistice and was re-organized in 1953 as "J" Battery, R.C.H.A. which is presently a sub-unit of "3 Regiment, Royal Canadian Horse Artillery (Regular)". "13 Field Battery" was relocated at Virden in 1965 thereby continuing a militia presence subsequent to the disbandment of the "12th Manitoba Dragoons" of which "Regimental Headquarters" and "B" Squadron were located at Virden. The battery was relocated at Portage la Prairie in 1970 and is presently a sub-unit of "26 Field Regiment (The Manitoba Rangers), R.C.A.".

Affiliated British Unit:

"13 (MARTINIQUE) Battery, R.A." fought on that Caribbean island in 1809 during the Napoleonic Wars.

14 (MIDLAND) Field Battery — COBOURG, Ontario

"14 Battery, C.F.A." fought in France during the Great War. "14 Field Battery R.C.A.", which fought in North-West Europe during the Second World War, was disbanded in 1970 as a sub-unit of "50 Field Regiment (The Prince of Wales' Rangers), R.C.A. (Militia)".

Affiliated British Unit:

"14 (Cole's Kop) Battery, R.A." fought at that battle in 1900 during the South African War and was more recently a sub-unit of "21 Locating Regiment, R.A.".

15 Field Battery — Moss Park Armoury, TORONTO, Ontario

"15 Battery, C.F.A." fought in France during the Great War. "15 Anti-Tank Battery, R.C.A." fought in both Italy and North-West Europe during the Second World War. "15 Field Battery" is presently a sub-unit of "7 Toronto Regiment, R.C.A.".

Affiliated British Unit:

"15 (GIBRALTAR) Battery, R.A." served at that fortress during the siege of 1779 to 1783.

16 Field Battery — GUELPH, Ontario

The "Wellington Field Battery" was formed in 1871 by the re-organization of a "Battery of Garrison Artillery" which had previously been a sub-unit of the "Wellington Battalion of Rifles". "16 Battery, C.F.A." fought in France during the Great War. "16 Field Battery, R.C.A." landed at Normandy and fought in North-West Europe during the Second World War and subsequently recruited a battery for service with the "27th Canadian Infantry Brigade Group" in West Germany. This battery fought in Korea and was re-organized in 1953 as "K" Battery, R.C.H.A. which was disbanded in 1970 as a sub-unit of "4 Regiment, Royal Canadian Horse Artillery (Regular)". "16 Field Battery" was relocated from Fergus in 1965 and is presently a sub-unit of "11 Field Regiment, R.C.A.".

Affiliated British Unit:

"16 Battery (Sandham's Company), R.A." fought at Waterloo in 1815.

17 Field Battery — WINNIPEG, Manitoba

"17 Battery, C.F.A." fought in France during the Great War. "17 Field Battery, R.C.A." fought in

North-West Europe during the Second World War. The battery maintained a detached troop at Emerson and was disbanded in 1965 as a sub-unit of "39 Field Regiment, R.C.A. (Militia)".
Affiliated British Unit:
"17 (CORUNNA) Battery, R.A." fought at that battle in Spain in 1809 during the Napoleonic Wars.

18 Field Battery — REGINA, Saskatchewan
"18 Battery, C.F.A." fought in France during the Great War. "18 Anti-Tank Battery, R.C.A." fought in North-West Europe during the Second World War. "18 Field Battery" is presently a sub-unit of "10 Field Regiment, R.C.A.".
Affiliated British Unit:
"18 (QUEBEC) Battery, R.A." fought at that battle in 1759 during the Seven-Years War (1756-1763).

19 Field Battery — NEEPAWA, Manitoba
"19 Battery, C.F.A." fought in France during the Great War. "19 Field Battery, R.C.A." fought in both Italy and North-West Europe during the Second World War. The battery was relocated from Winnipeg in 1965 thereby continuing a militia presence subsequent to the disbandment of the "12th Manitoba Dragoons" of which "A" and "C" Squadrons were located at Minnedosa and Neepawa, respectively. The battery, which maintained a detached troop at Minnedosa until 1968, was disbanded in 1970 as a sub-unit of "26 Field Regiment (The Manitoba Rangers), R.C.A. (Militia)".
Affiliated British Unit:
"19 (GIBRALTAR) Battery, R.A." served at that fortress during the siege of 1779 to 1783.

20 (Independent) Field Battery — LETHBRIDGE, Alberta
"20 Battery, C.F.A." fought in France during the Great War. "20 Anti-Tank Battery, R.C.A." fought in North-West Europe during the Second World War. "20 Field Battery" was a sub-unit of "18 Field Regiment, R.C.A. (Militia)" until 1970.
Affiliated British Unit:
"20 Battery, R.A." fought in Borneo as a sub-unit of "29 Commando Regiment, R.A." during the "Confrontation" with Indonesia. The battery was subsequently removed from the regiment.

21 (Independent) Medium Battery — SASKATOON, Saskatchewan
"21 Battery, C.F.A." fought in France during the Great War. "21 Field Battery, R.C.A." fought in North-West Europe during the Second World War. "21 (Independent) Medium Battery, R.C.A. (Militia)" was disbanded in 1965.
Affiliated British Unit:
"21 (GIBRALTAR) Battery, R.A.", which served at that fortress during the siege of 1779 to 1783 and is presently a sub-unit of "27 Field Regiment, R.A.", fought in the Falkland Islands during the South Atlantic Campaign (1982).

22 (Independent) Medium Battery — COBURG, Ontario
The battery originated as a "Company of Heavy Artillery" which was re-organized subsequent to the Great War as "22 Medium Battery" of "7 Toronto Regiment, Canadian Artillery (Non-Permanent Active Militia)". "22 (Independent) Medium Battery, R.C.A. (Militia)" was disbanded in 1965.
Affiliated British Unit:
"22 (GIBRALTAR) Battery, R.A." served at that fortress during the siege of 1779 to 1783.

23 Medium Battery — BANFF, Alberta
"23 Battery, C.F.A." fought in France during the Great War. "23 Anti-Tank Battery, R.C.A." fought in North-West Europe during the Second World War. "23 Medium Battery" was

disbanded in 1965 as a sub-unit of "19 Medium Regiment, R.C.A. (Militia)".
Affiliated British Unit:
"23 (GIBRALTAR) Battery, R.A." served at that fortress during the siege of 1779 to 1783.

24 (SHEFFORD) Field Battery — GRANBY, Quebec

The battery adopted the county designation in 1904 upon the disbandment of "The Shefford and Brome Regiment" which had originated in 1872 as the "Shefford Battalion of Infantry". "24 Battery, C.F.A." fought in France during the Great War. "24 Field Battery, R.C.A.", which served in Canada during the Second World War, was disbanded in 1970 as a sub-unit of "27 Field Regiment, R.C.A. (Militia)".
Affiliated British Unit:
"24 (IRISH) Battery, R.A." originated in the Royal Irish Artillery which was incorporated within the Royal Artillery in 1801.

25 Field Battery — KEMPTVILLE, Ontario

"25 Battery, C.F.A." fought in France during the Great War. "25 Light Anti-Aircraft Battery, R.C.A." served in Canada during the Second World War. "25 Field Battery" was relocted from Ottawa in 1954 thereby continuing an artillery presence subsequent to the disbandment of "181 Light Anti-Aircraft Battery, R.C.A. (Reserve Force)". The battery was disbanded in 1968 as a sub-unit of "30 Field Regiment, R.C.A. (Militia)" (The Bytown Gunners).
Affiliated British Unit:
25 Battery, R.A.

26 (LAMBTON) Field Battery — SARNIA, Ontario

"26 Battery, C.F.A." fought in France during the Great War. The county designation was adopted in 1936 upon the disbandment of "The Lambton Regiment (Non-Permanent Active Militia)" which had originated in 1866 as the "Lambton Battalion of Infantry". "26 Field Battery, R.C.A.", which fought in North-West Europe during the Second World War, was disbanded in 1965 as a sub-unit of "7 Field Regiment, R.C.A. (Militia)".
Affiliated British Unit:
26 Battery, R.A.

27 Field Battery — MONTREAL, Quebec

"27 Battery, C.F.A." fought in France during the Great War. "27 Anti-Tank Battery, R.C.A." fought in both Italy and North-West Europe during the Second World War. "27 Field Battery" was disbanded in 1965 as a sub-unit of "34 Field Regiment, R.C.A. (Militia)".
Affiliated British Unit:
"27 (Strange's) Battery, R.A." commemorates the receiving of the Victoria Cross by the battery's commander during the Indian Mutiny (1857-1858).

28 Field Battery — NEWCASTLE, New Brunswick

"28 Battery, C.F.A." fought in France during the Great War. "28 Field Battery, R.C.A." fought in North-West Europe during the Second World War. The battery, a sub-unit of "12 Field Regiment, R.C.A. (Reserve Force)", was incorporated within "2nd Battalion, The Royal New Brunswick Regiment, R.C.I.C. (Militia)" in 1954.
Affiliated British Unit:
28 Battery, R.A.

29 Field Battery — GUELPH, Ontario

"29 Battery, C.F.A." fought in France during the Great War. "29 Field Battery, R.C.A.", which fought in both Italy and North-West Europe during the Second World War, is presently a sub-unit of "11 Field Regiment, R.C.A.".
Affiliated British Unit:
"29 (CORUNNA) Battery, R.A." fought at that battle in Spain in 1809 during the Napoleonic Wars.

30 Field Battery —SAULT STE. MARIE, Ontario
"30 Battery, C.F.A." fought in France during the Great War. "30 Light Anti-Aircraft Battery, R.C.A." fought in North-West Europe during the Second World War. "30 Field Battery" is presently a sub-unit of "49 (Sault Ste. Marie) Field Regiment, R.C.A.".
Affiliated British Unit:
"30 Battery (Rogers' Company), R.A." fought at Waterloo in 1815.

31 Field Battery — VANCOUVER, British Columbia
"31 Battery, C.F.A." fought in France during the Great War. "31 Field Battery, R.C.A.", which fought in North-West Europe during the Second World War, is presently a sub-unit of "15 Field Regiment, R.C.A.".
Affiliated British Unit:
31 Battery, R.A.

32 Locating Battery (The Brockville Rifles) — BROCKVILLE, Ontario
The "Volunteer Militia Company of Foot Artillery of Kingston" was formed in 1855. "32 Battery, C.F.A." fought in France during the Great War. "32 Light Anti-Aircraft Battery, R.C.A." landed at Normandy and fought in North-West Europe during the Second World War. "32 Locating Battery (The Brockville Rifles), R.C.A. (Militia)" was formed in 1954 by the amalgamation of "32 Anti-Tank Battery" (a sub-unit of "9 Anti-Tank Regiment (The Argyll Light Infantry), R.C.A. (Reserve Force)") and "Headquarters, 60 Light Anti-Aircraft Regiment (The Brockville Rifles), R.C.A. (Reserve Force)". The battery was converted to infantry in 1959 and re-designated "The Brockville Rifles, R.C.I.C. (Militia)".
Affiliated British Unit:
"32 (MINDEN) Battery, R.A.", which originated in 1756 as a "Company of Miners", fought at that battle in Germany in 1759 during the Seven-Years War (1756-1763).

33 Field Battery — ST. CATHARINES, Ontario
"33 Battery, C.F.A." fought in France during the Great War. "33 Anti-Tank Battery, R.C.A." fought in North-West Europe during the Second World War. "33 Field Battery" was disbanded in 1965 as a sub-unit of "44 Field Regiment, R.C.A. (Militia)".
Affiliated British Unit:
"33 Battery (Brome's Company), R.A." fought at Waterloo in 1815.

34 Anti-Tank Battery — BELLEVILLE, Ontario
"34 Field Battery, R.C.A." landed at Normandy and fought in North-West Europe during the Second World War. "34 Anti-Tank Battery", a sub-unit of "9 Anti-Tank Regiment (The Argyll Light Infantry), R.C.A. (Reserve Force)", was incorporated within "The Hastings and Prince Edward Regiment, R.C.I.C. (Militia)" in 1954.
Affiliated British Unit:
"34 (SERINGAPATAM) Battery, R.A." fought at that battle in India 1799.

35 Field Battery — FARNHAM, Quebec
"35 Battery, C.F.A." fought in France during the Great War. "35 Light Anti-Aircraft Battery, R.C.A." fought in both Italy and North-West Europe during the Second World War. The battery was converted in 1944 and re-designated "35 Traffic Control Company, C.Pro.C." which fought in Italy prior to re-conversion to artillery in 1945. "35 Field Battery" was disbanded in 1970 as a sub-unit of "27 Field Regiment, R.C.A. (Militia)".
Affiliated British Unit:
35 Battery, R.A.

36 Heavy Anti-Aircraft Battery — SYDNEY, Nova Scotia
"36 Battery, C.F.A." fought in France during the Great War. "36 Field Battery. R.C.A." fought in North-West Europe during the Second World War. "36 Heavy Anti-Aircraft Battery" was

disbanded in 1954 as a sub-unit of "16 Heavy Anti-Aircraft Regiment, R.C.A. (Reserve Force)".
Affiliated British Unit:
"36 (ARCOT) Battery, R.A." fought at that battle in India in 1751.

37 Light Anti-Aircraft Battery — PORTAGE LA PRAIRIE, Manitoba
"37 Battery, C.F.A." fought in France during the Great War. The battery was re-formed in 1936 by the conversion and re-designation of "A" Company of "The Manitoba Rangers (Non-Permanent Active Militia)" which had originated in 1908. "37 Field Battery, R.C.A." fought in both Italy and North-West Europe during the Second World War. "37 Light Anti-Aircraft Battery" was disbanded in 1954 as a sub-unit of "67 Light Anti-Aircraft Regiment (The Manitoba Mounted Rifles), R.C.A. (Reserve Force)".
Affiliated British Unit:
37 Battery, R.A.

38 Field Battery — PORTAGE LA PRAIRIE, Manitoba
"38 Battery, C.F.A." fought in France during the Great War. "38 Light Anti-Aircraft Battery, R.C.A." fought in North-West Europe during the Second World War. "38 Field Battery" was disbanded in 1970 as a sub-unit of "26 Field Regiment (The Manitoba Rangers), R.C.A. (Militia)".
Affiliated British Unit:
"38 (SERINGAPATAM) Battery, R.A." fought at that battle in India in 1799.

39 Field Battery — LETHBRIDGE, Alberta
"39 Battery, C.F.A." fought in France during the Great War. "39 Field Battery, R.C.A.", which served in Canada during the Second World War, was disbanded in 1970 as a sub-unit of "18 Field Regiment, R.C.A. (Militia)".
Affiliated British Unit:
"39 (Roberts') Battery, R.A." commemorates the receiving of the Victoria Cross by the battery's commander during the Indian Mutiny (1857-1858).

40 Field Battery — HAMILTON, Ontario
"40 Battery, C.F.A." fought in France during the Great War. "40 Field Battery, R.C.A., which fought in both Italy and North-West Europe during the Second World War, was disbanded in 1970 as a sub-unit of "8 Field Regiment, R.C.A. (Militia)".
Affiliated British Unit:
40 Battery, R.A.

41 Medium Battery — SIMCOE, Ontario
"41 Battery, C.F.A." fought in France during the Great War. "41 Light Anti-Aircraft Battery, R.C.A." fought in both Italy and North-West Europe during the Second World War. "41 Medium Battery" was disbanded in 1954 as a sub-unit of "25 (Norfolk) Medium Regiment, R.C.A. (Reserve Force)".
Affiliated British Unit:
41 Battery, R.A.

42 Medium Battery — SIMCOE, Ontario
"42 Light Anti-Aircraft Battery, R.C.A." served in the United Kingdom during the Second World War. "42 Medium Battery" was disbanded in 1954 as a sub-unit of "25 (Norfolk) Medium Regiment, R.C.A. (Reserve Force)".
Affiliated British Unit:
42 Battery, R.A.

"25 (Norfolk) Medium Regiment, R.C.A. (Reserve Force)", having originated in 1936 by the conversion and re-designation of "The Norfolk Regiment (Non-Permanent Active Militia)" which had originated in 1866 as the "Norfolk Battalion of Rifles", was amalgamated with "56 Light Anti-Aircraft Regiment (The Dufferin and Haldimand Rifles of Canada), R.C.A. (Reserve Force)" in 1954 and re-designated "56 Field Regiment (The Dufferin and Haldimand Rifles of Canada), R.C.A. (Militia)".

43 Field Battery — GUELPH, Ontario
"43 Battery, C.F.A." fought in France during the Great War. "43 Field Battery, R.C.A.", which landed at Normandy and fought in North-West Europe during the Second World War, was disbanded in 1970 as a sub-unit of "11 Field Regiment, R.C.A.".
Affiliated British Unit:
"43 Battery (Lloyd's Company), R.A.", which fought at Waterloo in 1815 and is presently a sub-unit of "32 Guided-Weapons Regiment, R.A.", fought in the Falkland Islands during the South Atlantic Campaign (1982).

44 (Independent) Field Battery — PRINCE ALBERT, Saskatchewan
"44 Battery, C.F.A." fought in France during the Great War. "44 Field Battery, R.C.A." landed at Normandy and fought in North-West Europe during the Second World War. "44 (Independent) Field Battery, R.C.A. (Militia)" was disbanded in 1968.
Affiliated British Unit:
44 Battery, R.A.

45 (VICTORIA) Field Battery — LINDSAY, Ontario
"45 Battery, C.F.A." fought in France during the Great War. The county designation was adopted in 1936 upon the disbandment of "The Victoria and Haliburton Regiment (Non-Permanent Active Militia)" which had originated in 1866 as the "West Durham Battalion of Infantry" which provided one company for service with the "Midland Provisional Battalion" in Saskatchewan during the "Riel" Rebellion (1885). "45 Medium Battery, R.C.A." fought in North-West Europe during the Second World War. "45 (Victoria) Field Battery" was disbanded in 1970 as a sub-unit of "50 Field Regiment (The Prince of Wales' Rangers), R.C.A. (Militia)".
Affiliated British Unit:
45 Battery, R.A.

46 Field Battery — ST. CATHARINES, Ontario
"46 Battery, C.F.A." fought in France during the Great War. "46 Light Anti-Aircraft Battery, R.C.A." served on Kiska in the Aleutian Islands as a unit of the "13th Canadian Infantry Brigade Group" during the Second World War. "46 Field Battery" was disbanded in 1965 as a sub-unit of "44 Field Regiment, R.C.A. (Militia)".
Affiliated British Unit:
"46 (TALAVERA) Battery, R.A." fought at that battle in Spain in 1809 during the Napoleonic Wars.

47 (FRONTENAC) Medium Battery — NAPANEE, Ontario
"47 Battery, C.F.A." fought in France during the Great War. The county designation was adopted in 1936 upon the disbandment of "The Frontenac Regiment (Non-Permanent Active Militia)" which had originated in 1866 as the "Frontenac Battalion of Infantry" which provided one company for service with the "Midland Provisional Battalion" in Saskatchewan during the "Riel" Rebellion (1885). "47 Light Anti-Aircraft Battery, R.C.A." fought in both Italy and North-West Europe during the Second World War. "47 (Frontenac) Medium Battery" was disbanded in 1965 as a sub-unit of "33 Medium Regiment, R.C.A. (Militia)".
Affiliated British Unit:
47 Battery, R.A.

48 Field Battery — WATFORD, Ontario
"48 Battery, C.F.A." fought in France during the Great War. "48 Light Anti-Aircraft Battery,

R.C.A." served in Canada during the Second World War. "48 Field Battery" was disbanded in 1965 as a sub-unit of "7 Field Regiment, R.C.A. (Militia)".
Affiliated British Unit:
48 Battery, R.A.

49 Harbour Defence Troop, R.C.A. (Regular) — HALIFAX, Nova Scotia
"49 Battery, C.F.A." fought in France during the Great War. "49 Field Battery, R.C.A." served on Kiska in the Aleutian Islands as a unit of the "13th Canadian Infantry Brigade Group" during the Second World War. "49 Coast Battery, R.C.A. (Active Force)" was formed in 1946 and re-organized in 1954 as a harbour defence troop. "49 Harbour Defence Troop, R.C.A. (Regular)" was disbanded in 1956 at York Redoubt in Halifax.
Affiliated British Unit:
"49 (INKERMAN) Battery, R.A." fought at that battle in the Crimea in 1854 during the Anglo/French and Turkish war against the Russians (1854-1856).

50 Field Battery — MONTREAL, Quebec
"50 Medium Battery, R.C.A." fought in North-West Europe during the Second World War. "50 Field Battery" is presently a sub-unit of "2 Field Regiment, R.C.A.".
Affiliated British Unit:
50 (Queen Mary's) Battery, R.A.

51 Field Battery — HALIFAX, Nova Scotia
The battery originated in 1869 as a company of "The Halifax Brigade of Garrison Artillery" and was re-organized subsequent to the Great War as "51 Heavy Battery" of "1 (Halifax) Coast Brigade, Canadian Artillery (Non-Permanent Active Militia)". "51 Coast Battery, R.C.A." provided harbour defence for Halifax during the Second World War. "51 Field Battery" is presently a sub-unit of "1 Field Regiment, R.C.A.".
Affiliated British Unit:
51 Battery, R.A.

52 Field Battery — LIVERPOOL, Nova Scotia
The battery originated in 1869 as a company of "The Halifax Brigade of Garrison Artillery" and was re-organized subsequent to the Great War as "52 Heavy Battery" of "1 (Halifax) Coast Brigade, Canadian Artillery (Non-Permanent Active Militia)". "52 Coast Battery, R.C.A." provided harbour defence for Halifax during the Second World War. "52 Field Battery" was disbanded in 1970 as a sub-unit of "1 Field Regiment, R.C.A. (Militia)".
Affiliated British Unit:
"52 (NIAGARA) Battery, R.A." participated in the capture of the American fort at the mouth of the Niagara River in 1813 during the Anglo-American War of 1812 to 1814.

53 Medium Anti-Aircraft Battery — HALIFAX, Nova Scotia
The battery originated in 1869 as a company of "The Halifax Brigade of Garrison Artillery" and was re-organized subsequent to the Great War as "53 Heavy Battery" of "1 (Halifax) Coast Brigade, Canadian Artillery (Non-Permanent Active Militia)". "53 Coast Battery, R.C.A." provided harbour defence for Halifax during the Second World War. "53 Medium Anti-Aircraft Battery" was disbanded in 1959 as a sub-unit of "1 Medium Anti-Aircraft Regiment, R.C.A. (Militia)".
Affiliated British Unit:
"53 (LOUISBURG) Battery, R.A." fought at that battle on Cape Breton Island in 1758 during the Seven-Years War (1756-1763).

54 Field Battery — BRANTFORD, Ontario
"54 Light Anti-Aircraft Battery, R.C.A." fought in both Italy and North-West Europe during the Second World War. The battery is presently a sub-unit of "56 Field Regiment (The Dufferin and

Haldimand Rifles of Canada), R.C.A.".
Affiliated British Unit:
"54 (MAHARAJPUR) Battery, R.A." fought at that battle in India in 1843.

55 Medium Battery — LONDON, Ontario
"55 Battery, C.F.A." fought in France during the Great War. "55 Field Battery, R.C.A." landed at Normandy and fought in North-West Europe during the Second World War. "55 Medium Battery" was disbanded in 1954 as a sub-unit of "7 Medium Regiment, R.C.A. (Reserve Force)".
Affiliated British Unit:
"55 (RESIDENCY) Battery, R.A." fought in the defence of Lucknow in 1857 during the Indian Mutiny (1857-1858).

56 (GRENVILLE) Field Battery — LINDSAY, Ontario
The county designation was adopted in 1936 upon the disbandment of "The Grenville Regiment (Lisgar Rifles) (Non-Permanent Active Militia)" which had originated in 1867 as the "Grenville Battalion of Infantry". "56 Anti-Tank Battery, R.C.A." fought in North-West Europe during the Second World War. "56 (Grenville) Field Battery" was disbanded in 1954 as a sub-unit of "4 Field Regiment, R.C.A. (Reserve Force)".
Affiliated British Unit:
"56 (Olpherts') Battery, R.A." commemorates the receiving of the Victoria Cross by the battery's commander during the Indian Mutiny (1857-1858).

57 Field Battery — LEVIS, Quebec
The "Volunteer Militia Field Battery of Quebec City" was formed in 1855. "57 Anti-Tank Battery, R.C.A." fought in both Italy and North-West Europe during the Second World War. "57 Field Battery", which was re-organized in 1954 as a locating battery and disbanded in 1965, was re-formed in 1970 and is presently a sub-unit of "6ieme Regiment d'Artillerie du Canada".
Affiliated British Unit:
57 Battery, R.A.

58 Field Battery — Manege Grande-Allee, QUEBEC CITY
The battery originated as a "Company of Heavy Artillery" which was re-organized subsequent to the Great War as "58 Medium Battery" of "6 (Quebec and Levis) Medium Brigade, Canadian Artillery (Non-Permanent Active Militia)". "58 Medium Battery, R.C.A." fought in North-West Europe during the Second World War and subsequently recruited a battery for service with the "27th Canadian Infantry Brigade Group" in West Germany. This battery fought in Korea and was re-organized in 1953 as "L" Battery, R.C.H.A. which was disbanded in 1970 as a sub-unit of "4 Regiment, Royal Canadian Horse Artillery (Regular)". "58 Field Battery" was relocated from Levis in 1970 and is presently a sub-unit of "6ieme Regiment d'Artillerie du Canada".
Affiliated British Unit:
"58 (Eyre's) Battery, R.A." commemorates the receiving of the Victoria Cross by the battery's commander during the Indian Mutiny (1857-1858).

59 Field Battery — MONTMAGNY, Quebec
The battery originated as a "Company of Heavy Artillery" which was re-organized subsequent to the Great War as "59 Medium Battery" of "6 (Quebec and Levis) Medium Brigade, Canadian Artillery (Non-Permanent Active Militia)". "59 Coast Battery, R.C.A." provided harbour defence for Levis during the Second World War. "59 Field Battery", which was relocated from Levis in 1965 thereby continuing a militia presence subsequent to the relocation of "B" Company of "Les Fusiliers du St-Laurent", is presently a sub-unit of "6ieme Regiment d'Artillerie du Canada".
Affiliated British Unit:
"59 (ASTEN) Battery, R.A." fought at that battle in Germany in 1944 during the crossing of the Rhine River.

60 Anti-Tank Battery — ANEROID, Saskatchewan

"60 Battery, C.F.A." fought in France during the Great War. "60 Field Battery, R.C.A." fought in both Italy and North-West Europe during the Second World War. "60 Anti-Tank Battery" was disbanded in 1954 as a sub-unit of "48 Anti-Tank Regiment, R.C.A. (Reserve Force)".
Affiliated British Unit:
60 Battery, R.A.

61 Field Battery — Griesbach Barracks, EDMONTON, Alberta

"61 Battery, C.F.A." fought in France during the Great War. "61 Field Battery, R.C.A." fought in both Italy and North-West Europe during the Second World War. The battery, which maintained a detached troop at Beaumont until 1965, is presently a sub-unit of "20 Field Regiment, R.C.A.".
Affiliated British Unit:
61 Battery, R.A.

62 Anti-Tank Battery — COURTENAY, British Columbia

"62 Light Anti-Aircraft Battery, R.C.A." served in the United Kingdom during the Second World War. "62 Anti-Tank Battery", a sub-unit of "41 Anti-Tank Regiment, R.C.A. (Reserve Force)" was converted to infantry in 1954 and re-organized as "C" Company of "The Canadian Scottish Regiment, R.C.I.C. (Militia)".
Affiliated British Unit:
62 Battery, R.A.

63 (MIDDLESEX) Field Battery — STRATHROY, Ontario

"63 Field Battery, R.C.A." landed at Normandy and fought in North-West Europe during the Second World War. The county designation was adopted in 1946 upon the disbandment of "The Middlesex and Huron Regiment (Non-Permanent Active Militia)" which had been formed in 1936 by the amalgamation of "The Middlesex Light Infantry" and "The Huron Regiment", both of which had originated in 1866. The battery was disbanded in 1954 as a sub-unit of "31 Field Regiment, R.C.A. (Reserve Force)".
Affiliated British Unit:
63 Battery, R.A.

64 Field Battery — YORKTON, Saskatchewan

The battery was formed in 1936 by the conversion and re-designation of "The Yorkton Regiment (Non-Permanent Active Militia)" which had originated in 1924. "64 Field Battery, R.C.A." served in Canada during the Second World War. The battery, which maintained a detached troop at Kamsack until 1965, is presently a sub-unit of "10 Field Regiment, R.C.A.".
Affiliated British Unit:
64 Battery, R.A.

65 Field Battery — GRENFELL, Saskatchewan

The battery was formed in 1936 by the conversion and re-designation of "A" Company of "The Assiniboia Regiment (Non-Permanent Active Militia)" which had originated in 1905 as an element of the "Saskatchewan Rifles". "65 Anti-Tank Battery, R.C.A." fought in North-West Europe during the Second World War. "65 Field Battery" was disbanded in 1968 as a sub-unit of "10 Field Regiment, R.C.A. (Militia)".
Affiliated British Unit:
65 Battery, R.A.

66 Field Battery — MONTREAL, Quebec

"66 Battery, C.F.A." fought in France during the Great War. "66 Field Battery. R.C.A.", which landed at Normandy and fought in North-West Europe during the Second World War, is presently a sub-unit of "2 Field Regiment, R.C.A.".
Affiliated British Unit:
66 Battery, R.A.

67 Light Anti-Aircraft Battery — ROSETOWN, Saskatchewan
"67 (University of Toronto) Depot Battery, C.F.A.", served in Canada during the Great War. "67 Battery, C.F.A." fought at Archangel as a unit of the North Russian Expeditionary Force (1918-1919). "67 Light Anti-Aircraft Battery, R.C.A." served in the United Kingdom during the Second World War. The battery, a sub-unit of "17 Light Anti-Aircraft Regiment, R.C.A. (Reserve Force)", was incorporated within the "Saskatoon Light Infantry, R.C.I.C. (Militia)" (now "The North Saskatchewan Regiment") in 1954.
Affiliated British Unit:
67 Battery, R.A.

68 Field Battery — VANCOUVER, British Columbia
"68 Battery, C.F.A." fought at Archangel as a unit of the North Russian Expeditionary Force (1918-1919). "68 Coast Battery, R.C.A." provided harbour defence on Vancouver Island during the Second World War. "68 Medium Battery, R.C.A. (Active Force)" was formed in 1946 and disbanded in 1954. "68 Field Battery" was formed in 1970 and is presently a sub-unit of "15 Field Regiment, R.C.A.".
Affiliated British Unit:
68 Battery, R.A.

69 Field Battery — SIMCOE, Ontario
"69 Light Anti-Aircraft Battery, R.C.A." fought in both Italy and North-West Europe during the Second World War. "69 Field Battery" is presently a sub-unit of "56 Field Regiment (The Dufferin and Haldimand Rifles of Canada), R.C.A." and has maintained a detached troop at Niagara Falls since 1970 thereby continuing an artillery presence subsequent to the disbandment of "172 Field Battery, R.C.A. (Militia)".
Affiliated British Unit:
69 Battery, R.A.

70 Field Battery — DAUPHIN, Manitoba
The battery was formed in 1936 by the conversion and re-designation of "B" Company of "The Manitoba Rangers (Non-Permanent Active Militia)" which had originated in 1908. "70 Light Anti-Aircraft Battery, R.C.A." fought in North-West Europe during the Second World War. "70 Field Battery" was disbanded in 1970 as a sub-unit of "26 Field Regiment (The Manitoba Rangers), R.C.A. (Militia)".
Affiliated British Unit:
70 Battery, R.A.

71 Field Battery — BRANDON, Manitoba
The battery was formed in 1936 by the conversion and re-designation of "C" Company of "The Manitoba Rangers (Non-Permanent Active Militia)" which had originated in 1908. "71 Field Battery, R.C.A." fought in both Italy and North-West Europe during the Second World War. The battery, which maintained a detached troop at Dauphin until 1979 thereby continuing an artillery presence subsequent to the disbandment of "70 Field Battery, R.C.A. (Militia)", is presently a sub-unit of "26 Field Regiment (The Manitoba Rangers), R.C.A.".
Affiliated British Unit:
72 Battery, R.A.

72 Field Battery — COATICOOK, Quebec
The battery was formed in 1936 by the conversion and re-designation of "A" Squadron of "The Eastern Townships Mounted Rifles (Non-Permanent Active Militia)" which had originated in 1910 as the "Stanstead Dragoons". "72 Field Battery, R.C.A.", which served in Canada during the Second World War, was disbanded in 1968 as a sub-unit of "46 Field Regiment, R.C.A. (Militia)".
Affiliated British Unit:
72 Battery, R.A.

73 Field Battery — VICTORIAVILLE, Quebec
The battery was formed in 1936 by the conversion and re-designation of "B" Squadron of "The Eastern Townships Mounted Rifles (Non-Permanent Active Militia)" which had originated in 1910 as the "Stanstead Dragoons". "73 Field Battery, R.C.A.", which fought in North-West Europe during the Second World War, was relocated from Magog in 1954 and disbanded in 1968 as a sub-unit of "46 Field Regiment, R.C.A. (Militia)".
Affiliated British Unit:
"73 (SPHINX) Battery, R.A." fought at Alexandria in Egypt in 1801 during the Napoleonic Wars.

74 Field Battery — DRUMMONDVILLE, Quebec
The battery was formed in 1936 by the conversion and re-designation of "C" Squadron of "The Eastern Townships Mounted Rifles (Non-Permanent Active Militia)" which had originated in 1910 as the "Stanstead Dragoons". "74 Anti-Tank Battery, R.C.A." fought in North-West Europe during the Second World War. "74 Field Battery" was relocated from Rock Island in 1954 and disbanded in 1968 as a sub-unit of "46 Field Regiment, R.C.A.(Militia)".
Affiliated British Unit:
"74 Battery (The Battle-Axe Company), R.A.", which fought in the Caribbean during the Seven-Years War (1756-1763), is presently a sub-unit of "32 Guided-Weapons Regiment, R.A.".

75 Field Battery — COWANSVILLE, Quebec
The battery was formed in 1936 by the conversion and re-designation of the "13th Scottish Light Dragoons (Non-Permanent Active Militia)" which had originated in 1866 as the "Bedford Battalion of Infantry". "75 Field Battery, R.C.A.", which served in Canada during the Second World War, was disbanded in 1968 as a sub-unit of "27 Field Regiment, R.C.A. (Militia)".
Affiliated British Unit:
75 Battery, R.A.

76 Field Battery — INDIAN HEAD, Saskatchewan
The battery was formed in 1936 by the conversion and re-designation of "B" Company of "The Assiniboia Regiment (Non-Permanent Active Militia)" which had originated in 1905 as an element of the "Saskatchewan Rifles". "76 Field Battery, R.C.A." fought in both Italy and North-West Europe during the Second World War. The battery, which maintained a detached troop at Moosomin until 1965, was disbanded in 1970 as a sub-unit of "10 Field Regiment, R.C.A. (Militia)".
Affiliated British Unit:
"76 (Maude's) Battery, R.A." commemorates the receiving of the Victoria Cross by the battery's commander during the Indian Mutiny (1857-1858).

77 Field Battery — MOOSE JAW, Saskatchewan
"77 Field Battery, R.C.A.", which fought in both Italy and North-West Europe during the Second World War, was disbanded in 1946.
Affiliated British Unit:
77 Battery, R.A.

78 Field Battery — RED DEER, Alberta
"78 Field Battery, R.C.A.", which landed at Normandy and fought in North-West Europe during the Second World War, is presently a sub-unit of "20 Field Regiment, R.C.A.".
Affiliated British Unit:
78 Battery, R.A.

79 Medium Anti-Aircraft Battery — MONTREAL, Quebec
"79 Light Anti-Aircraft Battery, R.C.A." served in Canada during the Second World War. "79 Medium Anti-Aircraft Battery" was disbanded in 1959 as a sub-unit of "51 Medium Anti-Aircraft Regiment, R.C.A. (Militia)".

Affiliated British Unit:
"79 (KIRKEE) Battery, R.A.", which fought at that battle in India in 1817, fought as a sub-unit of "29 Commando Regiment, R.A." in Borneo during the "Confrontation" with Indonesia and in support of "3 Commando Brigade, Royal Marines" in the Falkland Islands during the South Atlantic Campaign (1982).

80 Field Battery — NEW RICHMOND, Quebec
"80 Field Battery, R.C.A.", which served in Canada during the Second World War, was disbanded in 1965 as a sub-unit of "6 Field Regiment, R.C.A. (Militia)".
Affiliated British Unit:
80 Battery, R.A.

81 Field Battery — SHAWINIGAN FALLS, Quebec
"81 Field Battery, R.C.A.", which landed at Normandy and fought in North-West Europe during the Second World War, is presently a sub-unit of "62ieme Regiment d'Artillerie du Canada".
Affiliated British Unit:
82 Battery, R.A.

82 Field Battery — BEAUPORT, Quebec
"82 Anti-Tank Battery, R.C.A." fought in both Italy and North-West Europe during the Second World War. "82 Field Battery" was disbanded in 1970 as a sub-unit of "6 Field Regiment, R.C.A. (Militia)".
Affiliated British Unit:
82 Battery, R.A.

83 Medium Battery — MONTREAL, Quebec
"83 Field Battery, R.C.A." fought in North-West Europe during the Second World War. "83 Medium Battery" was disbanded in 1965 as a sub-unit of "2 Medium Regiment, R.C.A. (Militia)".
Affiliated British Unit:
83 Battery, R.A.

84 (Independent) Field Battery — YARMOUTH, Nova Scotia
"84 Field Battery, R.C.A." served on Kiska in the Aleutian Islands as a unit of the "13th Canadian Infantry Brigade Group" during the Second World War and subsequently recruited a battery for service with the "27th Canadian Infantry Brigade Group" in West Germany. This battery fought in Korea and was re-organized in 1953 as "M" Battery, R.C.H.A. which was disbanded in 1964 as a sub-unit of "4 Regiment, Royal Canadian Horse Artillery (Regular)". "84 Field Battery" was a sub-unit of "14 Field Regiment, R.C.A. (Militia)" until 1970.
Affiliated British Unit:
84 Battery, R.A.

85 Field Battery — LADNER, British Columbia
"85 Battery, C.F.A." served at Vladivostock as a unit of the Canadian Siberian Expeditionary Force (1918-1919). "85 Coast Battery, R.C.A." provided harbour defence for Vancouver during the Second World War. "85 Field Battery" was disbanded in 1970 as a sub-unit of "15 Field Regiment, R.C.A. (Militia)".
Affiliated British Unit:
85 Battery, R.A.

86 Heavy Anti-Aircraft Battery — ANTIGONISH, Nova Scotia
"86 Coast Battery, R.C.A." provided harbour defence for Sydney during the Second World War. "86 Heavy Anti-Aircraft Battery" was disbanded in 1954 as a sub-unit of "16 Heavy Anti-Aircraft Regiment, R.C.A. (Reserve Force).
Affiliated British Unit:
86 Battery, R.A.

87 Field Battery — HALIFAX, Nova Scotia
"87 Medium Battery, R.C.A." fought in North-West Europe during the Second World War. "87 Field Battery" was relocated from Dartmouth in 1970 and is presently a sub-unit of "1 Field Regiment, R.C.A.".
Affiliated British Unit:
87 Battery, R.A.

88 Field Battery — WINDSOR, Nova SCOTIA
The battery was formed in 1936 by the conversion and re-designation of "The King's Canadian Hussars (Non-Permanent Active Militia)". "88 Light Anti-Airraft Battery, R.C.A." fought in both Italy and North-West Europe during the Second World War. "88 Field Battery" was disbanded in 1965 as a sub-unit of "14 Field Regiment, R.C.A. (Militia)".
Affiliated British Unit:
"88 (ARAKAN) Battery, R.A." fought at that battle in Burma in 1945.

89 Field Battery — WOODSTOCK, New Brunswick
"89 Light Anti-Aircraft Battery, R.C.A." fought in both Italy and North-West Europe during the Second World War. The battery was converted in 1944 and re-organized as a sub-unit of the "1st Light Anti-Aircraft Battalion, Canadian Infantry Corps" wich was subsequently re-designated "The Lanark and Renfrew Scottish Regiment". "89 Field Battery" is presently a sub-unit of "3 Field Regiment (The Loyal Company), R.C.A.".
Affiliated British Unit:
89 Battery, R.A.

90 Field Battery — FREDERICTON, New Brunswick
"90 Anti-Tank Battery, R.C.A." fought in both Italy and North-West Europe during the Second World War. "90 Field Battery" was disbanded in 1970 as a sub-unit of "3 Field Regiment (The Loyal Company), R.C.A. (Militia)".
Affiliated British Unit:
90 Battery, R.A.

91 Medium Battery — CALGARY, Alberta
"91 Field Battery, R.C.A." fought in North-West Europe during the Second World War. "91 Medium Battery" was disbanded in 1965 as a sub-unit of "19 Medium Regiment, R.C.A. (Militia)".
Affiliated British Unit:
91 Battery, R.A.

92 Medium Battery, — EDMONTON, Alberta
"92 Field Battery, R.C.A." fought in both Italy and North-West Europe during the Second World War. "92 Medium Battery" was disbanded in 1965 as a sub-unit of "20 Medium Regiment, R.C.A. (Militia)".
Affiliated British Unit:
92 Battery, R.A.

93 Field Battery — Kenyon Field, FORT MACLEOD, Alberta
The battery served in Canada during the Second World War and was disbanded in 1970 as a sub-unit of "18 Field Regiment, R.C.A. (Militia)".
Affiliated British Unit:
"93 (LE CATEAU) Battery, R.A." fought at that battle in 1914 during the withdrawal from Mons in Belgium at the beginning of the Great War.

94 Field Battery — QUEBEC CITY
"94 Anti-Tank Battery, R.C.A." fought in North-West Europe during the Second World War. "94 Field Battery" was disbanded in 1954 as a sub-unit of "13 Field Regiment, R.C.A. (Reserve

Force)''.
Affiliated British Unit:
''94 (NEW ZEALAND) Battery, R.A.'' fought in the Maori Wars of the nineteenth century.

95 Field Battery — Prince of Wales' Armoury, EDMONTON, Alberta
''95 Field Battery, R.C.A.'', which fought in North-West Europe during the Second World War, was disbanded in 1970 as a sub-unit of ''20 Field Regiment, R.C.A. (Militia)''.
Affiliated British Unit:
95 Battery, R.A.

96 Field Battery — Prince of Wales' Armoury, EDMONTON, Alberta
''96 Anti-Tank Battery, R.C.A.'' fought in North-West Europe during the Second World War. ''96 Field Battery'' was disbanded in 1970 as a sub-unit of ''20 Field Regiment, R.C.A. (Militia)''.
Affiliated British Unit:
''96 Battery, R.A.'', a sub-unit of ''33 (Parachute) Field Regiment, R.A.'', landed at Port Said in Egypt in 1956 during the Anglo/French invasion of the Suez Canal Zone.

97 (BRUCE) Field Battery — WALKERTON, Ontario
The battery was formed in 1936 by the conversion and re-designation of ''The Bruce Regiment (Non-Permanent Active Militia)'' which had originated in 1866 as the ''Bruce Battalion of Infantry''. ''97 Field Battery, R.C.A.'', which served in the United Kingdom during the Second World War, was disbanded in 1970 as a sub-unit of ''21 Field Regiment, R.C.A. (Militia)''.
Affiliated British Unit:
''97 Battery, R.A.'', a sub-unit of ''33 (Parachute) Field Regiment, R.A.'', landed at Port Said in Egypt in 1956 during the Anglo/French invasion of the Suez Canal Zone.

98 (HURON) Anti-Tank Battery — GODERICH, Ontario
''98 Anti-Tank Battery, R.C.A.'' fought in both Italy and North-West Europe during the Second World War. The county designation was adopted in 1946 upon the disbandment of ''The Middlesex and Huron Regiment (Non-Permanent Active Militia)'' which had been formed in 1936 by the amalgamation of ''The Middlesex Light Infantry'' and ''The Huron Regiment'', both of which had originated in 1866. The battery was disbanded in 1954 as a sub-unit of ''21 Anti-Tank Regiment, R.C.A. (Reserve Force)''.
Affiliated British Unit:
98 Battery, R.A.

99 Field Battery — WINGHAM, Ontario
The battery was formed in 1936 by the conversion, re-designation and relocation (from Guelph) of ''The Wellington Regiment (Non-Permanent Active Militia)'' which had originated in 1866 as the ''Wellington Battalion of Rifles''. ''99 Field Battery, R.C.A.'', which landed at Normandy and fought in North-West Europe during the Second World War, was disbanded in 1970 as a sub-unit of ''21 Field Regiment, R.C.A. (Militia)''.
Affiliated British Unit:
99 Searchlight Battery, R.A.

100 Field Battery — LISTOWEL, Ontario
The battery was formed in 1936 by the conversion and re-designation of the ''9th Grey's Horse (Non-Permanent Active Militia)'' which had originated in 1908. ''100 Light Anti-Aircraft Battery, R.C.A.'' fought in North-West Europe during the Second World War. ''100 Field Battery'' was disbanded in 1970 as a sub-unit of ''21 Field Regiment, R.C.A. (Militia)''.
Affiliated British Unit:
100 Battery, R.A.

101 Field Battery — MOOSOMIN, Saskatchewan
The battery was formed in 1936 by the conversion and re-designation of ''C'' Company of ''The

Assiniboia Regiment (Non-Permanent Active Militia)" which had originated in 1905 as an element of the "Saskatchewan Rifles". "101 Light Anti-Aircraft Battery, R.C.A." fought in North-West Europe during the Second World War. The battery, a sub-unit of "22 (Assiniboia) Field Regiment, R.C.A. (Reserve Force)", was re-organized in 1954 as a detached troop of "76 Field Battery, R.C.A. (Militia)".
Affiliated British Unit:
101 Battery, R.A.

102 (WENTWORTH) Field Battery — DUNDAS, Ontario
The battery was formed in 1936 by the conversion and re-designation of "D" Company of "The Wentworth (Non-Permanent Active Militia)" which had originated in 1872 as the "Wentworth Battalion of Infantry". (Note that "Headquarters" and "A", "B" and "C" Companies of "The Wentworth Regiment" were amalgamated with "The Royal Hamilton Light Infantry".) "102 Light Anti-Aircraft Battery, R.C.A." fought in North-West Europe during the Second World War. "102 Field Battery" was disbanded in 1970 as a sub-unit of "8 Field Regiment, R.C.A. (Militia)".
Affiliated British Unit:
102 Battery, R.A.

103 Harbour Defence Troop — ST. JOHN'S, Newfoundland
"103 Anti-Tank Battery, R.C.A." fought in North-West Europe during the Second World War and was converted in 1954 and re-organized as a sub-unit of the "East Coast Harbour Defence Battery, R.C.A. (Militia)" which, headquartered at Halifax, maintained detached troops at Saint John (New Brunswick), Sydney (Nova Scotia) and St. John's (Newfoundland). "103 Harbour Defence Troop, R.C.A. (Militia)" was disbanded in 1956.
Affiliated British Unit:
103 Battery, R.A.

104 Field Battery — FREDERICTON, New Brunswick
The battery was formed in 1936 by the conversion and re-designation of "A" Squadron of "The New Brunswick Dragoons (Non-Permanent Active Militia)" which had originated in 1911. "104 Anti-Tank Battery, R.C.A." fought in both Italy and North-West Europe during the Second World War. "104 Field Battery" was disbanded in 1965 as a sub-unit of "3 Field Regiment (The Loyal Company), R.C.A. (Militia)".
Affiliated British Unit:
104 Battery, R.A.

105 Medium Anti-Aircraft Battery — SAINT JOHN, New Brunswick
"105 Field Battery" was formed in 1936 by the conversion and re-designation of "B" Squadron of "The New Brunswick Dragoons (Non-Permanent Active Militia)" which had originated in 1911. "105 Anti-Tank Battery, R.C.A." landed at Normandy and fought in North-West Europe during the Second World War. "105 Medium Anti-Aircraft Battery" was disbanded in 1959 as a sub-unit of "3 Medium Anti-Aircraft Regiment (The Loyal Company), R.C.A. (Militia)".
Affiliated British Unit:
105 Battery, R.A.

106 Field Battery — MONTREAL, Quebec
"106 Coast Battery, R.C.A." provided harbour defence in Newfoundland during the Second World War. "106 Field Battery" was disbanded in 1965 as a sub-unit of "37 Field Regiment, R.C.A. (Militia)".
Affiliated British Unit:
106 Battery, R.A.

107 Medium Anti-Aircraft Battery — CRANBROOK, British Columbia
"107 Field Battery", which was formed in 1936 by the conversion and re-designation of "A"

Company of "The Kootenay Regiment (Non-Permanent Active Militia)", fought in both Italy and North-West Europe during the Second World War. "107 Medium Anti-Aircraft Battery" was disbanded in 1959 as a sub-unit of "24 (Kootenay) Medium Anti-Aircraft Regiment, R.C.A. (Militia)".
Affiliated British Unit:
107 Battery, R.A.

108 Anti-Tank Battery — KIMBERLEY, British Columbia
"108 Field Battery" was formed in 1936 by the conversion and re-designation of "B" Company of "The Kootenay Regiment (Non-Permanent Active Militia)" which had originated in 1914. "108 Anti-Tank Battery, R.C.A." fought in North-West Europe during the Second World War. The battery, a sub-unit of "41 Anti-Tank Regiment, R.C.A. (Reserve Force)", was concerted in 1954 and re-designated "17 Field Squadron, R.C.E. (Militia)".
Affiliated British Unit:
108 Battery, R.A.

109 Field Battery — TRAIL, British Columbia
"109 Field Battery" was formed in 1936 by the conversion and re-designation of "C" Company of "The Kootenay Regiment (Non-Permanent Active Militia)" which had originated in 1914. "109 Light Anti-Aircraft Battery, R.C.A." fought in both Italy and North-West Europe during the Second World War. The battery was converted in 1944 and re-organized as a sub-unit of the "1st Light Anti-Aircraft Battalion, Canadian Infantry Corps" which was subsequently re-designated "The Lanark and Renfrew Scottish Regiment". "109 Field Battery" was disbanded in 1965 as a sub-unit of "24 (Kootenay) Field Regiment, R.C.A. (Militia)".
Affiliated British Unit:
109 Battery, R.A.

110 Field Battery — BROADVIEW, Saskatchewan
The battery was formed in 1936 by the conversion and re-designation of "D" Company of "The Assiniboia Regiment (Non-Permanent Active Militia)" which had originated in 1905 as an element of the "Saskatchewan Rifles". "110 Field Battery, R.C.A.", which fought in North-West Europe during the Second World War, was disbanded in 1954 as a sub-unit of "22 (Assiniboia) Field Regiment, R.C.A. (Reserve Force)".
Affiliated British Unit:
110 Battery, R.A.

111 Field Battery — NELSON, British Columbia
The battery was formed in 1936 by the conversion and re-designation of "D" Company of "The Kootenay Regiment (Non-Permanent Active Militia)" which had originated in 1914. "111 Anti-Tank Battery, R.C.A." fought in both Italy and North-West Europe during the Second World War. "111 Field Battery", a sub-unit of 24 (Kootenay) Field Regiment, R.C.A. (Militia)", was converted in 1965 and re-organized as a detached troop of "44 Field Squadron, R.C.E. (Militia)".
Affiliated British Unit:
111 Battery, R.A.

112 Medium Anti-Aircraft Battery — MONTREAL, Quebec
"112 Light Anti-Aircraft Battery, R.C.A." fought in North-West Europe during the Second World War. "112 Medium Anti-Aircraft Battery" was disbanded in 1959 as a sub-unit of "51 Medium Anti-Aircraft Regiment, R.C.A. (Militia)".
Affiliated British Unit:
112 Battery, R.A.

113 Medium Battery — REGINA, Saskatchewan
"13 Siege Battery, C.G.A.", which served as a depot battery in the United Kingdom during the

Great War, was perpetuated by "13 Medium Battery" of "7 Medium Brigade, Canadian Artillery (Non-Permanent Active Militia)". (Note that "13" in the present battery list was provided by the pre-1939 series of field artillery.) "13 Medium Battery" was re-organized in 1936 and re-designated "113 Field Battery". "113 Anti-Tank Battery, R.C.A." fought in both Italy and North-West Europe during the Second World War. "113 Medium Battery" was disbanded in 1954 as a sub-unit of "10 Medium Regiment, R.C.A. (Reserve Force)".
Affiliated British Unit:
113 Battery, R.A.

114 Light Anti-Aircraft Battery — CHARLOTTETOWN, Prince Edward Island
"14 Siege Battery, C.G.A." was formed in 1920 and subsequently re-organized as "14 Medium Battery" of the "Prince Edward Island Medium Brigade, Canadian Artillery (Non-Permanent Active Militia)". (Note that "14" in the present battery list was provided by the pre-1939 series of field artillery.) "14 Medium Battery" was re-organized in 1946 and re-designated "114 Light Anti-Aircraft Battery" which, as a sub-unit of "28 Light Anti-Aircraft Regiment, R.C.A. (Reserve Force)", was incorporated within "A" Squadron of "The Prince Edward Island Regiment (R.C.A.C.) (Militia)" in 1954.
Affiliated British Unit:
114 Battery, R.A.

115 Field Battery — Barrack Green Armoury, SAINT JOHN, New Brunswick
"15 Siege Battery, C.G.A." was formed in 1920 and subsequently re-organized as "15 Heavy Battery" of "3 (New Brunswick) Coast Brigade (The Loyal Company), R.C.A. (Non-Permanent Active Militia)". (Note that "15" in the present battery list was provided by the pre-1939 series of field artillery.) "15 Heavy Battery" was re-organized in 1946 and re-designated "115 Heavy Anti-Aircraft Battery". This battery was re-organized in 1954 as a field battery which is presently a sub-unit of "3 Field Regiment (The Loyal Company), R.C.A.".
Affiliated British Unit:
115 Battery, R.A.

116 (Independent) Field Battery — KENORA, Ontario
"16 Medium Battery" was formed in 1936 as a sub-unit of "7 Medium Brigade, R.C.A. (Non-Permanent Active Militia)" by the conversion of "The Kenora Light Infantry (Non-Permanent Active Militia)" which had originated in 1908. (Note that "16" in the present battery list was provided by the pre-1939 series of field artillery.) "16 Medium Battery" was re-designated "116 Medium Battery" in 1946 and re-organized in 1965 as a field battery which maintained a detached troop at Fort Francis until 1979 thereby continuing an artillery presence subsequent to the disbandment of "121 Medium Battery, R.C.A. (Militia)".
Affiliated British Unit:
"116 Field Battery, R.A." fought in Korea.

117 Medium Anti-Aircraft Battery — SAINT JOHN, New Brunswick
The battery, which had originated in 1946 as "117 Heavy Anti-Aircraft Battery", was disbanded in 1959 as a sub-unit of "3 Medium Anti-Aircraft Regiment (The Loyal Company), R.C.A. (Militia)".
Affiliated British Unit:
117 Battery, R.A.

118 Medium Battery — PORT ARTHUR (THUNDER BAY), Ontario
"18 Medium Battery" was formed in 1936 as a sub-unit of "7 Medium Brigade, R.C.A. (Non-Permanent Active Militia)". (Note that "18" in the present battery list was provided by the pre-1939 series of field artillery.) "18 Medium Battery, R.C.A." fought in both Italy and North-West Europe during the Second World War. This battery was re-designated "118 Medium Battery" in

1946 and disbanded in 1965 as a sub-unit of "40 Medium Regiment, R.C.A. (Militia)".
Affiliated British Unit:
118 Battery, R.A.

119 Composite Anti-Aircraft Battery (Active Force) — ESQUIMALT (VICTORIA), B.C.
The battery was formed in 1950 and disbanded in 1953.
Affiliated British Unit:
119 Battery, R.A.

120 (Independent) Field Battery — PRINCE RUPERT, British Columbia
"102 (North British Columbia) Heavy Battery, R.C.A." was formed in 1936 by the conversion and re-designation of "The North British Columbia Regiment (Non-Permanent Active Militia)" which, having originated in 1910 as "Earl Grey's Own Rifles", perpetuated the "102nd (North British Columbia) Infantry Battalion, C.E.F." which fought in France during the Great War. (Note that "102" in the present battery list was provided by the pre-1939 series of field artillery.) "102 (North British Columbia) Coast Battery, R.C.A." provided harbour defence for Prince Rupert during the Second World War. This battery was re-designated "120 Coast Battery" in 1946 and re-organized in 1954 as a harbour defence troop which was further re-organized in 1956 as an independent field battery which was converted to infantry in 1958 and re-organized as "D" Company of "The Irish Fusiliers of Canada (Vancouver Regiment), R.C.I.C. (Militia)".
Affiliated British Unit:
"120 Pack Battery, R.A." served in Kurdistan subsequent to the Great War and was later re-organized as a light battery which fought in Korea.

121 Medium Battery — FORT FRANCES, Ontario
The battery was formed in 1946 by the re-designation of "21 Medium Battery" which originated subsequent to the Great War as a sub-unit of "7 Toronto Regiment, Canadian Artillery (Non-Permanent Active Militia)". (Note that "21" in the present battery list was provided by the pre-1939 series of field artillery.) "121 Medium Battery", after relocation from Toronto in 1954, was disbanded in 1965 as a sub-unit of "40 Medium Regiment, R.C.A. (Militia)".
Affiliated British Unit:
121 Battery, R.A.

122 Light Anti-Aircraft Battery — BASSANO, Alberta
The battery was formed in 1946 by the re-organization of "22 Field Battery, R.C.A. (Non-Permanent Active Militia)". (Note that "22" in the present battery list was provided by the pre-1939 series of garrison (coast, medium and anti-aircraft artillery.) "22 Battery, C.F.A." fought in France during the Great War. "22 Field Battery, R.C.A." landed at Normandy and fought in North-West Europe during the Second World War. "122 Light Anti-Aircraft Battery" was disbanded in 1954 as a sub-unit of "68 Light Anti-Aircraft Regiment (15th Alberta Light Horse), R.C.A. (Reserve Force)".
Affiliated British Unit:
122 Battery, R.A.

123 Medium Battery — Falaise Barracks, TORONTO, Ontario
The battery was formed in 1946 by the re-designation of "23 Medium Battery" which originated subsequent to the Great War as a sub-unit of "7 Toronto Regiment, Canadian Artillery (Non-Permanent Active Militia)". (Note that "23" in the present battery list was provided by the pre-1939 series of field artillery.) "23 Medium Battery, R.C.A." fought in both Italy and North-West Europe during the Second World War. "123 Medium Battery" was disbanded in 1965 as a sub-unit of "42 Medium Regiment, R.C.A. (Militia)".
Affiliated British Unit:
123 Battery, R.A.

124 Medium Anti-Aircraft Battery — SAINT JOHN, New Brunswick
The battery, which had originated in 1946 as "124 Heavy Anti-Aircraft Battery", was disbanded in 1959 as a sub-unit of "23 (New Brunswick) Medium Anti-Aircraft Regiment, R.C.A. (Militia)".
Affiliated British Unit:
124 Battery, R.A.

125 Medium Battery — Falaise Barracks, TORONTO, Ontario
The battery was formed in 1946 by the re-designation of "25 Medium Battery" which originated subsequent to the Great War as a sub-unit of "7 Toronto Regiment, Canadian Artillery (non-Permanent Active Militia)". (Note that "25" in the present battery list was provided by the pre-1939 series of field artillery.) "25 Medium Battery, R.C.A." fought in both Italy and North-West Europe during the Second World War. "125 Medium Battery" was disbanded in 1965 as a sub-unit of "42 Medium Regiment, R.C.A. (Militia)".
Affiliated British Unit:
125 Battery, R.A.

126 Medium Anti-Aircraft Battery — QUEBEC CITY
·The battery, which had originated in 1946 as "126 Heavy Anti-Aircraft Battery", was disbanded in 1959 as a sub-unit of "51 Medium Anti-Aircraft Regiment, R.C.A.(Militia)".
Affiliated British Unit:
126 Battery, R.A.

127 Composite A-A Battery (Active Force) — Craig Barracks, CAMP PICTON, Ontario
"127 Anti-Tank Battery, R.C.A. (Active Force)" was formed in 1946 and re-organized in 1950 as a composite anti-aircraft battery which was allocated to "1 Light Anti-Aircraft Regiment, R.C.A. (Regular)" in 1953 as "2 Light Anti-Aircraft Battery". This battery was re-organized in 1960 as "1 Surface-to-Surface Missile Battery, R.C.A. (Regular)" which was disbanded in 1970 at Soest in West Germany.
Affiliated British Unit:
127 Battery, R.A.

128 Air Defence Battery (Regular) — BADEN, West Germany
"128 Heavy Anti-Aircraft Battery, R.C.A. (Active Force)" was formed in 1946 and re-organized in 1950 as a composite anti-aircraft battery which was allocated to "1 Light Anti-Aircraft Regiment, R.C.A. (Regular)" in 1953 as "3 Light Anti-Aircraft Battery". This battery was re-organized in 1960 as "2 Surface-to-Surface Missile (Training) Battery, R.C.A. (Regular)" which was disbanded in 1970 at the Royal Canadian School of Artillery. "128 Air Defence Battery" was formed in 1976 to provide airfield defence for "1 Canadian Air Group" in West Germany.
Affiliated British Unit:
128 Battery, R.A.

129 Air Defence Battery (Regular) — LAHR, West Germany
"129 Light Anti-Aircraft Battery, R.C.A. (Active Force)" was formed in 1946 and re-organized in 1950 as a composite anti-aircraft battery which was allocated to "1 Light Anti-Aircraft Regiment, R.C.A. (Regular)" in 1953 as "4 Light Anti-Aircraft Battery". This battery was disbanded in 1957. "129 Air Defence Battery" was formed in 1976 to provide airfield defence for "1 Canadian Air Group" in West Germany.
Affiliated British Unit:
"129 (DRAGON) Battery, R.A." commemorates artillery service in China during the nineteenth century.

130 Field Battery — Moss Park Armoury, TORONTO, Ontario
The battery was formed in 1946 and is presently a sub-unit of "7 Toronto Regiment, R.C.A.".
Affiliated British Unit:
130 Battery, R.A.

131 Field Battery — LACHUTE, Quebec
The battery, which was disbanded in 1965 as a sub-unit of "37 Field Regiment, R.C.A. (Militia)", had been relocated from Montreal in 1954 thereby continuing a militia presence subsequent to "A" Company of "Le Regiment de Joliette", R.C.I.C. (Militia) being relocated at Joliette.
Affiliated British Unit:
131 Battery, R.A.

132 Anti-Tank Battery — QUEBEC CITY
The battery was disbanded in 1954 as a sub-unit of "35 Anti-Tank Regiment, R.C.A. (Reserve Force)".
Affiliated British Unit:
"132 Battery (The Bengal Rocket Troop), R.A.", which originated in the "Bengal Artillery", is presently a sub-unit of "The Support Regiment, R.A.".

133 Field Battery — LIVERPOOL, Nova Scotia
The battery was disbanded in 1968 as a sub-unit of "14 Field Regiment, R.C.A. (Militia)".
Affiliated British Unit:
133 Battery, R.A.

134 Locating Battery — Falaise Barracks, TORONTO, Ontario
The battery, which had originated in 1946 as "134 Field Battery", was disbanded in 1965 as a sub-unit of "1 Locating Regiment, R.C.A. (Militia)". This regiment perpetuates "1 Survey Regiment, R.C.A." which fought in both Italy and North-West Europe during the Second World War.
Affiliated British Unit:
134 Battery, R.A.

135 Anti-Tank Battery — OWEN SOUND, Ontario
The battery, a sub-unit of "45 Anti-Tank Regiment (The Grey and Simcoe Foresters), R.C.A. (Reserve Force)", was converted to armour in 1954 and re-organized as "A" Squadron of "The Grey and Simcoe Foresters (R.C.A.C.) (Militia)" which maintained detached troops at Durham (County of Grey) and Collingwood (County of Simcoe) until 1965.
Affiliated British Unit:
135 Battery, R.A.

136 Anti-Tank Battery — BARRIE, Ontario
The battery, a sub-unit of "45 Anti-Tank Regiment (The Grey and Simcoe Foresters), R.C.A.(Reserve Force)", was converted to armour in 1954 and re-organized as "B" Squadron of "The Grey and Simcoe Foresters (R.C.A.C.) (Militia)".
Affiliated British Unit:
136 Battery, R.A.

137 Anti-Tank Battery — ORILLIA, Ontario
The battery, a sub-unit of "45 Anti-Tank Regiment (The Grey and Simcoe Foresters), R.C.A. (Reserve Force)", was converted to armour in 1954 and re'organized as "D" Squadron of "The Grey and Simcoe Foresters (R.C.A.C.) (Militia)".
Affiliated British Unit:
"137 (JAVA) Battery, R.A." fought on that island in the Dutch East Indies in 1811 during the Napoleonic Wars.

138 Anti-Tank Battery — MEAFORD, Ontario
The battery was disbanded in 1954 as a sub-unit of "45 Anti-Tank Regiment (The Grey and Simcoe Foresters), R.C.A. (Reserve Force)".
Affiliated British Unit:
138 Battery, R.A.

139 Anti-Tank Battery — VICTORIAVILLE, Quebec
The battery was disbanded in 1954 as a sub-unit of "46 Anti-Tank Regiment, R.C.A. (Reserve Force)".
Affiliated British Unit:
139 Battery, R.A.

140 Anti-Tank Battery — DRUMMONDVILLE, Quebec
The battery was disbanded in 1954 as a sub-unit of "46 Anti-Tank Regiment, R.C.A. (Reserve Force)".
Affiliated British Unit:
140 Battery, R.A.

141 Anti-Tank Battery — SOREL, Quebec
The battery was disbanded in 1954 as a sub-unit of "46 Anti-Tank Regiment, R.C.A. (Reserve Force)".
Affiliated British Unit:
141 Battery, R.A.

142 Anti-Tank Battery — SOREL, Quebec
The battery was disbanded in 1954 as a sub-unit of "46 Anti-Tank Regiment, R.C.A. (Reserve Force)".
Affiliated British Unit:
142 Battery, R.A.

143 Anti-Tank Battery — QUEBEC CITY
The battery was disbanded in 1954 as a sub-unit of "35 Anti-Tank Regiment, R.C.A. (Reserve Force)".
Affiliated British Unit:
"143 Battery (Tombs' Troop), R.A." commemorates the receiving of the Victoria Cross by the battery's commander during the Indian Mutiny (1857-1858).

144 Anti-Tank Battery — LAUZON, Quebec
The battery was disbanded in 1954 as a sub-unit of "35 Anti-Tank Regiment, R.C.A. (Reserve Force)".
Affiliated British Unit:
144 Battery, R.A.

145 Anti-Tank Battery — GASPE, Quebec
The battery was disbanded in 1954 as a sub-unit of "35 Anti-Tank Regiment, R.C.A. (Reserve Force)".
Affiliated British Unit:
"145 (MAIWAND) Battery, R.A.", which fought at that battle in Afghanistan in 1880, fought in Borneo as a sub-unit of "29 Commando Regiment, R.A." during the "Confrontation" with Indonesia. The battery was subsequently removed from the regiment.

146 Anti-Tank Battery — WOLFVILLE, Nov Scotia
The battery was disbanded in 1954 as a sub-unit of "47 Anti-Tank Regiment, R.C.A. (Reserve Force)".
Affiliated British Unit:
146 Battery, R.A.

147 Anti-Tank Battery — WINNIPEG, Manitoba
The battery, which was disbanded in 1954 as a sub-unit of "48 Anti-Tank Regiment, R.C.A. (Reserve Force)", perpetuates the "Machine-Gun Squadron, C.E.F." which fought in France as a unit of the "Canadian Cavalry Brigade" during the Great War.
Affiliated British Unit:
147 Battery, R.A.

148 Field Battery — SAULT STE. MARIE, Ontario
The battery, which originated in 1946 as "148 Heavy Anti-Aircraft Battery", is presently a sub-unit of "49 (Sault Ste. Marie) Field Regiment, R.C.A.".
Affiliated British Unit:
"148 (MEIKTILA) Battery, R.A.", which fought at that battle in Burma in 1945, fought in Borneo as a sub-unit of "95 Commando Regiment, R.A." during the "Confrontation" with Indonesia. The battery was subsequently removed from the regiment and re-organized as "148 (MEIKTILA) Commando Forward Observation Battery, R.A." which fought in support of "3 Commando Brigade, Royal Marines" in the Falkland Islands during the South Atlantic Campaign (1982).

149 Field Battery — PETERBOROUGH, Ontario
The battery, which had originated in 1946 as "149 Heavy Anti-Aircraft Battery", was disbanded in 1970 as a sub-unit of "50 Field Regiment (The Prince of Wales' Rangers), R.C.A. (Militia)".
Affiliated British Unit:
149 Battery, R.A.

150 Field Battery — PETERBOROUGH, Ontario
The battery, which had originated in 1946 as "150 Heavy Anti-Aircraft Battery", was disbanded in 1965 as a sub-unit of "50 Field Regiment (The Prince of Wales' Rangers), R.C.A. (Militia)".
Affiliated British Unit:
150 Anti-Aircraft Fire-Control Battery, R.A.

151 Medium Anti-Aircraft Battery — PETERBOROUGH, Ontario
"151 Heavy Anti-Aircraft Battery" was formed in 1946 by the re-organization of "51 Field Battery, R.C.A. (Non-Permanent Active Militia)". (Note that "51" in the present battery list was provided by the pre-1939 series of garrison (coast, medium and anti-aircraft artillery.) "51 Battery, C.F.A." fought in France during the Great War. "51 Anti-Tank Battery, R.C.A." fought in both Italy and North-West Europe during the Second World War. "151 Medium Anti-Aircraft Battery" was disbanded in 1959 as a sub-unit of "50 Medium Anti-Aircraft Regiment (The Prince of Wales' Rangers), R.C.A. (Militia)".
Affiliated British Unit:
151 Battery, R.A.

"50 Medium Anti-Aircraft Regiment (The Prince of Wales' Rangers), R.C.A. (Militia)" originated in 1946 as "50 Heavy Anti-Aircraft Regiment (The Prince of Wales' Rangers), R.C.A. (Reserve Force)" by the conversion and re-designation of "The Prince of Wales' Rangers (Non-Permanent Active Militia)" which had been formed in 1936 by the amalgamation of the "3rd Prince of Wales' Canadian Dragoons" and "The Peterborough Rangers" which had originated in 1866 as the "Peterborough Battalion of Infantry". The "3rd Prince of Wales' Canadian Dragoons" originated in 1872 as a "provisional" regiment of cavalry which had been formed to administer the previously-independent troops of cavalry in "Military District 3".

3rd Provisional Regiment of Cavalry
"Headquarters" — COBOURG, Ontario
"1" Troop — COBOURG, Ontario
This troop originated in 1856 as the "Volunteer Militia Troop of Cavalry of the County of Northumberland".
"2" Troop — MILLBROOK, Ontario
"3" Troop — PETERBOROUGH, Ontario

152 Medium Anti-Aircraft Battery — SHELBURNE, Nova Scotia
"152 Heavy Anti-Aircraft Battery" was formed in 1946 by the re-organization of "52 Field Battery, R.C.A. (Non-Permanent Active Militia)". (Note that "52" in the present battery list was provided by the pre-1939 series of garrison (coast, medium and anti-aircraft artillery.) "52

Battery, C.F.A." fought in France during the Great War. "52 Anti-Tank Battery, R.C.A." fought in North-West Europe during the Second World War.

"152 Medium Anti-Aircraft Battery" was disbanded in 1959 as a sub-unit of "36 Medium Anti-Aircraft Regiment, R.C.A. (Militia)".

Affiliated British Unit:

"152 (INKERMAN) Battery, R.A." fought at that battle in the Crimea in 1854 during the Anglo/French and Turkish war against the Russians (1854-1856) and was more recently a sub-unit of "21 Locating Regiment, R.A.".

153 Field Battery — SAULT STE. MARIE, Ontario

"153 Heavy Anti-Aircraft Battery" was formed in 1946 by the re-organization of "53 Field Battery, R.C.A. (Non-Permanent Active Militia)". (Note that "53" in the present battery list was provided by the pre-1939 series of garrison (coast, medium and anti-aircraft artillery.) "53 Battery, C.F.A." fought in France during the Great War. "53 Light Anti-Aircraft Battery, R.C.A." served in the United Kingdom during the Second World War. "153 Field Battery" was disbanded in 1970 as a sub-unit of "49 (Sault Ste. Marie) Field Regiment, R.C.A. (Militia)".

Affiliated British Unit:

153 Battery, R.A.

154 Heavy Anti-Aircraft Battery — FLIN FLON, Manitoba

The battery was disbanded in 1954 as a sub-unit of "52 Heavy Anti-Aircraft Regiment, R.C.A. (Reserve Force)".

Affiliated British Unit:

154 Battery, R.A.

155 Heavy Anti-Aircraft Battery — VICTORIA, British Columbia

The battery originated in 1883 as a company of "The British Columbia Regiment of Garrison Artillery" and was re-organized subsequent to the Great War as "55 Heavy Battery" of "5 (British Columbia) Coast Brigade, Canadian Artillery (Non-Permanent Active Militia)". (Note that "55" in the present battery list was provided by the pre-1939 series of field artillery.) "55 Coast Battery, R.C.A.", which provided harbour defence for Victoria during the Second World War, was re-designated "155 Heavy Anti-Aircraft Battery" in 1946. This battery, a sub-unit of "5 Heavy Anti-Aircraft Regiment, R.C.A. (Reserve Force)", was re-organized in 1954 as a troop of "5 (West Coast) Harbour Defence Battery, R.C.A. (Militia)". The harbour defence battery was re-organized in 1956 as an independent medium battery which was further re-organized in 1965 and re-designated "5 (Independent) Field Battery, R.C.A. (Militia)".

Affiliated British Unit:

"155 Field Battery, R.A." fought at Sidi Nsir in the western desert of Egypt in 1941 during the North African campaign.

156 Heavy Anti-Aircraft Battery — VICTORIA, British Columbia

The battery originated in 1883 as a company of "The British Columbia Regiment of Garrison Artillery" and was re-organized subsequent to the Great War as "56 Heavy Battery" of "5 (British Columbia) Coast Brigade, Canadian Artillery (Non-Permanent Active Militia)". (Note that "56" in the present battery list was provided by the pre-1939 series of field artillery.) "56 Coast Battery, R.C.A., which provided harbour defence for Victoria during the Second World War, was re-designated "156 Heavy Anti-Aircraft Battery" in 1946. This battery, a sub-unit of "5 Heavy Anti-Aircraft Regiment, R.C.A. (Reserve Force)", was re-organized in 1954 as a troop of "5 (West Coast) Harbour Defence Battery, R.C.A. (Militia)". The harbour defence battery was re-organized in 1956 as an independent medium battery which was further re-organized in 1965 and re-designated "5 (Independent) Field Battery, R.C.A. (Militia)".

Affiliated British Unit:

"156 (INKERMAN) Battery, R.A." fought at that battle in the Crimea in 1854 during the Anglo/French and Turkish war against the Russians (1854-1856) and was more recently a sub-unit of "21 Locating Regiment, R.A.".

157 Heavy Anti-Aircraft Battery — DAUPHIN, Manitoba
The battery was disbanded in 1954 as a sub-unit of "52 Heavy Anti-Aircraft Regiment, R.C.A. (Reserve Force)".
Affiliated British Unit:
157 Battery, R.A.

158 Field Battery — VANCOUVER, British Columbia
"158 Heavy Anti-Aircraft Battery" was formed in 1946 by the re-organization of "58 Field Battery, R.C.A. (Non-Permanent Active Militia)". (Note that "58" in the present battery list was provided by the pre-1939 series of garrison (coast, medium and anti-aircraft artillery.) "58 Battery, C.F.A." fought in France during the Great War. "158 Field Battery" was disbanded in 1968 as a sub-unit of "15 Field Regiment, R.C.A. (Militia)".
Affiliated British Unit:
158 Battery, R.A.

159 Heavy Anti-Aircraft Battery — BRANDON, Manitoba
The battery was formed in 1946 by the re-organization of "59 Field Battery, R.C.A. (Non-Permanent Active Militia)". (Note that "59" in the present battery list was provided by the pre-1939 series of garrison (coast, medium and anti-aircraft artillery.) "159 Heavy Anti-Aircraft Battery" was disbanded in 1954 as a sub-unit of "52 Heavy Anti-Aircraft Regiment, R.C.A. (Reserve Force)".
Affiliated British Unit:
"159 (COLENSO) Battery, R.A." fought at that battle in 1900 during the South African War.

160 Heavy Anti-Aircraft Battery — VANCOUVER, British Columbia
The battery originated in 1883 as a company of "The British Columbia Regiment of Garrison Artillery" and was re-organized subsequent to the Great War as "60 Heavy Battery" of "5 (British Columbia) Coast Brigade, Canadian Artillery (Non-Permanent Active Militia)". (Note that "60" in the present battery list was provided by the pre-1939 series of field artillery.) "60 Coast Battery, R.C.A.", which provided harbour defence for Vancouver during the Second World War, was re-designated "160 Heavy Anti-Aircraft Battery" in 1946. This battery was disbanded in 1954 as a sub-unit of "5 Heavy Anti-Aircraft Regiment, R.C.A. (Reserve Force)".
Affiliated British Unit:
"160 (Middleton's) Battery. R.A." commemorates the battery's commander during the Indian Mutiny (1857-1858).

161 Heavy Anti-Aircraft Battery — SHERRIDON, Manitoba
The battery was disbanded in 1954 as a sub-unit of "53 Heavy Anti-Aircraft Regiment, R.C.A. (Reserve Force)".
Affiliated British Unit:
161 Battery, R.A.

162 Field Battery — MELVILLE, Saskatchewan
The battery, which originated in 1946 as "162 Heavy Anti-Aircraft Battery", was disbanded in 1965 as a sub-unit of "53 Field Regiment, R.C.A. (Militia)".
Affiliated British Unit:
162 Battery, R.A.

163 Light Anti-Aircraft Battery — KITCHENER, Ontario
The battery, a sub-unit of "54 Light Anti-Aircraft Regiment (The Scots Fusiliers of Canada), R.C.A. (Militia)", was converted to infantry in 1959 and re-organized as "A" Company of "The Scots Fusiliers of Canada, R.C.I.C. (Militia)".
Affiliated British Unit:
163 Battery, R.A.

164 Light Anti-Aircraft Battery — KITCHENER, Ontario
The battery, a sub-unit of "54 Light Anti-Aircraft Regiment (The Scots Fusiliers of Canada), R.C.A. (Militia)", was converted to infantry in 1959 and re-organized as "B" Company of "The Scots Fusiliers of Canada, R.C.I.C. (Militia)".
Affiliated British Unit:
164 Battery, R.A.

165 Light Anti-Aircraft Battery — KITCHENER, Ontario
The battery, a sub-unit of "54 Light Anti-Aircraft Regiment (The Scots Fusiliers of Canada), R.C.A. (Militia)", was converted to infantry in 1959 and re-organized as "C" Company of "The Scots Fusiliers of Canada, R.C.I.C. (Militia)".
Affiliated British Unit:
165 Battery, R.A.

166 Light Anti-Aircraft Battery — WINDSOR, Ontario
The battery was disbanded in 1954 as a sub-unit of "55 Light Anti-Aircraft Regiment, R.C.A. (Reserve Force)".
Affiliated British Unit:
"166 Amphibious Observation Battery, R.A." landed at Port Said in Egypt in 1956 during the Anglo/French invasion of the Suez Canal Zone.

167 Light Anti-Aircraft Battery — WINDSOR, Ontario
The battery was disbanded in 1954 as a sub-unit of "55 Light Anti-Aircraft Regiment, R.C.A. (Reserve Force)".
Affiliated British Unit:
167 Battery, R.A.

168 Light Anti-Aircraft Battery — WINDSOR, Ontario
The battery was disbanded in 1954 as a sub-unit of "55 Light Anti-Aircraft Regiment, R.C.A. (Reserve Force)".
Affiliated British Unit:
168 Battery, R.A.

169 Field Battery — BRANTFORD, Ontario
The battery, which had originated in 1946 as "169 Light Anti-Aircraft Battery", was relocated from Paris in 1965 and disbanded in 1970 as a sub-unit of "56 Field Regiment (The Dufferin and Haldimand Rifles of Canada), R.C.A. (Militia)".
Affiliated British Unit:
169 Battery, R.A.

"56 Field Regiment (The Dufferin and Haldimand Rifles of Canada), R.C.A. (Militia)" was formed in 1954 by the amalgamation of "25 (Norfolk) Medium Regiment, R.C.A. (Reserve Force)" and "56 Light Anti-Aircraft Regiment (The Dufferin and Haldimand Rifles of Canada), R.C.A. (Reserve Force)" which, having been formed in 1946 by the conversion and re-designation of "The Dufferin and Haldimand Rifles of Canada (Non-Permanent Active Militia)", had originated in 1866 as the "Brant Battalion of Infantry".

170 Field Battery — WELLAND, Ontario
The battery, which had originated in 1946 as "170 Light Anti-Aircraft Battery", was disbanded in 1965 as a sub-unit of "57 Field Regiment (2nd/10th Dragoons), R.C.A. (Militia)".
Affiliated British Unit:
"170 (IMJIN) Light Battery, R.A." fought at that battle in 1951 during the Korean War. The battery subsequently served in Malaya during the "Emergency" and on the Arabian Peninsula prior to the withdrawal from "East of Suez". "170 (IMJIN) Medium Battery, R.A." has since served in Northern Ireland.

171 Field Battery — FORT ERIE, Ontario
The battery, which had originated in 1946 as "171 Light Anti-Aircraft Battery", was disbanded in 1970 as a sub-unit of "57 Field Regiment (2nd/10th Dragoons), R.C.A. (Militia)".
Affiliated British Unit:
"171 (The Broken-Wheel) Battery, R.A.", which fought at Tel-el-Kebir in 1882 during the Egyptian Campaign, is presently a sub-unit of "32 Guided-Weapons Regiment, R.A.".

172 Field Battery — NIAGARA FALLS, Ontario
The battery, which had originated in 1946 as "172 Light Anti-Aircraft Battery", was disbanded in 1970 as a sub-unit of "57 Field Regiment (2nd/10th Dragoons), R.C.A. (Militia)".
Affiliated British Unit:
172 Battery, R.A.

"57 Field Regiment (2nd/10th Dragoons), R.C.A. (Militia)" originated in 1946 as "57 Light Anti-Aircraft Regiment (2nd/10th Dragoons), R.C.A. (Reserve Force)" by the conversion and re-designation of the "2nd/10th Dragoons (Non-Permanent Active Militia)" which, having originated in 1855 as the "Volunteer Militia Troop of Cavalry of St. Catharines", may be considered as perpetuating the "Provincial Dragoons" which served on the lines of communication between Montreal and the Niagara frontier during the Anglo-American War of 1812 to 1814.

173 Field Battery — SUDBURY, Ontario
The battery, a sub-unit of "58 (Sudbury) Field Regiment, R.C.A. (Militia)", originated in 1946 as "173 Light Anti-Aircraft Battery" and was converted to infantry in 1965 and re-organized as "A" Company of "2nd Battalion, The Irish Regiment of Canada, R.C.I.C. (Militia)".
Affiliated British Unit:
173 Battery, R.A.

174 Field Battery — SUDBURY, Ontario
The battery, a sub-unit of "58 (Sudbury) Field Regiment, R.C.A. (Militia)", originated in 1946 as "174 Light Anti-Aircraft Battery" and was converted to infantry in 1965 and re-organized as "B" Company of "2nd Battalion, The Irish Regiment of Canada, R.C.I.C. (Militia)".
Affiliated British Unit:
175 Battery, R.A.

175 Field Battery — SUDBURY, Ontario
The battery, a sub-unit of "58 (Sudbury) Field Regiment, R.C.A. (Militia)", originated in 1946 as "175 Light Anti-Aircraft Battery" and was converted to infantry in 1965 and re-organized as "C" Company of "2nd Battalion, The Irish Regiment of Canada, R.C.I.C. (Militia)".
Affiliated British Unit:
175 Battery, R.A.

176 Light Anti-Aircraft Battery — PERTH, Ontario
The battery (a sub-unit of "59 Light Anti-Aircraft Regiment (The Lanark and Renfrew Scottish Regiment), R.C.A. (Militia)"), which maintained detached troops at Carleton Place and Smith's Falls, was converted to infantry in 1959 and re-organized as "C" (Carleton Place) and "D" (Perth) Companies of "The Lanark and Renfrew Scottish Regiment, R.C.I.C. (Militia)".
Affiliated British Unit:
"176 (ABU KLEA) Battery, R.A.", which fought at that battle in Egypt in 1885, is presently a sub-unit of "The Support Regiment, R.A.".

177 Light Anti-Aircraft Battery — PEMBROKE, Ontario
The battery, a sub unit of "59 Light Anti-Aircraft Regiment (The Lanark and Renfrew Scottish Regiment), R.C.A. (Militia)", was converted to infantry in 1959 and re-organized as "B" Company of "The Lanark and Renfrew Scottish Regiment, R.C.I.C. (Militia)".
Affiliated British Unit:
177 Battery, R.A.

178 Light Anti-Aircraft Battery — RENFREW, Ontario
The battery, a sub-unit of "59 Light Anti-Aircraft Regiment (The Lanark and Renfrew Scottish Regiment), R.C.A. (Militia)", was converted to infantry in 1959 and re-organized as "A" Company of "The Lanark and Renfrew Scottish Regiment, R.C.I.C. (Militia)".
Affiliated British Unit:
178 Battery, R.A.

179 Light Anti-Aircraft Battery — BROCKVILLE, Ontario
The battery was disbanded in 1954 as a sub-unit of "60 Light Anti-Aircraft Regiment (The Brockville Rifles), R.C.A. (Reserve Force)".
Affiliated British Unit:
179 Battery, R.A.

180 Light Anti-Aircraft Battery — PRESCOTT, Ontario
The battery, which maintained a detached troop at Cardinal, was disbanded in 1954 as a sub-unit of "60 Light Anti-Aircraft Regiment (The Brockville Rifles), R.C.A. (Reserve Force)".
Affiliated British Unit:
180 Battery, R.A,

181 Light Anti-Aircraft Battery — KEMPTVILLE, Ontario
The battery, which maintained a detached troop at Merrickville, was disbanded in 1954 as a sub-unit of "60 Light Anti-Aircraft Regiment (The Brockville Rifles), R.C.A. (Reserve Force)".
Affiliated British Unit:
181 Battery, R.A.

182 Light Anti-Aircraft Battery — VERDUN (MONTREAL), Quebec
The battery was disbanded in 1959 as a sub-unit of "61 Light Anti-Aircraft Regiment, R.C.A. (Militia)".
Affiliated British Unit:
182 Battery, R.A.

183 Light Anti-Aircraft Battery — ST-LAMBERT (MONTREAL), Quebec
The battery was disbanded in 1959 as a sub-unit of "61 Light Anti-Aircraft Regiment, R.C.A. (Militia)".
Affiliated British Unit:
183 Battery, R.A.

184 Light Anti-Aircraft Battery — ST-LAMBERT (MONTREAL), Quebec
The battery was disbanded in 1959 as a sub-unit of "61 Light Anti-Aircraft Regiment, R.C.A. (Militia)".
Affiliated British Unit:
184 Battery, R.A.

185 Field Battery — SHAWINIGAN FALLS, Quebec
The battery, which originated in 1946 as "185 Light Anti-Aircraft Battery", is presently a sub-unit of "62ieme Regiment d'Artillerie du Canada".
Affiliated British Unit:
185 Battery, R.A.

186 Light Anti-Aircraft Battery — GRAN'MERE, Quebec
The battery was disbanded in 1959 as a sub-unit of "62 Light Anti-Aircraft Regiment, R.C.A. (Militia)".
Affiliated British Unit:
186 Battery, R.A.

187 Field Battery — ARVIDA, Quebec
The battery, which had originated in 1946 as "187 Light Anti-Aircraft Battery", was disbanded in 1965 as a sub-unit of "6 Field Regiment, R.C.A. (Militia)".
Affiliated British Unit:
"187 Light Anti-Aircraft Battery, R.A." served on the Arabian Peninsula prior to the withdrawal from "East of Suez".

188 Light Anti-Aircraft Battery — ARVIDA, Quebec
The battery was disbanded in 1954 as a sub-unit of "63 Light Anti-Aircraft Regiment, R.C.A. (Reserve Force)".
Affiliated British Unit:
"188 (ANTRIM) Heavy Battery, R.A." provided coast defence at various sites in Northern Ireland during the Second World War.

189 Light Anti-Aircraft Battery — STELLARTON, Nova Scotia
The battery, a sub-unit of "28 Light Anti-Aircraft Regiment, R.C.A. (Reserve Force)", was incorporated within "1st Battalion, The Nova Scotia Highlanders, R.C.I.C. (Militia)" in 1954.
Affiliated British Unit:
189 Battery, R.A.

190 Light Anti-Aircraft Battery — MONCTON, New Brunswick
The battery was disbanded in 1959 as a sub-unit of "64 (New Brunswick) Light Anti-Aircraft Regiment, R.C.A. (Militia)".
Affiliated British Unit:
190 Battery, R.A.

191 Light Anti-Aircraft Battery — SHEDIAC, New Brunswick
The battery was disbanded in 1959 as a sub-unit of "64 (New Brunswick) Light Anti-Aircraft Regiment, R.C.A. (Militia)".
Affiliated British Unit:
191 Battery, R.A.

192 Light Anti-Aircraft Battery — REXTON, New Brunswick
The battery was disbanded in 1959 as a sub-unit of "64 (New Brunswick) Light Anti-Aircraft Regiment, R.C.A. (Militia)".
Affiliated British Unit:
192 Battery, R.A.

"64 (New Brunswick) Light Anti-Aircraft Regiment, R.C.A. (Militia)" originated in 1946 as "64 (New Brunswick) Light Anti-Aircraft Regiment, R.C.A. (Reserve Force)" by the conversion and re-designation of "The New Brunswick Regiment (Tank) (Non-Permanent Active Militia)" which had been formed in 1936.

193 Light Anti-Aircraft Battery — VANCOUVER, British Columbia
The battery, a sub-unit of "65 Light Anti-Aircraft Regiment (The Irish Fusiliers of Canada), R.C.A. (Militia)", was converted to infantry in 1958 and re-organized as "A" Company of "The Irish Fusiliers of Canada (Vancouver Regiment), R.C.I.C. (Militia)".
Affiliated British Unit:
193 Battery, R.A.

194 Light Anti-Aircraft Battery — VANCOUVER, British Columbia
The battery, a sub-unit of "65 Light Anti-Aircraft Regiment (The Irish Fusiliers of Canada), R.C.A. (Militia)", was converted to infantry in 1958 and re-organized as "B" Company of "The Irish Fusiliers of Canada (Vancouver Regiment), R.C.I.C. (Militia)".
Affiliated British Unit:
194 Battery, R.A.

195 Light Anti-Aircraft Battery — VANCOUVER, British Columbia
The battery, a sub-unit of "65 Light Anti-Aircraft Regiment (The Irish Fusiliers of Canada), R.C.A. (Militia)", was converted to infantry in 1958 and re-organized as "C" Company of "The Irish Fusiliers of Canada (Vancouver Regiment), R.C.I.C. (Militia)".
Affiliated British Unit:
195 Battery, R.A.

196 Light Anti-Aircraft Battery — NANAIMO, British Columbia
The battery, a sub-unit of "66 Light Anti-Aircraft Regiment (2nd Battalion, The Canadian Scottish Regiment), R.C.A. (Reserve Force)", was converted to infantry in 1954 and re-organized as "B" Company of "The Canadian Scottish Regiment, R.C.I.C. (Militia)".
Affiliated British Unit:
196 Battery, R.A.

197 Light Anti-Aircraft Battery — PORT ALBERNI, British Columbia
The battery, a sub-unit of "66 Light Anti-Aircraft Regiment (2nd Battalion, The Canadian Scottish Regiment), R.C.A. (Reserve Force)", was converted to infantry in 1954 and re-organized as "D" Company of "The Canadian Scottish Regiment, R.C.I.C. (Militia)".
Affiliated British Unit:
197 Battery, R.A.

198 Light Anti-Aircraft Battery — DUNCAN, British Columbia
The battery was disbanded in 1954 as a sub-unit of "66 Light Anti-Aircraft Regiment (2nd Battalion, The Canadian Scottish Regiment), R.C.A. (Reserve Force)".
Affiliated British Unit:
198 Battery, R.A.

199 Light Anti-Aircraft Battery — CARMAN, Manitoba
The battery was disbanded in 1954 as a sub-unit of "67 Light Anti-Aircraft Regiment (The Manitoba Mounted Rifles), R.C.A. (Reserve Force)".
Affiliated British Unit:
199 Battery, R.A.

200 Light Anti-Aircraft Battery — MANITOU, Manitoba
The battery, which had been formed in 1946 by the conversion and re-designation of "The Manitoba Mounted Rifles (Non-Permanent Active Militia)", was disbanded in 1954 as a sub-unit of "67 Light Anti-Aircraft Regiment (The Manitoba Mounted Rifles), R.C.A. (Reserve Force)".
Affiliated British Unit:
200 (SUSSEX YEOMANRY) Field Battery, R.A. (Volunteers).

201 Field Battery — EASTERN PASSAGE (DARTMOUTH), Nova Scotia
The battery, which had originated in 1946 as "201 Heavy Anti-Aircraft Battery", was disbanded in 1965 as a sub-unit of "1 Field Regiment, R.C.A. (Militia)".
Affiliated British Unit:
201 (BEDFORDSHIRE and HERTFORDSHIRE YEOMANRY) Field Battery, R.A. (V)

202 Field Battery — YORKTON, Saskatchewan
The battery, which had originated in 1946 as "202 Heavy Anti-Aircraft Battery", maintained a detached troop at Canora and was disbanded in 1965 as a sub-unit of "53 Field Regiment, R.C.A. (Militia)".
Affiliated British Unit:
202 (NORFOLK and SUFFOLK YEOMANRY) Field Battery, R.A. (Volunteers)

203 Light Anti-Aircraft Battery — QUEBEC CITY
The battery was disbanded in 1954 as a sub-unit of "63 Light Anti-Aircraft Regiment, R.C.A. (Reserve Force)".
Affiliated British Unit:
203 (1st DURHAM) Field Battery, R.A. (Volunteers)

204 Light Anti-Aircraft Battery — MONTAGUE, Prince Edward Island
The battery was formed in 1946 by the amalgamation of "2 Medium Battery, R.C.A." and "8 Medium Battery, R.C.A.", both sub-units of the "Prince Edward Island Medium Brigade, R.C.A. (Non-Permanent Active Militia)" which had originated in 1882 as the "Prince Edward Island Brigade of Garrison Artillery". (Note that both "2" and "8" in the present battery list were provided by the pre-1939 series of field artillery.) "2 Medium Battery, R.C.A." fought in both Italy and North-West Europe during the Second World War. "8 Heavy Anti-Aircraft Battery, R.C.A." fought in North-West Europe during the Second World War. "204 Light Anti-Aircraft Battery", a sub-unit of "28 Light Anti-Aircraft Regiment, R.C.A. (Reserve Force)", was incorporated within "B" Squadron of "The Prince Edward Island Regiment (R.C.A.C.) (Militia)" in 1954.
Affiliated British Unit:
204 (TYNESIDE SCOTTISH) Field Battery, R.A. (Volunteers)

205 Medium Anti-Aircraft Battery — SYDNEY, Nova Scotia
The battery, which had originated in 1946 as "205 Heavy Anti-Aircraft Battery", was disbanded in 1959 as a sub-unit of "36 Medium Anti-Aircraft Regiment, R.C.A. (Militia)".
Affiliated British Unit:
205 (3rd DURHAM) Field Battery, R.A. (Volunteers)

206 Medium Anti-Aircraft Battery — GLACE BAY, Nova Scotia
The battery, which had originated in 1946 as "206 Heavy Anti-Aircraft Battery", was disbanded in 1959 as a sub-unit of "36 Medium Anti-Aircraft Regiment, R.C.A. (Militia)".
Affiliated British Unit:
206 (ULSTER) Air Defence Battery, R.A. (Volunteers)

207 Light Anti-Aircraft Battery — CALGARY, Alberta
The battery was disbanded in 1954 as a sub-unit of "68 Light Anti-Aircraft Regiment (15th Alberta Light Horse), R.C.A. (Reserve Force)".
Affiliated British Unit:
207 (LOWLAND) Air Defence Battery, R.A. (Volunteers)

208 Locating Battery — Falaise Barracks, TORONTO, Ontario
The battery, which had originated in 1946 as "208 Field Battery", was disbanded in 1965 as a sub-unit of "1 Locating Regiment, R.C.A. (Militia)". This regiment perpetuates "1 Survey Regiment, R.C.A." which fought in both Italy and North-West Europe during the Second World War.
Affiliated British Unit:
208 (3rd WEST LANCASHIRE) Air Defence Battery, R.A. (Volunteers)

209 Field Battery — VANCOUVER, British Columbia
The battery, which had originated in 1946 as "209 Heavy Anti-Aircraft Battery", was disbanded in 1965 as a sub-unit of "15 Field Regiment, R.C.A. (Militia)".
Affiliated British Unit:
209 Air Defence Battery, R.A. (Volunteers)

210 Field Battery — VANCOUVER, British Columbia
The battery, which had originated in 1946 as "210 Heavy Anti-Aircraft Battery", was disbanded in 1965 as a sub-unit of "15 Field Regiment, R.C.A. (Militia)".
Affiliated British Unit:
210 (STAFFORDSHIRE) Air Defence Battery, R.A. (Volunteers)

211 Medium Anti-Aircraft Battery — VANCOUVER, British Columbia
The battery, which had originated in 1946 as "211 Heavy Anti-Aircraft Battery", was disbanded in 1959 as a sub-unit of "43 Medium Anti-Aircraft Regiment, R.C.A. (Militia)".
Affiliated British Unit:
211 (SOUTH WALES) Air Defence Battery, R.A. (Volunteers)

212 Light Anti-Aircraft Battery — CALGARY, Alberta
The battery was disbanded in 1954 as a sub-unit of "68 Light Anti-Aircraft Regiment (15th Alberta Light Horse), R.C.A. (Reserve Force)".
Affiliated British Unit:
212 (HIGHLAND) Air Defence Battery, R.A. (Volunteers)

213 Field Battery — Buckmaster's Field, ST. JOHN'S, Newfoundland
The battery, which had been formed in 1949 as a sub-unit of "166 (Newfoundland) Field Regiment, R.C.A. (Reserve Force)", was incorporated within "Headquarters" of "The Royal Newfoundland Regiment, R.C.I.C. (Militia)" in 1961 as the "Saluting Battery".
Affiliated British Unit:
213 Air Defence Battery, R.A. (Volunteers)

214 Field Battery — BELL ISLAND, Newfoundland
The battery, which had been formed in 1949 as a sub-unit of "166 (Newfoundland) Field Regiment, R.C.A. (Reserve Force)", was incorporated within "C" Company of "The Royal Newfoundland Regiment, R.C.I.C. (Militia)" in 1961.
Affiliated British Unit:
214 Air Defence Battery, R.A. (Volunteers)

215 Field Battery — Gallipoli Armoury, CORNER BROOK, Newfoundland
The battery, which had been formed in 1949 as a sub-unit of "166 (Newfoundland) Field Regiment, R.C.A. (Reserve Force)", was incorporated within "A" Company of "The Royal Newfoundland Regiment, R.C.I.C. (Militia)" in 1961.

"166 (Newfoundland) Field Regiment, R.A." fought in both North Africa and Italy as a unit of the British 8th Army during the Second World War and may be considered as having been perpetuated by "166 (Newfoundland) Field Regiment, R.C.A. (Militia)" which, having been formed in 1949 upon the entry into confederation of the former British colony of Newfoundland, was disbanded in 1961.

"1 Air Observation Post Squadron, Royal Canadian Artillery", which had been formed in England in 1944, was re-organized as a unit of the Royal Canadian Air Force and re-designated "664 Air Observation Post Squadron, R.C.A.F.". The squadron flew operationally as a unit of "First Canadian Army" in North-West Europe during the Second World War and was disbanded in 1946.

"2 Air Observation Post Squadron, Royal Canadian Artillery", which had been formed in England in 1945, was re-organized as a unit of the Royal Canadian Air Force and re-designated "665 Air Observation Post Squadron, R.C.A.F.". The squadron flew operationally as a unit of "First Canadian Army" in North-West Europe during the Second World War and was disbanded in 1945.

"3 Air Observation Post Squadron, Royal Canadian Artillery", which had been formed in England in 1945, was re-organized as a unit of the Royal Canadian Air Force and re-designated "666 Air Observation Post Squadron, R.C.A.F." The squadron served in North-West Europe after the cessation of hostilities and was disbanded in 1945.

"1 Air Observation Post Flight, R.C.A. (Regular)" was formed in 1953 and disbanded in 1961 at Camp Petawawa, Ontario.

"2 Air Observation Post Flight, R.C.A. (Regular)" was formed in 1954 and disbanded in 1961 at Camp Shilo, Manitoba.

THE ROYAL CANADIAN HORSE ARTILLERY

Regimental Gallop-Past: *"BONNIE DUNDEE"*
Regimental Trot-Past: *"THE KEEL ROW"*
Regimental Mottoes: *"UBIQUE"* / *("EVERYWHERE")*
   "QUO FAS ET GLORIA DUCUNT"
   ("WHITHER RIGHT AND GLORY LEAD")

NOTE
Like-designated British batteries, although not officially affiliated, have been linked with their Canadian counterparts.

"A" Battery — LAHR, West Germany

The battery was formed in 1871 at Kingston as a permanent "Battery of Garrison Artillery" to "maintain warlike stores". "A" Battery fought in France as a sub-unit of the "Royal Canadian Horse Artillery Brigade" during the Great War and in both Italy and North-West Europe as a sub-unit of the "1st Field Regiment, R.C.H.A." during the Second World War. The battery fought in Korea and is presently a sub-unit of "1 Regiment, R.C.H.A." which is a unit of "4 Canadian Mechanized Brigade Group".

Affiliated British Unit:

"A" Battery (The Chestnut Troop), R.H.A., the honour-title of which commemorates the markings of the original horses, originated in 1793 and fought at Waterloo in 1815 during the Napoleonic Wars and in South Africa during the "Boer" War. The battery, which served in Mesopotamia subsequent to the Great War and fought in North Africa during the Second World War, is presently a sub-unit of "1 Regiment, R.H.A." which fought on the Arabian Peninsula during the withdrawal from "East of Suez".

"B" Battery — LAHR, West Germany

The battery was formed in 1871 at Quebec City as a permanent "Battery of Garrison Artillery" to "maintain warlike stores". "B" Battery fought in France as a sub-unit of the "Royal Canadian Horse Artillery Brigade" during the Great War and in both Italy and North-West Europe as a sub-unit of the "1st Field Regiment, R.C.H.A." during the Second World War. The battery fought in Korea and is presently a sub-unit of "1 Regiment, R.C.H.A." which is a unit of "4 Canadian Mechanized Brigade Group".

Affiliated British Unit:

"B" Battery, R.H.A. originated in 1793 and fought in Spain during the Napoleonic Wars and in the Crimea during the Anglo/French and Turkish war against the Russians (1854-1856). The battery, which served in Egypt subsequent to the Great War and fought in the withdrawal to Dunkirk during the Second World War, is presently a sub-unit of "1 Regiment, R.H.A." which fought on the Arabian Peninsula during the withdrawal from "East of Suez".

"C" Battery — LAHR, West Germany

The battery was formed in 1887 at Victoria, British Columbia. "C" Battery, R.C.F.A. fought in South Africa during the "Boer" War. "C" Battery, which served as a "depot battery" at Tete-de-Pont Barracks in Kingston during the Great War, fought in both Italy and North-West Europe as a sub-unit of the "1st Field Regiment, R.C.H.A." during the Second World War. The battery fought in Korea and is presently a sub-unit of "1 Regiment, R.C.H.A." which is a unit of "4 Canadian Mechanized Brigade Group".

Affiliated British Unit:

"C" Battery, R.H.A. originated in 1793 and fought in Spain during the Napoleonic Wars and in the Crimea during the Anglo/French and Turkish war against the Russians (1854-1856). The battery, which fought in the withdrawal from Mons in Belgium at the beginning of the Great War and in North Africa during the Second World War, is presently deployed as an anti-tank unit in the "British Army of the Rhine"

"D" Battery — CAMP PETAWAWA, Ontario

"D" Battery, R.C.F.A. fought in South Africa during the "Boer" War. "D" Battery, R.C.H.A., which was formed in 1951, fought in Korea and is presently a sub-unit of "2 Regiment, R.C.H.A." which is a unit of the "Special Service Force".

Affiliated British Unit:

"D" Battery, R.H.A. originated in 1794 and fought in Spain and at Waterloo during the Napoleonic Wars and in India during the Mutiny (1857-1858). The battery, which fought in the withdrawal from Mons in Belgium at the beginning of the Great War and in North Africa during the Second World War, is presently deployed as an anti-tank unit in the "British Army of the Rhine".

"E" (Parachute) Battery — CAMP PETAWAWA, Ontario
"E" Battery, R.C.A.F. fought in South Africa during the "Boer" War. "E" Battery, R.C.H.A., which was formed in 1951, fought in Korea and, while receiving its' parachute role in 1977, is presently a sub-unit of "2 Regiment, R.C.H.A." which is a unit of the "Special Service Force".
Affiliated British Unit:
"E" Battery, R.H.A. originated in 1794 and fought in Spain and at Waterloo during the Napoleonic Wars and in India during the Mutiny (1857-1858). The battery, which fought in the withdrawal from Mons in Belgium at the beginning of the Great War and in North Africa during the Second World War, is presently a sub-unit of "1 Regiment, R.H.A." which fought on the Arabian Peninsula during the withdrawal from "East of Suez".

"F" Battery — Brownfield Barracks, CAMP GAGETOWN, New Brunswick
"F" Battery, R.C.H.A., which was formed in 1951, fought in Korea and was disbanded in 1970 as a sub-unit of "2 Regiment, R.C.H.A.".
Affiliated British Unit:
"F" (Sphinx) Battery, R.H.A. originated in 1800 and fought at Alexandria in Egypt (1801), in Spain and at Waterloo in 1815 during the Napoleonic Wars. The battery, which fought in the withdrawal from Mons in Belgium at the beginning of the Great War and in North Africa during the Second World War, is presently a sub-unit of "7 Regiment, R.H.A." which fought on the Arabian Peninsula during the withdrawal from "East of Suez".

"G" Battery — CAMP SHILO, Manitoba
"G" Battery, R.C.H.A. was formed in 1953 by the re-designation of "205 Field Battery, R.C.A. (Active Force)" which had been recruited by "5 Field Battery, R.C.A. (Reserve Force)" and served in Korea as a sub-unit of "79 Field Regiment, R.C.A.". The battery is presently a sub-unit of "3 Regiment, R.C.H.A." which is a unit of "1 Canadian Brigade Group".
Affiliated British Unit:
"G" Battery, R.H.A. (Mercer's Troop), which originated in 1801, commemorates the commander of a troop of horse artillery which fought at Waterloo in 1815. The battery fought in India during the Mutiny (1857-1858) and in South Africa during the "Boer" War. "G" Battery, R.H.A., which served in the United Kingdom subsequent to the Great War and fought in North Africa during the Second World War, is presently a sub-unit of "7 Regiment, R.H.A." which fought on the Arabian Peninsula during the withdrawal from "East of Suez".

"H" Battery — CAMP SHILO, Manitoba
"H" Battery, R.C.H.A. was formed in 1953 by the re-designation of "209 Field Battery, R.C.A. (Active Force)" which had been recruited by "9 Field Battery, R.C.A. (Reserve Force)" and served in Korea as a sub-unit of "79 Field Regiment, R.C.A.". The battery was disbanded in 1970 as a sub-unit of "3 Regiment, R.C.H.A.".
Affiliated British Unit:
"H" Battery, R.H.A. (Ramsay's Troop), which originated in 1801, commemorates the commander of a troop of horse artillery which fought at Waterloo in 1815. The battery fought in India subsequent to the Great War and in North Africa during the Second World War after which it was removed from the Royal Horse Artillery but retained as a non-numerically designated field battery ("H" Field Battery, R.A.).

"I" Not Allocated
Affiliated British Unit:
"I" Battery (Bull's Troop), R.H.A., which originated in 1802 and fought in Spain during the Napoleonic Wars, commemorates the commander of a troop of horse artillery which fought at Waterloo in 1815. The battery, which fought in the withdrawal from Mons in Belgium at the beginning of the Great War and in North Africa during the Second World War, is presently a sub-unit of "7 Regiment, R.H.A." which fought on the Arabian Peninsula during the withdrawal from "East of Suez".

"J" Battery — CAMP SHILO, Manitoba

"J" Battery, R.C.H.A. was formed in 1953 by the re-designation of "213 Field Battery, R.C.A. (Active Force)" which had been recruited by "13 Field Battery, R.C.A. (Reserve Force)" and served in Korea as a sub-unit of "79 Field Regiment, R.C.A.". The battery is presently a sub-unit of "3 Regiment, R.C.H.A." which is a unit of "1 Canadian Brigade Group".

Affiliated British Unit:

"J" (Sidi Rezegh) Battery, R.H.A., which originated in 1805, fought in the withdrawal from Mons in Belgium at the beginning of the Great War and, during the Second World War, in North Africa where it distinguished itself at Sidi Rezegh in the western desert of Egypt. The battery fought on the Arabian Peninsula during the withdrawal from "East of Suez" and is presently deployed as an anti-tank unit in the "British Army of the Rhine".

"K" Battery — CAMP PETAWAWA, Ontario

"K" Battery, R.C.H.A. was formed in 1953 by the re-designation of "216 Field Battery, R.C.A. (Active Force)" which had been recruited by "16 Field Battery, R.C.A. (Reserve Force)" and fought in Korea as a sub-unit of "81 Field Regiment, R.C.A.". The battery, which received its mortar role in 1964, was disbanded in 1970 as a sub-unit of "4 Regiment, R.C.H.A.".

Affiliated British Unit:

"K" (Hondeghem) Battery, R.H.A., which originated in 1809, fought in the withdrawal from Mons in Belgium at the beginning of the Great War and, during the Second World War, in the withdrawal to Dunkirk during which it received its honour-title for the holding action at the village of Hondeghem in Belgium. The battery was disbanded after the Second World War as a sub-unit of "5 Regiment, R.H.A.".

"L" Battery — CAMP PETAWAWA, Ontario

"L" Battery, R.C.H.A. was formed in 1953 by the re-designation of "258 Field Battery, R.C.A. (Active Force)" which had been recruited by "58 Field Battery, R.C.A. (Reserve Force)" and fought in Korea as a sub-unit of "81 Field Regiment, R.C.A.". The battery, which received its mortar role in 1964, was disbanded in 1970 as a sub-unit of "4 Regiment, R.C.H.A.".

Affiliated British Unit:

"L" (Nery) Battery, R.H.A., which originated in 1809, fought during the Great War in France where it received its honour-title for the holding action at the village of Nery during the withdrawal from Mons. The battery fought in North Africa during the Second World War and subsequently in Malaya during the "Emergency" after which it was disbanded as a sub-unit of "2 Regiment, R.H.A.".

"M" Battery — CAMP PETAWAWA, Ontario

"M" Battery, R.C.H.A. was formed in 1953 by the re-designation of "284 Field Battery, R.C.A. (Active Force)" which had been recruited by "84 Field Battery, R.C.A. (Reserve Force)" and fought in Korea as a sub-unit of "81 Field Regiment, R.C.A.". The battery was disbanded in 1964 as a sub-unit of "4 Regiment, R.C.H.A.".

Affiliated British Unit:

"M" Battery, R.H.A., which originated in 1809, fought in North Africa during the Second World War after which it was disbanded as a sub-unit of "3 Regiment, R.H.A.". The battery was later re-formed and is presently deployed as an anti-tank unit in the "British Army of the Rhine".

"N" Not Allocated

Affiliated British Unit:

"N" Battery (The Eagle Troop), R.H.A., which originated in 1811, fought in Afghan during the First Afghanistan War, in North Africa during the Second World War and subsequently in Malaya during the "Emergency" after which it was disbanded as a sub-unit of "4 Regiment, R.H.A.".

"O" Not allocated
Affiliated British Unit:
"O" Battery (The Rocket Troop), R.H.A., which originated in 1813, fought in the "Battle of the Nations" at Leipzig in 1813 and at Waterloo in 1815 during the Napoleonic Wars. The battery served in the United Kingdom subsequent to the Great War and was captured in France prior to the evacuation from Dunkirk in 1940. "O" Battery, R.H.A. fought in Malaya during the "Emergency" after which it was disbanded as a sub-unit of "2 Regiment, R.H.A.".

"P" Not Allocated
Affiliated British Unit:
"P" Battery (The Dragon Troop), R.H.A., which originated in 1816, fought in China during the First China War and in South Africa during the "Boer" War. The battery fought in North Africa during the Second World War after which it was disbanded as a sub-unit of "4 Regiment, R.H.A.".

Batterie "Q" — CAMP VALCARTIER, Quebec
"Q" Battery, R.C.H.A. was formed in 1968 as a sub-unit of "5ieme Regiment d'Artillerie Legere du Canada (Regulier)".
Affiliated British Unit:
"Q" (Sanna's Post) Battery, R.H.A. fought during the "Boer" War in South Africa where it received its honour title for the defence of Sanna's Post (an outpost in the valley of the Korn Spruit). The battery fought in North Africa during the Second World War after which it was removed from the Royal Horse Artillery but retained as a non-numerically designated field battery ("Q" (Sanna's Post) Field Battery, R.A.).

"R" Not Allocated
Affiliated British Unit:
"R" Battery, R.H.A., which fought in South Africa during the "Boer" War, was removed from the Royal Horse Artillery after the Great War but retained as a non-numerically designated field battery ("R" Field Battery, R.A.).

"S" Not Allocated
Affiliated British Unit:
"S" Battery, R.H.A. was removed from the Royal Horse Artillery after the Great War but retained as a non-numerically designated field battery ("S" Field Battery, R.A.).

"T" Not Allocated
Affiliated British Unit:
"T" Battery (Shah Sujah's Troop), R.H.A. fought in Afghanistan during the First Afghan War and in South Africa during the "Boer" War. The battery fought in the withdrawal from Mons in Belgium at the beginning of the Great War after which it was removed from the Royal Horse Artillery but retained as a non-numerically designated field battery which was re-organized subsequent to the Second World War and re-designated "T" Air Defence Battery (Shah Sujah's Troop), R.A. which fought in the Falkland Islands as a sub-unit of "12 Air Defence Regiment, R.A." during the South Atlantic Campaign (1982).

"U" (Air Defence) Battery — CAMP SHILO, Manitoba
"U" Battery, R.C.H.A. was formed in 1977 as a sub-unit of "3 Regiment, R.C.H.A.".
Affiliated British Unit:
"U" Battery, R.H.A., which fought in South Africa during the "Boer" War, was removed from the Royal Horse Artillery after the Great War but retained as a non-numerically designated field battery ("U" Field Battery, R.A.) which fought in North Africa during the Second World War.

Batterie "V" (Defence de l'Air) — CAMP VALCARTIER, Quebec
"V" Battery, R.C.H.A. was formed in 1977 as a sub-unit of "5ieme Regiment d'Artillerie Legere

du Canada (Regulier)".
Affiliated British Unit:
"V" Battery, R.H.A. was removed from the Royal Horse Artillery after the Great War but retained as a non-numerically designated field battery ("V" Field Battery, R.A.).

"W" Battery — Brownfield Barracks, CAMP GAGETOWN, New Brunswick
"W" Battery, R.C.H.A. was formed in 1954 as a mortar battery in "4 Regiment, R.C.H.A." and, after service with the "United Nations Force" in Cyprus in 1965, was relocated at Camp Gagetown from Camp Petawawa in 1970 upon the replacement of the "3rd Canadian Infantry Brigade Group" by the "Combat Training Centre".
Affiliated British Unit:
"W" Battery, R.H.A. was removed from the Royal Horse Artillery after the Great War but retained as a non-numerically designated field battery ("W" Field Battery, R.A.).

Batterie "X" — CAMP VALCARTIER, Quebec
"X" Super-Heavy Battery, R.C.A. deployed railway guns in England throughout the period of imminent invasion (1940-1941) during the Second World War. "X" Battery, R.C.H.A. was formed in 1954 as a mortar battery in "3 Regiment, R.C.H.A." and was reorganized in 1958 as a medium battery which served with the "United Nations Force" in Cyprus in 1968 after which it was transferred to "5ieme Regiment d'Artillerie Legere du Canada (Regulier)".
Affiliated British Unit:
"X" Battery, R.H.A. was removed from the Royal Horse Artillery after the Great War but retained as a non-numerically designated field battery ("X" Field Battery, R.A.).

"Y" Battery — Brownfield Barracks, CAMP GAGETOWN, New Brunswick
"Y" Super-Heavy Battery, R.C.A. deployed railway guns in England throughout the period of imminent invasion (1940-1941) during the Second World War. "Y" Battery, R.C.H.A. was formed in 1954 as a mortar battery in "2 Regiment, R.C.H.A." and was re-organized in 1958 as a medium battery which was disbanded in 1970.
Affiliated British Unit:
"Y" Battery, R.H.A. was removed from the Royal Horse Artillery after the Great War but retained as a non-numerically designated field battery ("Y" Field Battery, R.A.).

"Z" Battery — CAMP SHILO, Manitoba
"Z" (Parachute) Battery, R.C.H.A., which had originated in 1951, was re-organized in 1954 as a mortar battery in "1 Regiment, R.C.H.A." and further re-organized in 1958 as a medium battery which was disbanded in 1964. "Z" Battery was re-formed in 1977 as a reinforcement battery for "1 Regiment, R.C.H.A.".
Affiliated British Unit:
"Z" Battery, R.H.A. was removed from the Royal Horse Artillery after the Great War but retained as a non-numerically designated field battery ("Z" Field Battery, R.A.).

THE CORPS OF ROYAL CANADIAN ENGINEERS

Corps March: "WINGS"
Corps Mottoes: "UBIQUE" / ("EVERYWHERE")
   "QUO FAS ET GLORIA DUCUNT"
   ("WHITHER RIGHT AND GLORY LEAD")
The Royal Canadian School of Military Engineering: CAMP CHILLIWACK, B.C.

NOTE (1)

Like-numbered British engineer units, although not officially affiliated, have been linked with their Canadian counterparts.

NOTE (2)

"Sappers" carry no battle honours but rather, upon their various badges and devices, bear the distinctions "UBIQUE" and "QUO FAS ET GLORIA DUCUNT"

1 Field Squadron (Militia) — SAINT JOHN, New Brunswick

A "Company of Engineers" was formed in 1880 at Brighton and re-designated "1 Field Company" in 1904. "1 Field Company" fought in France during the Great War and in both Italy and North-West Europe during the Second World War. "1 Field Squadron" was disbanded in 1965 as a sub-unit of "5 Field Engineer Regiment, R.C.E. (Militia)".

Affiliated British Unit:

"1 Fortress Squadron, R.E.", which originated in 1772 as a "Company of Military Articifers", served at Gibraltar as a sub-unit of the "Fortress Engineer Regiment, R.E.".

2 Field Squadron (Militia) — Fort York Armoury, TORONTO, Ontario

A "Company of Engineers" was formed in 1901 at Toronto and re-designated "2 Field Company" in 1904. "2 Field Company" fought in France during the Great War and in North-West Europe during the Second World War. "2 Field Squadron" is presently a sub-unit of "2 Field Engineer Regiment".

Affiliated British Unit:

2 Field Squadron, R.E.

3 Field Squadron (Militia) — OTTAWA, Ontario

A "Company of Engineers" was formed in 1902 at Ottawa and re-designated "3 Field Company" in 1904. "3 Field Company", which fought in France during the Great War, landed on Spitsbergen during the raid on that Norwegian island in the Barents Sea and fought in both Italy and North-West Europe during the Second World War. "3 Field Squadron" was a sub-unit of "2 Field Engineer Regiment, R.C.E. (Reserve Force)" until 1954.

Affiliated British Unit:

3 Field Squadron, R.E.

4 Field Squadron (Militia) — WESTMOUNT (MONTREAL), Quebec

A "Company of Engineers" was formed in 1903 at Montreal and re-designated "4 Field Company" in 1904. "4 Field Company" fought in France during the Great War and in both Italy and North-West Europe during the Second World War. "4 Field Squadron" is presently a sub-unit of "3 Field Engineer Regiment".

Affiliated British Unit:

4 Field Squadron, R.E.

5 Field Squadron (Reserve Force) — CHALK RIVER, Ontario

"5 Field Company" was formed in 1910 and fought in France during the Great War and in North-West Europe during the Second World War. "5 Field Squadron" was relocated from Kingston in 1946 and disbanded in 1954.

Affiliated British Unit:

5 Field Squadron, R.E.

6 Field Squadron (Militia) — NORTH VANCOUVER, British Columbia

"6 Field Company" was formed in 1911 and fought in France during the Great War and in North-West Europe during the Second World War. "6 Field Squadron" was a sub-unit of "7 Field Engineer Regiment, R.C.E. (Militia)" until 1965.

Affiliated British Units:

6 Field Squadron, R.E.

100 Field Squadron, Royal Monmouthshire Royal Engineers (Militia)

The "Royal Monmouthshire Royal Engineers", having originated in 1577 in the "trained bands" of Elizabethan England, provided reinforcements for the British Army during the Seven-Years War, American Revolution, Napoleonic Wars and the Crimean War. The "Regiment" was converted in 1877 and subsequently served as a field company in South Africa during the "Boer" War and in France during the Great War. "100 Field Company, Royal Monmouthshire Royal

Engineers" was captured at Dunkirk in 1940. The company, which was re-formed in England, landed at Normandy and fought in North-West Europe during the Second World War.

7 Field Squadron (Militia) — LONDON, Ontario
"7 Field Company" was formed in 1912 and fought in France during the Great War and in North-West Europe during the Second World War. "7 Field Squadron", which was disbanded in 1970, was a sub-unit of "1 Field Engineer Regiment, R.C.E. (Militia)" until 1965.
Affiliated British Unit:
7 Field Squadron, R.E.

8 Field Squadron (Militia) — NORTH BAY, Ontario
"8 Field Company" fought in France during the Great War and in North-West Europe during the Second World War. "8 Field Squadron", which was disbanded in 1970, was a sub-unit of "2 Field Engineer Regiment, R.C.E. (Reserve Force)" until 1954.
Affiliated British Unit:
8 Field Squadron, R.E.

9 Field Squadron (Militia) — NORANDA, Quebec
"9 Field Company" fought in France during the Great War and in North-West Europe during the Second World War".
Affiliated British Unit:
"9 (Independent) Parachute Squadron, R.E." originated as "9 Field Company, R.E." which fought in North Africa, Italy and North-West Europe as a unit of the "1st Airborne Division" during the Second World War after which it was re-organized as an independent parachute squadron which landed at Port Said in Egypt in 1956 during the Anglo-French invasion of the Suez Canal Zone and fought in the Falkland Islands during the South Atlantic Campaign (1982).

10 Field Squadron (Militia) — Manege Grande-Allee, QUEBEC CITY
"10 Field Company" fought in France during the Great War and in both Italy and North-West Europe during the Second World War. "10 Field Squadron" was a sub-unit of "4 Field Engineer Regiment, R.C.E. (Militia)" until 1965.
Affiliated British Unit:
10 Airfield Squadron, R.E.

11 (LAMBTON) Field Squadron (Militia) — SARNIA, Ontario
"11 Field Company" fought in France during the Great War and in North-West Europe during the Second World War. The county designation was adopted in 1936 upon the disbandment of "The Lambton Regiment (Non-Permanent Active Militia)" which had originated in 1866 as the "Lambton Battalion of Infantry". "11 Field Squadron" was disbanded in 1965 as a sub-unit of "1 Field Engineer Regiment, R.C.E. (Militia)".
Affiliated British Unit:
"11 Field Squadron, R.E." fought in the Falkland Islands during the South Atlantic Campaign (1982).

12 Field Squadron (Militia) — WINNIPEG, Manitoba
"12 Field Company" fought in France during the Great War and in both Italy and North-West Europe during the Second World War. "12 Field Squadron" was disbanded in 1965 as a sub-unit of "6 Field Engineer Regiment, R.C.E. (Militia)".
Affiliated British Unit:
12 (Nova Scotia) Field Squadron, R.E.

13 Field Squadron (Militia) — BROOKS, Alberta
"13 Field Company" fought in France during the Great War and in both Italy and North-West Europe during the Second World War. "13 Field Squadron", which maintained a detached troop

at Calgary until 1965, was disbanded in 1968 as a sub-unit of "8 Field Engineer Regiment, R.C.E. (Militia)".
Affiliated British Unit:
13 Map Production Squadron, R.E.

14 Field Squadron (Militia) — REGINA, Saskatchewan
"14 Field Company" fought in France during the Great War and in both Italy and North-West Europe during the Second World War. "14 Field Squadron" was disbanded in 1965 as a sub-unit of "6 Field Engineer Regiment, R.C.E. (Militia)".
Affiliated British Unit:
14 Field Squadron, R.E.

15 Field Squadron (Militia) — THETFORD MINES, Quebec
"15 Field Company" fought in France during the Great War and served in Atlantic Command (Canada) during the Second World War. "15 Field Squadron" was disbanded in 1965 as a sub-unit of "4 Field Engineer Regiment, R.C.E. (Militia)".
Affiliated British Unit:
15 Support Squadron, R.E.

16 Field Squadron (Militia) — WESTMOUNT (MONTREAL), Quebec
"16 Field Company" served at Vladivostok as a unit of the Canadian Siberian Expeditionary Force (1918-1919) and fought in North-West Europe during the Second World War. "16 Field Squadron" is presently a sub-unit of "3 Field Engineer Regiment".
Affiliated British Unit:
16 Field Squadron, R.E.

17 Field Squadron (Militia) — KIMBERLEY, British Columbia
The squadron, which maintained a detached troop at Creston until 1965, was disbanded in 1968 as a sub-unit of "8 Field Engineer Regiment, R.C.E. (Militia)".
Affiliated British Unit:
17 Field Squadron, R.E.

18 Field Squadron (Militia) — HAMILTON, Ontario
"18 Field Company, R.C.E." fought in North-West Europe during the Second World War. "18 Field Squadron" was disbanded in 1965 as a sub-unit of "2 Field Engineer Regiment, R.C.E. (Militia)".
Affiliated British Unit:
18 Field Squadron, R.E.

19 Field Squadron (Reserve Force) — DRUMMONDVILLE, Quebec
The squadron was disbanded in 1954 as a sub-unit of "4 Field Engineer Regiment, R.C.E. (Reserve Force)".
Affiliated British Unit:
19 Topographical Squadron, R.E.

20 Field Squadron (Reserve Force) — LUNENBURG, Nova Scotia
"20 Field Company, R.C.E." fought in North-West Europe during the Second World War. "20 Field Squadron" was disbanded in 1954 as a sub-unit of "5 Field Engineer Regiment, R.C.E. (Reserve Force)".
Affiliated British Unit:
20 Postal Communications Squadron, R.E.

21 Field Squadron (Militia) — FLIN FLON, Manitoba
"21 Field Company, R.C.E." served in Pacific Command (Canada) during the Second World War.
Affiliated British Unit:
21 Postal Communications Squadron, R.E.

22 Field Squadron (Regular) — CAMP GAGETOWN, New Brunswick
"22 Field Squadron, R.C.E." served in Pacific Command (Canada) during the Second World War. "22 Field Squadron" was disbanded in 1965 at Chilliwack in British Columbia as a sub-unit of "7 Field Engineer Regiment, R.C.E. (Militia)". The squadron was re-formed in 1977 to support the "Combat Training Centre".
Affiliated British Unit:
22 Field Squadron, R.E.

23 Field Squadron (Active Force) — CAMP CHILLIWACK, British Columbia
"23 Field Company, R.C.E." fought in North-West Europe during the Second World War. The company distinguished itself in 1944 at Arnhem in the Netherlands where it assisted in the evacuation of airborne troops following the abortive attempt to gain control of the Rhine bridges. "23 Field Squadron" was retained in the post-war "Active Force" and fought in Korea as a unit of the "25th Canadian Infantry Brigade". The squadron was re-organized in 1953 as "1 Field Squadron" of "1 Field Engineer Regiment, R.C.E. (Regular)" which had been formed to support the re- constituted "1st Canadian Infantry Division". "1 Field Squadron, R.C.E. (Regular)" was re-organized in 1958 as a unit of the "1st Canadian Infantry Brigade Group" and was further re-organized in 1977 and re-designated "1 Combat Engineer Regiment" which is a unit of "1 Canadian Brigade Group".
Affiliated British Unit:
23 Amphibious Squadron, R.E.

24 Field Squadron (Reserve Force) — EDMONTON, Alberta
"24 Field Company, R.C.E." served on Kiska in the Aleutian Islands as a unit of the "13th Canadian Infantry Brigade Group" during the Second World War. "24 Field Squadron" was disbanded in 1954 as a sub-unit of "8 Field Engineer Regiment, R.C.E. (Reserve Force)".
Affiliated British Unit:
24 Field Squadron, R.E.

25 Field Squadron (Militia) — EDMONTON, Alberta
"25 Field Company, R.C.E." served in Pacific Command (Canada) during the Second World War. "25 Field Squadron" is presently a sub-unit of "8 Field Engineer Regiment".
Affiliated British Unit:
25 Field Squadron, R.E.

26 Field Park Squadron (Reserve Force) — WINDSOR, Ontario
"26 Field Company, R.C.E." served in Pacific Command (Canada) during the Second World War. "26 Field Park Squadron" was formed in 1946 to support the "1st Division" (Reserve Force) and was disbanded in 1954 as a sub-unit of "1 Field Engineer Regiment, R.C.E. (Reserve Force)".
Affiliated British Unit:
26 Armoured Squadron, R.E.

27 Field Park Squadron (Reserve Force) — TORONTO, Ontario
"27 Field Company, R.C.E." served in Atlantic Command (Canada) during the Second World War. "27 Field Park Squadron" was formed in 1946 to support the "2nd Division (Reserve Force) and was disbanded in 1954 as a sub-unit of "2 Field Engineer Regiment, R.C.E. (Reserve Force)".
Affiliated British Unit:
27 Field Squadron, R.E.

28 Field Park Squadron (Reserve Force) — MONTREAL, Quebec
The squadron was formed in 1946 to support the "3rd Division" (Reserve Force) and was disbanded in 1954 as a sub-unit of "3 Field Engineer Regiment, R.C.E. (Reserve Force)".
Affiliated British Unit:
28 Training Squadron, R.E.

29 Field Park Squadron (Reserve Force) — QUEBEC CITY
"29 Field Company, R.C.E." fought in North-West Europe during the Second World War. "29 Field Park Squadron" was formed in 1946 to support the "4th Division" (Reserve Force) and was disbanded in 1954 as a sub-unit of "4 Field Engineer Regiment, R.C.E. (Reserve Force)".
Affiliated British Unit:
29 Field Squadron, R.E.

30 Field Squadron (Militia) — HALIFAX, Nova Scotia
"30 Field Company, R.C.E." fought in North-West Europe during the Second World War. "30 Field Park Squadron" was formed in 1946 to support the "5th Division" (Reserve Force) and was re-organized in 1954 as a field squadron which was a sub-unit of "5 Engineer Regiment, R.C.E. (Militia)" until 1965. "30 Field Squadron" was disbanded in 1970.
Affiliated British Unit:
30 Field Squadron, R.E.

31 Field Park Squadron (Reserve Force) — WINNIPEG, Manitoba
"31 Field Company, R.C.E." fought in North-West Europe during the Second World War. "31 Field Park Squadron" was formed in 1946 to support the "6th Division" (Reserve Force) and was disbanded in 1954 as a sub-unit of "6 Field Engineer Regiment, R.C.E. (Reserve Force)".
Affiliated British Unit:
31 Armoured Squadron, R.E.

32 Field Park Squadron (Reserve Force) — VANCOUVER, British Columbia
"32 Field Company, R.C.E." fought in North-West Europe during the Second World War. "32 Field Park Squadron" was formed in 1946 to support the "1st Corps" (Reserve Force) and was disbanded in 1954 as a sub-unit of "7 Field Engineer Regiment, R.C.E. (Reserve Force)".
Affiliated British Unit:
32 Field Squadron, R.E.

33 Field Squadron (Militia) — EDMONTON, Alberta
"33 Field Company, R.C.E." fought in North-West Europe during the Second World War. "33 Field Park Squadron" was formed in 1946 to support the "2nd Corps" (Reserve Force) and was re-organized in 1954 as a field squadron which is presently a sub-unit of "8 Field Engineer Regiment". "33 Field Squadron" was relocated at Edmonton from Lethbridge in 1970.
Affiliated British Unit:
33 Field Squadron, R.E.

34 Bridge Troop (Reserve Force) — WINDSOR, Ontario
The "1st Pontoon Bridging Transport Unit, C.E." fought in France as a unit of the "1st Canadian Division" during the Great War. "34 Field Company, R.C.E." fought in North-West Europe during the Second World War. "34 Bridge Troop" was formed in 1946 to support the "1st Division" (Reserve Force) and was disbanded in 1954 as a sub-unit of "1 Field Engineer Regiment, R.C.E. (Reserve Force)".
Affiliated British Unit:
34 Field Squadron, R.E.

35 Bridge Troop (Reserve Force) — TORONTO, Ontario
The "2nd Pontoon Bridging Transport Unit, C.E." fought in France as a unit of the "2nd Canadian Division" during the Great War. "35 Bridge Troop" was formed in 1946 to support the "2nd Division" (Reserve Force) and was disbanded in 1954 as a sub-unit of "2 Field Regiment, R.C.E. (Reserve Force)".
Affiliated British Unit:
35 Field Squadron, R.E.

36 Bridge Troop (Reserve Force) — MONTREAL, Quebec
The "3rd Pontoon Bridging Transport Unit, C.E." fought in France as a unit of the "3rd Canadian Division" during the Great War. "36 Bridge Troop" was formed in 1946 to support the "3rd Division" (Reserve Force) and was disbanded in 1954 as a sub-unit of "3 Field Engineer Regiment, R.C.E. (Reserve Force)".
Affiliated British Unit:
36 Field Squadron, R.E.

37 Bridge Troop (Reserve Force) — QUEBEC CITY
The "4th Pontoon Bridging Transport Unit, C.E." fought in France as a unit of the "4th Canadian Division" during the Great War. "37 Bridge Troop" was formed in 1946 to support the "4th Division" (Reserve Force) and was disbanded in 1954 as a sub-unit of "4 Field Engineer Regiment, R.C.E. (Reserve Force)".
Affiliated British Unit:
37 Field Squadron, R.E.

38 Bridge Troop (Reserve Force) — HALIFAX, Nova Scotia
The troop was formed in 1946 to support the "5th Division" (Reserve Force) and was disbanded in 1954 as a sub-unit of "5 Field Engineer Regiment, R.C.E. (Reserve Force)".
Affiliated British Unit:
38 Field Squadron, R.E.

39 Bridge Troop (Reserve Force) — WINNIPEG, Manitoba
The troop was formed in 1946 to support the "6th Division" (Reserve Force) and was disbanded in 1954 as a sub-unit of "6 Field Engineer Regiment, R.C.E. (Reserve Force)".
Affiliated British Unit:
39 Field Squadron, R.E.

40 Survey Squadron (Active Force) — OTTAWA, Ontario
The squadron was formed in 1946 and subsequently re-organized as the "Army Survey Establishment, R.C.E. (Regular)" which was re-designated "Canadian Forces Mapping and Charting Establishment" in 1968.
Affiliated British Unit:
40 Field Squadron, R.E.

41 Survey Squadron (Reserve Force) — TORONTO, Ontario
The squadron was formed in 1946 and disbanded in 1947.
Affiliated British Unit:
41 Field Squadron, R.E.

42 Electrical and Mechanical Troop (Reserve Force) — REGINA, Saskatchewan
The troop was formed in 1946 to support the "1st Corps" (Reserve Force) and was disbanded in 1954.
Affiliated British Unit:
42 Field Squadron, R.E.

43 Electrical and Mechanical Troop (Reserve Force) — LETHBRIDGE, Alberta
The troop was formed in 1946 to support the "2nd Corps" (Reserve Force) and was disbanded in 1954.
Affiliated British Unit:
43 Support Squadron, R.E.

44 Field Squadron (Militia) — TRAIL, British Columbia
The squadron, which was formed in 1947, was a sub-unit of "7 Field Engineer Regiment, R.C.E. (Militia)" until 1965 and maintained a detached troop at Nelson until 1968 thereby continuing a

militia presence subsequent to the disbandment of "111 Field Battery, R.C.A."
Affiliated British Unit:
44 Field Squadron, R.E.

45 Field Squadron (Militia) — SYDNEY, Nova Scotia
The squadron, which was formed in 1947, was a sub-unit of "5 Field Engineer Regiment, R.C.E. (Militia)" until 1965.
Affiliated British Unit:
45 Field Squadron, R.E.

46 Field Squadron (Militia) — PINE FALLS, Manitoba
The squadron was disbanded in 1965 as a sub-unit of "6 Field Engineer Regiment, R.C.E. (Militia)".
Affiliated British Unit:
46 Field Squadron, R.E.

47 Field Squadron (Militia) — Fort York Armoury, TORONTO, Ontario
The squadron, which was relocated from Welland in 1954, is presently a sub-unit of "2 Field Engineer Regiment".
Affiliated British Unit:
47 Field Squadron, R.E.

48 Field Squadron (Militia) — KITCHENER, Ontario
The squadron, which was disbanded in 1970, was a sub-unit of "1 Field Engineer Regiment, R.C.E. (Militia)" until 1965.
Affiliated British Unit:
48 Field Squadron, R.E.

49 Field Squadron (Reserve Force) — WESTMOUNT (MONTREAL), Quebec
The squadron was formed in 1947 and disbanded in 1954.
Affiliated British Unit:
"49 Explosive Ordnance Disposal Squadron, R.E." fought in the Falkland Islands during the South Atlantic Campaign (1982).

50 Field Squadron (Reserve Force) — LLOYDMINSTER, Saskatchewan
The squadron was incorporated within "The Prince Albert and Battleford Volunteers" (now "The North Saskatchewan Regiment") in 1954.
Affiliated British Unit:
50 Construction Squadron, R.E.

51 Field Squadron (Reserve Force) — MOOSE JAW, Saskatchewan
The squadron was formed in 1947 and disbanded in 1954.
Affiliated British Unit:
51 Airfield Squadron, R.E.

52 Field Squadron (Reserve Force) — SASKATOON, Saskatchewan
The squadron was formed in 1947 and disbanded in 1954.
Affiliated British Unit:
52 Airfield Squadron, R.E.

53 Field Squadron (Reserve Force) — CALGARY, Alberta
The squadron was formed in 1947 and disbanded in 1954.
Affiliated British Unit:
53 Field Squadron, R.E.

54 Field Squadron (Reserve Force) — VANCOUVER, British Columbia
The squadron was formed in 1947 and disbanded in 1954.
Affiliated British Unit:
54 Support Squadron, R.E.

55 Field Squadron (Militia) — KINGSTON, Ontario
The squadron, which had been relocated from St. Catharines in 1954, was disbanded in 1965.
Affiliated British Unit:
55 Training Squadron, R.E.

56 Field Squadron (Militia) — ST. JOHN'S, Newfoundland
The squadron was formed in 1949.
Affiliated British Unit:
56 Training Squadron, R.E.

57 Field Squadron (Militia) — ST-HILAIRE, Quebec
The squadron was formed in 1954 and disbanded in 1965 as a sub-unit of "3 Field Engineer Regiment, R.C.E. (Militia)". "57 Field Squadron" was originally formed in 1951 and, after service in Korea, was re-organized as "2 Field Squadron" of "1 Field Engineer Regiment, R.C.E. (Regular)" which had been formed in 1953 to support the re-constituted "1st Canadian Infantry Division". "2 Field Squadron, R.C.E. (Regular)" was re-organized in 1958 as a unit of the "2nd Canadian Infantry Brigade Group" and was further re-organized in 1977 and re-designated "2 Combat Engineer Regiment" which is a unit of the "Special Service Force" at Camp Petawawa.
Affiliated British Unit:
57 Training Squadron, R.E.

58 Field Squadron (Militia) — ASBESTOS, Quebec
The squadron was formed in 1954 and disbanded in 1965 as a sub-unit of "4 Field Engineer Regiment, R.C.E. (Militia)". "58 Field Squadron" was originally formed in 1951 for service with the "27th Canadian Infantry Brigade Group" in West Germany and was re-organized in 1953 as "3 Field Squadron" of "1 Field Engineer Regiment, R.C.E. (Regular)" which had been formed to support the re-constituted "1st Canadian Infantry Division". "3 Field Squadron, R.C.E. (Regular)" served in Korea subsequent to the armistice and was re-organized in 1958 as a unit of the "3rd Canadian Infantry Brigade Group". The squadron was disbanded in 1970 at Camp Gagetown upon the replacement of the "3rd Canadian Infantry Brigade Group" by the "Combat Training Centre".
Affiliated British Unit:
58 Field Squadron, R.E.

"59 Field Squadron (Active Force)" was formed for "rotation" with "57" and "58" Field Squadrons and, after service in Korea, was re-organized in 1953 as "4 Field Squadron", a sub-unit of "1 Field Engineer Regiment, R.C.E. (Regular)" which had been formed to support the re-constituted "1st Canadian Infantry Division". "4 Field Squadron, R.C.E. (Regular)" was re-organized in 1958 as a unit of the "4th Canadian Infantry Brigade Group" and was further re-organized in 1977 and re-designated "4 Combat Engineer Regiment" which is a unit of "4 Canadian Mechanized Brigade Group" at Lahr in West Germany.

Affiliated British Unit:
"59 (Independent) Commando Squadron, R.E." originated in 1900 as "59 Field Company, R.E." which fought in the withdrawal from Mons in Belgium at the beginning of the Great War and in both North Africa and Italy during the Second World War. The squadron fought in support of "3 Commando Brigade, Royal Marines" in the Falkland Islands during the South Atlantic Campaign (1982).

THE ROYAL CANADIAN CORPS OF SIGNALS

Corps March: "BEGONE DULL CARE"
Corps Motto: "VELOX-VERSATUS-VIGILANS"
    ("QUICK-ACCURATE-WATCHFUL")
The Royal Canadian School of Signals: Vimy Barracks, CAMP BARRIEFIELD, Ontario

NOTE

Signal companies formed for service during the Great War were organized as units of the "Canadian Engineers".

1st Divisional Signal Regiment (Reserve Force)
The "1st Divisional Signalling Company, C.E." fought in France during the Great War and was organized as follows:
1st Divisional Artillery Signal Section
1st Infantry Brigade Signal Section
2nd Infantry Brigade Signal Section
3rd Infantry Brigade Signal Section
The "1st Divisional Signals" fought in both Italy and North-West Europe during the Second World War and was organized as follows:
1st Divisional Signals, R.C. Signals
"A" Section provided radio communications between "Headquarters, 1st Canadian Infantry Division" and its' three infantry brigades.
"B" Section provided telephone communications between "Headquarters, 1st Canadian Infantry Division" and its' three infantry brigades.
"C" Section provided crews for the laying of field telephone lines.
"D" Section provided despatch riders.
"E" Section provided radio communications between "Headquarters, 1st Canadian Infantry Brigade" and its' supporting field artillery regiment.
"F" Section provided radio communications between "Headquarters, 2nd Canadian Infantry Brigade" and its' supporting field artillery regiment.
"G" Section provided radio communications between "Headquarters, 3rd Canadian Infantry Brigade" and its' supporting field artillery regiment.
"H" Section provided radio communications between "Headquarters, 1st Canadian Infantry Division" and its' supporting anti-tank regiment.
"I" Section was not allocated.
"J" Section provided radio communications between "Headquarters, 1st Canadian Infantry Brigade" and its' three infantry battalions.
"K" Section provided radio communications between "Headquarters, 2nd Canadian Infantry Brigade" and its' three infantry battalions.
"L" Section provided radio communications between "Headquarters, 3rd Canadian Infantry Brigade" and its' three infantry battalions.
"M" Section provided tradesmen for equipment maintenance.
"N" Section provided radio communications between "Headquarters, R.C.E., 1st Candian Infantry Division" and its' three field squadrons.
The "1st Divisional Signal Regiment (Reserve Force)", which had been formed in 1946 to perpetuate the wartime "1st Divisional Signals", was disbanded in 1954.
1st Divisional Signal Regiment (Reserve Force)
"Headquarters" was disbanded in 1954 at Hamilton.
"1" Squadron — HAMILTON, Ontario
The squadron, which provided communications for "3 Infantry Brigade", was re-organized in 1954 and re-designated "1st Independent Signal Squadron (Militia)".
"2" Squadron — LONDON, Ontario
The squadron, which provided communications for "2 Infantry Brigade", was re-organized in 1954 and re-designated "9th Independent Signal Squadron (Militia)".
"3" Squadron — WINDSOR, Ontario
The squadron, which provided communications for "1 Infantry Brigade", was disbanded in 1954.

2nd Divisional Signal Regiment (Reserve Force)

The "2nd Divisional Signalling Company, C.E." fought in France during the Great War and was organized as follows:

2nd Divisional Artillery Signal Section

4th Infantry Brigade Signal Section

5th Infantry Brigade Signal Section

6th Infantry Brigade Signal Section

The "2nd Divisional Signals" fought in North-West Europe during the Second World War and was organized as follows:

2nd Divisional Signals, R. C. Signals

"A" Section provided radio communications between "Headquarters, 2nd Canadian Infantry Division" and its' three infantry brigades.

"B" Section provided telephone communications between "Headquarters, 2nd Canadian Infantry Division" and its' three infantry brigades.

"C" Section provided crews for the laying of field telephone lines.

"D" Section provided despatch riders.

"E" Section provided radio communications between "Headquarters, 4th Canadian Infantry Brigade" and its' supporting field artillery regiment.

"F" Section provided radio communications between "Headquarters, 5th Canadian Infantry Brigade" and its' supporting field artillery regiment.

"G" Section provided radio communications between "Headquarters, 6th Canadian Infantry Brigade" and its' supporting field artillery regiment.

"H" Section provided radio communications between "Headquarters, 2nd Canadian Infantry Division" and its' supporting anti-tank regiment.

"I" Section was not allocated.

"J" Section provided radio communications between "Headquarters, 4th Canadian Infantry Brigade" and its' three infantry battalions.

"K" Section provided radio communications between "Headquarters, 5th Canadian Infantry Brigade" and its' three infantry battalions.

"L" Section provided radio communications between "Headquarters, 6th Canadian Infantry Brigade" and its' three infantry battalions.

"M" Section provided tradesmen for equipment maintenance.

"N" Section provided radio communications between "Headquarters, R.C.E., 2nd Canadian Infantry Division" and its' three field squadrons.

The "2nd Divisional Signal Regiment (Reserve Force)", which had been formed in 1946 to perpetuate the wartime "2nd Divisional Signals", was re-designated "2nd Signal Regiment (Militia)" in 1954.

2nd Divisional Signal Regiment (Reserve Force)

"Headquarters" — TORONTO, Ontario

"1" Squadron — TORONTO, Ontario

The squadron provided communications for "4 Infantry Brigade".

"2" Squadron — KINGSTON, Ontario

The squadron provided communications for "6 Infantry Brigade".

"3" Squadron — TORONTO, Ontario

The squadron provided communications for "5 Infantry Brigade".

3rd Divisional Signal Regiment (Reserve Force)

The "3rd Divisional Signalling Company, C.E." fought in France during the Great War and was organized as follows:

3rd Divisional Artillery Signal Section

7th Infantry Brigade Signal Section

8th Infantry Brigade Signal Section

9th Infantry Brigade Signal Section

The "3rd Divisional Signals" fought in North-West Europe during the Second World War and was organized as follows:

3rd Divisional Signals, R. C. Signals

"A" Section provided radio communications between "Headquarters, 3rd Canadian Infantry Division" and its' three infantry brigades.

"B" Section provided radio communications between "Headquarters, 3rd Canadian Infantry Division" and its' three infantry brigades.

"C" Section provided crews for the laying of field telephone lines.

"D" Section provided despatch riders.

"E" Section provided radio communications between "Headquarters, 7th Canadian Infantry Brigade" and its' supporting field artillery regiment.

"F" Section provided radio communications between "Headquarters, 8th Canadian Infantry Brigade" and its' supporting field artillery regiment.

"G" Section provided radio communications between "Headquarters, 9th Canadian Infantry Brigade" and its' supporting field artillery regiment.

"H" Section provided radio communications between "Headquarters, 3rd Canadian Infantry Division" and its' supporting anti-tank regiment.

"I" Section was not allocated.

"J" Section provided radio communications between "Headquarters, 7th Canadian Infantry Brigade" and its' three infantry battalions.

"K" Section provided radio communications between "Headquarters, 8th Canadian Infantry Brigade" and its' three infantry battalions.

"L" Section provided radio communications between "Headquarters, 9th Canadian Infantry Brigade" and its' three infantry battalions.

"M" Section provided tradesmen for equipment maintenance.

"N" Section provided radio communications between "Headquarters, R.C.E., 3rd Canadian Infantry Division" and its' three field squadrons.

The "3rd Divisional Signal Regiment (Reserve Force)", which had been formed in 1946 to perpetuate the wartime "3rd Divisional Signals", was re-designated "3rd Signal Regiment (Militia)" in 1954.

3rd Divisional Signal Regiment (Reserve Force)

Headquarters — OTTAWA, Ontario

"1" Squadron provided communications for "7 Infantry Brigade".

"2" Squadron provided communications for "8 Infantry Brigade".

"3" Squadron provided communications for "9 Infantry Brigade".

4th Divisional Signal Regiment (Reserve Force)

The "4th Divisional Signalling Company. C.E." fought in France during the Great War and was organized as follows:

4th Divisional Artillery Signal Section

10th Infantry Brigade Signal Section

11th Infantry Brigade Signal Section

12th Infantry Brigade Signal Section

The "4th Divisional Signals" fought in North-West Europe during the Second World War and was perpetuated by the "4th Divisional Signal Regiment (Reserve Force)" which was disbanded in 1954.

4th Divisional Signal Regiment (Reserve Force)

"Headquarters" was disbanded in 1954 at Montreal.

"1" Squadron — MONTREAL, Quebec

The squadron, which provided communications for "10 Infantry Brigade", was re-organized in 1954 and re-designated "11th Independent Signal Squadron (Militia)".

"2" Squadron — SHERBROOKE, Quebec

The squadron, which provided communications for "11 Infantry Brigade", was re-organized in 1954 and re-designated "12th Independent Signal Squadron (Militia)".

"3" Squadron — QUEBEC CITY

The squadron, which provided communications for "12 Infantry Brigade", was re-organized in 1954 and re-designated "3rd Independent Signal Squadron (Militia)".

5th Divisional Signal Regiment (Reserve Force)

5th Divisional Signalling Company, C.E.

The "5th Divisional Artillery Signal Section" fought in France during the Great War.

The "13th Infantry Brigade Signal Section" served in the United Kingdom during the Great War.

The "14th Infantry Brigade Signal Section" served in the United Kingdom during the Great War.

The "15th Infantry Brigade Signal Section" served in the United Kingdom during the Great War.

The "5th Divisional Signals" fought in both Italy and North-West Europe during the Second World War and was perpetuated by the "5th Divisional Signal Regiment (Reserve Force)" which was re-designated "5th Signal Regiment (Militia)" in 1954.

5th Divisional Signal Regiment (Reserve Force)

"Headquarters" — CHARLOTTETOWN, Prince Edward Island

"1" Squadron — CHARLOTTETOWN, Prince Edward Island

The squadron provided communications for "13 Infantry Brigade".

"2" Squadron — FREDERICTON, New Brunswick

The squadron, which provided communications for "14 Infantry Brigade", was re-organized in 1954 and re-designated "6th Independent Signal Squadron (Militia)".

"3" Squadron — VANCOUVER, British Columbia

The squadron, which provided communications for "15 Infantry Brigade", was disbanded in 1954.

6th Divisional Signal Regiment (Reserve Force)

The "6th Signalling Company, C.E." served at Vladivostok as a unit of the Canadian Siberian Expeditionary Force (1918-1919).

The "6th Divisional Signal Regiment" was formed in 1946 and disbanded in 1954.

"Headquarters" was disbanded in 1954 at Winnipeg.

"1" Squadron — WINNIPEG, Manitoba

The squadron, which provided communications for "16 Infantry Brigade", was re-organized in 1954 and re-designated "10th Independent Signal Squadron (Militia)".

"2" Squadron — REGINA, Saskatchewan

The squadron, which provided communications for "17 Infantry Brigade", was re-organized in 1954 and re-designated "2nd Independent Signal Squadron (Militia)".

"3" Squadron — CALGARY, Alberta

The squadron, which provided communications for "18 Infantry Brigade", was re-organized in 1954 and re-designated "7th Independent Signal Squadron (Militia)".

19 Armoured Brigade Signal Squadron (Reserve Force)
The squadron was authorized (but not formed) to provide communications for "19 Armoured Brigade".

20 Armoured Brigade Signal Squadron (Reserve Force) — MONTREAL, Quebec
The squadron, which provided communications for "20 Armoured Brigade", was disbanded in 1954.

21 Armoured Brigade Signal Squadron (Reserve Force) — MONCTON, New Brunswick
The squadron, which provided communications for "21 Armoured Brigade", was re-organized in 1954 and re-designated "4th Independent Signal Squadron (Militia)".

22 Armoured Brigade Signal Squadron (Reserve Force)
The squadron was authorized (but not formed) to provide communications for "22 Armoured Brigade".

23 Infantry Brigade Group Signal Troop (Active Force)
— Vimy Barracks, CAMP BARRIEFIELD, Ontario
The troop, which had been formed in 1946 to support the "23rd Canadian Infantry Brigade Group", was incorporated within the "1st Infantry Divisional Signal Regiment (Regular)" in 1953.

"24" Not Allocated

"25 Infantry Brigade Signal Troop" fought in Korea as a unit of the "25th Canadian Infantry Brigade".

"26" Not Allocated

"27 Infantry Brigade Group Signal Squadron" was formed in 1951 for service with the "27th Canadian Infantry Brigade Group" in West Germany.

1st Corps Signal Regiment (Reserve Force) — TORONTO, Ontario
The "Canadian Corps Signalling Company, C.E." fought in France during the Great War. The "1st Corps Signals" fought in both Italy and North-West Europe during the Second World War and was perpetuated by the "1st Corps Signal Regiment" which was re-designated "8th Signal Regiment (Militia)" in 1954.

2nd Corps Signal Regiment (Reserve Force) — MONTREAL, Quebec
The "2nd Corps Signals" fought in North-West Europe during the Second World War and was perpetuated by the "2nd Corps Signal Regiment" which was disbanded in 1954.

East Coast Signal Regiment (Reserve Force)
The regiment was re-designated "East Coast Signal Regiment (Militia)" in 1954.
"Headquarters" — HALIFAX, Nova Scotia
1st Area Signal Squadron — HALIFAX, Nova Scotia
2nd Area Signal Squadron — SAINT JOHN, New Brunswick
The "2nd Area Signal Squadron" was re-organized in 1954 and re-designated "5th Independent Signal Squadron (Militia)".

West Coast Signal Regiment (Reserve Force)
The regiment was re-designated "West Coast Signal Regiment (Militia)" in 1954.
"Headquarters" — VANCOUVER, British Columbia.
3rd Area Signal Squadron — VANCOUVER, British Columbia
4th Area Signal Squadron — VANCOUVER, British Columba
5th Area Signal Squadron — VICTORIA, British Columbia

1st Airborne Signal Squadron (Regular) — CAMP BARRIEFIELD, Ontario
The squadron, which had been formed in 1948 to support the "Mobile Striking Force", was disbanded in 1958.

1st Infantry Divisional Signal Regiment (Regular) — CAMP BORDEN, Ontario
The regiment, which had been formed in 1953 to support the re-constituted "1st Canadian Infantry Division", was disbanded in 1958.

2nd Signal Regiment (Militia)
The regiment was amalgamated with the "8th Signal Regiment (Militia)" in 1965 and re-designated "Toronto Signal Regiment (Militia)".
"Headquarters" was incorporated within the "Toronto Signal Regiment".
"1" Squadron — TORONTO, Ontario
The squadron was re-organized in 1965 as "1" Squadron of the "Toronto Signal Regiment".
"2" Squadron — PORT CREDIT, Ontario
The squadron, which had been relocated from Kingston in 1954, was disbanded in 1965.
"3" Squadron — TORONTO, Ontario
The squadron was re-organized in 1965 as "3" Squadron of the "Toronto Signal Regiment".

3rd Signal Regiment (Militia) — OTTAWA, Ontario
The regiment was re-organized in 1970 and re-designated "703 (Reserve) Communications Regiment".

5th Signal Regiment (Militia) — CHARLOTTETOWN, Prince Edward Island
The regiment was re-organized in 1970 and re-designated "721 (Reserve) Communications Regiment".

8th Signal Regiment (Militia) — TORONTO, Ontario
The regiment was amalgamated with the "2nd Signal Regiment (Militia)" in 1965 and re-designated "Toronto Signal Regiment (Militia)".
"Headquarters" was incorporated within the "Toronto Signal Regiment".
"1" Squadron was disbanded in 1965.
"2" Squadron was re-organized in 1965 as "2" Squadron of the "Toronto Signal Regiment".
"3" Squadron was disbanded in 1965.

1st Independent Signal Squadron (Militia) — HAMILTON, Ontario
The squadron was re-organized in 1970 and re-designated "705 (Reserve) Communications Squadron".

2nd Independent Signal Squadron (Militia) — REGINA, Saskatchewan
The squadron, which maintained a detached troop at Saskatoon until 1965, was re-organized in 1970 and re-designated "734 (Reserve) Communications Squadron".

3rd Independent Signal Squadron (Militia) — QUEBEC CITY
The squadron was re-organized in 1970 and re-designated "713 (Reserve) Communications Regiment".

4th Independent Signal Squadron (Militia) — MONCTON, New Brunswick
The squadron was disbanded in 1965.

5th Independent Signal Squadron (Militia) — SAINT JOHN, New Brunswick
The squadron was re-organized in 1970 and re-designated "722 (Reserve) Communications Squadron".

6th Independent Signal Squadron (Militia) — FREDERICTON, New Brunswick
The squadron was disbanded in 1965.

7th Independent Signal Squadron (Militia) —CALGARY, Alberta
The squadron was re-organized in 1970 and re-designated "746 (Reserve) Communications Squadron".

8th Independent Signal Squadron (Militia) — EDMONTON, Alberta
The squadron, which maintained a detached troop at Wetaskiwin until 1965, was re-organized in 1970 and re-designated "745 (Reserve) Communications Squadron".

9th Independent Signal Squadron (Militia) — LONDON, Ontario
The squadron was disbanded in 1970.

10th Independent Signal Squadron (Militia) — WINNIPEG, Manitoba
The squadron was re-organized in 1970 and re-designated "735 (Reserve) Communications Regiment".

11th Independent Signal Squadron (Militia) —WESTMOUNT (MONTREAL), Quebec
The squadron was re-organized in 1970 and re-designated "712 (Reserve) Communications Squadron".

12th Independent Signal Squadron (Militia) — SHERBROOKE, Quebec
The squadron was re-organized in 1970 and re-designated "714 (Reserve) Communications Squadron".

East Coast Signal Regiment (Militia)
"Headquarters" was disbanded in 1965 at Halifax.
1st Area Signal Squadron — HALIFAX, Nova Scotia
The "1st Area Signal Squadron" was re-organized in 1970 and re-designated "723 (Reserve) Communications Squadron".
2nd Area Signal Squadron — HALIFAX, Nova Scotia
The "2nd Area Signal Squadron", which was re-formed in 1954 to replace the original squadron which had been re-organized as the "5th Independent Signal Squadron (Militia)", was disbanded in 1965.

West Coast Signal Regiment (Militia)
"Headquarters" was disbanded in 1965 at Vancouver.
3rd Area Signal Squadron — VANCOUVER, British Columbia
The "3rd Area Signal Squadron" was re-organized in 1970 and re-designated "744 (Reserve) Communications Regiment".
The "4th Area Signal Squadron" was disbanded in 1965 at Vancouver.
The "5th Area Signal Squadron" was disbanded in 1965 at Victoria.

1st Signal Squadron (Regular) — CALGARY, Alberta
The squadron, which had been formed in 1958 to support the "1st Canadian Infantry Brigade Group", was re-organized in 1977 and re-designated "1 Canadian Brigade Group Headquarters and Signal Squadron".

2nd Signal Squadron (Regular) — CAMP PETAWAWA, Ontario
The squadron, which had been formed in 1958 to support the "2nd Canadian Infantry Brigade Group", was re-organized in 1977 and re-designated "Special Service Force Headquarters and Signal Squadron".

3rd Signal Squadron (Regular) — CAMP GAGETOWN, New Brunswick
The squadron, which had been formed in 1958 to support the "3rd Canadian Infantry Brigade Group", was disbanded in 1970 upon the replacement of the "3rd Canadian Infantry Brigade Group" by the "Combat Training Centre".

4th Signal Squadron (Regular) — SOEST, West Germany
The squadron, which had been formed in 1958 to support the "4th Canadian Infantry Brigade Group", was re-organized in 1977 and re-designated "4 Canadian Mechanized Brigade Group Headquarters and Signal Squadron".

5th Signal Squadron (Regular) — CAMP BARRIEFIELD, Ontario
The squadron, which had been formed in 1958 for electronic counter-measures, was incorporated within the "1st Canadian Signal Regiment (Regular)" in 1968.

6th Signal Squadron (Regular) — CAMP VALCARTIER, Quebec
The squadron, which had been formed in 1961 to support the "Defence of Canada Force", was re-designated "5ieme Escadron des Transmissions" in 1968.

1st Airborne Signal Troop (Regular) — CALGARY, Alberta
The troop, which had been formed in 1958 to support the airborne elements of the "1st Canadian Infantry Brigade Group", was disbanded in 1968.

2nd Airborne Signal Troop (Regular) — CAMP BORDEN, Ontario
The troop, which had been formed in 1958 to support the airborne elements of the "2nd Canadian Infantry Brigade Group", was disbanded in 1968.

3rd Airborne Signal Troop (Regular) — CAMP GAGETOWN, New Brunswick
The troop, which had been formed in 1958 to support the airborne elements of the "3rd Canadian Infantry Brigade Group", was disbanded in 1968.

Toronto Signal Regiment (Militia) — Fort York Armoury, TORONTO, Ontario
The regiment, which maintained a detached troop at Newmarket until 1970, was re-organized in 1970 and re-designated "709 (Reserve) Communications Regiment".

1st Canadian Signal Regiment — MacNaughton Barracks, CAMP BARRIEFIELD, Ontario
The regiment was formed in 1968 and provided the "Canadian Signal Squadron" which served with the "United Nations Interim Force" in Lebanon in 1978.

700 (Reserve) Communications Squadron — CAMP BORDEN, Ontario
The squadron was formed in 1977.

701 Communications Squadron (Regular) — CARP, Ontario
The squadron was formed in 1970.

702 Communications Squadron (Regular) — CAMP PETAWAWA, Ontario
The squadron was formed in 1970 by the re-organization and re-designation of the "Camp Petawawa Signal Troop (Regular)".

703 (Reserve) Communications Regiment — OTTAWA, Ontario
The regiment was re-designated "763 (Reserve) Communications Regiment" in 1977.

704 Communications Squadron (Regular) — OTTAWA, Ontario
The squadron, which had been formed in 1970 by the re-organization and re-designation of the "Eastern Ontario Signal Squadron (Regular)", was re-designated "764 Communications Squadron (Regular)" in 1977.

705 (Reserve) Communications Squadron — HAMILTON, Ontario

706 Communications Squadron (Regular) — CAMP BORDEN, Ontario
The squadron was formed in 1970 by the re-organization and re-designation of the "Central Ontario Signal Squadron (Regular)".

707 Communications Squadron (Regular) —NORTH BAY, Ontario
The squadron was formed in 1970.

708 Communications Squadron (Regular) — TRENTON, Ontario
The squadron was formed in 1970.

709 (Reserve) Communications Regiment — Fort York Armoury, TORONTO, Ontario

"710" Not Allocated

711 Communications Squadron (Regular) — CAMP VALCARTIER, Quebec
The squadron was formed in 1970 by the re-organization and re-designation of the "Eastern Quebec Signal Troop (Regular)".

712 (Reserve) Communications Squadron — MONTREAL, Quebec

713 (Reserve) Communications Regiment — BEAUPORT, Quebec

714 (Reserve) Communications Squadron — SHERBROOKE, Quebec

715 Communications Squadron (Regular) — ST-HUBERT, Quebec
The squadron was formed in 1970 by the re-organization and re-designation of the "Western Quebec Signal Squadron (Regular)".

"716" Not Allocated

"717" Not Allocated

"718" Not Allocated

"719" Not Allocated

720 Communications Squadron (Regular) — CAMP DEBERT, Nova Scotia
The squadron was formed in 1970.

721 (Reserve) Communications Regiment — CHARLOTTETOWN, Prince Edward Island

722 (Reserve) Communications Squadron — SAINT JOHN, New Brunswick

723 (Reserve) Communications Squadron — HALIFAX, Nova Scotia

724 Communications Squadron (Regular) — CAMP GAGETOWN, New Brunswick
The squadron was formed in 1970 by the re-organization and re-designation of the "New Brunswick Signal Troop (Regular)".

"725" Not Allocated

726 Communications Squadron (Regular) — HALIFAX, Nova Scotia
The squadron was formed in 1970 by the re-organization and re-designation of the "Nova Scotia Signal Squadron (Regular)".

727 Communications Squadron (Regular) — ST. JOHN'S, Newfoundland
The squadron was formed in 1970 by the re-organization and re-designation of the "Newfoundland Signal Troop (Regular)".

728 (Reserve) Communications Squadron — ST. JOHN'S, Newfoundland
The squadron was formed in 1970.

"729" Not Allocated

"730" Not Allocated

731 Communications Squadron (Regular) — CAMP SHILO, Manitoba
The squadron was formed in 1970 by the re-organization and re-designation of the "Manitoba Signal Squadron (Regular)".

"732" Not Allocated

"733" Not Allocated

734 (Reserve) Communications Squadron — REGINA, Saskatchewan

735 (Reserve) Communications Regiment — WINNIPEG, Manitoba

736 (Reserve) Communications Squadron — THUNDER BAY, Ontario

737 (Reserve) Communications Troop — SASKATOON, Saskatchewan
The troop was formed in 1977.

"738" Not Allocated

"739" Not Allocated

740 Communications Squadron (Regular) — NANAIMO, British Columba
The squadron was formed in 1970.

741 (Reserve) Communications Squadron — VICTORIA, British Columbia
The squadron was formed in 1970.

742 Communications Squadron (Regular) — EDMONTON, Alberta
The squadron was formed in 1970 by the re-organization and re-desination of the "Alberta Signal Squadron (Regular)".

743 Communications Squadron (Regular) — PENHOLD, Alberta
The squadron was formed in 1970.

744 (Reserve) Communications Regiment — VANCOUVER, British Columbia

745 (Reserve) Communications Squadron — EDMONTON, Alberta

746 (Reserve) Communications Squadron — CALGARY, Alberta

747 Communications Squadron (Regular) — ESQUIMALT (VICTORIA), British Columbia
The squadron was formed in 1970.

748 (Reserve) Communications Troop — NANAIMO, British Columbia
The troop was formed in 1977.

749 (Reserve) Communications Troop — RED DEER, Alberta
The troop was formed in 1977.

750 Communications Squadron (Regular) — LAHR, West Germany
The squadron was formed in 1970.

"751" Not Allocated

"752" Not Allocated

"753" Not Allocated

"754" Not Allocated

"755" Not Allocated

"56 Canadian Signal Squadron", which was formed in 1956, served with the "United Nations Emergency Force" in the Middle East until disbanded in 1967.

"57 Canadian Signal Squadron", which was formed in 1960, served with the "United Nations Organization" in the Congo until disbanded in 1964.

"758" Not Allocated

"759" Not Allocated

"760" Not Allocated

"761" Not Allocated

"762" Not Allocated

763 (Reserve) Communications Regiment — OTTAWA, Ontario

764 Communications Squadron (Regular) — OTTAWA, Ontario

"765" Not Allocated

"766" Not Allocated

"767" Not Allocated

"768" Not Allocated

"769" Not Allocated

770 Communications Research Squadron (Regular) — GANDER, Newfoundland

THE ROYAL CANADIAN ARMY SERVICE CORPS

Corps March: *"WAIT FOR THE WAGON"*
Corps Motto: *"NIL SINE LABORE"*
   ("NOTHING WITHOUT LABOUR")
Corps School: CAMP BORDEN, Ontario

NOTE

A "Corps of Military Staff Clerks" provided personnel for administrative support at the various headquarters during both the Great War and the Second World War. These duties were subsequently undertaken by the "Royal Canadian Army Service Corps".

1 Transport Company (Reserve Force) — LONDON, Ontario
"1 Company, C.A.S.C." was formed in 1901 at London. "1 Infantry Brigade Company, R.C.A.S.C." served in both Italy and North-West Europe during the Second World War and was perpetuated by "1 Transport Company" which supported "1 Infantry Brigade", a formation of the "1st Division" (Reserve Force). "1 Transport Company" was amalgamated with "2 Transport Company" in 1954 and re-designated "132 Transport Company, R.C.A.S.C. (Militia)".

2 Transport Company (Reserve Force) — LONDON, Ontario
"2 Company, C.A.S.C." was formed in 1901 at Toronto. "2 Infantry Brigade Company, R.C.A.S.C." served in both Italy and North-West Europe during the Second World War and was perpetuated by "2 Transport Company" which supported "2 Infantry Brigade", a formation of the "1st Division" (Reserve Force). "2 Transport Company" was amalgamated with "1 Transport Company" in 1954 and re-designated "132 Transport Company, R.C.A.S.C. (Militia)".

3 Transport Company (Reserve Force) — KITCHENER, Ontario
"3 Company, C.A.S.C." was formed in 1901 at Kingston. "3 Infantry Brigade Company, R.C.A.S.C." served in both Italy and North-West Europe during the Second World War and was perpetuated by "3 Transport Company" which supported "3 Infantry Brigade", a formation of the "1st Division" (Reserve Force). "3 Transport Company" was re-designated "137 Transport Company, R.C.A.S.C. (Militia)" in 1954.

4 Transport Company (Reserve Force) — TORONTO, Ontario
"4 Company, C.A.S.C." was formed in 1901 at Montreal. "4 Infantry Brigade Company, R.C.A.S.C." served in North-West Europe during the Second World War and was perpetuated by "4 Transport Company" which supported "4 Infantry Brigade", a formation of the "2nd Division" (Reserve Force). "4 Transport Company" was re-designated "134 Transport Company, R.C.A.S.C. (Militia)" in 1954.

5 Transport Company (Reserve Force) — TORONTO, Ontario
"5 Company, C.A.S.C." was formed in 1903 at Ottawa. "5 Infantry Brigade Company, R.C.A.S.C." served in North-West Europe during the Second World War and was perpetuated by "5 Transport Company" which supported "5 Infantry Brigade", a formation of the "2nd Division" (Reserve Force). "5 Transport Company" was re-designated "135 Transport Company, R.C.A.S.C. (Militia)" in 1954.

6 Transport Company (Reserve Force) — TORONTO, Ontario
"6 Company, C.A.S.C." was formed in 1903 at Sherbrooke. "6 Infantry Brigade Company, R.C.A.S.C." served in North-West Europe during the Second World War and was perpetuated by "6 Transport Company" which supported "6 Infantry Brigade", a formation of the "2nd Division" (Reserve Force). "6 Transport Company" was re-designated "136 Transport Company, R.C.A.S.C. (Militia)" in 1954.

7 Transport Company (Reserve Force) — VERDUN (MONTREAL), Quebec
"7 Company, C.A.S.C." was formed in 1903 at Saint John. "7 Infantry Brigade Company, R.C.A.S.C." served in North-West Europe during the Second World War and was perpetuated by "7 Transport Company" which supported "7 Infantry Brigade", a formation of the "3rd Division" (Reserve Force). "7 Transport Company" was re-designated "122 Transport Company, R.C.A.S.C. (Militia)" in 1954.

8 Transport Company (Reserve Force) — VERDUN (MONTREAL), Quebec
"8 Company, C.A.S.C." was formed in 1903 at Kentville, Nova Scotia. "8 Infantry Brigade Company, R.C.A.S.C." served in North-West Europe during the Second World War and was perpetuated by "8 Transport Company" which supported "8 Infantry Brigade", a formation of the "3rd Division" (Reserve Force). "8 Transport Company" was re-designated "123 Transport Company, R.C.A.S.C. (Militia)" in 1954.

9 Transport Company (Reserve Force) — VERDUN (MONTREAL), Quebec
"9 Company, C.A.S.C." was formed in 1905 at Hamilton. "9 Infantry Brigade Company, R.C.A.S.C." served in North-West Europe during the Second World War and was perpetuated by "9 Transport Company" which supported "9 Infantry Brigade", a formation of the "3rd Division" (Reserve Force). "9 Transport Company" was re-designated "124 Transport Company, R.C.A.S.C. (Militia)" in 1954.

10 Transport Company (Reserve Force) — SHERBROOKE, Quebec
"10 Company, C.A.S.C." was formed in 1905 at Quebec City. "10 Infantry Brigade Company, R.C.A.S.C." served in North-West Europe during the Second World War and was perpetuated by "10 Transport Company" which supported "10 Infantry Brigade", a formation of the "4th Division" (Reserve Force). "10 Transport Company" was re-designated "125 Transport Company, R.C.A.S.C. (Militia)" in 1954.

11 Transport Company (Reserve Force) — VERDUN (MONTREAL), Quebec
"11 Company, C.A.S.C." was formed in 1905 at Winnipeg. "11 Infantry Brigade Company, R.C.A.S.C." served in both Italy and North-West Europe during the Second World War and was perpetuated by "11 Transport Company" which supported "11 Infantry Brigade", a formation of the "4th Division" (Reserve Force). "11 Transport Company" was disbanded in 1954.

12 Transport Company (Reserve Force) — VERDUN (MONTREAL), Quebec
"12 Company, C.A.S.C." was formed in 1907 at Toronto. "12 Infantry Brigade Company, R.C.A.S.C." served in Italy during the Second World War and was perpetuated by "12 Transport Company" which supported "12 Infantry Brigade", a formation of the "4th Division" (Reserve Force). "12 Transport Company" was disbanded in 1954.

13 Transport Company (Reserve Force) — HALIFAX, Nova Scotia
The company, which supported "13 Infantry Brigade", a formation of the "5th Division" (Reserve Force), was amalgamated with "14 Transport Company" in 1954 and re-designated "110 Transport Company, R.C.A.S.C. (Militia)".

14 Transport Company (Reserve Force) — HALIFAX, Nova Scotia
"14 Company, C.A.S.C." was formed in 1910 at Calgary. "14 Transport Company", which supported "14 Infantry Brigade", a formation of the "5th Division" (Reserve Force), was amalgamated with "13 Transport Company" in 1954 and re-designated "110 Transport Company, R.C.A.S.C. (Militia)".

15 Transport Company (Reserve Force) — VANCOUVER, British Columbia
15 Company, C.A.S.C." was formed in 1910 at Montreal. "15 Transport Company", which supported "15 Infantry Brigade", a formation of the "5th Division" (Reserve Force), was re-designated "156 Transport Company, R.C.A.S.C. (Militia)" in 1954.

16 Transport Company (Reserve Force) — WINNIPEG, Manitoba
"16 Company, C.A.S.C." was formed in 1912 at London. "16 Transport Company", which supported "16 Infantry Brigade", a formation of the "6th Division" (Reserve Force), was re-designated "140 Transport Company, R.C.A.S.C. (Militia)" in 1954.

17 Transport Company (Reserve Force) — WINNIPEG, Manitoba
"17 Company, C.A.S.C." was formed in 1912 at St-Raymond, Quebec. "17 Transport Company", which supported "17 Infantry Brigade", a formation of the "6th Division" (Reserve Force), was re-designated "141 Transport Company, R.C.A.S.C. (Militia)" in 1954 and relocated at Brandon.

18 Transport Company (Reserve Force) — WINNIPEG, Manitoba
"18 Company, C.A.S.C." was formed in 1912 at Winnipeg. "18 Transport Company", which

supported "18 Infantry Brigade", a formation of the "6th Division" (Reserve Force), was re-designated "143 Transport Company, R.C.A.S.C. (Militia)" in 1954.

19 Transport Company (Reserve Force) — HAMILTON, Ontario
"19 Company, C.A.S.C." was formed in 1912 at Vancouver. "1 Armoured Brigade Company, R.C.A.S.C." served in both Italy and North-West Europe during the Second World War and was perpetuated by "19 Transport Company" which supported "19 Armoured Brigade" (Reserve Force). "19 Transport Company" was re-designated "133 Transport Company, R.C.A.S.C. (Militia)" in 1954.

20 Transport Company (Reserve Force) — VERDUN (MONTREAL), Quebec
"2 Armoured Brigade Company, R.C.A.S.C." served in North-West Europe during the Second World War and was perpetuated by "20 Transport Company" which supported "20 Armoured Brigade" (Reserve Force). "20 Transport Company" was disbanded in 1954.

21 Transport Company (Reserve Force) — SAINT JOHN, New Brunswick
"4 Armoured Brigade Company, R.C.A.S.C." served in North-West Europe during the Second World War and was perpetuated by "21 Transport Company" which supported "21 Armoured Brigade" (Reserve Force). "21 Transport Company" was re-designated "112 Transport Company, R.C.A.S.C. (Militia)" in 1954.

22 Transport Company (Reserve Force) — REGINA, Saskatchewan
"5 Armoured Brigade Company, R.C.A.S.C." served in both Italy and North-West Europe during the Second World War and was perpetuated by "22 Transport Company" which supported "22 Armoured Brigade" (Reserve Force). "22 Transport Company" was re-designated "142 Transport Company, R.C.A.S.C. (Militia)" in 1954.

23 Transport Company (Active Force) — CAMP BORDEN, Ontario
The company, which had been formed in 1946 as "23 Brigade Group Company, R.C.A.S.C." to support the "23rd Canadian Infantry Brigade Group", served in Korea and was subsequently re-designated "1 Transport Company", a sub-unit of the "1st Infantry Divisional Column, R.C.A.S.C. (Regular)" which had been formed in 1953 to support the re-constituted "1st Canadian Infantry Division". "1 Transport Company, R.C.A.S.C. (Regular)" was re-organized in 1958 as a unit of the "1st Canadian Infantry Brigade Group" and was further re-organized in 1965 as a sub-unit of "1 Service Battalion". The company was further re-organized in 1970 as the "transport company" of "1 Service Battalion" which is a unit of "1 Canadian Brigade Group" at Calgary.

24 Transport Company (Reserve Force) — WINDSOR, Ontario
The "1st Divisional Train, C.A.S.C." served in France during the Great War. The "1st Divisional Troops Company, R.C.A.S.C." served in both Italy and North-West Europe during the Second World War. "24 Transport Company", which had been formed in 1946 to support the "1st Division" (Reserve Force), was disbanded in 1954.

25 Transport Company (Reserve Force) — TORONTO, Ontario
The "2nd Divisional Train, C.A.S.C." served in France during the Great War. The "2nd Divisional Troops Company, R.C.A.S.C." served in North-West Europe during the Second World War. "25 Transport Company", which had been formed in 1946 to support the "2nd Division" (Reserve Force), was disbanded in 1954.

26 Transport Company (Reserve Force) — VERDUN (MONTREAL), Quebec
The "3rd Divisional Train, C.A.S.C." served in France during the Great War. The "3rd Divisional Troops Company, R.C.A.S.C." served in North-West Europe during the Second World War. "26 Transport Company", which had been formed in 1946 to support the "3rd Division" (Reserve Force), was disbanded in 1954.

27 Transport Company (Reserve Force) — VERDUN (MONTREAL), Quebec
The "4th Divisional Train, C.A.S.C." served in France during the Great War. The "4th Divisional Troops Company, R.S.C.A.S.C." served in North-West Europe during the Second World War. "27 Transport Company", which had been formed in 1946 to support the "4th Division" (Reserve Force), was disbanded in 1954.

28 Transport Company (Reserve Force) — PICTOU, Nova Scotia
The "5th Divisional Troops Company, R.C.A.S.C." served in both Italy and North-West Europe during the Second World War. "28 Transport Company", which had been formed in 1946 to support the "5th Division" (Reserve Force), was disbanded in 1954.

29 Transport Company (Reserve Force) — WINNIPEG, Manitoba
The company, which had been formed in 1946 to support the "6th Division" (Reserve Force), was disbanded in 1954.

30 Transport Company (Reserve Force) — OTTAWA, Ontario
The company, which had been formed in 1946 to support the "1st Corps" (Reserve Force), was re-designated "130 Transport Company, R.C.A.S.C. (Militia)" in 1954.

31 Supply Company (Reserve Force) — CARLETON PLACE, Ontario
"31 Corps Troops Company, R.C.A.S.C." served in both Italy and North-West Europe during the Second World War. "31 Supply Company", which had been formed in 1946 to support the "1st Corps" (Reserve Force), was disbanded in 1954.

32 Transport Company (Reserve Force) — CALGARY, Alberta
"32 Corps Troops Company, R.C.A.S.C." served in both Italy and North-West Europe during the Second World War. "32 Transport Company", which had been formed in 1946 to support the "2nd Corps" (Reserve Force), was re-designated "150 Transport Company, R.C.A.S.C. (Militia)" in 1954.

33 Supply Company (Reserve Force) — EDMONTON, Alberta
"33 Corps Troops Company, R.C.A.S.C." served in North-West Europe during the Second World War. "33 Supply Company", which had been formed in 1946 to support the "2nd Corps" (Reserve Force), was disbanded in 1954.

34 Transport Company (Reserve Force) — OTTAWA, Ontario
"34 Corps Troops Company, R.C.A.S.C." served in North-West Europe during the Second World War. "34 Transport Company", which had been formed in 1946 to support the "1st Corps" (Reserve Force), was disbanded in 1954.

35 Transport Company (Reserve Force) — CALGARY, Alberta
"35 Composite Company, R.C.A.S.C." served in North-West Europe during the Second World War. "35 Transport Company", which had been formed in 1946 to support the "2nd Corps" (Reserve Force), was disbanded in 1954.

"36" Not Allocated

"37" Not Allocated

38 Medium Regiment Platoon (Reserve Force) — LONDON, Ontario

The platoon, which had been formed in 1946 to support the medium artillery of the "1st Division" (Reserve Force), was disbanded in 1954.

39 Medium Regiment Platoon (Reserve Force) — HAMILTON, Ontario
The platoon, which had been formed in 1946 to support the medium artillery of the "2nd Division" (Reserve Force), was disbanded in 1954.

40 Medium Regiment Platoon (Reserve Force) — TORONTO, Ontario
The platoon, which had been formed in 1946 to support the medium artillery of the "3rd Division" (Reserve Force), was disbanded in 1954.

41 Medium Regiment Platoon (Reserve Force) — OTTAWA, Ontario
The platoon, which had been formed in 1946 to support the medium artillery of the "4th Division" (Reserve Force), was disbanded in 1954.

42 Medium Regiment Platoon (Reserve Force) — VERDUN (MONTREAL), Quebec
The platoon, which had been formed in 1946 to support the medium artillery of the "5th Division" (Reserve Force), was disbanded in 1954.

43 Medium Regiment Platoon (Reserve Force) — WINNIPEG, Manitoba
The platoon, which had been formed in 1946 to support the medium artillery of the "6th Division" (Reserve Force), was disbanded in 1954.

44 Medium Regiment Platoon (Reserve Force) — REGINA, Saskatchewan
The platoon, which had been formed in 1946 to support the medium artillery of the "1st Corps" (Reserve Force), was disbanded in 1954.

45 Medium Regiment Platoon (Reserve Force) — CALGARY, Alberta
The platoon, which had been formed in 1946 to support the medium artillery of the "2nd Corps" (Reserve Force), was disbanded in 1954.

"46" Not Allocated

"47" Not Allocated

48 Tipper Company (Reserve Force) — ARNPRIOR, Ontario
The company, which had been formed in 1946 to support the "1st Corps" (Reserve Force), was disbanded in 1954.

49 Tipper Company (Reserve Force) — DAWSON CREEK, British Columbia
The company, which had been formed in 1946 to support the "2nd Corps" (Reserve Force), was disbanded in 1954.

50 Transport Company (Reserve Force) — KINGSTON, Ontario
The company, which had been formed in 1946 to support the "1st Corps" (Reserve Force), was re-organized in 1954 as a detached platoon of "130 Transport Company, R.C.A.S.C. (Militia)".

51 Transport Company (Reserve Force) — EDMONTON, Alberta
The company, which had been formed in 1946 to support the "2nd Corps" (Reserve Force), was re-designated "154 Transport Company, R.C.A.S.C. (Militia)" in 1954.

"52" Not Allocated

"53" Not Allocated

"54 Transport Company" served in Korea and was subsequently re-designated "2 Transport Company", a sub-unit of the "1st Infantry Divisional Column, R.C.A.S.C. (Regular)" which had been formed in 1953 to support the re-constituted "1st Canadian Infantry Division". "2 Transport Company, R.C.A.S.C. (Regular)" was re-organized in 1958 as a unit of the "2nd Canadian Infantry Brigade Group" and was further re-organized in 1965 as a sub-unit of "2 Service Battalion". The company was further re-organized in 1970 as the "transport company" of "2 Service Battalion" which supports the "Special Service Force" at Camp Petawawa.

"55 Transport Company" was re-designated "3 Transport Company" which served in Korea subsequent to the armistice after which it was re-organized as a sub-unit of the "1st Infantry Divisional Column, R.C.A.S.C. (Regular)" which had been formed in 1953 to support the re-constituted "1st Canadian Infantry Division". "3 Transport Company, R.C.A.S.C. (Regular)" was re-organized in 1958 as a unit of the "3rd Canadian Infantry Brigade Group" and was further re-organized in 1965 as a sub-unit of "3 Service Battalion". The company was disbanded in 1970 at Camp Gagetown upon the replacement of the "3rd Canadian Infantry Brigade Group" by the "Combat Training Centre".

"56 Transport Company" served in Korea and was subsequently re-designated "4 Transport Company", a sub-unit of the "1st Infantry Divisional Column, R.C.A.S.C. (Regular)" which had been formed in 1953 to support the re-constituted "1st Canadian Infantry Division". "4 Transport Company, R.C.A.S.C. (Regular)" was re-organized in 1958 as a unit of the "4th Canadian Infantry Brigade Group" and was further re-organized in 1965 as a sub-unit of "4 Service Battalion". The company was further re-organized in 1970 as the "transport company" of "4 Service Battalion" which is a unit of "4 Canadian Mechanized Brigade Group" at Lahr in West Germany.

"57 Transport Company" served in Japan as an element of "Canadian Base Units, Korea".

"58 Transport Company" served in Japan as an element of "Canadian Base Units, Korea".

"1 Airborne Platoon, R.C.A.S.C. (Regular)" was disbanded in 1958 as a unit of the "Mobile Striking Force".

110 Transport Company (Militia) — HALIFAX, Nova Scotia
The company, which maintained a detached platoon at Charlottetown, P.E.I. until 1965, was a sub-unit of "1 Column, R.C.A.S.C." until 1965 when it was re-organized as a sub-unit of the "Halifax Service Battalion" and was re-organized in 1970 as the "transport company" of the battalion which was re-designated "33 (Halifax) Service Battalion" in 1975.

111 Transport Company (Militia) — SYDNEY, Nova Scotia
The company, which maintained a detached platoon at St. John's, Newfoundland until 1965, was a sub-unit of "1 Column, R.C.A.S.C." until 1965 when it was re-organized as a sub-unit of the "Sydney Service Battalion" and was re-organized in 1970 as the "transport company" of the battalion which was re-designated "35 (Sydney) Service Battalion" in 1975.

112 Transport Company (Militia) — SAINT JOHN, New Brunswick
The company was a sub-unit of "1 Column, R.C.A.S.C." until 1965 when it was re-organized as a sub-unit of the "Saint John Service Battalion" and was re-organized in 1970 as the "transport company" of the battalion which was re-designated "31 (Saint John) Service Battalion" in 1975.

113 Transport Company (Militia) — MONCTON, New Brunswick
The company was a sub-unit of "1 Column, R.C.A.S.C." until 1965 when it was re-organized as a sub-unit of the "Moncton Service Battalion" and was re-organized in 1970 as the "transport company" of the battalion which was re-designated "32 (Moncton) Service Battalion" in 1975.

120 Transport Company (Militia) — QUEBEC CITY
The company, a sub-unit of "2 Column, R.C.A.S.C.", was re-organized in 1965 as a sub-unit of the "Quebec Service Battalion" and was re-organized in 1970 as the "transport company" of the battalion which was re-designated "55 (Quebec) Bataillon des Services" in 1975.

121 Transport Company (Militia) — QUEBEC CITY
The company was disbanded in 1965 as a sub-unit of "2 Column, R.C.A.S.C.".

122 Transport Company (Militia) — MONTREAL, Quebec
The company, a sub-unit of "3 Column, R.C.A.S.C.", was re-organized in 1965 as a sub-unit of the "1st Montreal Service Battalion" and was amalgamated with "124 Transport Company" in 1970 and re-organized as the "transport company" of the "Montreal Service Battalion" which was re-designated "51 (Montreal) Service Battalion" in 1975.

123 Transport Company (Militia) — MONTREAL, Quebec
The company was disbanded in 1965 as a sub-unit of "3 Column, R.C.A.S.C.".

124 Transport Company (Militia) — MONTREAL, Quebec
The company, a sub-unit of "3 Column, R.C.A.S.C.", was re-organized in 1965 as a sub-unit of the "2nd Montreal Service Battalion" and was amalgamated with "122 Transport Company" in 1970 and re-organized as the "transport company" of the "Montreal Service Battalion" which was re-designated "51 (Montreal) Service Battalion" in 1975.

125 Transport Company (Militia) — SHERBROOKE, Quebec
The company was disbanded in 1965 as a sub-unit of "2 Column, R.C.A.S.C.".

126 Transport Company (Militia) — TROIS-RIVIERES, Quebec
The company was disbanded in 1965 as a sub-unit of "2 Column, R.C.A.S.C.".

130 Transport Company (Militia) — OTTAWA, Ontario
The company, which maintained a detached platoon at Kingston until 1965, was a sub-unit of "4 Column, R.C.A.S.C." until 1965 when it was re-organized as a sub-unit of the "Ottawa Service Battalion" and was re-organized in 1970 as the "transport company" of the battalion which was re-designated "28 (Ottawa) Service Battalion" in 1975.

131 Transport Company (Militia) — PETERBOROUGH, Ontario
The company was disbanded in 1965 as a sub-unit of "4 Column, R.C.A.S.C.".

132 Transport Company (Militia) — LONDON, Ontario
The company was a sub-unit of "4 Column, R.C.A.S.C." until 1965 when it was re-organized as a sub-unit of the "London Service Battalion" and was re-organized in 1970 as the "transport company" of the battalion which was re-designated "22 (London) Service Battalion" in 1975.

133 Transport Company (Militia) — HAMILTON, Ontario
The company was a sub-unit of "5 Column, R.C.A.S.C." until 1965 when it was re-organized as a sub-unit of the "Hamilton Service Battalion" and was re-organized in 1970 as the "transport company" of the battalion which was re-designated "23 (Hamilton) Service Battalion" in 1975.

134 Transport Company (Militia) — Denison Armoury, DOWNSVIEW (TORONTO), Ontario
The company was a sub-unit of "5 Column, R.C.A.S.C." until 1965 when it was re-organized as a sub-unit of the "1st Toronto Service Battalion" and was amalgamated with "136 Transport Company" in 1970 and re-organized as the "transport company" of the "Toronto Service Battalion" which was re-designated "25 (Toronto) Service Battalion" in 1975.

135 Transport Company (Militia) — Denison Armoury, DOWNSVIEW (TORONTO), Ontario
The company was disbanded in 1965 as a sub-unit of "5 Column, R.C.A.S.C.".

136 Transport Company (Militia) — Moss Park Armoury, TORONTO, Ontario
The company was a sub-unit of "5 Column, R.C.A.S.C." until 1965 when it was re-organized as a sub-unit of the "2nd Toronto Service Battalion" and was amalgamated with "134 Transport Company" in 1970 and re-organized as the "transport company" of the "Toronto Service Battalion" which was re-designated "25 (Toronto) Service Battalion" in 1975.

"5 Column, R.C.A.S.C. (Militia)", prior to disbandment in 1965, maintained a detached platoon at Owen Sound.

137 Transport Company (Militia) — KITCHENER, Ontario
The company was disbanded in 1965 as a sub-unit of "4 Column, R.C.A.S.C.".

138 Transport Company (Militia) — PORT ARTHUR (THUNDER BAY), Ontario
The company was formed in 1954 and re-organized in 1965 as a sub-unit of the "Lakehead Service Battalion" and was re-organized in 1970 as the "transport company" of the battalion which was re-designated "18 (Thunder Bay) Service Battalion" in 1975.

140 Transport Company (Militia) — WINNIPEG, Manitoba
The company was a sub-unit of "6 Column, R.C.A.S.C." until 1965 when it was re-organized as a sub-unit of the "Winnipeg Service Battalion" and was re-organized in 1970 as the "transport company" of the battalion which was re-designated "17 (Winnipeg) Service Battalion" in 1975.

141 Transport Company (Militia) — BRANDON, Manitoba
The company was disbanded in 1965 as a sub-unit of "6 Column, R.C.A.S.C.".

142 Transport Company (Militia) — REGINA, Saskatchewan
The company, which maintained a detached platoon at Moose Jaw until 1965, was a sub-unit of "6 Column, R.C.A.S.C." until 1965 when it was re-organized as a sub-unit of the "Regina Service Battalion" and was re-organized in 1970 as the "transport company" of the battalion which was re-designated "16 (Regina) Service Battalion" in 1975.

143 Transport Company (Militia) — WINNIPEG, Manitoba
The company was disbanded in 1965 as a sub-unit of "6 Column, R.C.A.S.C.".

150 Transport Company (Militia) — CALGARY, Alberta
The company was a sub-unit of "7 Column, R.C.A.S.C." until 1965 when it was re-organized as a

sub-unit of the "Calgary Service Battalion" and was re-organized in 1970 as the "transport company" of the battalion which was re-designated "14 (Calgary) Service Battalion" in 1975.

151 Transport Company (Militia) — RED DEER, Alberta
The company was disbanded in 1965 as a sub-unit of "7 Column, R.C.A.S.C.".

152 Transport Company (Militia) — ABBOTSFORD, British Columbia
The company was disbanded in 1965 as a sub-unit of "8 Column, R.C.A.S.C.".

153 Transport Company (Militia) — HIGH RIVER, Alberta
The company, which maintained a detached platoon at Medicine Hat, was disbanded in 1965 as a sub-unit of "7 Column, R.C.A.S.C.".

154 Transport Company (Militia) — EDMONTON, Alberta
The company was a sub-unit of "7 Column, R.C.A.S.C." until 1965 when it was re-organized as a sub-unit of the "Edmonton Service Battalion" and was re-organized in 1970 as the "transport company" of the battalion which was re-designated "15 (Edmonton) Service Battalion" in 1975.

155 Transport Company (Militia) — VICTORIA, British Columbia
The company was a sub-unit of "8 Column, R.C.A.S.C." until 1965 when it was re-organized as a sub-unit of the "Victoria Service Battalion" and was re-organized in 1970 as the "transport company" of the battalion which was re-designated "11 (Victoria) Service Battalion" in 1975.

156 Transport Company (Militia) — VANCOUVER, British Columbia
The company was a sub-unit of "8 Column, R.C.A.S.C." until 1965 when it was re-organized as a sub-unit of the "Vancouver Service Battalion" and was re-organized in 1970 as the "transport company" of the battalion which was re-designated "12 (Vancouver) Service Battalion" in 1975.

"1 Helicopter Transport Platoon, R.C.A.S.C. (Regular)" was disbanded in 1970.

THE ROYAL CANADIAN ORDNANCE CORPS

Corps March: *"THE VILLAGE BLACKSMITH"*
Corps School: LONGUE POINTE (MONTREAL), Quebec

1st Divisional Ordnance Field Park (Reserve Force) — HAMILTON, Ontario
"1 Detachment, Canadian Ordnance Corps (Non-Permanent Active Militia)" was formed in 1920 at London. The "1st Divisional Ordnance Field Park, R.C.O.C." served in both Italy and North-West Europe during the Second World War and was re-formed in 1946 to support the "1st Division" (Reserve Force). The unit was re-organized in 1954 and re-designated "4 Ordnance Company, R.C.O.C. (Militia)".

2nd Divisional Ordnance Field Park (Reserve Force) — TORONTO, Ontario
"2 Detachment, Canadian Ordnance Corps (Non-Permanent Active Militia)" was formed in 1920 at Niagara Falls. The "2nd Divisional Ordnance Field Park, R.C.O.C." served in North-West Europe during the Second World War and was re-formed in 1946 to support the "2nd Division" (Reserve Force). The unit was re-organized in 1954 and re-designated "A" Company of "4 Ordnance Battalion, R.C.O.C. (Militia)".

3rd Divisional Ordnance Field Park (Reserve Force) — OTTAWA, Ontario
"3 Detachment, Canadian Ordnance Corps (Non-Permanent Active Militia)" was formed in 1920 at Kingston. The "3rd Divisional Ordnance Field Park, R.C.O.C." served in North-West Europe during the Second World War and was reformed in 1946 to support the "3rd Division" (Reserve Force). The unit was re-organized in 1954 and re-designated "3 Ordnance Company, R.C.O.C. (Militia)".

4th Divisional Ordnance Field Park (Reserve Force) — QUEBEC CITY
"4 Detachment, Canadian Ordnance Corps (Non-Permanent Active Militia)" was formed in 1920 at Montreal. The "4th Divisional Ordnance Field Park, R.C.O.C." served in North-West Europe during the Second World War and was re-formed in 1946 to support the "4th Division" (Reserve Force). The unit was re-organized in 1954 and re-designated "2 Ordnance Battalion, R.C.O.C. (Militia)".

5th Divisional Ordnance Field Park (Reserve Force) — HALIFAX, Nova Scotia
"5 Detachment, Canadian Ordnance Corps (Non-Permanent Active Militia)" was formed in 1920 at Quebec City. The "5th Divisional Ordnance Field Park, R.C.O.C." served in both Italy and North-West Europe during the Second World War and was reformed in 1946 to support the "5th Division" (Reserve Force). The unit was re-organized in 1954 and re-designated "1 Ordnance Battalion, R.C.O.C. (Militia)".

6th Divisional Ordnance Field Park (Reserve Force) — WINNIPEG, Manitoba
"6 Detachment, Canadian Ordnance Corps (Non-Permanent Active Militia)" was formed in 1920 at Halifax. The "6th Divisional Ordnance Field Park" was formed in 1946 to support the "6th Division" (Reserve Force) and was re-organized in 1954 and re-designated "6 Ordnance Battalion, R.C.O.C. (Militia)".

1st Corps Ordnance Field Park (Reserve Force) — TORONTO, Ontario
The "1st Corps Troops Sub-Park, R.C.O.C." served in both Italy and North-West Europe during the Second World War and was perpetuated by the "1st Corps Ordnance Field Park" which was formed in 1946 to support the "1st Corps" (Reserve Force). The "1st Corps Ordnance Field Park" was re-organized in 1954 and re-designated "B" Company of "4 Ordnance Battalion, R.C.O.C. (Militia)".

2nd Corps Ordnance Field Park (Reserve Force) — REGINA, Saskatchewan
The "2nd Corps Troops Sub-Park, R.C.O.C." served in North-West Europe during the Second World War and was perpetuated by the "2nd Corps Ordnance Field Park" which was formed in 1946 to support the "2nd Corps" (Reserve Force). The "2nd Corps Ordnance Field Park" was re-organized in 1954 and re-designated "5 Ordnance Company, R.C.O.C. (Militia)".

"9 Detachment, Canadian Ordnance Corps" served at Vladivostok as a unit of the Canadian Siberian Expeditionary Force (1918-1919).

"25 Infantry Brigade Ordnance Company" served in Korea as a unit of the "25th Canadian Infantry Brigade" and was re-organized in 1951 as the Canadian element of the "1st Commonwealth Divisional Ordnance Field Park".

"27 Infantry Brigade Ordnance Company" was formed in 1951 for service with the "27th Canadian Infantry Brigade Group" in West Germany and was re-designated "4 Ordnance Field Park, R.C.O.C. (Regular)" in 1954.

1 Ordnance Field Park (Regular) — CALGARY, Alberta
"1 Ordnance Field Park", a unit of the "1st Canadian Infantry Brigade Group", was incorporated within "1 Service Battalion" in 1965 and re-organized in 1970 as the "supply company" of the battalion which is a unit of "1 Canadian Brigade Group".

2 Ordnance Field Park (Regular) — CAMP PETAWAWA, Ontario
"2 Ordnance Field Park", a unit of the "2nd Canadian Infantry Brigade Group", was incorporated within "2 Service Battalion" in 1965 and re-organized in 1970 as the "supply company" of the battalion which is a unit of the "Special Service Force".

3 Ordnance Field Park (Regular) — CAMP GAGETOWN, New Brunswick
"3 Ordnance Field Park", a unit of the "3rd Canadian Infantry Brigade Group", was incorporated within "3 Service Battalion" in 1965 and disbanded in 1970 upon the replacement of the "3rd Canadian Infantry Brigade Group" by the "Combat Training Centre".

4 Ordnance Field Park (Regular) — SOEST, West Germany
"4 Ordnance Field Park", a unit of the "4th Canadian Infantry Brigade Group", was incorporated within "4 Service Battalion" in 1965 and re-organized in 1970 as the "supply company" of the battalion which is a unit of "4 Canadian Mechanized Brigade Group" at Lahr.

1 Ordnance Battalion (Militia) — HALIFAX, Nova Scotia
The battalion was re-organized in 1965 and re-designated "9 Ordnance Company, R.C.O.C. (Militia)".

2 Ordnance Battalion (Militia) — QUEBEC CITY
The battalion was re-organized in 1965 as "10" and "11" Ordnance Companies.

3 Ordnance Battalion (Militia) — MONTREAL, Quebec
The battalion was formed in 1954 and re-organized in 1965 as "7" and "8" Ordnance Companies.

4 Ordnance Battalion (Militia) — TORONTO, Ontario
The battalion was re-organized in 1965 as "12" and "13" Ordnance Companies.

5 Ordnance Battalion (Militia) — LONDON, Ontario
The battalion was formed in 1954 and re-organized in 1965 as "14 Ordnance Company, R.C.O.C. (Militia)".

6 Ordnance Battalion (Militia) — WINNIPEG, Manitoba
The battalion was re-organized in 1965 and re-designated "15 Ordnance Company, R.C.O.C. (Militia)".

7 Ordnance Battalion (Militia) — EDMONTON, Alberta
The battalion was formed in 1954 and re-organized in 1965 as "16 Ordnance Company, R.C.O.C. (Militia)".

8 Ordnance Battalion (Militia) — VANCOUVER, British Columbia
The battalion was formed in 1954 and re-organized in 1965 as "17 Ordnance Company, R.C.O.C (Militia)".

"1" Not Allocated

"2" Not Allocated

3 Ordnance Company (Militia) — OTTAWA, Ontario
The company was incorporated within the "Ottawa Service Battalion" in 1965 and re-organized in 1970 as the "supply company" of the battalion which was re-designated "28 (Ottawa) Service Battalion" in 1975.

4 Ordnance Company (Militia) — HAMILTON, Ontario
The company was incorporated within the "Hamilton Service Battalion" in 1965 and re-organized in 1970 as the "supply company" of the battalion which was re-designated "23 (Hamilton) Service Battalion" in 1975.

5 Ordnance Company (Militia) — REGINA, Saskatchewan
The company was incorporated within the "Regina Service Battalion" in 1965 and re-organized in 1970 as the "supply company" of the battalion which was re-designated "16 (Regina) Service Battalion" in 1975.

6 Ordnance Company (Militia) — CALGARY, Alberta
The company, which was formed in 1954, was incorporated within the "Calgary Service Battalion" in 1965 and re-organized in 1970 as the "supply company" of the battalion which was re-designated "14 (Calgary) Service Battalion" in 1975.

7 Ordnance Company (Militia) — MONTREAL, Quebec
The company was incorporated within the "1st Montreal Service Battalion" in 1965 and, upon amalgamation with "8 Ordnance Company", re-organized in 1970 as the "supply company" of the "Montreal Service Battalion" which was re-designated "51 (Montreal) Service Battalion" in 1975.

8 Ordnance Company (Militia) — STE-THERESE, Quebec
The company was incorporated within the "2nd Montreal Service Battalion" in 1965 and, upon amalgamation with "7 Ordnance Company", re-organized in 1970 as the "supply company" of the "Montreal Service Battalion" which was re-designated "51 (Montreal) Service Battalion" in 1975.

9 Ordnance Company (Militia) — HALIFAX, Nova Scotia
The company was incorporated within the "Halifax Service Battalion" in 1965 and re-organized in 1970 as the "supply company" of the battalion which was re-designated "33 (Halifax) Service Battalion" in 1975.

10 Ordnance Company (Militia) — QUEBEC CITY
The company was incorporated within the "Quebec Service Battalion" in 1965 and, upon amalgamation with "11 Ordnance Company", re-organized in 1970 as the "supply company" of the battalion which was re-designated "55 (Quebec) Bataillon des Services" in 1975.

11 Ordnance Company (Militia) — BEAUPORT, Quebec
The company was amalgamated with "10 Ordnance Company" in 1970 and re-organized as the "supply company" of the "Quebec Service Battalion" which was re-designated "55 (Quebec) Bataillon des Services" in 1975.

12 Ordnance Company (Militia) — Denison Armoury, DOWNSVIEW (TORONTO), Ontario
The company was incorporated within the "1st Toronto Service Battalion" in 1965 and, upon amalgamation with "13 Ordnance Company", re-organized in 1970 as the "supply company" of the "Toronto Service Battalion" which was re-designated "25 (Toronto) Service Battalion" in 1975.

13 Ordnance Company (Militia) — Moss Park Armoury, TORONTO, Ontario
The company was incorporated within the "2nd Toronto Service Battalion" in 1965 and, upon

amalgamation with "12 Ordnance Company", re-organized in 1970 as the "supply company" of the "Toronto Service Battalion" which was re-designated "25 (Toronto) Service Battalion" in 1975.

14 Ordnance Company (Militia) — LONDON, Ontario
The company was incorporated within the "London Service Battalion" in 1965 and re-organized in 1970 as the "supply company" of the battalion which was re-designated "22 (London) Service Battalion" in 1975.

15 Ordnance Company (Militia) — WINNIPEG, Manitoba
The company was incorporated within the "Winnipeg Service Battalion" in 1965 and re-organized in 1970 as the "supply company" of the battalion which was re-designated "17 (Winnipeg) Service Battalion" in 1975.

16 Ordnance Company (Militia) — EDMONTON, Alberta
The company was incorporated within the "Edmonton Service Battalion" in 1965 and re-organized in 1970 as the "supply company" of the battalion which was re-designated "15 (Edmonton) Service Battalion" in 1975.

17 Ordnance Company (Militia) — VANCOUVER, British Columbia
The company was incorporated within the "Vancouver Service Battalion" in 1965 and re-organized in 1970 as the "supply company" of the battalion which was re-designated "11 (Vancouver) Service Battalion" in 1975.

THE ROYAL CANADIAN ELECTRICAL AND MECHANICAL ENGINEERS

Corps March: "AUPRES DE MA BLONDE"
Corps School: MacNaughton Barracks, CAMP BARRIEFIELD (KINGSTON), Ontario

1st Infantry Brigade Workshop (Reserve Force)— WALLACEBURG, Ontario
The "1st Infantry Brigade Workshop, R.C.E.M.E." served in both Italy and North-West Europe during the Second World War and was re-formed in 1946 to support "1 Infantry Brigade", a formation of the "1st Division" (Reserve Force). The unit was disbanded in 1954.

2nd Infantry Brigade Workshop (Reserve Force) — KITCHENER, Ontario
The "2nd Infantry Brigade Workshop, R.C.E.M.E." served in both Italy and North-West Europe during the Second World War and was reformed in 1946 to support "2 Infantry Brigade", a formation of the "1st Division" (Reserve Force). The unit was disbanded in 1954.

3rd Infantry Brigade Workshop (Reserve Force) — HAMILTON, Ontario
The "3rd Infantry Brigade Workshop, R.C.E.M.E." served in both Italy and North-West Europe during the Second World War and was re-formed in 1946 to support "3 Infantry Brigade", a formation of the "1st Division" (Reserve Force). The unit was re-organized in 1954 and re-designated "5 Technical Regiment, R.C.E.M.E. (Militia)" which was re-organized in 1965 and re-designated "47 Technical Squadron, R.C.E.M.E. (Militia)".

4th Infantry Brigade Workshop (Reserve Force) — TORONTO, Ontario
The "4th Infantry Brigade Workshop, R.C.E.M.E." served in North-West Europe during the Second World War and was re-formed in 1946 to support "4 Infantry Brigade", a formation of the "2nd Division" (Reserve Force). The unit was re-organized in 1954 as "A" Squadron of "4 Technical Regiment, R.C.E.M.E. (Militia)". This squadron was re-organized in 1965 and re-designated "45 Technical Squadron, R.C.E.M.E. (Militia)".

5th Infantry Brigade Workshop (Reserve Force) — TORONTO, Ontario
The "5th Infantry Brigade Workshop, R.C.E.M.E." served in North-West Europe during the Second World War and was re-formed in 1946 to support "5 Infantry Brigade", a formation of the "2nd Division" (Reserve Force). The unit was re-organized in 1954 as "B" Squadron of "4 Technical Regiment, R.C.E.M.E. (Militia)". This squadron was re-organized in 1965 and re-designated "46 Technical Squadron, R.C.E.M.E. (Militia)".

6th Infantry Brigade Workshop (Reserve Force) — KINGSTON, Ontario
The "6th Infantry Brigade Workshop, R.C.E.M.E." served in North-West Europe during the Second World War and was re-formed in 1946 to support "6 Infantry Brigade", a formation of the "2nd Division" (Reserve Force). The unit was disbanded in 1954.

7th Infantry Brigade Workshop (Reserve Force) — OTTAWA, Ontario
The "7th Infantry Brigade Workshop, R.C.E.M.E." served in North-West Europe during the Second World War and was re-formed in 1946 to support "7 Infantry Brigade", a formation of the "3rd Division" (Reserve Force). The unit was amalgamated with "30 Medium Workshop" in 1954 and re-designated "26 Technical Squadron, R.C.E.M.E. (Militia)".

8th Infantry Brigade Workshop (Reserve Force) — MONTREAL, Quebec
The "8th Infantry Brigade Workshop, R.C.E.M.E." served in North-West Europe during the Second World War and was re-formed in 1946 to support "8 Infantry Brigade", a formation of the "3rd Division" (Reserve Force). The unit was amalgamated with the "20th Armoured Brigade Workshop" and "35 Corps Workshop" in 1954 and re-designated "2 Technical Regiment, R.C.E.M.E. (Militia)" which was re-organized in 1965 and re-designated "43 Technical Squadron, R.C.E.M.E.(Militia)".

9th Infantry Brigade Workshop (Reserve Force) — MONTREAL, Quebec
The "9th Infantry Brigade Workshop, R.C.E.M.E." served in North-West Europe during the Second World War and was re-formed in 1946 to support "9 Infantry Brigade", a formation of the "3rd Division" (Reserve Force). The unit was amalgamated with "27 Medium Workshop" and "38 Heavy Anti-Aircraft Workshop" in 1954 and re-designated "3 Technical Regiment, R.C.E.M.E. (Militia)" which was re-organized in 1965 and re-designated "44 Technical Squadron, R.C.E.M.E. (Militia)".

10th Infantry Brigade Workshop (Reserve Force) — SHERBROOKE, Quebec
The "10th Infantry Brigade Workshop, R.C.E.M.E." served in North-West Europe during the Second World War and was re-formed in 1946 to support "10 Infantry Brigade", a formation of the "4th Division" (Reserve Force). The unit was re-organized in 1954 and re-designated "24 Technical Squadron, R.C.E.M.E. (Militia)".

11th Infantry Brigade Workshop (Reserve Force) — QUEBEC CITY
The "11th Infantry Brigade Workshop, R.C.E.M.E." served in both Italy and North-West Europe during the Second World War and was re-formed in 1946 to support "11 Infantry Brigade", a formation of the "4th Division" (Reserve Force). The unit was amalgamated with the "12th Infantry Brigade Workshop in 1954 and re-designated "42 Technical Squadron, R.C.E.M.E. (Militia)".

12th Infantry Brigade Workshop (Reserve Force) — QUEBEC CITY
The "12th Infantry Brigade Workshop, R.C.E.M.E." served in Italy during the Second World War and was re-formed in 1946 to support "12 Infantry Brigade", a formation of the "4th Division" (Reserve Force). The unit was amalgamated with the "11th Infantry Brigade Workshop" in 1954 and re-designated "42 Technical Squadron, R.C.E.M.E. (Militia)".

13th Infantry Brigade Workshop (Reserve Force) — SYDNEY, Nova Scotia
The unit, which had been formed in 1946 to support "13 Infantry Brigade", a formation of the "5th Division" (Reserve Force), was disbanded in 1954.

14th Infantry Brigade Workshop (Reserve Force) — MONCTON, New Brunswick
The unit, which had been formed in 1946 to support "14 Infantry Brigade", a formation of the "5th Division" (Reserve Force), was amalgamated with "28 Medium Workshop" in 1954 and re-designated "21 Technical Squadron, R.C.E.M.E. (Militia)".

15th Infantry Brigade Workshop (Reserve Force) — VANCOUVER, British Columbia
The unit, which had been formed in 1946 to support "15 Infantry Brigade", a formation of the "5th Division" (Reserve Force), was amalgamated with "41 Heavy Anti-Aircraft Workshop" in 1954 and re-designated "8 Technical Regiment, R.C.E.M.E. (Militia)" which was re-organized in 1965 and re-designated "49 Technical Squadron, R.C.E.M.E. (Militia)".

16th Infantry Brigade Workshop (Reserve Force) — MOOSE JAW, Saskatchewan
The unit, which had been formed in 1946 to support "16 Infantry Brigade", a formation of the "6th Division" (Reserve Force), was amalgamated with the "17th Infantry Brigade Workshop" in 1954 and re-designated "37 Technical Squadron, R.C.E.M.E. (Militia)".

17th Infantry Brigade Workshop (Reserve Force) — SASKATOON, Saskatchewan
The unit, which had been formed in 1946 to support "17 Infantry Brigade", a formation of the "6th Division (Reserve Force), was amalgamated with the "16th Infantry Brigade Workshop" in 1954 and re-designated "37 Technical Squadron, R.C.E.M.E. (Militia)".

18th Infantry Brigade Workshop (Reserve Force) — DRUMHELLER, Alberta
The unit, which had been formed in 1946 to support "18 Infantry Brigade", a formation of the "6th Division" (Reserve Force), was amalgamated with the "22nd Armoured Brigade Workshop" in 1954 and re-designated "31 Technical Squadron, R.C.E.M.E. (Militia)".

19th Armoured Brigade Workshop (Reserve Force) — OSHAWA, Ontario
The "1st Armoured Brigade Workshop, R.C.E.M.E." served in both Italy and North-West Europe during the Second World War and was perpetuated by the "19th Armoured Brigade Workshop" which was formed in 1946 to support "19 Armoured Brigade" (Reserve Force). The unit was disbanded in 1954.

20th Armoured Brigade Workshop (Reserve Force) — MONTREAL, Quebec
The "2nd Armoured Brigade Workshop, R.C.E.M.E." served in North-West Europe during the Second World War and was perpetuated by the "20th Armoured Brigade Workshop" which was formed in 1946 to support "20 Armoured Brigade" (Reserve Force). The "20th Armoured Brigade Workshop" was amalgamated with the "8th Infantry Brigade Workshop" and "35 Corps Workshop" in 1954 and re-designated "2 Technical Regiment, R.C.E.M.E. (Militia)".

21st Armoured Brigade Workshop (Reserve Force) — HALIFAX, Nova Scotia
The "4th Armoured Brigade Workshop, R.C.E.M.E." served in North-West Europe during the Second World War and was perpetuated by the "21st Armoured Brigade Workshop" which was formed in 1946 to support "21 Armoured Brigade" (Reserve Force). This unit was re-organized in 1954 as "A" Squadron of "1 Technical Regiment, R.C.E.M.E. (Militia)" which was re-organized in 1965 and re-designated "20 Technical Squadron, R.C.E.M.E. (Militia)".

22nd Armoured Brigade Workshop (Reserve Force) — BLAIRMORE, Alberta
The "5th Armoured Brigade Workshop, R.C.E.M.E." served in both Italy and North-West Europe during the Second World War and was perpetuated by the "22nd Armoured Brigade Workshop" which was formed in 1946 to support "22 Armoured Brigade" (Reserve Force). The "22nd Armoured Brigade Workshop" was amalgamated with the "18th Infantry Brigade Workshop" in 1954 and re-designated "31 Technical Squadron, R.C.E.M.E. (Militia)".

23 Infantry Workshop (Active Force) — CAMP PETAWAWA, Ontario
The unit was formed in 1946 as "23 Composite Brigade Group Workshop" to support the "23rd Canadian Infantry Brigade Group" and served in Korea as a unit of the "25th Canadian Infantry Brigade".

24 Medium Workshop (Reserve Force) — WINDSOR, Ontario
The unit was formed in 1946 to support the medium artillery of the "1st Division" (Reserve Force) and was re-organized in 1954 and re-designated "39 Technical Squadron, R.C.E.M.E. (Militia)".

25 Medium Workshop (Reserve Force) — SUDBURY, Ontario
The unit was formed in 1946 to support the medium artillery of the "2nd Division" (Reserve Force) and was re-organized in 1954 and re-designated "33 Technical Squadron, R.C.E.M.E. (Militia)".

26 Medium Workshop (Reserve Force) — ST. CATHARINES, Ontario
The unit was formed in 1946 to support the medium artillery of the "3rd Division" (Reserve Force) and was re-organized in 1954 and re-designated "30 Technical Squadron, R.C.E.M.E. (Militia)".

27 Medium Workshop (Reserve Force) — MONTREAL, Quebec
The unit, which had been formed in 1946 to support the medium artillery of the "4th Division" (Reserve Force), was amalgamated with the "9th Infantry Brigade Workshop" and "38 Heavy Anti-Aircraft Workshop" in 1954 and re-designated "3 Technical Regiment, R.C.E.M.E. (Militia)" which was re-organized in 1965 and re-designated "44 Technical Squadron, R.C.E.M.E. (Militia)".

28 Medium Workshop (Reserve Force) — MONCTON, New Brunswick
The unit, which had been formed in 1946 to support the medium artillery of the "5th Division" (Reserve Force), was amalgamated with the "14th Infantry Brigade Workshop" in 1954 and re-designated "21 Technical Squadron, R.C.E.M.E. (Militia)".

29 Medium Workshop (Reserve Force) — FORT WILLIAM, Ontario
The unit was formed in 1946 to support the medium artillery of the "6th Division" (Reserve Force) and was re-organized in 1954, re-designated "35 Technical Squadron, R.C.E.M.E. (Militia)", and relocated at Port Arthur.

30 Medium Workshop (Reserve Force) — OTTAWA, Ontario
The unit, which had been formed in 1946 to support the medium artillery of the "1st Corps" (Reserve Force), was amalgamated with the "7th Infantry Brigade Workshop" in 1954 and re-designated "26 Technical Squadron, R.C.E.M.E. (Militia)".

31 Armoured Recovery Unit (Reserve Force) — SAINT JOHN, New Brunswick
The "1st Recovery Company, R.C.E.M.E." served in both Italy and North-West Europe during the Second World War and was perpetuated by "31 Armoured Recovery Unit" which had been formed in 1946 to support the "1st Corps" (Reserve Force). "31 Armoured Recovery Unit" was disbanded in 1954.

32 Medium Workshop (Reserve Force) — WINNIPEG, Manitoba
The unit was formed in 1946 to support the medium artillery of the "2nd Corps" (Reserve Force) and was re-organized in 1954 and re-designated "36 Technical Squadron, R.C.E.M.E. (Militia)".

33 Armoured Recovery Unit (Reserve Force) — MOOSE JAW, Saskatchewan
The "2nd Recovery Company, R.C.E.M.E." served in North-West Europe during the Second World War and was perpetuated by "33 Armoured Recovery Unit" which had been formed in 1946 to support the "2nd Corps" (Reserve Force). "33 Armoured Recovery Unit" was disbanded in 1954.

34 Corps Workshop (Reserve Force) — TORONTO, Ontario
The "1st Corps Workshop, R.C.E.M.E." served in both Italy and North-West Europe during the Second World War and was perpetuated by "34 Corps Workshop" which had been formed in 1946 to support the "1st Corps" (Reserve Force). "34 Corps Workshop" was disbanded in 1954.

35 Corps Workshop (Reserve Force) — MONTREAL, Quebec
The "2nd Corps Workshop, R.C.E.M.E." served in North-West Europe during the Second World War and was perpetuated by "35 Corps Workshop" which had been formed in 1946 to support the "2nd Corps" (Reserve Force). "35 Corps Workshop" was amalgamated with the "8th Infantry Brigade Workshop" and the "20th Armoured Brigade Workshop" in 1954 and re-designated "2 Technical Regiment, R.C.E.M.E. (Militia)" which was re-organized in 1965 and re-designated "43 Technical Squadron, R.C.E.M.E. (Militia)".

36 Heavy Anti-Aircraft Workshop (Reserve Force) — SAULT STE. MARIE, Ontario
The unit, which had been formed in 1946 to support "49 Heavy Anti-Aircraft Regiment, R.C.A. (Reserve Force)", was re-organized in 1954 and re-designated "34 Technical Squadron, R.C.E.M.E. (Militia)".

37 Heavy Anti-Aircraft Workshop (Reserve Force) — PETERBOROUGH, Ontario
The unit, which had been formed in 1946 to support "50 Heavy Anti-Aircraft Regiment (The Prince of Wales' Rangers), R.C.A. (Reserve Force)", was re-organized in 1954 and re-designated "28 Technical Squadron, R.C.E.M.E. (Militia)".

38 Heavy Anti-Aircraft Workshop (Reserve Force) — MONTREAL, Quebec
The unit, which had been formed in 1946 to support "51 Heavy Anti-Aircraft Regiment, R.C.A. (Reserve Force)", was amalgamated with the "9th Infantry Brigade Workshop" and "27 Medium Workshop" in 1954 and re-designated "3 Technical Regiment, R.C.E.M.E. (Militia)" which was re-organized in 1965 and re-designated "44 Technical Squadron, R.C.E.M.E. (Militia)".

39 Heavy Anti-Aircraft Workshop (Reserve Force) — HALIFAX, Nova Scotia
The unit, which had been formed in 1946 to support "36 Heavy Anti-Aircraft Regiment, R.C.A. (Reserve Force)", was re-organized in 1954 as "B" Squadron of "1 Technical Regiment, R.C.E.M.E. (Militia)" which was re-organized in 1965 and re-designated "20 Technical Squadron, R.C.E.M.E. (Militia)".

"40 Infantry Workshop" served in Korea as a unit of the "25th Canadian Infantry Brigade".

41 Heavy Anti-Aircraft Workshop (Reserve Force) — VANCOUVER, British Columbia
The unit, which had been formed in 1946 to support "43 Heavy Anti-Aircraft Regiment, R.C.A.
(Reserve Force)", was amalgamated with the "15th Infantry Brigade Workshop" in 1954 and re-
designated "8 Technical Regiment, R.C.E.M.E. (Militia)" which was re-organized in 1965 and re-
designated "49 Technical Squadron, R.C.E.M.E. (Militia)".

"42 Infantry Workshop" served in Korea as a unit of the "25th Canadian Infantry Brigade".

1 Field Workshop (Regular) — CALGARY, Alberta
The unit was incorporated within "1 Service Battalion" in 1965 and re-organized in 1970 as the
"maintenance company" of the battalion which is a unit of "1 Canadian Brigade Group".

2 Field Workshop (Regular) — CAMP PETAWAWA, Ontario
The unit was incorporated within "2 Service Battalion" in 1965 and re-organized in 1970 as the
"maintenance company" of the battalion which is a unit of the "Special Service Force".

3 Field Workshop (Regular) — CAMP GAGETOWN, New Brunswick
The unit was incorporated within "3 Service Battalion" which was disbanded in 1970 upon the
replacement of the "3rd Canadian Infantry Brigade Group" by the "Combat Training Centre".

4 Field Workshop (Regular) — SOEST, West Germany
The unit was incorporated within "4 Service Battalion" in 1965 and re-organized in 1970 as the
"maintenance company" of the battalion which is a unit of "4 Canadian Mechanized Brigade
Group".

20 Technical Squadron (Militia) — HALIFAX, Nova Scotia
The squadron was incorporated within the "Halifax Service Battalion" in 1965 and re-organized in 1970 as the "maintenance company" of the battalion which was re-designated "33 (Halifax) Service Battalion" in 1975.

21 Technical Squadron (Militia) — MONCTON, New Brunswick
The squadron was incorporated within the "Moncton Service Battalion" in 1965 and re-organized in 1970 as the "maintenance company" of the battalion which was re-designated "32 (Moncton) Service Battalion" in 1975.

22 Technical Squadron (Militia) — CAP DE LA MADELEINE, Quebec
The squadron was disbanded in 1965.

23 Technical Squadron (Militia) — TROIS-RIVIERES, Quebec
The squadron was disbanded in 1965.

24 Technical Squadron (Militia) — SHERBROOKE, Quebec
The squadron was disbanded in 1965.

25 Technical Squadron (Militia) — JONQUIERE, Quebec
The squadron was disbanded in 1965.

26 Technical Squadron (Militia) — OTTAWA, Ontario
The squadron was disbanded in 1965.

27 Technical Squadron (Militia)
The squadron was disbanded in 1965.

28 Technical Squadron (Militia) — PETERBOROUGH, Ontario
The squadron, which was disbanded in 1970, had been incorporated within the "Ottawa Service Battalion" in 1965.

29 Technical Squadron (Militia) — LONDON, Ontario
The squadron was incorporated within the "London Service Battalion" in 1965 and re-organized in 1970 as the "maintenance company" of the battalion which was re-designated "22 (London) Service Battalion" in 1975.

30 Technical Squadron (Militia) — ST. CATHARINES, Ontario
The squadron was disbanded in 1970.

31 Technical Squadron (Militia) — BLAIRMORE, Alberta
The squadron was disbanded in 1965.

32 Technical Squadron (Militia) — LETHBRIDGE, Alberta
The squadron was disbanded in 1965.

33 Technical Squadron (Militia) — SUDBURY, Ontario
The squadron, which maintained a detached troop at Espanola, was disbanded in 1970.

34 Technical Squadron (Militia) — SAULT STE. MARIE, Ontario
The squadron was disbanded in 1970.

35 Technical Squadron (Militia) — PORT ARTHUR (THUNDER BAY), Ontario
The squadron was incorporated within the "Lakehead Service Battalion" in 1965 and re-organized in 1970 as the "maintenance company" of the battalion which was re-designated "18 (Thunder Bay) Service Battalion" in 1975.

36 Technical Squadron (Militia) — WINNIPEG, Manitoba
The squadron was incorporated within the "Winnipeg Service Battalion" in 1965 and re-organized in 1970 as the "maintenance company" of the battalion which was re-designated "17 (Winnipeg) Service Battalion" in 1975.

37 Technical Squadron (Militia) — SASKATOON, Saskatchewan
The squadron, which maintained a detached troop at Radisson until 1965, was disbanded in 1970.

38 Technical Squadron (Militia) — EDMONTON, Alberta
The squadron was incorporated within the "Edmonton Service Battalion" in 1965 and re-organized in 1970 as the "maintenance company" of the battalion which was re-designated "15 (Edmonton) Service Battalion" in 1975.

39 Technical Squadron (Militia) — WINDSOR, Ontario
The squadron was re-organized in 1970 as the "maintenance company" of the "Windsor Service Battalion" which was re-designated "21 (Windsor) Service Battalion" in 1975.

40 Technical Squadron (Militia) — VICTORIA, British Columbia
The squadron was incorporated within the "Victoria Service Battalion" in 1965 and re-organized in 1970 as the "maintenance company" of the battalion which was re-designated "11 (Victoria) Service Battalion" in 1975.

41 Technical Squadron (Militia) — ARVIDA, Quebec
The squadron was disbanded in 1965.

42 Technical Squadron (Militia) — QUEBEC CITY
The squadron was incorporated within the "Quebec Service Battalion" in 1965 and re-organized in 1970 as the "maintenance company" of the battalion which was re-designated "55 (Quebec) Bataillon des Services" in 1975.

43 Technical Squadron (Militia) — MONTREAL, Quebec
The squadron was incorporated within the "1st Montreal Service Battalion" in 1965 and, upon amalgamation with "44 Technical Squadron", re-organized in 1970 as the "maintenance company" of the "Montreal Service Battalion" which was re-designated "51 (Montreal) Service Battalion" in 1975.

44 Technical Squadron (Militia) — MONTREAL, Quebec
The squadron was incorporated within the "2nd Montreal Service Battalion" in 1965 and, upon amalgamation with "43 Technical Squadron", re-organized in 1970 as the "maintenance company" of the "Montreal Service Battalion" which was re-designated "51 (Montreal) Service Battalion" in 1975.

45 Technical Squadron (Militia) — Denison Armoury, DOWNSVIEW (TORONTO), Ontario
The squadron was incorporated within the "1st Toronto Service Battalion" in 1965 and, upon amalgamation with "46 Technical Squadron", re-organized in 1970 as the "maintenance company" of the "Toronto Service Battalion" which was re-designated "25 (Toronto) Service Battalion" in 1975.

46 Technical Squadron (Militia) — Moss Park Armoury, TORONTO, Ontario
The squadron was incorporated within the "2nd Toronto Service Battalion" in 1965 and, upon amalgamation with "45 Technical Squadron", re-organized in 1970 as the "maintenance company" of the "Toronto Service Battalion" which was re-designated "25 (Toronto) Service Battalion" in 1975.

47 Technical Squadron (Militia) — HAMILTON, Ontario
The squadron was incorporated within the "Hamilton Service Battalion" in 1965 and re-organized in 1970 as the "maintenance company" of the battalion which was re-designated "23 (Hamilton) Service Battalion" in 1975.

48 Technical Squadron (Militia) — CALGARY, Alberta
The squadron was incorporated within the "Calgary Service Battalion" in 1965 and re-organized in 1970 as the "maintenance company" of the battalion which was re-designated "14 (Calgary) Service Battalion" in 1975.

49 Technical Squadron (Militia) — VANCOUVER, British Columbia

The squadron was incorporated within the "Vancouver Service Battalion" in 1965 and re-organized in 1970 as the "maintenance company" of the battalion which was re-designated "12 (Vancouver) Service Battalion" in 1975.

THE ROYAL CANADIAN ARMY MEDICAL CORPS

Corps March: *"HERE'S A HEALTH UNTO HER MAJESTY"*
Corps Motto: *"IN ARDUIS FIDELIS"* / (*"FAITHFUL IN ADVERSITY"*)
The Canadian Forces Medical Services Training Centre: CAMP BORDEN, Ontario

NOTE
Prior to the organization of a "medical service", two "field hospitals" (recruited at Montreal and Toronto, respectively) served in Saskatchewan during the "Riel" Rebellion (1885). A "Canadian Field Hospital" served with the Canadian contingent in South Africa during the "Boer" War.

1 Field Ambulance (Reserve Force) — KINGSTON, Ontario
"1 Field Ambulance" served in France as a unit of the "1st Canadian Division" during the Great War and in Pacific Command (Canada) during the Second World War. The unit was re-organized in 1954 and re-designated "11 Medical Company, R.C.A.M.C. (Militia)".

2 Field Ambulance (Reserve Force) — TORONTO, Ontario
"2 Field Ambulance" served in France as a unit of the "1st Canadian Division" during the Great War and in both Italy and North-West Europe during the Second World War. The unit was amalgamated with "7" and "16" Field Ambulances in 1954 and re-designated "26 Medical Company, R.C.A.M.C. (Militia)".

3 Field Ambulance (Reserve Force) — WINNIPEG, Manitoba
"3 Field Ambulance" served in France as a unit of the "1st Canadian Division" during the Great World War and in Pacific Command (Canada) during the Second World War. The unit was re-organized in 1954 and re-designated "18 Medical Company, R.C.A.M.C. (Militia)".

4 Field Ambulance (Reserve Force) — FORT WILLIAM, Ontario
"4 Field Ambulance" served in France as a unit of the "2nd Canadian Division" during the Great War and in both Italy and North-West Europe during the Second World War. The unit was re-organized in 1954, re-designated "17 Medical Company, R.C.A.M.C. (Militia)", and relocated at Port Arthur.

5 Field Ambulance (Reserve Force) — HAMILTON, Ontario
"5 Field Ambulance" served in France as a unit of the "2nd Canadian Division" during the Great War and in both Italy and North-West Europe during the Second World War. The unit was re-organized in 1954 and re-designated "16 Medical Company, R.C.A.M.C. (Militia)".

6 Field Ambulance (Reserve Force) — MONTREAL, Quebec
"6 Field Ambulance" served in France as a unit of the "2nd Canadian Division" during the Great War and at Camp Valcartier in Quebec during the Second World War. The unit was amalgamated with "9" and "20" Field Ambulances in 1954 and re-designated "25 Medical Company, R.C.A.M.C. (Militia)".

7 Field Ambulance (Reserve Force) — TORONTO, Ontario
"7 (Cavalry) Field Ambulance, C.A.M.C." served in France as a unit of the "Canadian Cavalry Brigade" during the Great War. "7 Field Ambulance, R.C.A.M.C." served in both Italy and North-West Europe during the Second World War. The unit was amalgamated with "2" and "16" Field Ambulances in 1954 and re-designated "26 Medical Company, R.C.A.M.C. (Militia)".

8 Field Ambulance (Reserve Force) — CALGARY, Alberta
"8 Field Ambulance" served in France as a unit of the "3rd Canadian Division" during the Great War and in Italy during the Second World War. The unit was re-organized in 1954 and re-designated "21 Medical Company, R.C.A.M.C. (Militia)".

9 Field Ambulance (Reserve Force) — MONTREAL, Quebec
"9 Field Ambulance" served in France as a unit of the "3rd Canadian Division" during the Great War and in both Italy and North-West Europe during the Second World War. The unit was amalgamated with "6" and "20" Field Ambulances in 1954 and re-designated "25 Medical Company, R.C.A.M.C. (Militia)".

10 Field Ambulance (Reserve Force) — WEYBURN, Saskatchewan
"10 Field Ambulance" served in France as a unit of the "3rd Canadian Division" during the Great War and in North-West Europe during the Second World War. The unit, which maintained a detached company at Outlook, was disbanded in 1954.

11 Field Ambulance (Reserve Force) — GUELPH, Ontario
"11 Field Ambulance" served in France as a unit of the "4th Canadian Division" during the Great War and in North-West Europe during the Second World War. The unit was disbanded in 1954.

12 Field Ambulance (Reserve Force) — VANCOUVER, British Columbia
"12 Field Ambulance" served in France as a unit of the "4th Canadian Division" during the Great War and in North-West Europe during the Second World War. The unit was re-organized in 1954 and re-designated "24 Medical Company, R.C.A.M.C. (Militia)".

13 Field Ambulance (Reserve Force) — VICTORIA, British Columbia
"13 Field Ambulance" served in France as a unit of the "4th Canadian Division" during the Great War and in Canada during the Second World War. The unit was disbanded in 1954.

14 Field Ambulance (Reserve Force) — MONCTON, New Brunswick
"14 Field Ambulance" served in France as a unit of the "Canadian Corps" during the Great War and in North-West Europe during the Second World War. The unit was re-organized in 1954 and re-designated "3 Medical Company, R.C.A.M.C. (Militia)".

15 Field Ambulance (Reserve Force) — LONDON, Ontario
"15 Field Ambulance" served in the United Kingdom during the Great War and in North-West Europe during the Second World War. The unit was re-organized in 1954 and re-designated "15 Medical Company, R.C.A.M.C. (Militia)".

16 Field Ambulance (Reserve Force) — TORONTO, Ontario
"16 Field Ambulance" served at Vladivostok as a unit of the Canadian Siberian Expeditionary Force (1918-1919) and in Canada during the Second World War. The unit was amalgamated with "2" and "7" Field Ambulances in 1954 and re-designated "26 Medical Company, R.C.A.M.C. (Militia)".

17 Field Ambulance (Reserve Force) — PONOKA, Alberta
"17 Field Ambulance, R.C.A.M.C." served in North-West Europe during the Second World War. The unit was re-organized in 1954 and re-designated "22 Medical Company, R.C.A.M.C. (Militia)".

18 Field Ambulance (Reserve Force) — QUEBEC CITY
"18 Field Ambulance, R.C.A.M.C." served in North-West Europe during the Second World War. The unit was amalgamated with "19 Field Ambulance" in 1954 and re-designated "7 Medical Company, R.C.A.M.C. (Militia)".

19 Field Ambulance (Reserve Force) — QUEBEC CITY
"19 Field Ambulance, R.C.A.M.C." served at Camp Valcartier in Quebec during the Second World War. The unit was amalgamated with "18 Field Ambulance" in 1954 and re-designated "7 Medical Company, R.C.A.M.C. (Militia)".

20 Field Ambulance (Reserve Force) — MONTREAL, Quebec
"20 Field Ambulance, R.C.A.M.C" served in Atlantic Command (Canada) during the Second World War. The unit was amalgamated with "6" and "9" Field Ambulances in 1954 and re-designated "25 Medical Company, R.C.A.M.C. (Militia)".

21 Field Ambulance (Reserve Force) — CHARLOTTETOWN, Prince Edward Island
"21 Field Ambulance, R.C.A.M.C." served in Atlantic Command (Canada) during the Second World War. The unit, which maintained a detached company at Sydney, was re-organized in 1954 and re-designated "5 Medical Company, R.C.A.M.C. (Militia)". The detached company at Sydney was re-designated "6 Medical Company, R.C.A.M.C. (Militia)".

22 Field Ambulance (Reserve Force) — HALIFAX, Nova Scotia
"22 Field Ambulance, R.C.A.M.C." served in North-West Europe during the Second World War. The unit was re-organized in 1954 and re-designated "2 Medical Company, R.C.A.M.C. (Militia)".

23 Field Ambulance (Active Force) — CAMP PETAWAWA, Ontario
"23 Field Ambulance, R.C.A.M.C." served in North-West Europe during the Second World War and was retained in the post-war "Active Force".

24 Field Ambulance (Reserve Force) — KITCHENER, Ontario
"24 Field Ambulance, R.C.A.M.C." served in both Italy and North-West Europe during the Second World War. The unit was re-organized in 1954 and re-designated "12 Medical Company, R.C.A.M.C. (Militia)".

"25 Field Ambulance, R.C.A.M.C." served on Kiska in the Aleutian Islands as a unit of the "13th Canadian Infantry Brigade Group" during the Second World War and was re-formed in 1950 for service with the "25th Canadian Infantry Brigade" in Korea.

"26 Field Ambulance, R.C.A.M.C." served in Canada during the Second World War.

"27 Field Ambulance, R.C.A.M.C." served in Atlantic Command (Canada) during the Second World War and was re-formed in 1951 for service with the "27th Canadian Infantry Brigade Group" in West Germany.

1 Field Ambulance (Regular) —CALGARY, Alberta
"1 Field Ambulance" is a unit of "1 Canadian Brigade Group".

2 Field Ambulance (Regular) — CAMP PETAWAWA, Ontario
"2 Field Ambulance" is a unit of the "Special Service Force".

3 Field Ambulance (Regular) — CAMP GAGETOWN, New Brunswick
"3 Field Ambulance", which served in Korea subsequent to the armistice, was disbanded in 1970 upon the replacement of the "3rd Canadian Infantry Brigade Group" by the "Combat Training Centre".

4 Field Ambulance (Regular) — LAHR, West Germany
"4 Field Ambulance" is a unit of "4 Canadian Mechanized Brigade Group".

5ieme Ambulance de Campagne (Regulier) — CAMP VALCARTIER, Quebec
"5ieme Ambulance de Campagne" est un unit de "5ieme Groupe-Brigade du Canada".

1 Medical Company (Militia) — ST. JOHN'S, Newfoundland
The company, which maintained a detached platoon at Corner Brook until 1970, was re-organized as the "medical section" of the "Newfoundland Service Battalion".

2 Medical Company (Militia) — HALIFAX, Nova Scotia
The company, which was disbanded in 1970, had been incorporated within the "Halifax Service Battalion" in 1965.

3 Medical Company (Militia) — MONCTON, New Brunswick
The company, which was disbanded in 1970, had been incorporated within the "Moncton Service Battalion" in 1965.

4 Medical Company (Militia) — SAINT JOHN, New Brunswick
The company, which was disbanded in 1970, had been incorporated within the "Saint John Service Battalion" in 1965.

5 Medical Company (Militia) —CHARLOTTETOWN, Prince Edward Island
The company was disbanded in 1970.

6 Medical Company (Militia) — SYDNEY, Nova Scotia
The company was incorporated within the "Sydney Service Battalion" in 1965, re-organized in 1970 as the "medical company" of the battalion, and re-designated "35 (Sydney) Medical Company" in 1975.

7 Medical Company (Militia) — QUEBEC CITY
The company was incorporated within the "Quebec Service Battalion" in 1965, re-organized in 1970 as the "medical company" of the battalion, and re-designated "55 (Quebec) Medical Company" in 1975.

8 Medical Company (Militia) — SHERBROOKE, Quebec
The company was re-designated "52 (Sherbrooke) Medical Company" in 1975.

9 Medical Company (Militia) — CORNWALL, Ontario
The company was disbanded in 1965.

10 Medical Company (Militia) — OTTAWA, Ontario
The company, which was disbanded in 1970, had been incorporated within the "Ottawa Service Battalion" in 1965.

11 Medical Company (Militia) — KINGSTON, Ontario
The company was disbanded in 1965.

12 Medical Company (Militia) — KITCHENER, Ontario
The company was disbanded in 1970.

13 Medical Company (Militia) — OWEN SOUND, Ontario
The company, which was disbanded in 1970, had been incorporated within the "1st Toronto Service Battalion' in 1965.

14 Medical Company (Militia) — WINDSOR, Ontario
The company was disbanded in 1965.

15 Medical Company (Militia) — LONDON, Ontario
The company, which was disbanded in 1970, had been incorporated within the "London Service Battalion" in 1965.

16 Medical Company (Militia) — HAMILTON, Ontario
The company was incorporated within the "Hamilton Service Battalion" in 1965, re-organized in 1970 as the "medical company" of the battalion, and re-designated "23 (Hamilton Medical Company" in 1975.

17 Medical Company (Militia) — PORT ARTHUR (THUNDER BAY), Ontario
The company was incorporated within the "Lakehead Service Battalion" in 1965, re-organized in 1970 as the "medical company" of the battalion, and re-designated "18 (Thunder Bay) Medical Company" in 1975.

18 Medical Company (Militia) — WINNIPEG, Manitoba
The company was incorporated within the "Winnipeg Service Battalion" in 1965, re-organized in 1970 as the "medical company" of the battalion, and re-designated "17 (Winnipeg) Medical Company" in 1975.

19 Medical Company (Militia) — REGINA, Saskatchewan
The company, which maintained a detached platoon at Moose Jaw until 1965, was incorporated within the "Regina Service Battalion" in 1965, re-organized in 1970 as the "medical company" of the battalion, and re-designated "16 (Regina) Medical Company" in 1975.

20 Medical Company (Militia) — SASKATOON, Saskatchewan
The company was disbanded in 1965.

21 Medical Company (Militia) — CALGARY, Alberta
The company, which was disbanded in 1970, had been incorporated within the "Calgary Service Battalion" in 1965.

22 Medical Company (Militia) — PONOKA, Alberta
The company was disbanded in 1965.

23 Medical Company (Militia) — EDMONTON, Alberta
The company was incorporated within the "Edmonton Service Battalion" in 1965, re-organized in 1970 as the "medical company" of the battalion, and re-designated "15 (Edmonton) Medical Company" in 1975.

24 Medical Company (Militia) — VANCOUVER, British Columbia
The company was incorporated within the "Vancouver Service Battalion" in 1965, re-organized in 1970 as the "medical company" of the battalion, and re-designated "12 (Vancouver) Medical Company" in 1975.

25 Medical Company (Militia) — MONTREAL, Quebec
The company was incorporated within the "1st Medical Battalion, R.C.A.M.C. (Militia)" of which "A" and "B" Companies, which had been incorporated within the "1st" and "2nd" Montreal Service Battalions in 1965, were amalgamated in 1970 and re-organized as the "medical company" of the "Montreal Service Battalion" and re-designated "51 (Montreal) Medical Company" in 1975.

26 Medical Company (Militia) — Moss Park Armoury, TORONTO, Ontario
The company was incorporated within the "2nd Toronto Service Battalion" in 1965, re-organized in 1970 as the "medical company" of the "Toronto Service Battalion", and re-designated "25 (Toronto) Medical Company" in 1975.

1st Airborne Medical Section (Regular) — CALGARY, Alberta
The unit, which had been formed in 1958 to support the airborne elements of the "1st Canadian Infantry Brigade Group", was disbanded in 1968.

2nd Airborne Medical Section (Regular) — CAMP BORDEN, Ontario
The unit, which had been formed in 1958 to support the airborne elements of the "2nd Canadian Infantry Brigade Group", was disbanded in 1968.

3rd Airborne Medical Section (Regular) — CAMP VALCARTIER, Quebec
The unit, which had been formed in 1958 to support the airborne elements of the "3rd Canadian Infantry Brigade Group", was disbanded in 1968.

THE ROYAL CANADIAN DENTAL CORPS

Corps March: "*MARCH-PAST OF THE ROYAL CANADIAN DENTAL CORPS*"
Corps School: CAMP BORDEN, Ontario

"1 Dental Company, C.D.C." served in both Italy and North-West Europe as a unit of the "1st Canadian Infantry Division" during the Second World War.

"2 Dental Company, C.D.C." served in North-West Europe as a unit of the "2nd Canadian Infantry Division" during the Second World War.

"3 Dental Company, C.D.C." served in both Italy and North-West Europe as a unit of the "1st Canadian Corps" during the Second World War.

"4 Dental Company, C.D.C." served in North-West Europe as a unit of the "First Canadian Army" during the Second World War.

"5 Dental Company, C.D.C." served in North-West Europe as a unit of the "3rd Canadian Infantry Division" during the Second World War.

"6 Dental Company, C.D.C." served in North-West Europe as a unit of the "4th Canadian Armoured Division" during the Second World War.

"7 Dental Company, C.D.C." was authorized (but not formed) for service in the Far East during the Second World War.

"8 Dental Company, C.D.C." served in both Italy and North-West Europe as a unit of the "5th Canadian Armoured Division" during the Second World War.

"9 Dental Company, C.D.C." served in North-West Europe as a unit of the "2nd Canadian Corps" during the Second World War.

"10 Dental Company, C.D.C." served in Newfoundland during the Second World War.

"11 Dental Company, C.D.C." provided dental services to personnel of "Canadian Base Units, Italy" during the Second World War.

"12 Dental Company, C.D.C." provided dental services to personnel of "Canadian Base Units, North-West Europe" during the Second World War.

"13" Not Allocated

"14" Not Allocated

"15 Dental Company, C.D.C." provided dental services to personnel of "Canadian Base Units, England" during the Second World War.

"16 Dental Company, C.D.C." provided dental services to personnel of "Canadian Base Units, England" during the Second World War.

"17 Dental Company, C.D.C." provided dental services to personnel of "Canadian Military Headquarters, London" during the Second World War.

"18 Dental Company, C.D.C." provided dental services to personnel of "Headquarters, R.C.A.F., London" during the Second World War.

"19 Dental Company, C.D.C." provided dental services to personnel of "6 (R.C.A.F.) Bomber Group" in the United Kingdom during the Second World War.

"20 Dental Company, C.D.C." provided dental services to personnel of the Royal Canadian Air Force in the United Kingdom during the Second World War.

"21 Dental Company, C.D.C." provided dental services to units in "Military District 1" (South-Western Ontario) during the Second World War.

"22 Dental Company, C.D.C." provided dental services to units in "Military District 2" (Central Ontario) during the Second World War.

"23 Dental Company, C.D.C." provided dental services to units in "Military District 3" (Eastern Ontario) during the Second World War.

"24 Dental Company, C.D.C." provided dental services to units in "Military District 4" (Western Quebec) during the Second World War.

"25 Dental Company, C.D.C." provided dental services to units in "Military District 5" (Eastern Quebec) during the Second World War.

"26 Dental Company, C.D.C." provided dental services to units in "Military District 6" (Nova Scotia) during the Second World War.

"27 Dental Company, C.D.C." provided dental services to units in "Military District 7" (New Brunswick) during the Second World War.

"28 Dental Company, C.D.C." provided dental services to personnel at Camp Borden during the Second World War.

"29 Dental Company, C.D.C." provided dental services to personnel of "Army Headquarters" at Ottawa during the Second World War.

"30 Dental Company, C.D.C." provided dental services to units in "Military District 10" (Manitoba) during the Second World War.

"31 Dental Company, C.D.C." provided dental services to units in "Military District 11" (British Columbia) during the Second World War.

"32 Dental Company, C.D.C." provided dental services to units in "Military District 12" (Saskatchewan) during the Second World War.

"33 Dental Company, C.D.C." provided dental services to units in "Military District 13" (Alberta) during the Second World War.

"34 Dental Company, C.D.C." provided dental services to personnel of "R.C.A.F. Headquarters" at Ottawa during the Second World War.

"35 Dental Company, C.D.C." provided dental services to personnel of the Royal Canadian Air Force at Halifax during the Second World War.

"36 Dental Company, C.D.C." provided dental services to personnel of the Royal Canadian Air Force at Trenton during the Second World War.

"37 Dental Company, C.D.C." provided dental services to personnel of the Royal Canadian Air Force at Vancouver during the Second World War.

"38 Dental Company, C.D.C." provided dental services to personnel of the Royal Canadian Air Force at Winnipeg during the Second World War.

"39 Dental Company, C.D.C." provided dental services to personnel of the Royal Canadian Air Force at Montreal during the Second World War.

"40 Dental Company, C.D.C." provided dental services to personnel of the Royal Canadian Air Force at Calgary during the Second World War.

50 Dental Unit (Militia) — HALIFAX, Nova Scotia
"50 Dental Company, C.D.C." provided dental services to personnel of the Royal Canadian Navy at Halifax during the Second World War. "50 Dental Unit", which had been formed in 1946 as "5 Dental Company" to support the "5th Division" (Reserve Force), was disbanded in 1965.

51 Dental Unit (Milita) — SAINT JOHN, New Brunswick
"51 Dental Company, C.D.C." provided dental services to personnel of the Royal Canadian Navy at Toronto during the Second World War. "51 Dental Unit", which had been formed in 1954, was disbanded in 1965.

52 Dental Unit (Militia) — QUEBEC CITY
"52 Dental Company, C.D.C." provided dental services to personnel of the Royal Canadian Navy at Esquimalt (Victoria) during the Second World War. "52 Dental Unit", which had been formed in 1946 as "4 Dental Company" to support the "4th Division" (Reserve Force), was disbanded in 1965.

53 Dental Unit (Militia) — MONTREAL, Quebec
"53 Dental Company, C.D.C." provided dental services to personnel of "Headquarters, Royal Canadian Navy, London" during the Second World War. "53 Dental Unit", which had been formed in 1946 as "3 Dental Company" to support the "3rd Division" (Reserve Force), was disbanded in 1965.

54 Dental Unit (Militia) — OTTAWA, Ontario
"54 Dental Unit", which had been formed in 1946 as "7 Dental Company" to support the "1st Corps" (Reserve Force), was disbanded in 1965.

55 Dental Unit (Militia) — LONDON, Ontario
"55 Dental Unit", which had been formed in 1946 as "1 Dental Company" to support the "1st Division" (Reserve Force), was disbanded in 1965.

56 Dental Unit (Militia) — TORONTO, Ontario
"56 Dental Unit", which had been formed in 1946 as "2 Dental Company" to support the "2nd Division" (Reserve Force), was disbanded in 1965.

57 Dental Unit (Militia) — WINNIPEG, Manitoba
"57 Dental Unit", which had been formed in 1946 as "6 Dental Company" to support the "6th Division" (Reserve Force), was disbanded in 1965.

58 Dental Unit (Militia) — REGINA, Saskatchewan
"58 Dental Unit", which had been formed in 1954, was disbanded in 1965.

59 Dental Unit (Militia) — CALGARY, Alberta
"59 Dental Unit", which had been formed in 1954, was disbanded in 1965.

60 Dental Unit (Militia) — EDMONTON, Alberta
"60 Dental Unit", which had been formed in 1954, was disbanded in 1965.

61 Dental Unit (Militia) — VANCOUVER, British Columbia
"61 Dental Unit", which had been formed in 1946 as "8 Dental Company" to support the "2nd Corps" (Reserve Force), was disbanded in 1965.

1 Dental Unit (Regular) — OTTAWA, Ontario
This unit provides dental services to personnel of "Canadian Forces Headquarters".

4 Field Dental Company, R.C.D.C. (Regular) — SOEST, West Germany
The company was disbanded in 1970 as a unit of the "4th Canadian Infantry Brigade Group".

11 Dental Unit (Regular) — ESQUIMALT (VICTORIA) British Columbia
Detachment — CAMP CHILLIWACK, British Columbia

12 Dental Unit (Regular) — HALIFAX, Nova Scotia
Detachment — CAMP GAGETOWN, New Brunswick

13 Dental Unit (Regular) — TRENTON, Ontario
Detachment — CAMP PETAWAWA, Ontario

14 Dental Unit (Regular) — WINNIPEG, Manitoba
Detachment — CAMP SHILO, Manitoba

15 Dental Unit (Regular) — MONTREAL, Quebec
Detachment — CAMP VALCARTIER, Quebec

"25 Field Dental Company, R.C.D.C." served in Korea as a unit of the "25th Canadian Infantry Brigade".

"27 Field Dental Company, R.C.D.C.", which had been formed in 1951 for service with the "27th Canadian Infantry Brigade Group" in West Germany, was re-designated "4 Field Dental Company, R.C.D.C. (Regular)" in 1954.

35 Dental Unit (Regular) — LAHR, West Germany
Detachment — BADEN, West Germany
This unit provides dental services to personnal of both "4 Canadian Mechanized Brigade Group" and "1 Canadian Air Group".

THE CANADIAN PROVOST CORPS

Corps March: *"DISCIPLINE BY EXAMPLE"*
Corps Motto: *"THROUGH NIGHT TO LIGHT"*
Corps School: CAMP BORDEN, Ontario

1 Provost Company — GUELPH, Ontario

"1 Detachment, C.M.P.C." served in "Military District 1" (South-Western Ontario) during the Great War. "1 Provost Company, C.Pro.C. (R.C.M.P.)" fought in both Italy and North-West Europe during the Second World War and was perpetuated by "1 Provost Company (Reserve Force)" which, having been formed in 1946 to support the "1st Division" (Reserve Force), was re-organized in 1954 as a detached platoon of "6 Provost Company (Militia)".

2 Provost Company — Denison Armoury, DOWNSVIEW (TORONTO), Ontario

"2 Detachment, C.M.P.C." served in "Military District 2" (Central Ontario) during the Great War. "2 Provost Company, C.Pro.C." fought in North-West Europe during the Second World War and was perpetuated by "2 Provost Company (Reserve Force)" which had been formed in 1946 to support the "2nd Division" (Reserve Force). "2 Provost Company (Militia)", which maintained a detached platoon at Markham from 1965 until 1968, was incorporated within the "1st Toronto Service Battalion" in 1965 and, upon amalgamation with "7 Provost Company", re-organized in 1970 as the "security platoon" of the "Toronto Service Battalion" which was re-designated "25 (Toronto) Service Battalion" in 1975.

3 Provost Company — MONTREAL, Quebec

"3 Detachment, C.M.P.C." served in "Military District 3" (Eastern Ontario) during the Great War. "3 Provost Company, C.Pro.C." fought in both Italy and North-West Europe during the Second World War and was perpetuated by "3 Provost Company (Reserve Force)" which had been formed in 1946 to support the "3rd Division" (Reserve Force). "3 Provost Company (Militia)", which maintained detached platoons at Drummondville and Three Rivers until 1965, provided a provost platoon for both the "1st" and "2nd" Montreal Service Battalions in 1965. These platoons were amalgamated in 1970 and re-organized as the "security platoon" of the "Montreal Service Battalion" which was re-designated "51 (Montreal) Service Battalion" in 1975.

4 Provost Company — QUEBEC CITY

"4 Detachment, C.M.P.C." served in "Military District 4" (Western Quebec) during the Great War. "4 Provost Company, C.Pro.C." fought in North-West Europe during the Second World War and was perpetuated by "4 Provost Company (Reserve Force)" which had been formed in 1946 to support the "4th Division" (Reserve Force). "4 Provost Company (Militia)" was incorporated within the "Quebec Service Battalion" in 1965 and re-organized in 1970 as the "security platoon" of the battalion which was re-designated "55 (Quebec) Bataillon des Services" in 1975.

5 Provost Company — HALIFAX, Nova Scotia

"5 Detachment, C.M.P.C." served in "Military District 5" (Eastern Quebec) during the Great War. "5 Provost Company, C.Pro.C." fought in both Italy and North-West Europe during the Second World War and was perpetuated by "5 Provost Company (Reserve Force)" which had been formed in 1946 to support the "5th Division" (Reserve Force). "5 Provost Company (Militia)", which maintained a detached platoon at Charlottetown until 1965, was incorporated within the "Halifax Service Battalion" in 1965 and re-organized in 1970 as the "security platon" of the battalion which was re-designated "33 (Halifax) Service Battalion" in 1965.

6 Provost Company — LONDON, Ontario

"6 Detachment, C.M.P.C." served in "Military District 6" (Nova Scotia) during the Great War. "6 Provost Company (Militia)", which maintained a detached platoon at Guelph until 1965, was incorporated within the "London Service Battalion" in 1965 and re-organized in 1970 as the "security platoon" of the battalion which was re-designated "22 (London) Service Battalion" in 1975.

7 Provost Company — Moss Park Armoury, TORONTO, Ontario
"7 Detachment, C.M.P.C." served in "Military District 7" (New Brunswick and Prince Edward Island) during the Great War. "7 Provost Company, C.Pro.C." fought in North-West Europe during the Second World War. "7 Provost Company (Militia)", which had been formed in 1965 as a sub-unit of the "2nd Toronto Service Battalion", was amalgamated with "2 Provost Company" in 1970 and re-organized as the "security platoon" of the "Toronto Service Battalion" which was re-designated "25 (Toronto) Service Battalion" in 1975.

8 Provost Company — VANCOUVER, British Columbia
"8 Detachment, C.M.P.C." fought in France during the Great War. "8 Provost Company, C.Pro.C." fought in North-West Europe during the Second World War and was perpetuated by "8 Provost Company (Reserve Force)" which, having been formed in 1946, maintained detached platoons at Vernon and Victoria until 1954. "8 Provost Company (Militia)" was incorporated within the "Vancouver Service Battalion" in 1965 and re-organized in 1970 as the "security platoon" of the battalion which was redesignated "12 (Vancouver) Service Battalion" in 1975.

"9 Detachment, C.M.P.C." fought in France during the Great War.

"10 Detachment, C.M.P.C." served in "Military District 10" (Manitoba) during the Great War.

"11 Detachment, C.M.P.C." served in "Military District 11" (British Columbia) during the Great War. "11 Provost Company, C.Pro.C." fought in North-West Europe during the Second World War.

"12 Detachment, C.M.P.C." served in "Military District 12" (Saskatchewan) during the Great War.

13 Provost Company — WINNPEG, Manitoba
"13 Detachment, C.M.P.C." served in "Military District 13" (Alberta) during the Great War. "13 Provost Company, C.Pro.C." fought in North-West Europe during the Second World War and was perpetuated by "13 Provost Company (Reserve Force)" which had been formed in 1946. "13 Provost Company (Militia)" was incorporated within the "Winnipeg Service Battalion" in 1965 and re-organized in 1970 as the "security platoon" of the battalion which was re-designated "17 (Winnipeg) Service Battalion" in 1975.

14 Provost Company — CALGARY, Alberta
"14 Provost Company (Militia)", which had been formed in 1954, was incorporated within the "Calgary Service Battalion" in 1965 and re-organized in 1970 as the "security platoon" of the battalion which was re-designated "14 (Calgary) Service Battalion" in 1975.

15 Provost Company — EDMONTON, Alberta
"15 Provost Company, C.Pro.C." fought in North-West Europe during the Second World War. "15 Provost Company (Militia)", which had been formed in 1954, was incorporated within the "Edmonton Service Battalion" in 1965 and re-organized in 1970 as the "security platoon" of the battalion which was re-designated "15 (Edmonton) Service Battalion" in 1975.

16 Provost Company — MONCTON, New Brunswick
"16 Provost Company, C.Pro.C." fought in North-West Europe during the Second World War. "16 Provost Company (Militia)", which had been formed in 1954, was incorporated within the "Moncton Service Battalion" in 1965 and re-organized in 1970 as the "security platoon" of the battalion which was re-designated "32 (Moncton) Service Battalion" in 1975.

"25 Provost Detachment, C.Pro.C." served in Korea as a unit of the "25th Canadian Infantry Brigade".

"27 Provost Detachment, C.Pro.C." served in West Germany as a unit of the "27th Canadian Infantry Brigade Group".

"35 Traffic Control Company, C.Pro.C.", which had been formed in 1944 by the conversion and re-designation of "35 Light Anti-Aircraft Battery, R.C.A.", fought in Italy prior to re-conversion to artillery in 1945.

1 Provost Platoon (Regular) — CALGARY, Alberta
The platoon was formed to support the "1st Canadian Infantry Brigade Group" and was re-organized in 1970 as the "military police platoon" of "1 Canadian Brigade Group'.

2 Provost Platoon (Regular) — CAMP PETAWAWA, Ontario
The platoon was formed to support the "2nd Canadian Infantry Brigade Group" and was re-organized in 1970 as the "military police platoon" of the "Special Service Force".

3 Provost Platoon (Regular) — CAMP GAGETOWN, New Brunswick
The platoon, which had been formed to support the "3rd Canadian Infantry Brigade Group", was disbanded in 1970 upon the replacement of the "3rd Canadian Infantry Brigade Group" by the "Combat Training Centre".

4 Provost Platoon (Regular) — LAHR, West Germany
The platoon was formed to support the "4th Canadian Infantry Brigade Group" and was re-organized in 1970 as the "military police platoon" of "4 Canadian Mechanized Brigade Group".

5ieme Peloton de Police Militaire — CAMP VALCARTIER, Quebec
Le peloton, qui a forme en 1970, est un unit de "5ieme Group-Brigade du Canada".

THE CANADIAN INTELLIGENCE CORPS

Corps March: *"SILVER AND GREEN"*
Corps Motto: *"ACTION FROM KNOWLEDGE"*
The Canadian School of Military Intelligence: CAMP BORDEN, Ontario

NOTE

An "intelligence corps" consisting of land surveyors, who through their profession were familiar with the surrounding countryside, provided reconnaissance for the various "columns" advancing towards the Metis and Indian forces during the "Riel" Rebellion in Saskatchewan (1885). The "Corps of Guides", which performed intelligence duties, served from 1903 until 1929 as an element of the "Non-Permanent Active Militia". A "Canadian Corps Intelligence Section" served in France as a unit of the Canadian Expeditionary Force during the Great War.

1 Detachment, Corps of Guides — LONDON, Ontario

2 Detachment, Corps of Guides — TORONTO, Ontario

3 Detachment, Corps of Guides — KINGSTON, Ontario

4 Detachment, Corps of Guides — MONTREAL, Quebec

5 Detachment, Corps of Guides — QUEBEC CITY

6 Detachment, Corps of Guides — HALIFAX, Nova Scotia

7 Detachment, Corps of Guides — SAINT JOHN, New Brunswick

"8" Not Allocated

"9" Not Allocated

10 Detachment, Corps of Guides — WINNIPEG, Manitoba

11 Detachment, Corps of Guides — VICTORIA, British Columbia

12 Detachment, Corps of Guides — REGINA, Saskatchewan

13 Detachment, Corps of Guides — CALGARY, Alberta

1 Cyclist Company, Corps of Guides — LONDON, Ontario

2 Cyclist Company, Corps of Guides — TORONTO, Ontario

3 Cyclist Company, Corps of Guides — KINGSTON, Ontario

4 Cyclist Company, Corps of Guides — MONTREAL, Quebec

5 Cyclist Company, Corps of Guides — LAKE MEGANTIC, Quebec

6 Cyclist Company, Corps of Guides — NEW GLASGOW, Nova Scotia

7 Cyclist Company, Corps of Guides — WOODSTOCK, New Brunswick

8 Cyclist Company, Corps of Guides — TORONTO, Ontario

"9" Not Allocated

10 Cyclist Company, Corps of Guides — WINNIPEG, Manitoba

11 Cyclist Company, Corps of Guides — VICTORIA, British Columbia

12 Cyclist Company, Corps of Guides — REGINA, Saskatchewan

13 Cyclist Company, Corps of Guides — CALGARY, Alberta

"1 Field Security Section, C.Int.C." fought in both Italy and North-West Europe during the Second World War.

"2 Field Security Section, C.Int.C." fought at Dieppe and in North-West Europe during the Second World War.

"3 Field Security Section, C.Int.C." fought in North-West Europe during the Second World War.

"4 Field Security Section, C.Int.C." fought in North-West Europe during the Second World War.

"5 Field Security Section, C.Int.C." served in Canada during the Second World War.

"6 Field Security Section, C.Int.C." served in Canada during the Second World War.

"7 Field Security Section, C.Int.C." fought in both Italy and North-West Europe during the Second World War.

"8 Field Security Section, C.Int.C." served in Canada during the Second World War.

"9" Not Allocated

"10 Not Allocated

"11 Field Security Section, C.Int.C." fought in both Italy and North-West Europe during the Second World War.

"12 Field Security Section, C.Int.C." served in the United Kingdom during the Second World War.

"13 Field Security Section, C.Int.C." served in the United Kingdom during the Second World War.

"14 Field Security Section, C.Int.C." fought in both Italy and North-West Europe during the Second World War.

"15 Field Security Section, C.Int.C." fought in North-West Europe during the Second World War.

"16 Field Security Section, C.Int.C." fought in North-West Europe during the Second World War.

"17 Field Security Section, C.Int.C." fought in North-West Europe during the Second World War.

"18 Field Security Section, C.Int.C." fought in North-West Europe during the Second World War.

"19 Field Security Section, C.Int.C." served on Kiska in the Aleutian Islands as a unit of the "13th Canadian Infantry Brigade Group" during the Second World War.

"20 Field Security Section, C.Int.C." fought in North-West Europe during the Second World War.

1 Intelligence Training Company (Militia) — MONTREAL, Quebec
The company, which had been formed in 1947, was incorporated within the "security platoon" of the "Montreal Service Battalion" in 1970.

2 Intelligence Training Company (Militia) — TORONTO, Ontario
The company, which had been formed in 1947, was incorporated within the "security platoon" of the "Toronto Service Battalion" in 1970.

3 Intelligence Training Company (Militia) — HALIFAX, Nova Scotia
The company, which had been formed in 1950, was incorporated within the "security platoon" of the "Halifax Service Battalion" in 1970.

4 Intelligence Training Company (Militia) — VANCOUVER, British Columbia
The company, which had been formed in 1950, maintained detached sections at Victoria (until 1965) and Edmonton (until 1962) and was incorporated within the "security platoon" of the "Vancouver Service Battalion" in 1970.

5 Intelligence Training Company (Militia) — WINNIPEG, Manitoba
The company, which had been formed in 1951, maintained a detached section at Regina until 1953 and was incorporated within the "security platoon" of the "Winnipeg Service Battalion" in 1970.

6 Intelligence Training Company (Militia) — EDMONTON, Alberta
The company, which had been formed in 1962 by the re-organization of a detached section of "4 Intelligence Training Company", was incorporated within the "security platoon" of the "Edmonton Service Battalion" in 1970.

"1 Field Security Section, C.Int.C." served in Korea as a unit of the "25th Canadian Infantry Brigade".

"2 Field Security Section, C.Int.C." served in West Germany as a unit of the "27th Canadian Infantry Brigade Group".

THE ROYAL CANADIAN ARMY PAY CORPS

Corps March: *"PRIMROSE AND BLUE"*
Corps School: CAMP BARRIEFIELD (KINGSTON), Ontario

The "Canadian Army Pay Corps" provided paymasters and pay sergeants for service with all elements of the Canadian Expeditionary Force during the Great War. Personnel of the "Royal Canadian Army Pay Corps" served with all units of the Canadian Army during both the Second World War and the Korean War.

"1 Army Pay Ledger Unit, R.C.A.P.C." maintained pay and pension records for personnel of the Canadian Army (Regular).

Battalion-sized units of both the Regular and Militia components of the Canadian Army maintained, within their particular organization, a paymaster and finance clerk of the "Royal Canadian Army Pay Corps".

THE ROYAL CANADIAN POSTAL CORPS

Corps March: "THE POST-HORN GALLOP"
Corps Motto: "SERVIRE ARMATIS"
("TO SERVE THE ARMED FORCES")

The "Canadian Postal Corps" provided postal clerks for the Canadian Expeditionary Force during the Great War and the Canadian Army during both the Second World War and the Korean War. The "Royal Canadian Postal Corps" provided personnel for all formations and units of the Canadian Army (Regular) as well as for installations of the Royal Canadian Navy and Royal Canadian Air Force.

THE ROYAL CANADIAN ARMY CHAPLAIN CORPS

The "Canadian Chaplain Service" provided chaplains for the Canadian Expeditionary Force during the Great War and the Canadian Army during the Second World War. The "Royal Canadian Army Chaplain Corps" provided chaplains for service during the Korean War. Army chaplains, prior to the unification of the armed forces in 1968, were administered through "command chaplain units" from which they were posted to units and formations as required.

SERVICE BATTALIONS

NOTE (1)

Regular service battalions, upon formation, incorporated those units of the RCASC, RCOC and RCEME that were in direct support of their respective brigade group. Each battalion therefore consisted of a transport company, ordnance field park (subsequently re-designated "supply company") and a field workshop (subsequently re-designated "maintenance company").

NOTE (2)

Militia service battalions, upon formation, incorporated those units of the RCASC, RCOC, RCEME, RCAMC and CProC that were located (with some exceptions) in the same general area.

1 Service Battalion (Regular) — CALGARY, Alberta
1 Transport Company, R.C.A.S.C. (Regular) — CALGARY
1 Ordnance Field Park, R.C.O.C. (Regular) — CALGARY
1 Field Workshop, R.C.E.M.E. (Regular) CALGARY

2 Service Battalion (Regular) — CAMP PETAWAWA, Ontario
2 Transport Company, R.C.A.S.C. (Regular) — CAMP PETAWAWA
2 Ordnance Field Park, R.C.O.C. (Regular) — CAMP PETAWAWA
2 Field Workshop, R.C.E.M.E. (Regular) — CAMP PETAWAWA

3 Service Battalion (Regular) — CAMP GAGETOWN, New Brunswick
3 Transport Company, R.C.A.S.C. (Regular) — CAMP GAGETOWN
3 Ordnance Field Park, R.C.O.C. (Regular) — CAMP GAGETOWN
3 Field Workshop, R.C.E.M.E. (Regular) — CAMP GAGETOWN

4 Service Battalion (Regular) — SOEST, West Germany
4 Transport Company, R.C.A.S.C. (Regular) — SOEST
4 Ordnance Field Park, R.C.O.C. (Regular) — SOEST
4 Field Workshop, R.C.E.M.E. (Regular) — SOEST

5 Bataillon des Services (Regulier) — CAMP VALCARTIER, Quebec

The Newfoundland Service Battalion (Militia)
Headquarters — ST. JOHN'S, Newfoundland
1 Medical Company, R.C.A.M.C. (Militia) — ST. JOHN'S

The Halifax Service Battalion (Militia)
Headquarters — HALIFAX, Nova Scotia
110 Transport Company, R.C.A.S.C. (Militia) — HALIFAX
9 Ordnance ompany, R.C.O.C. (Militia) — HALIFAX
20 Technical Squadron, R.C.E.M.E. (Militia) — HALIFAX
2 Medical Company, R.C.A.M.C. (Militia) — HALIFAX
5 Provost Company, C.Pro.C. (Militia) — HALIFAX

The Sydney Service Battalion (Militia)
Headquarters — SYDNEY, Nova Scotia
111 Transport Company, R.C.A.S.C. (Militia) — SYDNEY
6 Medical Company, R.C.A.M.C. (Militia) — SYDNEY

The Saint John Service Battalion (Militia)
Headquarters — SAINT JOHN, New Brunswick
112 Transport Company, R.C.A.S.C. (Militia) — SAINT JOHN
4 Medical Company, R.C.A.M.C. (Militia) — SAINT JOHN

The Moncton Service Battalion (Militia)
Headquarters — MONCTON, New Brunswick
113 Transport Company, R.C.A.S.C. (Militia) — MONCTON
21 Technical Squadron, R.C.E.M.E. (Militia) — MONCTON
3 Medical Company, R.C.A.M.C. (Militia) — MONCTON
16 Provost Company, C.Pro.C. (Militia) — MONCTON

The Quebec Service Battalion (Militia)
Headquarters — QUEBEC CITY
120 Transport Company, R.C.A.S.C. (Militia) — QUEBEC CITY
10 Ordnance Company, R.C.O.C. (Militia) — QUEBEC CITY
42 Technical Squadron, R.C.E.M.E. (Militia) — QUEBEC CITY
7 Medical Company, R.C.A.M.C. (Militia) — QUEBEC CITY
4 Provost Company, C.Pro.C. (Militia) — QUEBEC CITY

1st Montreal Service Battalion (Militia)
Headquarters — MONTREAL, Quebec
122 Transport Company, R.C.A.S.C. (Militia) — MONTREAL
7 Ordnance Company, R.C.O.C. (Militia) — MONTREAL
43 Technical Squadron, R.C.E.M.E. (Militia) — MONTREAL
"A" Company, 1st Medical Battalion, R.C.A.M.C. (Militia) — MONTREAL
1 Platoon, 3 Provost Company, C.Pro.C. (Militia) — MONTREAL

2nd Montreal Service Battalion (Militia)
Headquarters — MONTREAL, Quebec
124 Transport Company, R.C.A.S.C. (Militia) — MONTREAL
8 Ordnance Company, R.C.O.C. (Militia) — STE-THERESE, Quebec
44 Technical Squadron, R.C.E.M.E. (Militia) — MONTREAL
"B" Company, 1st Medical Battalion, R.C.A.M.C. (Militia) — MONTREAL
2 Platoon, 3 Provost Company, C.Pro.C. (Militia) — MONTREAL

The Ottawa Service Battalion (Militia)
Headquarters — OTTAWA, Ontario
130 Transport Company, R.C.A.S.C. (Militia) — OTTAWA
3 Ordnance Company, R.C.O.C. (Militia) — OTTAWA
28 Technical Squadron, R.C.E.M.E. (Militia) — PETERBOROUGH, Ontario
10 Medical Company, R.C.A.M.C. (Militia) — OTTAWA

1st Toronto Service Battalion (Militia)
Headquarters — Denison Armoury, DOWNSVIEW (TORONTO), Ontario
134 Transport Company, R.C.A.S.C. (Militia) — DOWNSVIEW
12 Ordnance Company, R.C.O.C. (Militia) — DOWNSVIEW
45 Technical Squadron, R.C.E.M.E. (Militia) — DOWNSVIEW
13 Medical Company, R.C.A.M.C. (Militia) — OWEN SOUND, Ontario
2 Provost Company, C.Pro.C. (Militia) — DOWNSVIEW

2nd Toronto Service Battalion (Militia)
Headquarters — Moss Park Armoury, TORONTO, Ontario
136 Transport Company, R.C.A.S.C. (Militia) — TORONTO
13 Ordnance Company, R.C.O.C. (Militia) — TORONTO
46 Technical Squadron, R.C.E.M.E. (Militia) — TORONTO
26 Medical Company, R.C.A.M.C. (Militia) — TORONTO
7 Provost Company, C.Pro.C. (Militia) — TORONTO

The Hamilton Service Battalion (Militia)
Headquarters — HAMILTON, Ontario
133 Transport Company, R.C.A.S.C. (Militia) — HAMILTON
4 Ordnance Company, R.C.O.C. (Militia) — HAMILTON
47 Technical Squadron, R.C.E.M.E. (Militia) — HAMILTON
16 Medical Company, R.C.A.M.C. (Militia) — HAMILTON

The London Service Battalion (Militia)
Headquarters — LONDON, Ontario
132 Transport Company, R.C.A.S.C. (Militia) — LONDON
14 Ordnance Company, R.C.O.C. (Militia) — LONDON
29 Technical Squadron, R.C.E.M.E. (Militia) — LONDON
15 Medical Company, R.C.A.M.C. (Militia) — LONDON
6 Provost Company, C. Pro.C. (Militia) — LONDON

The Windsor Service Battalion (Militia)
Headquarters — WINDSOR, Ontario
39 Technical Squadron, R.C.E.M.E. (Militia) — WINDSOR

The Lakehead Service Battalion (Militia)
Headquarters — THUNDER BAY, Ontario
138 Transport Company, R.C.A.S.C. (Militia) — THUNDER BAY
35 Technical Squadron, R.C.E.M.E. (Militia) — THUNDER BAY
17 Medical Company, R.C.A.M.C. (Militia) — THUNDER BAY

The Winnipeg Service Battalion (Militia)
Headquarters — WINNIPEG, Manitoba
140 Transport Company, R.C.A.S.C. (Militia) — WINNIPEG
15 Ordnance Company, R.C.O.C. (Militia) — WINNIPEG
36 Technical Squadron, R.C.E.M.E. (Militia) — WINNIPEG
18 Medical Company, R.C.A.M.C. (Militia) — WINNIPEG
13 Provost Company, C.Pro.C. (Militia) — WINNIPEG

The Regina Service Battalion (Militia)
Headquarters — REGINA, Saskatchewan
142 Transport Company, R.C.A.S.C. (Militia) — REGINA
5 Ordnance Company, R.C.O.C. (Militia) — REGINA
19 Medical Company, R.C.A.M.C. (Militia) — REGINA

The Calgary Service Battalion (Militia)
Headquarters — CALGARY, Alberta
150 Transport Company, R.C.A.S.C. (Militia) — CALGARY
6 Ordnance Company, R.C.O.C. (Militia) — CALGARY
48 Technical Squadron, R.C.E.M.E. (Militia) — CALGARY
21 Medical Company, R.C.A.M.C. (Militia) — CALGARY
14 Provost Company, C.Pro.C. (Militia) — CALGARY

The Edmonton Service Battalion (Militia)
Headquarters — EDMONTON, Alberta
154 Transport Company, R.C.A.S.C. (Militia) — EDMONTON
16 Ordnance Company, R.C.O.C. (Militia) — EDMONTON
38 Technical Squadron, R.C.E.M.E. (Militia) — EDMONTON
23 Medical Company, R.C.A.M.C. (Militia) — EDMONTON
15 Provost Company, C.Pro.C. (Militia) — EDMONTON

The Vancouver Service Battalion (Militia)
Headquarters — VANCOUVER, British Columbia
156 Transport Company, R.C.A.S.C. (Militia) — VANCOUVER
17 Ordnance Company, R.C.O.C. (Militia) — VANCOUVER
49 Technical Squadron, R.C.E.M.E. (Militia) — VANCOUVER
24 Medical Company, R.C.A.M.C. (Militia) — VANCOUVER
8 Provost Company, C.Pro.C. (Militia) — VANCOUVER

The Victoria Service Battalion (Militia)
Headquarters — VICTORIA, British Columbia
155 Transport Company, R.C.A.S.C. (Militia) — VICTORIA
40 Technical Squadron, R.C.E.M.E. (Militia) — VICTORIA

CURRENT REGULAR FORMATIONS

1st CANADIAN BRIGADE GROUP

Headquarters and Signal Squadron — CALGARY, Alberta
1st Battalion, P.P.C.L.I. — Currie Barracks, CALGARY, Alberta
2nd Battalion, P.P.C.L.I. — Kapyong Barracks, WINNIPEG, Manitoba
3rd Battalion, P.P.C.L.I. — Work Point Barracks, ESQUIMALT (VICTORIA), B.C.
Lord Strathcona's Horse (Royal Canadians) — Sarcee Barracks, CALGARY, Alberta
  "A" Squadron
  "B" Squadron
  "C" Squadron
3rd Regiment, R.C.H.A. — CAMP SHILO, Manitoba
  "G" Battery
  "J" Battery
  "U" (Air Defence) Battery
1st Combat Engineer Regiment — CAMP CHILLIWACK, British Columbia
1st Service Battalion — CALGARY, Alberta
1st Field Ambulance — CALGARY, Alberta
1st Military Police Platoon — CALGARY, Alberta

THE SPECIAL SERVICE FORCE

Headquarters and Signal Squadron — CAMP PETAWAWA, Ontario
1st Battalion, The Royal Canadian Regiment — Wolseley Barracks, LONDON, Ontario
The Canadian Airborne Regiment — CAMP PETAWAWA, Ontario
  1iere Commando (Aeroporte)
  2nd (Airborne) Commando
  3rd (Airborne) Commando
  Airborne Service Commando
8th Canadian Hussars (Princess Louise's) — CAMP PETAWAWA, Ontario
  "A" Squadron
  "B" Squadron
  "C" Squadron
2nd Regiment, R.C.H.A. — CAMP PETAWAWA, Ontario
  "D" Battery
  "E" (Parachute) Battery
  Air Defence Troop
2nd Combat Engineer Regiment — CAMP PETAWAWA, Ontario
2nd Service Battalion — CAMP PETAWAWA, Ontario
2nd Field Ambulance — CAMP PETAWAWA, Ontario
2nd Military Police Platoon — CAMP PETAWAWA, Ontario

THE COMBAT TRAINING CENTRE

Headquarters — CAMP GAGETOWN, New Brunswick
"C" Squadron, Royal Canadian Dragoons — Carleton Barracks, CAMP GAGETOWN
"W" Battery, R.C.H.A. — Brownfield Barracks, CAMP GAGETOWN, New Brunswick
22 Field Engineer Squadron — CAMP GAGETOWN, New Brunswick

4th CANADIAN MECHANIZED BRIGADE GROUP

Headquarters and Signal Squadron — LAHR, West Germany
3rd Battalion, The Royal Canadian Regiment — BADEN, West Germany
1iere Battaillon, Royal Vingt-Deuxieme Regiment — LAHR, West Germany
The Royal Canadian Dragoons — LAHR, West Germany
   "A" Squadron
   "B" Squadron
1st Regiment, R.C.H.A. — LAHR, West Germany
   "A" Battery
   "B" Battery
   "C" Battery
   "Z" (Reinforcement) Battery — CAMP SHILO, Manitoba
   Air Defence Troop
128 Air Defence Battery — BADEN, West Germany
129 Air Defence Battery — LAHR, West Germany
4th Combat Engineer Regiment — LAHR, West Germany
4th Service Battalion — LAHR, West Germany
4th Field Ambulance — LAHR, West Germany
4th Military Police Platoon — LAHR, West Germany

5ieme Groupe-Brigade du Canada

Quartier-General et Escadron des Transmissions — CAMP VALCARTIER, Quebec
2nd Battalion, The Royal Canadian Regiment — CAMP GAGETOWN, New Brunswick
2ieme Bataillon, Royal Vingt-Deuxieme Regiment — La Citadelle, QUEBEC CITY
3ieme Bataillon, Royal Vingt-Deuxieme Regiment — CAMP VALCARTER, Quebec
12ieme Regiment Blinde du Canada — CAMP VALCARTIER, Quebec
   Escadron "A"
   Escadron "B"
   Escadron "C"
5ieme Regiment d'Artillerie Legere du Canada — CAMP VALCARTIER, Quebec
   Batterie "Q"
   Batterie "V" (Defence de l'Air)
   Batterie "X"
5ieme Regiment du Genie — CAMP VALCARTIER, Quebec
5ieme Bataillon des Services — CAMP VALCARTER, Quebec
5ieme Ambulance de Campagne — CAMP VALCARTIER, Quebec
5ieme Peloton de Police Militaire — CAMP VALCARTIER, Quebec

THE ROYAL CANADIAN NAVAL RESERVE

March-Past: *"HEART OF OAK"*

Canadian naval tradition may be considered as having originated in "His Majesty's Provincial Marine" which, locally-recruited, fought on Lake Champlain and Lake George during the Seven-Years War (1756-1763) and was established on the Great Lakes in 1775 where it stood guard during the American Revolution/War of Independence (1775-1783). The "Provincial Marine" fought on the Great Lakes during the Anglo-American War of 1812 to 1814 after which it was disbanded according to the terms of peace. The Militia Act of 1855 authorized the formation of "naval companies" which were "commissioned" as follows:

The "Dunnville Naval Company" (authorized on 31 January 1862) was disbanded in 1869.

The "Hamilton Naval Company" (authorized on 31 January 1862), which was disbanded in 1870, may be considered as being perpetuated by "H.M.C.S. Star" (the naval reserve unit in Hamilton).

The "Kingston Naval Company" (authorized on 31 January 1862), which was disbanded in 1866, may be considered as being perpetuated by "H.M.C.S. Cataraqui" (the naval reserve unit in Kingston).

The "Oakville Naval Company" (authorized on 31 January 1862) was disbanded in 1866.

The "Port Stanley Naval Company" (authorized on 31 January 1862), was disbanded in 1869.

The "Toronto Naval Company" (authorized on 3 July 1862), which was disbanded in 1869, may be considered as being perpetuated by "H.M.C.S. York" (the naval reserve unit in Toronto).

The "Garden Island Naval Company" (authorized on 16 January 1863 for the County of Frontenac) was disbanded in 1869.

In 1909, the Government of Canada passed the "Naval Service Act" which provided for a permanent naval service that was established in 1910 as the "Naval Service of Canada" which was re-designated "Royal Canadian Navy" in 1911. Authorization for a "Royal Naval Canadian Volunteer Reserve" whose members were enrolled for wartime service with either the Royal Navy or the Royal Canadian Navy was given in July of 1914 and "companies" were organized at Victoria ("1" Company) and Vancouver ("2" Company). In 1923, the "Royal Canadian Naval Volunteer Reserve" was organized in "half-companies" which were re-designated "naval reserve divisions" in 1936 as follows:

The "Naval Reserve Division, Charlottetown" (authorized in 1923) was "commissioned" "H.M.C.S. Queen Charlotte" in 1941. This establishment was "paid-off" (de-commissioned) in 1964.

The "Naval Reserve Division, Saint John" (authorized in 1923) was "commissioned" "H.M.C.S. Brunswicker" in 1941. This establishment is still in existence.

The "Naval Reserve Division, Quebec City" (authorized in 1923) was "commissioned" "H.M.C.S. Montcalm" in 1941. This establishment is still in existence.

The "Naval Reserve Division, Montreal" (authorized in 1923) was "commissioned" "H.M.C.S. Donnaconna" in 1941. This establishment is still in existence.

The "Naval Reserve Division, Ottawa" (authorized in 1923) was "commissioned" "H.M.C.S. Carleton" in 1941. This establishment is still in existence.

The "Naval Reserve Division, Toronto" (authorized in 1923) was "commissioned" "H.M.C.S. York" in 1941. This establishment is still in existence.

The "Naval Reserve Division, Hamilton" (authorized in 1923) was "commissioned" "H.M.C.S. Star" in 1941. This establishment is still in existence.

The "Naval Reserve Division, Winnipeg" (authorized in 1923) was "commissioned" "H.M.C.S. Chippewa" in 1941. This establishment is still in existence.

The "Naval Reserve Division, Regina" (authorized in 1923) was "commissioned" "H.M.C.S. Queen" in 1941. This establishment is still in existence.

The "Naval Reserve Division, Saskatoon" (authorized in 1923) was "commissioned" "H.M.C.S. Unicorn" in 1941. This establishment is still in existence.

The "Naval Reserve Division, Calgary" (authorized in 1923) was "commissioned" "H.M.C.S. Tecumseh" in 1941. This establishment is still in existence.

The "Naval Reserve Division, Edmonton" (authorized in 1923) was "commissioned" "H.M.C.S. Nonsuch" in 1941. This establishment is still in existence.

The "Naval Reserve Division, Vancouver" (authorized in 1924) was "commissioned" "H.M.C.S. Discovery" in 1941. This establishment is still in existence.

The "Naval Reserve Division, Prince Rupert" (authorized in 1924) was "commissioned" "H.M.C.S. Chatham" in 1941. This establishment was "paid off" (de-commissioned) in 1964.

The "Naval Reserve Division, Halifax" (authorized in 1925) was "commissioned" "H.M.C.S. Scotian" in 1941. This establishment is still in existence.

The "Naval Reserve Division, Port Arthur" (authorized in 1937) was "commissioned" "H.M.C.S. Griffon" in 1941. This establishment is still in existence.

The "Naval Reserve Division, London" (authorized in 1938) was "commissioned" "H.M.C.S. Prevost" in 1941. This establishment was "paid off" (de-commissioned) in 1964.

The "Naval Reserve Division, Kingston" (authorized in 1939) was "commissioned" "H.M.C.S. Cataraqui" in 1941. This establishment is still in existence.

The "Naval Reserve Division, Windsor" (authorized in 1939) was "commissioned" "H.M.C.S. Hunter" in 1941. This establishment is still in existence.

"H.M.C.S. Malahat" was "commissioned" in 1947 at Victoria, British Columbia. This establishment is still in existence.

"H.M.C.S. Cabot" was "commissioned" in 1949 at St. John's, Newfoundland. This establishment is still in existence.

"H.M.C.S. Caribou" was "commissioned" in 1953 at Corner Brook, Newfoundland. This establishment was "paid off" (de-commissioned) in 1964.

THE MARCH TO THE BATTLEFIELD or CANADA'S MEN ON THE WAY
1914-1915

NOTE
A battle honour for "THE GREAT WAR" indicates that the battalion served in the United Kingdom for the period specified by the accompanying year-date. These battalions, although they did not serve in France, were integral to the Canadian Expeditionary Force in that they provided the administrative structure through which personnel were recruited in Canada and forwarded to the United Kingdom for further training in the "reserve battalions" prior to being posted to France as reinforcements for battalions of the "Canadian Corps" in the field.

1st (Western Ontario) Infantry Battalion, C.E.F. — CAMP VALCARTIER, Quebec
The battalion, which comprised volunteers from London and south-western Ontario, fought in France as a unit of the "1st Infantry Brigade" and is perpetuated by "4th Battalion, The Royal Canadian Regiment (London and Oxford Fusiliers) (Militia)".
Major Battle Honours:
VIMY RIDGE — PURSUIT TO MONS — FRANCE AND FLANDERS, 1915-1918

2nd (Eastern Ontario) Infantry Battalion, C.E.F. — CAMP VALCARTIER, Quebec
The battalion, which comprised volunteers from Ottawa and eastern Ontario, fought in France as a unit of the "1st Infantry Brigade" and is perpetuated by "The Governor-General's Foot Guards (5th Battalion, The Canadian Guards)".
Major Battle Honours:
VIMY RIDGE — PURSUIT TO MONS — FRANCE AND FLANDERS, 1915-1918

3rd Infantry Battalion (The Toronto Regiment), C.E.F. — CAMP VALCARTIER, Quebec
The battalion, which comprised volunteers from Toronto, fought in France as a unit of the "1st Infantry Brigade" and is perpetuated jointly by "The Queen's Own Rifles of Canada" and "The Royal Regiment of Canada".
Major Battle Honours:
VIMY RIDGE — PURSUIT TO MONS — FRANCE AND FLANDERS, 1915-1918

4th (Central Ontario) Infantry Battalion, C.E.F. — CAMP VALCARTIER, Quebec
The battalion, which comprised volunteers from Hamilton and central Ontario, fought in France as a unit of the "1st Infantry Brigade" and is perpetuated by "The Royal Hamilton Light Infantry (Wentworth Regiment)".
Major Battle Honours:
VIMY RIDGE — PURSUIT TO MONS — FRANCE AND FLANDERS, 1915-1918

5th (Western Cavalry) Infantry Battalion, C.E.F. —CAMP VALCARTIER, Quebec
The battalion, which comprised volunteers from Saskatchewan, fought in France as a unit of the "2nd Infantry Brigade" and is perpetuated by "The North Saskatchewan Regiment".
Major Battle Honours:
VIMY RIDGE — PURSUIT TO MONS — FRANCE AND FLANDERS, 1915-1918

6th Infantry Battalion, C.E.F. — CAMP VALCARTIER, Quebec
The battalion, which comprised volunteers from Manitoba and is perpetuated by the "12th Manitoba Dragoons", served in the United Kingdom where it was re-organized as the "Canadian Cavalry Depot" from which "The Fort Garry Horse, C.E.F." was mobilized. (Note that the "12th Manitoba Dragoons" was disbanded in 1965.)
Battle Honour: THE GREAT WAR, 1914-1915

7th (1st British Columbia) Infantry Battalion, C.E.F. — CAMP VALCARTIER, Quebec
The battalion, which comprised volunteers from British Columbia, fought in France as a unit of the "2nd Infantry Brigade" and is perpetuated by "The British Columbia Regiment (R.C.A.C.)".
Major Battle Honours:
VIMY RIDGE — PURSUIT TO MONS — FRANCE AND FLANDERS, 1915-1918

8th Infantry Battalion (90th Rifles), C.E.F. — CAMP VALCARTIER, Quebec
The battalion, which comprised volunteers from Winnipeg, fought in France as a unit of the "2nd Infantry Brigade" and is perpetuated by "The Royal Winnipeg Rifles".
Major Battle Honours:
VIMY RIDGE — PURSUIT TO MONS — FRANCE AND FLANDERS, 1915-1918

9th Infantry Battalion, C.E.F. — CAMP VALCARTIER, Quebec
The battalion, which comprised volunteers from Edmonton and is perpetuated by the "19th Alberta Dragoons", was disbanded in the United Kingdom and its' personnel incorporated within a "reserve battalion" for further training prior to their being posted to France as reinforcements for battalions of the "Canadian Corps" in the field. (Note that the "19th Alberta Dragoons" was disbanded in 1965.)
Battle Honour: THE GREAT WAR, 1914-1917

10th Infantry Battalion, C.E.F. — CAMP VALCARTIER, Quebec
The battalion, which comprised volunteers from the prairie provinces, fought in France as a unit of the "2nd Infantry Brigade" and is perpetuated jointly by "The Royal Winnipeg Rifles" and "The Calgary Highlanders".
Major Battle Honours:
VIMY RIDGE — PURSUIT TO MONS — FRANCE AND FLANDERS, 1915-1918

11th Infantry Battalion, C.E.F — CAMP VALCARTIER, Quebec
The battalion, which comprised volunteers from the prairie provinces and is perpetuated by "The Winnipeg Grenadiers", was disbanded in the United Kingdom and its' personnel incorporated within a "reserve battalion" for further training prior to their being posted to France as reinforcements for battalions of the "Canadian Corps" in the field. (Note that "The Winnipeg Grenadiers" was disbanded in 1965.)
Battle Honour: THE GREAT WAR, 1914-1917

12th Infantry Battalion, C.E.F. — CAMP VALCARTIER, Quebec
The battalion, which comprised volunteers from the maritime provinces and is perpetuated by "1st Battalion, The Royal New Brunswick Regiment", was disbanded in the United Kingdom and its' personnel incorporated within a "reserve battalion" for further training prior to their being posted to France as reinforcements for battalions of the "Canadian Corps" in the field.
Battle Honour: THE GREAT WAR, 1914-1917

13th Infantry Battalion (Royal Highlanders of Canada), C.E.F. — CAMP VALCARTIER, Quebec
The battalion, which comprised volunteers from Montreal, fought in France as a unit of the "3rd Infantry Brigade" and is perpetuated by "The Black Watch (Royal Highland Regiment) of Canada".
Major Battle Honours:
VIMY RIDGE — PURSUIT TO MONS — FRANCE AND FLANDERS, 1915-1918

14th Infantry Battalion (The Royal Montreal Regiment), C.E.F. — CAMP VALCARTIER, Quebec
The battalion, which comprised volunteers from Montreal, fought in France as a unit of the "3rd Infantry Brigade" and is perpetuated by "The Royal Montreal Regiment".
Major Battle Honours:
VIMY RIDGE — PURSUIT TO MONS — FRANCE AND FLANDERS, 1915-1918

15th Infantry Battalion (48th Highlanders of Canada), C.E.F. — CAMP VALCARTIER, Quebec
The battalion, which comprised volunteers from Toronto, fought in France as a unit of the "3rd Infantry Brigade" and is perpetuated by the "48th Highlanders of Canada".
Major Battle Honours:
VIMY RIDGE — PURSUIT TO MONS — FRANCE AND FLANDERS, 1915-1918

16th (Canadian Scottish) Infantry Battalion, C.E.F. — CAMP VALCARTIER, Quebec
The battalion, which comprised volunteers from Victoria, fought in France as a unit of the "3rd Infantry Brigade" and is perpetuated by "The Canadian Scottish Regiment".
Major Battle Honours:
VIMY RIDGE — PURSUIT TO MONS — FRANCE AND FLANDERS, 1915-1918

17th Infantry Battalion (Nova Scotia Highlanders), C.E.F. — TRURO, Nova Scotia
The battalion, which is perpetuated by "1st Battalion, The Nova Scotia Highlanders", was disbanded in the United Kingdom and its' personnel incorporated within a "reserve battalion" for further training prior to their being posted to France as reinforcements for battalions of the "Canadian Corps" in the field.
Battle Honour: THE GREAT WAR, 1914-1917

18th (Western Ontario) Infantry Battalion, C.E.F. — LONDON, Ontario
The battalion fought in France as a unit of the "4th Infantry Brigade" and is perpetuated by "The Essex and Kent Scottish Regiment".
Major Battle Honours:
VIMY RIDGE — PURSUIT TO MONS — FRANCE AND FLANDERS, 1915-1918

19th (Central Ontario) Infantry Battalion, C.E.F. — TORONTO, Ontario
The battalion fought in France as a unit of the "4th Infantry Brigade" and is perpetuated by "The Argyll and Sutherland Highlanders of Canada".
Major Battle Honours:
VIMY RIDGE — PURSUIT TO MONS — FRANCE AND FLANDERS, 1915-1918

20th (Central Ontario) Infantry Battalion, C.E.F. — TORONTO, Ontario
The battalion fought in France as a unit of the "4th Infantry Brigade" and is perpetuated by "The Queen's York Rangers (1st American Regiment) (R.C.A.C.)".
Major Battle Honours:
VIMY RIDGE — PURSUIT TO MONS — FRANCE AND FLANDERS, 1915-1918

21st (Eastern Ontario) Infantry Battalion, C.E.F. — KINGSTON, Ontario
The battalion fought in France as a unit of the "4th Infantry Brigade" and is perpetuated by "The Princess of Wales' Own Regiment".
Major Battle Honours:
VIMY RIDGE — PURSUIT TO MONS — FRANCE AND FLANDERS, 1915-1918

22nd (Canadien-Francais) Infantry Battalion, C.E.F. — ST. JOHN'S, Quebec
The battalion fought in France as a unit of the "5th Infantry Brigade" and is perpetuated by "Le Royal Vingt-Deuxieme Regiment (Regulier)".
Major Battle Honours:
VIMY RIDGE — PURSUIT TO MONS — FRANCE AND FLANDERS, 1915-1918

23rd Infantry Battalion, C.E.F. — QUEBEC CITY
The battalion, which is perpetuated by "The Royal Montreal Regiment", was disbanded in the United Kingdom and its' personnel incorporated within a "reserve battalion" for further training prior to their being posted to France as reinforcements for battalions of the "Canadian Corps" in the field.
Battle Honour: THE GREAT WAR, 1915-1917

24th Infantry Battalion (Victoria Rifles of Canada), C.E.F. — MONTREAL, Quebec
The battalion fought in France as a unit of the "5th Infantry Brigade" and is perpetuated by "The Victoria Rifles of Canada". (Note that "The Victoria Rifles of Canada" was disbanded in 1965.)
Major Battle Honours:
VIMY RIDGE — PURSUIT TO MONS — FRANCE AND FLANDERS, 1915-1918

25th Infantry Battalion (Nova Scotia Rifles), C.E.F. — HALIFAX, Nova Scotia
The battalion fought in France as a unit of the "5th Infantry Brigade" and is perpetuated by "1st Battalion, The Nova Scotia Highlanders".
Major Battle Honours:
VIMY RIDGE — FRANCE AND FLANDERS, 1915-1918

26th (New Brunswick) Infantry Battalion, C.E.F. — SAINT JOHN, New Brunswick
The battalion fought in France as a unit of the "5th Infantry Brigade" and is perpetuated by "1st Battalion, The Royal New Brunswick Regiment".
Major Battle Honours:
VIMY RIDGE — FRANCE AND FLANDERS, 1915-1918

27th (City of Winnipeg) Infantry Battalion, C.E.F. — WINNIPEG, Manitoba
The battalion fought in France as a unit of the "6th Infantry Brigade" and is perpetuated by "The Manitoba Regiment". (Note that "The Manitoba Regiment" was disbanded in 1936.)
Major Battle Honours:
.VIMY RIDGE — PURSUIT TO MONS — FRANCE AND FLANDERS, 1915-1918

28th (North-West) Infantry Battalion, C.E.F. — WINNIPEG, Manitoba
The battalion fought in France as a unit of the "6th Infantry Brigade" and is perpetuated by "The Regina Rifle Regiment".
Major Battle Honours:
VIMY RIDGE — PURSUIT TO MONS — FRANCE AND FLANDERS, 1915-1918

29th Infantry Battalion, C.E.F. — VANCOUVER, British Columbia
The battalion fought in France as a unit of the "6th Infantry Brigade" and is perpetuated by "The Irish Fusiliers of Canada (Vancouver Regiment)". (Note that "The Irish Fusiliers of Canada (Vancouver Regiment)" was disbanded in 1965.)
Major Battle Honours:
VIMY RIDGE — FRANCE AND FLANDERS, 1915-1918

30th Infantry Battalion, C.E.F. — VANCOUVER, British Columbia
The battalion, which is perpetuated by "The Irish Fusiliers of Canada (Vancouver Regiment)", was disbanded in the United Kingdom and its' personnel incorporated within a "reserve battalion" for further training prior to their being posted to France as reinforcements for battalions of the "Canadian Corps" in the field. (Note that "The Irish Fusiliers of Canada (Vancouver Regiment)" was disbanded in 1965.)
Battle Honour: THE GREAT WAR, 1915-1917

31st (Alberta) Infantry Battalion, C.E.F. — CALGARY, Alberta
The battalion fought in France as a unit of the "6th Infantry Brigade" and is perpetuated by "The South Alberta Light Horse".
Major Battle Honours:
VIMY RIDGE — PURSUIT TO MONS — FRANCE AND FLANDERS, 1915-1918

32nd Infantry Battalion, C.E.F. — CALGARY, Alberta
The battalion, which is perpetuated by the "12th Manitoba Dragoons", was disbanded in the United Kingdom and its' personnel incorporated within a "reserve battalion" for further training prior to their being posted to France as reinforcements for battalions of the "Canadian Corps" in the field. (Note that the "12th Manitoba Dragoons" was disbanded in 1965.)
Battle Honour: THE GREAT WAR, 1915-1917

33rd Infantry Battalion, C.E.F. — LONDON, Ontario
The battalion, which is perpetuated by "4th Battalion, The Royal Canadian Regiment (London and Oxford Fusiliers) (Militia)", was disbanded in the United Kingdom and its' personnel incorporated within a "reserve battalion" for further training prior to their being posted to France as reinforcements for battalions of the "Canadian Corps" in the field.
Battle Honour: THE GREAT WAR, 1916

34th Infantry Battalion, C.E.F. — GUELPH, Ontario
The battalion, which is perpetuated by "The Highland Fusiliers of Canada", was disbanded in the United Kingdom and its' personnel incorporated within a "reserve battalion" for further training prior to their being posted to France as reinforcements for battalions of the "Canadian Corps" in the field.
Battle Honour: THE GREAT WAR, 1915-1916

35th (Central Ontario) Infantry Battalion, C.E.F. — TORONTO, Ontario
The battalion, which is perpetuated by "The Queen's York Rangers (1st American Regiment) (R.C.A.C.)", was disbanded in the United Kingdom and its' personnel incorporated within a "reserve battalion" for further training prior to their being posted to France as reinforcements for battalions of the "Canadian Corps" in the field.
Battle Honour: THE GREAT WAR, 1915-1917

36th Infantry Battalion, C.E.F. — HAMILTON, Ontario
The battalion, which is perpetuated by "The Dufferin and Haldimand Rifles of Canada", was disbanded in the United Kingdom and its' personnel incorporated within a "reserve battalion" for further training prior to their being posted to France as reinforcements for battalions of the "Canadian Corps" in the field. (Note that "The Dufferin and Haldimand Rifles of Canada" was converted in 1946 and re-designated "56 Light Anti-Aircraft Regiment (The Dufferin and Haldimand Rifles of Canada), R.C.A.".)
Battle Honour: THE GREAT WAR, 1915-1917

37th Infantry Battalion, C.E.F. — TORONTO, Ontario
The battalion, which is perpetuated by "The Lorne Scots (Peel, Dufferin and Halton Regiment)", was disbanded in the United Kingdom and its' personnel incorporated within a "reserve battalion" for further training prior to their being posted to France as reinforcements for battalions of the "Canadian Corps" in the field.
Battle Honour: THE GREAT WAR, 1915-1916

38th Infantry Battalion, C.E.F. — OTTAWA, Ontario
The battalion, which served in Bermuda at the beginning of the Great War, fought in France as a unit of the "12th Infantry Brigade" and is perpetuated by "The Cameron Highlanders of Ottawa".
Major Battle Honours:
VIMY RIDGE — FRANCE AND FLANDERS, 1916-1918

39th Infantry Battalion, C.E.F. — BELLEVILLE, Ontario
The battalion, which is perpetuated by "The Hastings and Prince Edward Regiment", was disbanded in the United Kingdom and its' personnel incorporated within a "reserve battalion" for further training prior to their being posted to France as reinforcements for battalions of the "Canadian Corps" in the field.
Battle Honour: THE GREAT WAR, 1915-1917

40th Infantry Battalion, C.E.F. — HALIFAX, Nova Scotia
The battalion, which is perpetuated by "The Halifax Rifles (R.C.A.C.)", was disbanded in the United Kingdom and its' personnel incorporated within a "reserve battalion" for further training prior to their being posted to France as reinforcements for battalions of the "Canadian Corps" in the field. (Note that "The Halifax Rifles (R.C.A.C.)" was disbanded in 1965.)
Battle Honour: THE GREAT WAR, 1915-1917

41st Infantry Battalion, C.E.F. — QUEBEC CITY
The battalion, which is perpetuated by "Le Regiment de Maisonneuve", was disbanded in the United Kingdom and its' personnel incorporated within a "reserve battalion" for further training prior to their being posted to France as reinforcements for battalions of the "Canadian Corps" in the field.
Battle Honour: THE GREAT WAR, 1915-1916

42nd Infantry Battalion (Royal Highlanders of Canada), C.E.F. — MONTREAL, Quebec
The battalion fought in France as a unit of the "7th Infantry Brigade" and is perpetuated by "The Black Watch (Royal Highland Regiment) of Canada".
Major Battle Honours:
VIMY RIDGE — PURSUIT TO MONS — FRANCE AND FLANDERS, 1915-1918

43rd Infantry Battalion (Cameron Highlanders), C.E.F. — WINNIPEG, Manitoba
The battalion fought in France as a unit of the "9th Infantry Brigade" and is perpetuated by "The Queen's Own Cameron Highlanders of Canada".
Major Battle Honours:
VIMY RIDGE — PURSUIT TO MONS — FRANCE AND FLANDERS, 1916-1918

44th (Manitoba) Infantry Battalion, C.E.F. — WINNIPEG, Manitoba
The battalion fought in France as a unit of the "10th Infantry Brigade" and is perpetuated by "The Royal Winnipeg Rifles".
Major Battle Honours:
VIMY RIDGE — FRANCE AND FLANDERS, 1916-1918

45th Infantry Battalion, C.E.F. — BRANDON, Manitoba
The battalion, which is perpetuated by "The Manitoba Rangers", was disbanded in the United Kingdom and its' personnel incorporated within a "reserve battalion" for further training prior to their being posted to France as reinforcements for battalions of the "Canadian Corps" in the field. (Note that "The Manitoba Rangers" was converted in 1936 and re-designated "26 Field Brigade (The Manitoba Rangers), R.C.A.".)
Battle Honour: THE GREAT WAR, 1916

46th (South Saskatchewan) Infantry Battalion, C.E.F. — REGINA, Saskatchewan
The battalion fought in France as a unit of the "10th Infantry Brigade" and is perpetuated by "The Saskatchewan Dragoons".
Major Battle Honours:
VIMY RIDGE — FRANCE AND FLANDERS, 1916-1918

47th (British Columbia) Infantry Battalion, C.E.F. — NEW WESTMINSTER, British Columbia
The battalion fought in France as a unit of the "10th Infantry Brigade" and is perpetuated by "The Royal Westminster Regiment".
Major Battle Honours:
VIMY RIDGE —FRANCE AND FLANDERS, 1916-18

48th Infantry Battalion, C.E.F. — VICTORIA, British Columbia
The battalion, which is perpetuated by "The Canadian Scottish Regiment", was re-designated "3rd (48th Canadian) Pioneer Battalion, C.E.F." which fought in France as a unit of the "3rd Canadian Division".
Major Battle Honours:
VIMY RIDGE —FRANCE AND FLANDERS, 1916-1917

49th Infantry Battalion, C.E.F. — EDMONTON, Alberta
The battalion fought in France as a unit of the "7th Infantry Brigade" and is perpetuated by "The Loyal Edmonton Regiment (4th Battalion, P.P.C.L.I.) (Militia)".
Major Battle Honours:
VIMY RIDGE — PURSUIT TO MONS — FRANCE AND FLANDERS, 1915-1918

50th Infantry Battalion, C.E.F. — CALGARY, Alberta
The battalion fought in France as a unit of the "10th Infantry Brigade" and is perpetuated by "The King's Own Calgary Regiment (R.C.A.C.)".
Major Battle Honours:
VIMY RIDGE —FRANCE AND FLANDERS, 1916-1918

51st Infantry Battalion, C.E.F. — EDMONTON, Alberta
The battalion, which is perpetuated by "The Loyal Edmonton Regiment (4th Battalion, P.P.C.L.I.) (Militia)", was disbanded in the United Kingdom and its' personnel incorporated within a "reserve battalion" for further training prior to their being posted to France as reinforcements for battalions of the "Canadian Corps" in the field.
Battle Honour: THE GREAT WAR, 1916-1917

52nd (New Ontario) Infantry Battalion, C.E.F. — PORT ARTHUR, Ontario
The battalion fought in France as a unit of the "9th Infantry Brigade" and is perpetuated by "The Lake Superior Scottish Regiment".
Major Battle Honours:
VIMY RIDGE —FRANCE AND FLANDERS, 1916-1918

53rd Infantry Battalion, C.E.F. — PRINCE ALBERT, Saskatchewan
The battalion, which is perpetuated by "The North Saskatchewan Regiment", was disbanded in the United Kingdom and its' personnel incorporated within a "reserve battalion" for further training prior to their being posted to France as reinforcements for battalions of the "Canadian Corps" in the field.
Battle Honour: THE GREAT WAR, 1916-1917

54th (Kootenay) Infantry Battalion, C.E.F. — NELSON, British Columbia
The battalion fought in France as a unit of the "11th Infantry Brigade" and is perpetuated by "The Kootenay Regiment". (Note that "The Kootenay Regiment" was converted in 1936 and redesignated "24 (Kootenay) Field Brigade, R.C.A.".)
Major Battle Honours:
VIMY RIDGE —FRANCE AND FLANDERS, 1916-1918

55th (New Brunswick and P.E.I.) Infantry Battalion, C.E.F.— SUSSEX, New Brunswick
The battalion, which is perpetuated by "1st Battalion, The Royal New Brunswick Regiment", was disbanded in the United Kingdom and its' personnel incorporated within a "reserve battalion" for further training prior to their being posted to France as reinforcements for battalions of the "Canadian Corps" in the field.
Battle Honour: THE GREAT WAR, 1915-1916

56th Infantry Battalion, C.E.F. — CALGARY, Alberta
The battalion, which is perpetuated by "The Calgary Highlanders", was disbanded in the United Kingdom and its' personnel incorporated within a "reserve battalion" for further training prior to their being posted to France as reinforcements for battalions of the "Canadian Corps" in the field.
Battle Honour: THE GREAT WAR, 1916

57th Infantry Battalion, C.E.F. — QUEBEC CITY
The battalion, which is perpetuated by "Les Voltigeurs de Quebec", was disbanded in the United Kingdom and its' personnel incorporated within a "reserve battalion" for further training prior to their being posted to France as reinforcements for battalions of the "Canadian Corps" in the field
Battle Honour: THE GREAT WAR, 1916

58th (Central Ontario) Infantry Battalion, C.E.F. — TORONTO, Ontario
The battalion fought in France as a unit of the "9th Infantry Brigade" and is perpetuated by "The Royal Regiment of Canada".
Major Battle Honours:
VIMY RIDGE — PURSUIT TO MONS — FRANCE AND FLANDERS, 1916-1918

59th Infantry Battalion, C.E.F. — BROCKVILLE, Ontario
The battalion, which is perpetuated by "The Princess of Wales' Own Regiment", was disbanded in the United Kingdom and its' personnel incorporated within a "reserve battalion" for further training prior to their being posted to France as reinforcements for battalions of the "Canadian Corps" in the field.
Battle Honour: THE GREAT WAR, 1916

60th Infantry Battalion (Victoria Rifles of Canada), C.E.F. — MONTREAL, Quebec
The battalion fought in France as a unit of the "9th Infantry Brigade" and is perpetuated by "The Victoria Rifles of Canada".(Note that "The Victoria Rifles of Canada" was disbanded in 1965.)
Major Battle Honours:
VIMY RIDGE —FRANCE AND FLANDERS, 1916-1917

61st Infantry Battalion (90th Rifles) C.E.F. — WINNIPEG, Manitoba
The battalion, which is perpetuated by "The Royal Winnipeg Rifles", was disbanded in the United Kingdom and its' personnel incorporated within a "reserve battalion" for further training prior to their being posted to France as reinforcements for battalions of the "Canadian Corps" in the field.
Battle Honour: THE GREAT WAR, 1916

62nd Infantry Battalion, C.E.F. — VANCOUVER, British Columbia
The battalion, which is perpetuated by "The British Columbia Regiment (R.C.A.C.)", was disbanded in the United Kingdom and its' personnel incorporated within a "reserve battalion" for further training prior to their being posted to France as reinforcements for battalions of the "Canadian Corps" in the field.
Battle Honour: THE GREAT WAR, 1916

63rd Infantry Battalion, C.E.F. — EDMONTON, Alberta
The battalion, which is perpetuated by "The Loyal Edmonton Regiment (4th Battalion, P.P.C.L.I.) (Militia)", was disbanded in the United Kingdom and its' personnel incorporated within a "reserve battalion" for further training prior to their being posted to France as reinforcements for battalions of the "Canadian Corps" in the field.
Battle Honour: THE GREAT WAR, 1916

64th Infantry Battalion, C.E.F. — HALIFAX, Nova Scotia
The battalion, which is perpetuated by "The Princess Louise Fusiliers", was disbanded in the United Kingdom and its' personnel incorporated within a "reserve battalion" for further training prior to their being posted to France as reinforcements for battalions of the "Canadian Corps" in the field.
Battle Honour: THE GREAT WAR, 1916-1917

65th Infantry Battalion, C.E.F. — SASKATOON, Saskatchewan
The battalion, which is perpetuated by "The North Saskatchewan Regiment", was disbanded in the United Kingdom and its' personnel incorporated within a "reserve battalion" for further training prior to their being posted to France as reinforcements for battalions of the "Canadian Corps" in the field.
Battle Honour: THE GREAT WAR, 1916

66th Infantry Battalion, C.E.F. — EDMONTON, Alberta
The battalion, which is perpetuated by the "19th Alberta Dragoons", was disbanded in the United Kingdom and its' personnel incorporated within a "reserve battalion" for further training prior to their being posted to France as reinforcements for battalions of the "Canadian Corps" in the field.
(Note that the "19th Alberta Dragoons" was disbanded in 1965.)
Battle Honour: THE GREAT WAR, 1916

67th (Western Scots) Infantry Battalion, C.E.F. — VICTORIA, British Columbia
The battalion, which is perpetuated by "The Canadian Scottish Regiment", was re-designated "67th (Western Scots) Pioneer Battalion, C.E.F." which fought in France as a unit of the "4th Canadian Division".
Major Battle Honours:
VIMY RIDGE —FRANCE AND FLANDERS, 1916-1917

68th Infantry Battalion, C.E.F. — REGINA, Saskatchewan
The battalion, which is perpetuated by "The Regina Rifle Regiment", was disbanded in the United Kingdom and its' personnel incorporated within a "reserve battalion" for further training prior to their being posted to France as reinforcements for battalions of the "Canadian Corps" in the field.
Battle Honour: THE GREAT WAR, 1916

69th Infantry Battalion, C.E.F. — ST. JOHN'S, Quebec
The battalion, which is perpetuated by "Les Fusiliers Mont-Royal", was disbanded in the United Kingdom and its' personnel incorporated within a "reserve battalion" for further training prior to their being posted to France as reinforcements for battalions of the "Canadian Corps" in the field.
Battle Honour: THE GREAT WAR, 1916-1917

70th Infantry Battalion, C.E.F. — LONDON, Ontario
The battalion, which is perpetuated by "The Lambton Regiment", was disbanded in the United Kingdom and its' personnel incorporated within a "reserve battalion" for further training prior to their being posted to France as reinforcements for battalions of the "Canadian Corps" in the field. (Note that "The Lambton Regiment" was disbanded in 1936 and its' personnel absorbed by "26 Field Battery, R.C.A." and "11 Field Company, R.C.E." which both then received the county designation "LAMBTON".)
Battle Honour: THE GREAT WAR, 1916

71st Infantry Battalion, C.E.F. — WOODSTOCK, Ontario
The battalion, which is perpetuated by "4th Battalion, The Royal Canadian Regiment (London and Oxford Fusiliers) (Militia)", was disbanded in the United Kingdom and its' personnel incorporated within a "reserve battalion" for further training prior to their being posted to France as reinforcements for battalions of the "Canadian Corps" in the field.
Battle Honour: THE GREAT WAR, 1916

72nd Infantry Battalion (Seaforth Highlanders), C.E.F. — VANCOUVER, British Columbia
The battalion fought in France as a unit of the "12th Infantry Brigade" and is perpetuated by "The Seaforth Highlanders of Canada".
Major Battle Honours:
VIMY RIDGE —FRANCE AND FLANDERS, 1916-1918

73rd Infantry Battalion (Royal Highlanders of Canada), C.E.F. — MONTREAL, Quebec
The battalion fought in France as a unit of the "12th Infantry Brigade" and is perpetuated by "The Black Watch (Royal Highland Regiment) of Canada".
Major Battle Honours:
VIMY RIDGE —FRANCE AND FLANDERS, 1916-1917

74th Infantry Battalion, C.E.F. — TORONTO, Ontario
The battalion, which is perpetuated by "The Lorne Scots (Peel, Dufferin and Halton Regiment)", was disbanded in the United Kingdom and its' personnel incorporated within a "reserve battalion" for further training prior to their being posted to France as reinforcements for battalions of the "Canadian Corps" in the field.
Battle Honour: THE GREAT WAR, 1916

75th (Mississauga) Infantry Battalion, C.E.F. — TORONTO, Ontario
The battalion fought in France as a unit of the "11th Infantry Brigade" and is perpetuated by "The Toronto Scottish Regiment".
Major Battle Honours:
VIMY RIDGE —FRANCE AND FLANDERS, 1916-1918

76th Infantry Battalion, C.E.F. — BARRIE, Ontario
The battalion, which is perpetuated by "The Lorne Scots (Peel, Dufferin and Halton Regiment)", was disbanded in the United Kingdom and its' personnel incorporated within a "reserve battalion" for further training prior to their being posted to France as reinforcements for battalions of the "Canadian Corps" in the field.
Battle Honour: THE GREAT WAR, 1916

77th Infantry Battalion, C.E.F — OTTAWA, Ontario
The battalion, which is perpetuated by "The Governor-General's Foot Guards (5th Battalion, The Canadian Guards)", was disbanded in the United Kingdom and its' personnel incorporated within a "reserve battalion" for further training prior to their being posted to France as reinforcements for battalions of the "Canadian Corps" in the field.
Battle Honour: THE GREAT WAR, 1916

78th Infantry Battalion (Winnipeg Grenadiers), C.E.F. — WINNIPEG, Manitoba
The battalion fought in France as a unit of the "12th Infantry Brigade" and is perpetuated by "The Winnipeg Grenadiers". (Note that "The Winnipeg Grenadiers" was disbanded in 1965.)
Major Battle Honours:
VIMY RIDGE —FRANCE AND FLANDERS, 1916-1918

79th (Manitoba) Infantry Battalion, C.E.F. — BRANDON, Manitoba
The battalion, which is perpetuated by "The Manitoba Rangers", was disbanded in the United Kingdom and its' personnel incorporated within a "reserve battalion" for further training prior to their being posted to France as reinforcements for battalions of the "Canadian Corps" in the field. (Note that "The Manitoba Rangers" was converted in 1936 and re-designated "26 Field Brigade (The Manitoba Rangers), R.C.A.".)
Battle Honour: THE GREAT WAR, 1916

80th Infantry Battalion, C.E.F. — BELLEVILLE, Ontario
The battalion, which is perpetuated by "The Hastings and Prince Edward Regiment", was disbanded in the United Kingdom and its' personnel incorporated within a "reserve battalion" for further training prior to their being posted to France as reinforcements for battalions of the "Canadian Corps" in the field.
Battle Honour: THE GREAT WAR, 1916

81st Infantry Battalion, C.E.F. — TORONTO, Ontario
The battalion, which is perpetuated by "The Lincoln and Welland Regiment", was disbanded in the United Kingdom and its' personnel incorporated within a "reserve battalion" for further training prior to their being posted to France as reinforcements for battalions of the "Canadian Corps" in the field.
Battle Honour: THE GREAT WAR, 1916

82nd Infantry Battalion, C.E.F. — CALGARY, Alberta
The battalion, which is perpetuated by "The Calgary Highlanders", was disbanded in the United Kingdom and its' personnel incorporated within a "reserve battalion" for further training prior to their being posted to France as reinforcements for battalions of the "Canadian Corps" in the field.
Battle Honour: THE GREAT WAR, 1916

83rd Infantry Battalion (Queen's Own Rifles of Canada), C.E.F. — TORONTO, Ont.
The battalion, which is perpetuated by "The Queen's Own Rifles of Canada", was disbanded in the United Kingdom and its' personnel incorporated within a "reserve battalion" for further training prior to their being posted to France as reinforcements for battalions of the "Canadian Corps" in the field.
Battle Honour: THE GREAT WAR, 1916

84th Infantry Battalion, C.E.F. — TORONTO, Ontario
The battalion, which is perpetuated by "The Toronto Scottish Regiment", was disbanded in the United Kingdom and its' personnel incorporated within a "reserve battalion" for further training prior to their being posted to France as reinforcements for battalions of the "Canadian Corps" in the field.
Battle Honour: THE GREAT WAR, 1916

85th Infantry Battalion (Nova Scotia Highlanders), C.E.F. — HALIFAX, N.S.
The battalion fought in France as a unit of the "12th Infantry Brigade" and is perpetuated by "2nd Battalion, The Nova Scotia Highlanders".
Major Battle Honours:
VIMY RIDGE —FRANCE AND FLANDERS, 1917-1918

86th Infantry Battalion, C.E.F. — HAMILTON, Ontario
The battalion, which is perpetuated by "The Royal Hamilton Light Infantry (Wentworth Regiment)", was re-organized in the United Kingdom as the "Canadian Machine-Gun Depot".
Battle Honour: THE GREAT WAR, 1916

87th Infantry Battalion (Canadian Grenadier Guards), C.E.F. — MONTREAL, Quebec
The battalion fought in France as a unit of the "11th Infantry Brigade" and is perpetuated by "The Canadian Grenadier Guards (6th Battalion, The Canadian Guards)".
Major Battle Honours:
VIMY RIDGE —FRANCE AND FLANDERS, 1916-1918

88th Infantry Battalion (Victoria Fusiliers), C.E.F. — VICTORIA, B.C.
The battalion, which is perpetuated by "The Canadian Scottish Regiment", was disbanded in the United Kingdom and its' personnel incorporated within a "reserve battalion" for further training prior to their being posted to France as reinforcements for battalions of the "Canadian Corps" in the field.
Battle Honour: THE GREAT WAR, 1916

89th Infantry Battalion, C.E.F. — CALGARY, Alberta
The battalion, which is perpetuated by "The King's Own Calgary Regiment (R.C.A.C.)", was disbanded in the United Kingdom and its' personnel incorporated within a "reserve battalion" for further training prior to their being posted to France as reinforcements for battalions of the "Canadian Corps" in the field.
Battle Honour: THE GREAT WAR, 1916

90th Infantry Battalion (90th Rifles), C.E.F. — WINNIPEG, Manitoba
The battalion, which is perpetuated by "The Royal Winnipeg Rifles", was disbanded in the United Kingdom and its' personnel incorporated within a "reserve battalion" for further training prior to their being posted to France as reinforcements for battalions of the "Canadian Corps" in the field.
Battle Honour: THE GREAT WAR, 1916

91st (Elgin) Infantry Battalion, C.E.F. — ST. THOMAS, Ontario
The battalion, which is perpetuated by "The Elgin Regiment (R.C.A.C.)", was disbanded in the United Kingdom and its' personnel incorporated within a "reserve battalion" for further training prior to their being posted to France as reinforcements for battalions of the "Canadian Corps" in the field.
Battle Honour: THE GREAT WAR, 1916

92nd Infantry Battalion (48th Highlanders of Canada), C.E.F. — TORONTO, Ontario
The battalion, which is perpetuated by the "48th Highlanders of Canada", was disbanded in the United Kingdom and its' personnel incorporated within a "reserve battalion" for further training prior to their being posted to France as reinforcements for battalions of the "Canadian Corps" in the field.
Battle Honour: THE GREAT WAR, 1916-1917

93rd Infantry Battalion, C.E.F. — PETERBOROUGH, Ontario
The battalion, which is perpetuated by "The Prince of Wales' Rangers (Peterborough Regiment)", was disbanded in the United Kingdom and its' personnel incorporated within a "reserve battalion" for further training prior to their being posted to France as reinforcements for battalions of the "Canadian Corps" in the field. (Note that "The Prince of Wales' Rangers (Peterborough Regiment)" was converted in 1946 and re-designated "50 Heavy Anti-Aircraft Regiment (The Prince of Wales' Rangers), R.C.A.".)
Battle Honour: THE GREAT WAR, 1916

94th Infantry Battalion, C.E.F. — PORT ARTHUR, Ontario
The battalion, which is perpetuated by "The Kenora Light Infantry", was disbanded in the United Kingdom and its' personnel incorporated within a "reserve battalion" for further training prior to their being posted to France as reinforcements for battalions of the "Canadian Corps" in the field. (Note that "The Kenora Light Infantry" was converted in 1936 and re-designated "16 Medium Battery, R.C.A.".)
Battle Honour: THE GREAT WAR, 1916

95th Infantry Battalion (Queen's Own Rifles of Canada), C.E.F. — TORONTO, Ontario
The battalion, which is perpetuated by "The Queen's Own Rifles of Canada", was disbanded in the United Kingdom and its' personnel incorporated within a "reserve battalion" for further training prior to their being posted to France as reinforcements for battalions of the "Canadian Corps" in the field.
Battle Honour: THE GREAT WAR, 1916-1917

96th Infantry Battalion (Canadian Highlanders), C.E.F. — SASKATOON, Saskatchewan
The battalion, which is not perpetuated, was disbanded in the United Kingdom and its' personnel incorporated within a "reserve battalion" for further training prior to their being posted to France as reinforcements for battalions of the "Canadian Corps" in the field.
Battle Honour: THE GREAT WAR, 1916

97th (American) Infantry Battalion, C.E.F. — TORONTO, Ontario
The battalion, which is not perpetuated, was disbanded in the United Kingdom and its' personnel incorporated within a "reserve battalion" for further training prior to their being posted to France as reinforcements for battalions of the "Canadian Corps" in the field.
Battle Honour: THE GREAT WAR, 1916

98th (Lincoln and Welland) Infantry Battalion, C.E.F. — WELLAND, Ontario
The battalion, which is perpetuated by "The Lincoln and Welland Regiment", was disbanded in the United Kingdom and its' personnel incorporated within a "reserve battalion" for further training prior to their being posted to France as reinforcements for battalions of the "Canadian Corps" in the field.
Battle Honour: THE GREAT WAR, 1916

99th (Essex) Infantry Battalion, C.E.F. — WINDSOR, Ontario
The battalion, which is perpetuated by "The Essex and Kent Scottish Regiment", was disbanded in the United Kingdom and its' personnel incorporated within a "reserve battalion" for further training prior to their being posted to France as reinforcements for battalions of the "Canadian Corps" in the field.
Battle Honour: THE GREAT WAR, 1916

100th Infantry Battalion (Winnipeg Grenadiers), C.E.F. — WINNIPEG, Manitoba
The battalion, which is perpetuated by "The Winnipeg Grenadiers", was disbanded in the United
Kingdom and its' personnel incorporated within a "reserve battalion" for further training prior to
their being posted to France as reinforcements for battalions of the "Canadian Corps" in the field.
(Note that "The Winnipeg Grenadiers" was disbanded in 1965.)
Battle Honour: THE GREAT WAR, 1916-1917

101st Infantry Battalion (90th Rifles), C.E.F. — WINNIPEG, Manitoba
The battalion, which is perpetuated by "The Royal Winnipeg Rifles", was disbanded in the United
Kingdom and its' personnel incorporated within a "reserve battalion" for further training prior to
their being posted to France as reinforcements for battalions of the "Canadian Corps" in the field.
Battle Honour: THE GREAT WAR, 1916

102nd (North British Columbia) Infantry Battalion, C.E.F. — VICTORIA, British Columbia
The battalion fought in France as a unit of the "11th Infantry Brigade" and is perpetuated by "The
Irish Fusiliers of Canada (Vancouver Regiment)". (Note that "The Irish Fusiliers of Canada
(Vancouver Regiment)" was disbanded in 1965.)
Major Battle Honours:
VIMY RIDGE —FRANCE AND FLANDERS, 1916-1918

103rd Infantry Battalion, C.E.F. — VICTORIA, British Columbia
The battalion, which is perpetuated by "The Canadian Scottish Regiment", was disbanded in the
United Kingdom and its' personnel incorporated within a "reserve battalion" for further training
prior to their being posted to France as reinforcements for battalions of the "Canadian Corps" in
the field.
Battle Honour: THE GREAT WAR, 1916-1917

104th Infantry Battalion, C.E.F. — SUSSEX, New Brunswick
The battalion, which is perpetuated by "1st Battalion, The Royal New Brunswick Regiment", was
disbanded in the United Kingdom and its' personnel incorporated within a "reserve battalion" for
further training prior to their being posted to France as reinforcements for battalions of the
"Canadian Corps" in the field.
Battle Honour: THE GREAT WAR, 1916-1918

105th Infantry Battalion (The Prince Edward Island Highlanders), C.E.F. — CHARLOTTE-
TOWN, Prince Edward Island
The battalion, which is perpetuated by "The Prince Edward Island Regiment (R.C.A.C.)", was
disbanded in the United Kingdom and its' personnel incorporated within a "reserve battalion" for
further training prior to their being posted to France as reinforcements for battalions of the
"Canadian Corps" in the field.
Battle Honour: THE GREAT WAR, 1916-1917

106th Infantry Battalion (Nova Scotia Rifles), C.E.F. — TRURO, Nova Scotia
The battalion, which is perpetuated by "1st Battalion, The Nova Scotia Highlanders", was
disbanded in the United Kingdom and its' personnel incorporated within a "reserve battalion" for
further training prior to their being posted to France as reinforcements for battalions of the
"Canadian Corps" in the field.
Battle Honour: THE GREAT WAR, 1916

107th Infantry Battalion, C.E.F. — WINNIPEG, Manitoba
The battalion, which is not perpetuated, was re-designated "107th Pioneer Battalion, C.E.F."
which fought in France as a unit of the "1st Canadian Division".
Major Battle Honours:
VIMY RIDGE —FRANCE AND FLANDERS, 1917-1918

108th Infantry Battalion, C.E.F. — SELKIRK, Manitoba
The battalion, which is not perpetuated, was disbanded in the United Kingdom and its' personnel incorporated within a "reserve battalion" for further training prior to their being posted to France as reinforcements for battalions of the "Canadian Corps" in the field.
Battle Honour: THE GREAT WAR, 1916-1917

109th (Victoria and Haliburton) Infantry Battalion, C.E.F. — LINDSAY, Ontario
The battalion, which is perpetuated by "'The Victoria and Haliburton Regiment'", was disbanded in the United Kingdom and its' personnel incorporated within a "reserve battalion" for further training prior to their being posted to France as reinforcements for battalions of the "Canadian Corps" in the field. (Note that "The Victoria and Haliburton Regiment" was disbanded in 1936 and its' personnel absorbed by "45 Field Battery, R.C.A." which then received the county designation "VICTORIA".)
Battle Honour: THE GREAT WAR, 1916

110th Infantry Battalion, C.E.F. — STRATFORD, Ontario
The battalion, which is perpetuated by "The Perth Regiment", was disbanded in the United Kingdom and its' personnel incorporated within a "reserve battalion" for further training prior to their being posted to France as reinforcements for battalions of the "Canadian Corps" in the field. (Note that "The Perth Regiment" was disbanded in 1965.)
Battle Honour: THE GREAT WAR, 1916-1917

111th (South Waterloo) Infantry Battalion, C.E.F. — GALT, Ontario
The battalion, which is perpetuated by "The Highland Fusiliers of Canada", was disbanded in the United Kingdom and its' personnel incorporated within a "reserve battalion" for further training prior to their being posted to France as reinforcements for battalions of the "Canadian Corps" in the field.
Battle Honour: THE GREAT WAR, 1916

112th (Nova Scotia) Infantry Battalion, C.E.F. — WINDSOR, Nova Scotia
The battalion, which is perpetuated by "The West Nova Scotia Regiment", was disbanded in the United Kingdom and its' personnel incorporated within a "reserve battalion" for further training prior to their being posted to France as reinforcements for battalions of the "Canadian Corps" in the field.
Battle Honour: THE GREAT WAR, 1916-1917

113th Infantry Battalion (Lethbridge Highlanders), C.E.F. — LETHBRIDGE, Alberta
The battalion, which is perpetuated by "The South Alberta Light Horse", was disbanded in the United Kingdom and its' personnel incorporated within a "reserve battalion" for further training prior to their being posted to France as reinforcements for battalions of the "Canadian Corps" in the field.
Battle Honour: THE GREAT WAR, 1916

114th (Haldimand) Infantry Battalion (Brock's Rangers), C.E.F. — CAYUGA, Ontario
The battalion, which is perpetuated by "The Dufferin and Haldimand Rifles of Canada", was disbanded in the United Kingdom and its' personnel incorporated within a "reserve battalion" for further training prior to their being posted to France as reinforcements for battalions of the "Canadian Corps" in the field. (Note that "The Dufferin and Haldimand Rifles of Canada" was converted in 1946 and re-designated "56 Light Anti-Aircraft Regiment (The Dufferin and Haldimand Rifles of Canada), R.C.A.".)
Battle Honour: THE GREAT WAR, 1916

115th Infantry Battalion, C.E.F. — SAINT JOHN, New Brunswick
The battalion, which is perpetuated by "1st Battalion, The Royal New Brunswick Regiment", was disbanded in the United Kingdom and its' personnel incorporated within a "reserve battalion" for further training prior to their being posted to France as reinforcements for battalions of the "Canadian Corps" in the field.
Battle Honour: THE GREAT WAR, 1916

116th (County of Ontario) Infantry Battalion, C.E.F. — UXBRIDGE, Ontario
The battalion fought in France as a unit of the "9th Infantry Brigade" and is perpetuated by "The Ontario Regiment (R.C.A.C.)".
Major Battle Honours:
VIMY RIDGE —FRANCE AND FLANDERS, 1917-1918

117th (Eastern Townships) Infantry Battalion, C.E.F. — SHERBROOKE, Quebec
The battalion, which is perpetuated by "The Sherbrooke Hussars", was disbanded in the United Kingdom and its' personnel incorporated within a "reserve battalion" for further training prior to their being posted to France as reinforcements for battalions of the "Canadian Corps" in the field.
Battle Honour: THE GREAT WAR, 1916-1917

118th (North Waterloo) Infantry Battalion, C.E.F. — KITCHENER, Ontario
The battalion, which is perpetuated by "The Highland Fusiliers of Canada", was disbanded in the United Kingdom and its' personnel incorporated within a "reserve battalion" for further training prior to their being posted to France as reinforcements for battalions of the "Canadian Corps" in the field.
Battle Honour: THE GREAT WAR, 1917

119th (Algoma) Infantry Battalion, C.E.F. — SAULT STE. MARIE, Ontario
The battalion, which is perpetuated by "The Sault Ste. Marie and Sudbury Regiment", was disbanded in the United Kingdom and its' personnel incorporated within a "reserve battalion" for further training prior to their being posted to France as reinforcements for battalions of the "Canadian Corps" in the field. (Note that "The Ste. Marie and Sudbury Regiment" was converted in 1946 and re-organized as "49 (Sault Ste. Marie) Heavy Anti-Aircraft Regiment, R.C.A." and "58 (Sudbury) Light Anti-Aircraft Regiment, R.C.A.".)
Battle Honour: THE GREAT WAR, 1916-1918

120th Infantry Battalion, C.E.F. — HAMILTON, Ontario
The battalion, which is perpetuated by "The Royal Hamilton Light Infantry (Wentworth Regiment)", was disbanded in the United Kingdom and its' personnel incorporated within a "reserve battalion" for further training prior to their being posted to France as reinforcements for battalions of the "Canadian Corps" in the field.
Battle Honour: THE GREAT WAR, 1916-1917

121st (Western Irish) Infantry Battalion, C.E.F. — NEW WESTMINSTER, British Columbia
The battalion, which is perpetuated by "The Irish Fusiliers of Canada (Vancouver Regiment)", was disbanded in the United Kingdom and its' personnel incorporated within a "reserve battalion" for further training prior to their being posted to France as reinforcements for battalions of the "Canadian Corps" in the field. (Note that "The Irish Fusiliers of Canada (Vancouver Regiment)" was disbanded in 1965.)
Battle Honour: THE GREAT WAR, 1916-1917

122nd Infantry Battalion, C.E.F. — HUNTSVILLE, Ontario
The battalion, which is perpetuated by "The Algonquin Regiment", was disbanded in the United Kingdom and its' personnel incorporated within a "reserve battalion" for further training prior to their being posted to France as reinforcements for battalions of the "Canadian Corps" in the field.
Battle Honour: THE GREAT WAR, 1917

123rd Infantry Battalion (The Royal Grenadiers), C.E.F. — TORONTO, Ontario
The battalion, which is perpetuated by "The Royal Regiment of Canada", was re-designated "123rd Pioneer Battalion, C.E.F." which fought in France as a unit of the "3rd Canadian Division".
Major Battle Honours:
VIMY RIDGE —FRANCE AND FLANDERS, 1917-1918

124th Infantry Battalion (Governor-General's Body Guard), C.E.F. — TORONTO, Ontario
The battalion, which is perpetuated by "The Royal Regiment of Canada", was re-designated "124th Pioneer Battalion, C.E.F." which fought in France as a unit of the "4th Canadian Division".
Major Battle Honours:
VIMY RIDGE —FRANCE AND FLANDERS, 1917-1918

125th Infantry Battalion, C.E.F. — BRANTFORD, Ontario
The battalion, which is perpetuated by "The Dufferin and Haldimand Rifles of Canada", was disbanded in the United Kingdom and its' personnel incorporated within a "reserve battalion" for further training prior to their being posted to France as reinforcements for battalions of the "Canadian Corps" in the field. (Note that "The Dufferin and Haldimand Rifles of Canada" was converted in 1946 and re-designated "56 Light Anti-Aircraft Regiment (The Dufferin and Haldimand Rifles of Canada), R.C.A.".)
Battle Honour: THE GREAT WAR, 1916-1918

126th (Peel) Infantry Battalion, C.E.F. — TORONTO, Ontario
The battalion, which is perpetuated by "The Lorne Scots (Peel, Dufferin and Halton Regiment)", was disbanded in the United Kingdom and its' personnel incorporated within a "reserve battalion" for further training prior to their being posted to France as reinforcements for battalions of the "Canadian Corps" in the field.
Battle Honour: THE GREAT WAR, 1916

127th Infantry Battalion (York Rangers), C.E.F. — TORONTO, Ontario
The battalion, which is perpetuated by "The Queen's York Rangers (1st American Regiment) (R.C.A.C.)", fought in France and was converted in 1917 and re-designated "2nd Battalion, Canadian Railway Troops, C.E.F." which fought in France as a unit of the "Canadian Corps".
Major Battle Honours:
POLYGON WOOD — FRANCE AND FLANDERS, 1917-1918

128th Infantry Battalion, C.E.F. — MOOSE JAW, Saskatchewan
The battalion, which is perpetuated by "The Saskatchewan Dragoons", was disbanded in the United Kingdom and its' personnel incorporated within a "reserve battalion" for further training prior to their being posted to France as reinforcements for battalions of the "Canadian Corps" in the field.
Battle Honour: THE GREAT WAR, 1916-1917

129th Infantry Battalion, C.E.F — DUNDAS, Ontario
The battalion, which is perpetuated by "The Royal Hamilton Light Infantry (Wentworth Regiment)", was disbanded in the United Kingdom and its' personnel incorporated within a "reserve battalion" for further training prior to their being posted to France as reinforcements for battalions of the "Canadian Corps" in the field.
Battle Honour: THE GREAT WAR, 1916

130th (Lanark and Renfrew) Infantry Battalion, C.E.F. — PERTH, Ontario
The battalion, which is perpetuated by "The Lanark and Renfrew Scottish Regiment", was disbanded in the United Kingdom and its' personnel incorporated within a "reserve battalion" for further training prior to their being posted to France as reinforcements for battalions of the "Canadian Corps" in the field.
Battle Honour: THE GREAT WAR, 1916

131st Infantry Battalion, C.E.F. — NEW WESTMINSTER, British Columbia
The battalion, which is perpetuated by "The Royal Westminster Regiment", was disbanded in the United Kingdom and its' personnel incorporated within a "reserve battalion" for further training prior to their being posted to France as reinforcements for battalions of the "Canadian Corps" in the field.
Battle Honour: THE GREAT WAR, 1916

132nd (North Shore) Infantry Battalion, C.E.F. — CHATHAM, New Brunswick
The battalion, which is perpetuated by "2nd Battalion, The Royal New Brunswick Regiment", was disbanded in the United Kingdom and its' personnel incorporated within a "reserve battalion" for further training prior to their being posted to France as reinforcements for battalions of the "Canadian Corps" in the field.
Battle Honour: THE GREAT WAR, 1916-1917

133rd (Norfolk's Own) Infantry Battalion, C.E.F. — SIMCOE, Ontario
The battalion, which is perpetuated by "The Norfolk Regiment", was disbanded in the United Kingdom and its' personnel incorporated within a "reserve battalion" for further training prior to their being posted to France as reinforcements for battalions of the "Canadian Corps" in the field. (Note that "The Norfolk Regiment" was converted in 1936 and re-designated "25 (Norfolk) Field Brigade, R.C.A.".)
Battle Honour: THE GREAT WAR, 1916

134th Infantry Battalion (48th Highlanders of Canada), C.E.F. — TORONTO, Ontario
The battalion, which is perpetuated by the "48th Highlanders of Canada", was disbanded in the United Kingdom and its' personnel incorporated within a "reserve battalion" for further training prior to their being posted to France as reinforcements for battalions of the "Canadian Corps" in the field.
Battle Honour: THE GREAT WAR, 1916-1918

135th (Middlesex) Infantry Battalion, C.E.F. — LONDON, Ontario
The battalion, which is perpetuated by "The Middlesex and Huron Regiment", was disbanded in the United Kingdom and its' personnel incorporated within a "reserve battalion" for further training prior to their being posted to France as reinforcements for battalions of the "Canadian Corps" in the field. (Note that "The Middlesex and Huron Regiment" was disbanded in 1946 and its' personnel absorbed by "63 Field Battery, R.C.A." and "98 Anti-Tank Battery, R.C.A." which then received the county designations "MIDDLESEX" and "HURON", respectively.)
Battle Honour: THE GREAT WAR, 1916

136th (Durham) Infantry Battalion, C.E.F. — PORT HOPE, Ontario
The battalion, which is perpetuated by "The Hastings and Prince Edward Regiment", was disbanded in the United Kingdom and its' personnel incorporated within a "reserve battalion" for further training prior to their being posted to France as reinforcements for battalions of the "Canadian Corps" in the field.
Battle Honour: THE GREAT WAR, 1916

137th Infantry Battalion, C.E.F. — CALGARY, Alberta
The battalion, which is perpetuated by "The King's Own Calgary Regiment (R.C.A.C.)", was disbanded in the United Kingdom and its' personnel incorporated within a "reserve battalion" for further training prior to their being posted to France as reinforcements for battalions of the "Canadian Corps" in the field.
Battle Honour: THE GREAT WAR, 1916-1917

138th Infantry Battalion, C.E.F. — EDMONTON, Alberta
The battalion, which is perpetuated by the "19th Alberta Dragoons", was disbanded in the United Kingdom and its' personnel incorporated within a "reserve battalion" for further training prior to their being posted to France as reinforcements for battalions of the "Canadian Corps" in the field. (Note that the "19th Alberta Dragoons" was disbanded in 1965.)
Battle Honour: THE GREAT WAR, 1916

139th Infantry Battalion, C.E.F. — COBOURG, Ontario
The battalion, which is perpetuated by "The Hastings and Prince Edward Regiment", was disbanded in the United Kingdom and its' personnel incorporated within a "reserve battalion" for further training prior to their being posted to France as reinforcements for battalions of the "Canadian Corps" in the field.
Battle Honour: THE GREAT WAR, 1916

140th Infantry Battalion, C.E.F. — SAINT JOHN, New Brunswick
The battalion, which is perpetuated by "1st Battalion, The Royal New Brunswick Regiment", was disbanded in the United Kingdom and its' personnel incorporated within a "reserve battalion" for further training prior to their being posted to France as reinforcements for battalions of the "Canadian Corps" in the field.
Battle Honour: THE GREAT WAR, 1916

141st Infantry Battalion, C.E.F. — FORT FRANCES, Ontario
The battalion, which is perpetuated by "The Lake Superior Scottish Regiment", was disbanded in the United Kingdom and its' personnel incorporated within a "reserve battalion" for further training prior to their being posted to France as reinforcements for battalions of the "Canadian Corps" in the field.
Battle Honour: THE GREAT WAR, 1917

142nd Infantry Battalion, C.E.F. — LONDON, Ontario
The battalion, which is perpetuated by "4th Battalion, The Royal Canadian Regiment (London and Oxford Fusiliers) (Militia)", was disbanded in the United Kingdom and its' personnel incorporated within a "reserve battalion" for further training prior to their being posted to France as reinforcements for battalions of the "Canadian Corps" in the field.
Battle Honour: THE GREAT WAR, 1916

143rd Infantry Battalion, C.E.F. — VICTORIA, British Columbia
The battalion, which is perpetuated by "The Canadian Scottish Regiment", was disbanded in the United Kingdom and its' personnel incorporated within a "reserve battalion" for further training prior to their being posted to France as reinforcements for battalions of the "Canadian Corps" in the field.
Battle Honour: THE GREAT WAR, 1917

144th Infantry Battalion (90th Rifles), C.E.F. — WINNIPEG, Manitoba
The battalion, which is perpetuated by "The Royal Winnipeg Rifles", was disbanded in the United Kingdom and its' personnel incorporated within a "reserve battalion" for further training prior to their being posted to France as reinforcements for battalions of the "Canadian Corps" in the field.
Battle Honour: THE GREAT WAR, 1916-1917

145th Infantry Battalion, C.E.F. — MONCTON, New Brunswick
The battalion, which is perpetuated by "1st Battalion, The Royal New Brunswick Regiment", was disbanded in the United Kingdom and its' personnel incorporated within a "reserve battalion" for further training prior to their being posted to France as reinforcements for battalions of the "Canadian Corps" in the field.
Battle Honour: THE GREAT WAR, 1916

146th Infantry Battalion, C.E.F. — KINGSTON, Ontario
The battalion, which is perpetuated by "The Frontenac Regiment", was disbanded in the United Kingdom and its' personnel incorporated within a "reserve battalion" for further training prior to their being posted to France as reinforcements for battalions of the "Canadian Corps" in the field. (Note that "The Frontenac Regiment" was disbanded in 1936 and its' personnel absorbed by "47 Field Battery, R.C.A." which then received the county designation "FRONTENAC".)
Battle Honour: THE GREAT WAR, 1916

147th Infantry Battalion, C.E.F. — OWEN SOUND, Ontario
The battalion, which is perpetuated by "The Grey and Simcoe Foresters", was disbanded in the United Kingdom and its' personnel incorporated within a "reserve battalion" for further training prior to their being posted to France as reinforcements for battalions of the "Canadian Corps" in the field.
Battle Honour: THE GREAT WAR, 1916-1917

148th Infantry Battalion. C.E.F. — MONTREAL, Quebec
The battalion, which is perpetuated by the "McGill University Contingent, C.O.T.C.", was disbanded in the United Kingdom and its' personnel incorporated within a "reserve battalion" for further training prior to their being posted to France as reinforcements for battalions of the "Canadian Corps" in the field. (Note that all contingents of the "Canadian Officers Training Corps" were disbanded in 1965.)
Battle Honour: THE GREAT WAR, 1916-1917

149th Infantry Battalion, C.E.F. — WATFORD, Ontario
The battalion, which is perpetuated by "The Lambton Regiment", was disbanded in the United Kingdom and its' personnel incorporated within a "reserve battalion" for further training prior to their being posted to France as reinforcements for battalions of the "Canadian Corps" in the field. (Note that "The Lambton Regiment" was disbanded in 1936 and its' personnel absorbed by "26 Field Battery, R.C.A." and "11 Field Company, R.C.E." which both then received the county designation "LAMBTON".)
Battle Honour: THE GREAT WAR, 1917

150th Infantry Battalion (Caribiniers Mont-Royal), C.E.F. — MONTREAL, Quebec
The battalion, which is perpetuated by "Les Fusiliers Mont-Royal", was disbanded in the United Kingdom and its' personnel incorporated within a "reserve battalion" for further training prior to their being posted to France as reinforcements for battalions of the "Canadian Corps" in the field.
Battle Honour: THE GREAT WAR, 1916-1918

151st (Central Alberta) Infantry Battalion, C.E.F. — STRATHCONA, Alberta
The battalion, which is perpetuated by "The North Alberta Regiment", was disbanded in the United Kingdom and its' personnel incorporated within a "reserve battalion" for further training prior to their being posted to France as reinforcements for battalions of the "Canadian Corps" in the field. (Note that "The North Alberta Regiment" was disbanded in 1936.)
Battle Honour: THE GREAT WAR, 1916

152nd Infantry Battalion, C.E.F. — WEYBURN, Saskatchewan
The battalion, which is perpetuated by "The South Saskatchewan Regiment", was disbanded in the United Kingdom and its' personnel incorporated within a "reserve battalion" for further training prior to their being posted to France as reinforcements for battalions of the "Canadian Corps" in the field. (Note that "The South Saskatchewan Regiment" was disbanded in 1968.)
Battle Honour: THE GREAT WAR, 1916

153rd Infantry Battalion, C.E.F. — GUELPH, Ontario
The battalion, which is perpetuated by "The Wellington Regiment", was disbanded in the United Kingdom and its' personnel incorporated within a "reserve battalion" for further training prior to their being posted to France as reinforcements for battalions of the "Canadian Corps" in the field. (Note that "The Wellington Regiment" was converted in 1936 and re-designated "99 Field Battery, R.C.A.".)
Battle Honour: THE GREAT WAR, 1917

154th (Stormont, Dundas and Glengarry) Infantry Battalion, C.E.F. — CORNWALL, Ontario
The battalion, which is perpetuated by "The Stormont, Dundas and Glengarry Highlanders", was disbanded in the United Kingdom and its' personnel incorporated within a "reserve battalion" for further training prior to their being posted to France as reinforcements for battalions of the "Canadian Corps" in the field.
Battle Honour: THE GREAT WAR, 1916-1917

155th Infantry Battalion, C.E.F. — BELLEVILLE, Ontario
The battalion, which is perpetuated by "The Hastings and Prince Edward Regiment", was disbanded in the United Kingdom and its' personnel incorporated within a "reserve battalion" for further training prior to their being posted to France as reinforcements for battalions of the "Canadian Corps" in the field.
Battle Honour: THE GREAT WAR, 1916

156th (Leeds and Grenville) Infantry Battalion, C.E.F. — BROCKVILLE, Ontario
The battalion, which is perpetuated by "The Brockville Rifles", was disbanded in the United Kingdom and its' personnel incorporated within a "reserve battalion" for further training prior to their being posted to France as reinforcements for battalions of the "Canadian Corps" in the field.
Battle Honour: THE GREAT WAR, 1916-1918

157th Infantry Battalion (Simcoe Foresters), C.E.F. — BARRIE, Ontario
The battalion, which is perpetuated by "The Grey and Simcoe Foresters", was disbanded in the United Kingdom and its' personnel incorporated within a "reserve battalion" for further training prior to their being posted to France as reinforcements for battalions of the "Canadian Corps" in the field.
Battle Honour: THE GREAT WAR, 1916

158th (Duke of Connaught's Own) Infantry Battalion, C.E.F. — VANCOUVER, British Columbia
The battalion, which is perpetuated by "The Irish Fusiliers of Canada (Vancouver Regiment)", was disbanded in the United Kingdom and its' personnel incorporated within a "reserve battalion" for further training prior to their being posted to France as reinforcements for battalions of the "Canadian Corps" in the field. (Note that "The Irish Fusiliers of Canada (Vancouver Regiment)" was disbanded in 1965.)
Battle Honour: THE GREAT WAR, 1916-1917

159th (1st Algonquin) Infantry Battlion, C.E.F. — HAILEYBURY, Ontario
The battalion, which is perpetuated by "The Algonquin Regiment", was disbanded in the United Kingdom and its' personnel incorporated within a "reserve battalion" for further training prior to their being posted to France as reinforcements for battalions of the "Canadian Corps" in the field.
Battle Honour: THE GREAT WAR, 1916-1917

160th (Bruce) Infantry Battalion, C.E.F. — WALKERTON, Ontario
The battalion, which is perpetuated by "The Bruce Regiment", was disbanded in the United Kingdom and its' personnel incorporated within a "reserve battalion" for further training prior to their being posted to France as reinforcements for battalions of the "Canadian Corps" in the field. (Note that "The Bruce Regiment" was converted in 1936 and re-designated "97 (Bruce) Field Battery, R.C.A.".)
Battle Honour: THE GREAT WAR, 1916-1918

161st (Huron) Infantry Battalion, C.E.F. — CLINTON, Ontario
The battalion, which is perpetuated by "The Middlesex and Huron Regiment", was disbanded in the United Kingdom and its' personnel incorporated within a "reserve battalion" for further training prior to their being posted to France as reinforcements for battalions of the "Canadian Corps" in the field. (Note that "The Middlesex and Huron Regiment" was disbanded in 1946 and its' personnel absorbed by "63 Field Battery, R.C.A." and "98 Anti-Tank Battery, R.C.A." which then received the county designations "MIDDLESEX" and "HURON", respectively.
Battle Honour: THE GREAT WAR, 1916-1918

162nd Infantry Battalion, C.E.F. — PARRY SOUND, Ontario
The battalion, which is perpetuated by "The Algonquin Regiment", was disbanded in the United Kingdom and its' personnel incorporated within a "reserve battalion" for further training prior to their being posted to France as reinforcements for battalions of the "Canadian Corps" in the field.
Battle Honour: THE GREAT WAR, 1916-1917

163rd (Canadien-Francais) Infantry Battalion, C.E.F. — MONTREAL, Quebec
The battalion, which served in Bermuda at the beginning of the Great War, is perpetuated by "Les Fusiliers de Sherbrooke" and was disbanded in the United Kingdom and its' personnel incorporated within a "reserve battalion" for further training prior to their being posted to France as reinforcements for battalions of the "Canadian Corps" in the field.
Battle Honour: THE GREAT WAR, 1916-1917

164th (Halton and Dufferin) Infantry Battalion, C.E.F. — MILTON, Ontario
The battalion, which is perpetuated by "The Lorne Scots (Peel, Dufferin and Halton Regiment)", was disbanded in the United Kingdom and its' personnel incorporated within a "reserve battalion" for further training prior to their being posted to France as reinforcements for battalions of the "Canadian Corps" in the field.
Battle Honour: THE GREAT WAR, 1917-1918

165th (French-Acadian) Infantry Battalion, C.E.F. — MONCTON, New Brunswick
The battalion, which is perpetuated by "2nd Battalion, The Royal New Brunswick Regiment", was disbanded in the United Kingdom and its' personnel incorporated within a "reserve battalion" for further training prior to their being posted to France as reinforcements for battalions of the "Canadian Corps" in the field.
Battle Honour: THE GREAT WAR, 1917

166th Infantry Battalion (Queen's Own Rifles of Canada), C.E.F. — TORONTO, Ont.
The battalion, which is perpetuated by "The Queen's Own Rifles of Canada", was disbanded in the United Kingdom and its' personnel incorporated within a "reserve battalion" for further training prior to their being posted to France as reinforcements for battalions of the "Canadian Corps" in the field.
Battle Honour: THE GREAT WAR, 1916-1917

167th Infantry Battalion, C.E.F. — QUEBEC CITY
The battalion, which is perpetuated by "Les Chasseurs Canadiens", was disbanded in Canada in 1917 and its' personnel incorporated within the "Quebec Regiment, C.E.F." for further training prior to their being forwarded to the United Kingdom. (Note that "Les Chasseurs Canadiens" was disbanded in 1936).

168th Infantry Battalion, C.E.F. — WOODSTOCK, Ontario
The battalion, which is perpetuated by "4th Battalion, The Royal Canadian Regiment (London and Oxford Fusiliers) (Militia)", was disbanded in the United Kingdom and its' personnel incorporated within a "reserve battalion" for further training prior to their being posted to France as reinforcements for battalions of the "Canadian Corps" in the field.
Battle Honour: THE GREAT WAR, 1916-1917

169th Infantry Battalion, C.E.F. — TORONTO, Ontario
The battalion, which is not perpetuated, was disbanded in the United Kingdom and its' personnel incorporated within a "reserve battalion" for further training prior to their being posted to France as reinforcements for battalions of the "Canadian Corps" in the field.
Battle Honour: THE GREAT WAR, 1916-1917

170th Infantry Battalion (Mississauga Horse), C.E.F. — TORONTO, Ontario
The battalion, which is perpetuated by "The Royal Regiment of Canada", was disbanded in the United Kingdom and its' personnel incorporated within a "reserve battalion" for further training prior to their being posted to France as reinforcements for battalions of the "Canadian Corps" in the field.
Battle Honour: THE GREAT WAR, 1916

171st Infantry Battalion (Quebec Rifles), C.E.F. — QUEBEC CITY
The battalion, which is perpetuated by "The Royal Rifles of Canada", was disbanded in the United Kingdom and its' personnel incorporated within a "reserve battalion" for further training prior to their being posted to France as reinforcements for battalions of the "Canadian Corps" in the field. (Note that "The Royal Rifles of Canada" was disbanded in 1966.)
Battle Honour: THE GREAT WAR, 1916

172nd Infantry Battalion (Rocky Mountain Rangers), C.E.F. — KAMLOOPS, British Columbia
The battalion, which is perpetuated by "The Rocky Mountain Rangers", was disbanded in the United Kingdom and its' personnel incorporated within a "reserve battalion" for further training prior to their being posted to France as reinforcements for battalions of the "Canadian Corps" in the field.
Battle Honour: THE GREAT WAR, 1916-1917

173rd Infantry Battalion (Canadian Highlanders), C.E.F. — HAMILTON, Ontario
The battalion, which is perpetuated by "The Argyll and Sutherland Highlanders of Canada", was disbanded in the United Kingdom and its' personnel incorporated within a "reserve battalion" for further training prior to their being posted to France as reinforcements for battalions of the "Canadian Corps" in the field.
Battle Honour: THE GREAT WAR, 1916-1917

174th Infantry Battalion (Cameron Highlanders of Canada), C.E.F. — WINNIPEG, Manitoba
The battalion, which is perpetuated by "The Queen's Own Cameron Highlanders of Canada", was disbanded in the United Kingdom and its' personnel incorporated within a "reserve battalion" for further training prior to their being posted to France as reinforcements for battalions of the "Canadian Corps" in the field.
Battle Honour: THE GREAT WAR, 1917

175th Infantry Battalion, C.E.F. — MEDICINE HAT, Alberta
The battalion, which is perpetuated by "The South Alberta Light Horse", was disbanded in the United Kingdom and its' personnel incorporated within a "reserve battalion" for further training prior to their being posted to France as reinforcements for battalions of the "Canadian Corps" in the field.
Battle Honour: THE GREAT WAR, 1916-1917

176th Infantry Battalion (Niagara Rangers), C.E.F. — ST. CATHARINES, Ontario
The battalion, which is perpetuated by "The Lincoln and Welland Regiment", was disbanded in the United Kingdom and its' personnel incorporated within a "reserve battalion" for further training prior to their being posted to France as reinforcements for battalions of the "Canadian Corps" in the field.
Battle Honour: THE GREAT WAR, 1917

177th Infantry Battalion (Simcoe Foresters), C.E.F. — BARRIE, Ontario
The battalion, which is perpetuated by "The Grey and Simcoe Foresters", was disbanded in the United Kingdom and its' personnel incorporated within a "reserve battalion" for further training prior to their being posted to France as reinforcements for battalions of the "Canadian Corps" in the field.
Battle Honour: THE GREAT WAR, 1917

178th (Canadien-Francais) Infantry Battalion, C.E.F. — VICTORIAVILLE, Quebec
The battalion, which is perpetuated by the "12ieme Regiment Blinde du Canada (Milice)", was disbanded in the United Kingdom and its' personnel incorporated within a "reserve battalion" for further training prior to their being posted to France as reinforcements for battalions of the "Canadian Corps" in the field.
Battle Honour: THE GREAT WAR, 1917

179th Infantry Battalion (Cameron Highlanders of Canada), C.E.F. — WINNIPEG, Manitoba
The battalion, which is perpetuated by "The Queen's Own Cameron Highlanders of Canada", was disbanded in the United Kingdom and its' personnel incorporated within a "reserve battalion" for further training prior to their being posted to France as reinforcements for battalions of the "Canadian Corps" in the field.
Battle Honour: THE GREAT WAR, 1916

180th (Sportsmen's) Infantry Battlion, C.E.F. — TORONTO, Ontario
The battalion, which is perpetuated by "The Irish Regiment of Canada", was disbanded in the United Kingdom and its' personnel incorporated within a "reserve battalion" for further training prior to their being posted to France as reinforcements for battalions of the "Canadian Corps" in the field. (Note that "The Irish Regiment of Canada" was disbanded in 1965.)
Battle Honour: THE GREAT WAR, 1916-1917

181st Infantry Battalion, C.E.F. — BRANDON, Manitoba
The battalion, which is perpetuated by "The Manitoba Rangers", was disbanded in the United Kingdom and its' personnel incorporated within a "reserve battalion" for further training prior to their being posted to France as reinforcements for battalions of the "Canadian Corps" in the field. (Note that "The Manitoba Rangers" was converted in 1936 and re-designated "26 Field Brigade (The Manitoba Rangers), R.C.A.".)
Battle Honour: THE GREAT WAR, 1917

182nd (County of Ontario) Infantry Battalion, C.E.F. — WHITBY, Ontario
The battalion, which is perpetuated by "The Ontario Regiment (R.C.A.C.)", was disbanded in the United Kingdom and its' personnel incorporated within a "reserve battalion" for further training prior to their being posted to France as reinforcements for battalions of the "Canadian Corps" in the field.
Battle Honour: THE GREAT WAR, 1917

183rd Infantry Battalion (Manitoba Beavers), C.E.F. — WINNIPEG, Manitoba
The battalion, which is not perpetuated, was disbanded in the United Kingdom and its' personnel incorporated within a "reserve battalion" for further training prior to their being posted to France as reinforcements for battalions of the "Canadian Corps" in the field.
Battle Honour: THE GREAT WAR, 1916-1917

184th Infantry Battalion, C.E.F. — WINNIPEG, Manitoba
The battalion, which is not perpetuated, was disbanded in the United Kingdom and its' personnel incorporated within a "reserve battalion" for further training prior to their being posted to France as reinforcements for battalions of the "Canadian Corps" in the field.
Battle Honour: THE GREAT WAR, 1916

185th Infantry Battalion (Cape Breton Highlanders), C.E.F. — HALIFAX, N.S.
The battalion, which is perpetuated by "2nd Battalion, The Nova Scotia Highlanders", was disbanded in the United Kingdom and its' personnel incorporated within a "reserve battalion" for further training prior to their being posted to France as reinforcements for battalions of the "Canadian Corps" in the field.
Battle Honour: THE GREAT WAR, 1916-1918

186th Infantry Battalion, C.E.F. —CHATHAM, Ontario
The battalion, which is perpetuated by "The Essex and Kent Scottish Regiment", was disbanded in the United Kingdom and its' personnel incorporated within a "reserve battalion" for further training prior to their being posted to France as reinforcements for battalions of the "Canadian Corps" in the field.
Battle Honour: THE GREAT WAR, 1917

187th (Central Alberta) Infantry Battalion, C.E.F. — RED DEER, Alberta
The battalion, which is perpetuated by "The South Alberta Light Horse", was disbanded in the United Kingdom and its' personnel incorporated within a "reserve battalion" for further training prior to their being posted to France as reinforcements for battalions of the "Canadian Corps" in the field.
Battle Honour: THE GREAT WAR, 1916-1917

188th (Saskatchewan) Infantry Battalion, C.E.F. — PRINCE ALBERT, Saskatchewan
The battalion, which is perpetuated by "The Yorkton Regiment", was disbanded in the United Kingdom and its' personnel incorporated within a "reserve battalion" for further training prior to their being posted to France as reinforcements for battalions of the "Canadian Corps" in the field. (Note that "The Yorkton Regiment" was converted in 1936 and re-designated "64 Field Battery, R.C.A.".)
Battle Honour: THE GREAT WAR, 1916-1917

189th Infantry Battalion, C.E.F. — FRAZIERVILLE, Quebec
The battalion, which is perpetuated by "Les Fusiliers du St-Laurent (5ieme Bataillon, Royal Vingt-Deuxieme Regiment (Milice)", was disbanded in the United Kingdom and its' personnel incorporated within a "reserve battalion" for further training prior to their being posted to France as reinforcements for battalions of the "Canadian Corps" in the field.
Battle Honour: THE GREAT WAR, 1916

190th Infantry Battalion (90th Rifles), C.E.F. — WINNIPEG, Manitoba
The battalion, which is perpetuated by "The Royal Winnipeg Rifles", was disbanded in the United Kingdom and its' personnel incorporated within a "reserve battalion" for further training prior to their being posted to France as reinforcements for battalions of the "Canadian Corps" in the field.
Battle Honour: THE GREAT WAR, 1917

191st (South Alberta) Infantry Battalion, C.E.F. — FORT MACLEOD, Alberta
The battalion, which is perpetuated by "The North Alberta Regiment", was disbanded in the United Kingdom and its' personnel incorporated within a "reserve battalion" for further training prior to their being posted to France as reinforcements for battalions of the "Canadian Corps" in the field. (Note that "The North Alberta Regiment" was disbanded in 1936.)
Battle Honour: THE GREAT WAR, 1917

192nd (Crow's Nest Pass) Infantry Battalion, C.E.F. — BLAIRMORE, Alberta
The battalion, which is perpetuated by "The North Alberta Regiment", was disbanded in the United Kingdom and its' personnel incorporated within a "reserve battalion" for further training prior to their being posted to France as reinforcements for battalions of the "Canadian Corps" in the field. (Note that "The North Alberta Regiment" was disbanded in 1936.)
Battle Honour: THE GREAT WAR, 1916

193rd Infantry Battalion (Nova Scotia Highlanders), C.E.F — TRURO, Nova Scotia
The battalion, which is perpetuated by "1st Battalion. The Nova Scotia Highlanders", was disbanded in the United Kingdom and its' personnel incorporated within a "reserve battalion" for further training prior to their being posted to France as reinforcements for battalions of the "Canadian Corps" in the field.
Battle Honour: THE GREAT WAR, 1916-1917

194th Infantry Battalion (Edmonton Highlanders), C.E.F. — EDMONTON, Alberta
The battalion, which is not perpetuated, was disbanded in the United Kingdom and its' personnel incorporated within a "reserve battalion" for further training prior to their being posted to France as reinforcements for battalions of the "Canadian Corps" in the field.
Battle Honour: THE GREAT WAR, 1916-1917

195th Infantry Battalion, C.E.F. — REGINA, Saskatchewan
The battalion, which is perpetuated by "The Regina Rifle Regiment", was disbanded in the United Kingdom and its' personnel incorporated within a "reserve battalion" for further training prior to their being posted to France as reinforcements for battalions of the "Canadian Corps" in the field.
Battle Honour: THE GREAT WAR, 1916

196th (Western Universities) Infantry Battalion, C.E.F. — WINNIPEG, Manitoba,
The battalion, which is not perpetuated, was disbanded in the United Kingdom and its' personnel incorporated within a "reserve battalion" for further training prior to their being posted to France as reinforcements for battalions of the "Canadian Corps" in the field.
Battle Honour: THE GREAT WAR, 1916-1917

197th Infantry Battalion (Vikings of Canada), C.E.F. — WINNIPEG, Manitoba
The battalion, which is not perpetuated, was disbanded in the United Kingdom and its' personnel incorporated within a "reserve battalion" for further training prior to their being posted to France as reinforcements for battalions of the "Canadian Corps" in the field.
Battle Honour: THE GREAT WAR, 1917

198th Infantry Battalion (Canadian Buffs), C.E.F. — TORONTO, Ontario
The battalion, which is perpetuated by "The Queen's Own Rifles of Canada", was disbanded in the United Kingdom and its' personnel incorporated within a "reserve battalion" for further training prior to their being posted to France as reinforcements for battalions of the "Canadian Corps" in the field.
Battle Honour: THE GREAT WAR, 1917-1918

199th Infantry Battalion (Irish-Canadian Rangers), C.E.F. — MONTREAL, Quebec
The battalion, which is perpetuated by "The Irish Canadian Rangers", was disbanded in the United Kingdom and its' personnel incorporated within a "reserve battalion" for further training prior to their being posted to France as reinforcements for battalions of the "Canadian Corps" in the field. (Note that "The Irish Canadian Rangers" was disbanded in 1936.)
Battle Honour: THE GREAT WAR, 1916-1917

200th Infantry Battalion, C.E.F. — WINNIPEG, Manitoba
The battalion, which is not perpetuated, was disbanded in the United Kingdom and its' personnel incorporated within a "reserve battalion" for further training prior to their being posted to France as reinforcements for battalions of the "Canadian Corps" in the field.
Battle Honour: THE GREAT WAR, 1917

201st Infantry Battalion (Toronto Light Infantry), C.E.F. — TORONTO, Ontario
The battalion, which is not perpetuated, was disbanded in Canada in 1916 and its' personnel incorporated within the "Central Ontario Regiment, C.E.F." for further training prior to their being forwarded to the United Kingdom and subsequent posting to France.

202nd (Sportmen's) Infantry Battalion, C.E.F. — EDMONTON, Alberta
The battalion, which is perpetuated by the "19th Alberta Dragoons", was disbanded in the United Kingdom and its' personnel incorporated within a "reserve battalion" for further training prior to their being posted to France as reinforcements for battalions of the "Canadian Corps" in the field. (Note that the "19th Alberta Dragoons" was disbanded in 1965.)
Battle Honour: THE GREAT WAR, 1916-1917

203rd Infantry Battalion (90th Rifles), C.E.F. — WINNIPEG, Manitoba
The battalion, which is perpetuated by "The Royal Winnipeg Rifles", was disbanded in the United Kingdom and its' personnel incorporated within a "reserve battalion" for further training prior to their being posted to France as reinforcements for battalions of the "Canadian Corps" in the field.
Battle Honour: THE GREAT WAR, 1916-1917

204th Infantry Battalion (The Beavers), C.E.F. — TORONTO, Ontario
The battalion, which is perpetuated by "The Royal Regiment of Canada", was disbanded in the United Kingdom and its' personnel incorporated within a "reserve battalion" for further training prior to their being posted to France as reinforcements for battalions of the "Canadian Corps" in the field.
Battle Honour: THE GREAT WAR, 1917

205th Infantry Battalion, C.E.F. — HAMILTON, Ontario
The battalion, which is perpetuated by "The Royal Hamilton Light Infantry (Wentworth Regiment)", was re-organized in Canada as a "draft-giving machine-gun battalion" which forwarded successive drafts to the "Canadian Machine-Gun Depot" in the United Kingdom for further training prior to their being posted to France as reinforcements for machine-gun battalions of the "Canadian Corps" in the field.

206th (Canadien-Francais) Infantry Battalion, C.E.F. — MONTREAL, Quebec
The battalion, which is perpetuated by "Le Regiment de Maisonneuve", was disbanded in Canada in 1916 and its' personnel incorporated within the "Quebec Regiment, C.E.F." for further training prior to their being forwarded to the United Kingdom and subsequent posting to France.

207th (Ottawa and Carleton) Infantry Battalion, C.E.F. — OTTAWA, Ontario
The battalion, which is perpetuated by "The Cameron Highlanders of Ottawa", was disbanded in the United Kingdom and its' personnel incorporated within a "reserve battalion" for further training prior to their being posted to France as reinforcements for battalions of the "Canadian Corps" in the field.
Battle Honour: THE GREAT WAR, 1917

208th (Canadian Irish) Infantry Battalion, C.E.F. — TORONTO, Ontario
The battalion, which is perpetuated by "The Irish Regiment of Canada", was disbanded in the United Kingdom and its' personnel incorporated within a "reserve battalion" for further training prior to their being posted to France as reinforcements for battalions of the "Canadian Corps" in the field. (Note that "The Irish Regiment of Canada" was disbanded in 1965.)
Battle Honour: THE GREAT WAR, 1917-1918

209th Infantry Battalion, C.E.F. — SWIFT CURRENT, Saskatchewan
The battalion, which is perpetuated by the "14th Canadian Hussars", was disbanded in the United Kingdom and its' personnel incorporated within a "reserve battalion" for further training prior to their being posted to France as reinforcements for battalions of the "Canadian Corps" in the field. (Note that the "14th Canadian Hussars" was disbanded in 1968.)
Battle Honour: THE GREAT WAR, 1916

210th Infantry Battalion (Frontiersmen), C.E.F. — MOOSE JAW, Saskatchewan
The battalion, which is not perpetuated, was disbanded in the United Kingdom and its' personnel incorporated within a "reserve battalion" for further training prior to their being posted to France as reinforcements for battalions of the "Canadian Corps" in the field.
Battle Honour: THE GREAT WAR, 1917

211th (American) Infantry Battalion, C.E.F. — VANCOUVER, British Columbia
The battalion, which is not perpetuated, was disbanded in the United Kingdom and its' personnel incorporated, along with those of the "218th (Edmonton Irish) Infantry Battalion, C.E.F.", within the "Canadian Railway Troops Depot" where they were re-organized as the "8th Battalion, Canadian Railway Troops, C.E.F." which fought in France as a unit of the "Canadian Corps".
Battle Honour: THE GREAT WAR, 1916-1917

212th (American) Infantry Battalion, C.E.F. — WINNIPEG, Manitoba
The battalion, which is not perpetuated, was disbanded in Canada in 1916 and its' personnel incorporated within the "Manitoba Regiment, C.E.F." for further training prior to their being forwarded to the United Kingdom and subsequent posting to France.

213th (American) Infantry Battalion, C.E.F. — TORONTO, Ontario
The battalion, which is not perpetuated, was disbanded in Canada in 1917 and its' personnel incorporated within the "Central Ontario Regiment, C.E.F." for further training prior to their being forwarded to the United Kingdom and subsequent posting to France.

214th Infantry Battalion, C.E.F. — WADENA, Saskatchewan
The battalion, which is not perpetuated, was disbanded in the United Kingdom and its' personnel incorporated within a "reserve battalion" for further training prior to their being posted to France as reinforcements for battalions of the "Canadian Corps" in the field.
Battle Honour: THE GREAT WAR, 1917

215th Infantry Battalion, C.E.F. — BRANTFORD, Ontario
The battalion, which is perpetuated by "The Dufferin and Haldimand Rifles of Canada", was disbanded in the United Kingdom and its' personnel incorporated within a "reserve battalion" for further training prior to their being posted to France as reinforcements for battalions of the "Canadian Corps" in the field. (Note that "The Dufferin and Haldimand Rifles of Canada" was converted in 1946 and re-designated "56 Light Anti-Aircraft Regiment (The Dufferin and Haldimand Rifles of Canada), R.C.A.".)
Battle Honour: THE GREAT WAR, 1917

216th (Bantam) Infantry Battalion, C.E.F. — TORONTO, Ontario
The battalion, which is perpetuated by "The Governor-General's Horse Guards", was disbanded in the United Kingdom and its' personnel incorporated within a "reserve battalion" for further training prior to their being posted to France as reinforcements for battalions of the "Canadian Corps" in the field.
Battle Honour: THE GREAT WAR, 1917

217th Infantry Battalion, C.E.F. — MOOSOMIN, Saskatchewan
The battalion, which is perpetuated by "The Assiniboia Regiment", was disbanded in the United Kingdom and its' personnel incorporated within a "reserve battalion" for further training prior to their being posted to France as reinforcements for battalions of the "Canadian Corps" in the field. (Note that "The Assiniboia Regiment" was converted in 1936 and re-designated "22 (Assiniboia) Field Brigade, R.C.A.".)
Battle Honour: THE GREAT WAR, 1917

218th (Edmonton Irish) Infantry Battalion, C.E.F. — EDMONTON, Alberta
The battalion, which is not perpetuated, was disbanded in the United Kingdom and its' personnel incorporated, along with those of the "211th (American) Infantry Battalion, C.E.F.", within the "Canadian Railway Troops Depot" where they were re-organized as the "8th Battalion, Canadian Railway Troops, C.E.F." which fought in France as a unit of the "Canadian Corps".
Battle Honour: THE GREAT WAR, 1916-1917

219th Infantry Battalion (Nova Scotia Highlanders), C.E.F. — HALIFAX, N.S.
The battalion, which is perpetuated by "The West Nova Scotia Regiment", was disbanded in the United Kingdom and its' personnel incorporated within a "reserve battalion" for further training prior to their being posted to France as reinforcements for battalions of the "Canadian Corps" in the field.
Battle Honour: THE GREAT WAR, 1916-1917

220th Infantry Battalion (York Rangers), C.E.F. — TORONTO, Ontario
The battalion, which is perpetuated by "The Queen's York Rangers (1st American Regiment) (R.C.A.C.)", was disbanded in the United Kingdom and its' personnel incorporated within a "reserve battalion" for further training prior to their being posted to France as reinforcements for battalions of the "Canadian Corps" in the field.
Battle Honour: THE GREAT WAR, 1917

221st Infantry Battalion, C.E.F. — WINNIPEG, Manitoba
The battalion, which is not perpetuated, was disbanded in the United Kingdom and its' personnel incorporated within a "reserve battalion" for further training prior to their being posted to France as reinforcements for battalions of the "Canadian Corps" in the field.
Battle Honour: THE GREAT WAR, 1917

222nd Infantry Battalion (90th Rifles) C.E.F.— WINNIPEG, Manitoba
The battalion, which is perpetuated by "The Royal Winnipeg Rifles", was disbanded in the United Kingdom and its' personnel incorporated within a "reserve battalion" for further training prior to their being posted to France as reinforcements for battalions of the "Canadian Corps" in the field.
Battle Honour: THE GREAT WAR, 1916-1917

223rd (Scandinavian) Infantry Battalion, C.E.F. — WINNIPEG, Manitoba
The battalion, which is not perpetuated, was disbanded in the United Kingdom and its' personnel incorporated within a "reserve battalion" for further training prior to their being posted to France as reinforcements for battalions of the "Canadian Corps" in the field.
Battle Honour: THE GREAT WAR, 1917

224th Infantry Battalion, C.E.F. — OTTAWA, Ontario
The battalion, which is not perpetuated, was re-organized in the United Kingdom and re-designated "224th Forestry Battalion, C.E.F." which was subsequently incorporated within the "Canadian Forestry Corps, C.E.F.".
Battle Honour: THE GREAT WAR, 1916

225th (Kootenay) Infantry Battalion, C.E.F. — FERNIE, British Columbia
The battalion, which is perpetuated by "The Kootenay Regiment", was disbanded in the United Kingdom and its' personnel incorporated within a "reserve battalion" for further training prior to their being posted to France as reinforcements for battalions of the "Canadian Corps" in the field. (Note that "The Kootenay Regiment" was converted in 1936 and re-designated "24 (Kootenay) Field Brigade, R.C.A.".)
Battle Honour: THE GREAT WAR, 1917

226th Infantry Battalion (Men of the North), C.E.F. — DAUPHIN, Manitoba
The battalion, which is perpetuated by "The Royal Winnipeg Rifles", was disbanded in the United Kingdom and its' personnel incorporated within a "reserve battalion" for further training prior to their being posted to France as reinforcements for battalions of the "Canadian Corps" in the field.
Battle Honour: THE GREAT WAR, 1916-1917

227th Infantry Battalion (Men of the North), C.E.F. — SAULT STE. MARIE, Ontario
The battalion, which is perpetuated by "The Sault Ste. Marie and Sudbury Regiment", was disbanded in the United Kingdom and its' personnel incorporated within a "reserve battalion" for further training prior to their being posted to France as reinforcements for battalions of the "Canadian Corps" in the field. (Note that "The Sault Ste. Marie and Sudbury Regiment" was converted in 1946 and re-organized as "49 (Sault Ste. Marie) Heavy Anti-Aircraft Regiment, R.C.A." and "58 (Sudbury) Light Anti-Aircraft Regiment, R.C.A.".)
Battle Honour: THE GREAT WAR, 1917

228th Infantry Battalion (Northern Pioneers), C.E.F. — NORTH BAY, Ontario
The battalion, which is perpetuated by "The Algonquin Regiment", was re-organized in the United Kingdom and re-designated "6th Battalion, Canadian Railway Troops, C.E.F." which fought in France as a unit of the "Canadian Corps".
Battle Honour: FRANCE AND FLANDERS, 1917-1918

229th (South Saskatchewan) Infantry Battalion, C.E.F. — MOOSE JAW, Saskatchewan
The battalion, which is not perpetuated, was disbanded in the United Kingdom and its' personnel incorporated within a "reserve battalion" for further training prior to their being posted to France as reinforcements for battalions of the "Canadian Corps" in the field.
Battle Honour: THE GREAT WAR, 1917

230th Infantry Battalion (Voltigeurs Canadien-Francais), C.E.F. — HULL, Quebec
The battalion, which is perpetuated by "Le Regiment de Hull (R.C.A.C.)", was re-organized in the United Kingdom and re-designated "230th Forestry Battalion, C.E.F." which was subsequently incorporated within the "Canadian Forestry Corps, C.E.F.".
Battle Honour: THE GREAT WAR, 1917

231st Infantry Battalion (Seaforth Highlanders), C.E.F. — VANCOUVER, British Columbia
The battalion, which is perpetuated by "The Seaforth Highlanders of Canada", was disbanded in the United Kingdom and its' personnel incorporated within a "reserve battalion" for further training prior to their being posted to France as reinforcements for battalions of the "Canadian Corps" in the field.
Battle Honour: THE GREAT WAR, 1917

232nd Infantry Battalion, C.E.F. — BATTLEFORD, Saskatchewan
The battalion, which is perpetuated by "The North Saskatchewan Regiment", was disbanded in the United Kingdom and its' personnel incorporated within a "reserve battalion" for further training prior to their being posted to France as reinforcements for battalions of the "Canadian Corps" in the field.
Battle Honour: THE GREAT WAR, 1917

233rd Infantry Battalion, C.E.F. — EDMONTON, Alberta
The battalion, which is not perpetuated, was disbanded in Canada in 1917 and its' personnel incorporated within the "Alberta Regiment, C.E.F." for further training prior to their being forwarded to the United Kingdom and subsequent posting to France.

234th (Peel) Infantry Battalion, C.E.F. — TORONTO, Ontario
The battalion, which is perpetuated by "The Lorne Scots (Peel, Dufferin and Halton Regiment)", was disbanded in the United Kingdom and its' personnel incorporated within a "reserve battalion" for further training prior to their being posted to France as reinforcements for battalions of the "Canadian Corps" in the field.
Battle Honour: THE GREAT WAR, 1917

235th Infantry Battalion, C.E.F. — BELLEVILLE, Ontario
The battalion, which is perpetuated by "The Hastings and Prince Edward Regiment", was disbanded in the United Kingdom and its' personnel incorporated within a "reserve battalion" for further training prior to their being posted to France as reinforcements for battalions of the "Canadian Corps" in the field.
Battle Honour: THE GREAT WAR, 1917

236th Infantry Battalion (McLean Highlanders), C.E.F. — FREDERICTON, New Brunswick
The battalion, which is perpetuated by "1st Battalion, The Royal New Brunswick Regiment", was disbanded in the United Kingdom and its' personnel incorporated within a "reserve battalion" for further training prior to their being posted to France as reinforcements for battalions of the "Canadian Corps" in the field.
Battle Honour: THE GREAT WAR, 1917-1918

237th (American) Infantry Battalion, C.E.F. — SUSSEX, New Brunswick
The battalion, which is not perpetuated, was disbanded in Canada in 1916 and its' personnel incorporated within the "New Brunswick Regiment, C.E.F." for further training prior to their being forwarded to the United Kingdom and subsequent posting to France.

238th Infantry Battalion, C.E.F. — VALCARTIER, Quebec
The battalion, which is not perpetuated, was re-organized in the United Kingdom and re-designated "238th Forestry Battalion, C.E.F." which was subsequently incorporated within the "Canadian Forestry Corps, C.E.F.".
Battle Honour: THE GREAT WAR, 1916

239th Infantry Battalion, C.E.F. — WINDSOR, Nova Scotia
The battalion, which is not perpetuated, was re-organized in Canada in 1916 and re-designated "3rd Battalion, Canadian Railway Troops, C.E.F." which fought in France as a unit of the "Canadian Corps".

240th (Lanark and Renfrew) Infantry Battalion, C.E.F. — RENFREW, Ontario
The battalion, which is perpetuated by "The Lanark and Renfrew Scottish Regiment", was disbanded in the United Kingdom and its' personnel incorporated within a "reserve battalion" for further training prior to their being posted to France as reinforcements for battalions of the "Canadian Corps" in the field.
Battle Honour: THE GREAT WAR, 1917

241st Infantry Battalion (Canadian Scottish Borderers), C.E.F. — WINDSOR, Ontario
The battalion, which is perpetuated by "The Essex and Kent Scottish Regiment", was disbanded in the United Kingdom and its' personnel incorporated within a "reserve battalion" for further training prior to their being posted to France as reinforcements for battalions of the "Canadian Corps" in the field.
Battle Honour: THE GREAT WAR, 1917

242nd Infantry Battalion, C.E.F. — MONTREAL, Quebec
The battalion, which is not perpetuated, was re-organized in the United Kingdom and re-designated "242nd Forestry Battalion, C.E.F." which was subsequently incorporated within the "Canadian Forestry Corps, C.E.F.".
Battle Honour: THE GREAT WAR, 1916-1917

243rd Infantry Battalion, C.E.F. — PRINCE ALBERT, Saskatchewan
The battalion, which is not perpetuated, was disbanded in the United Kingdom and its' personnel incorporated within a "reserve battalion" for further training prior to their being posted to France as reinforcements for battalions of the "Canadian Corps" in the field.
Battle Honour: THE GREAT WAR, 1917

244th (Kitchener's Own) Infantry Battalion, C.E.F. — MONTREAL, Quebec
The battalion, which is perpetuated by "The Victoria Rifles of Canada", was disbanded in the United Kingdom and its' personnel incorporated within a "reserve battalion" for further training prior to their being posted to France as reinforcements for battalions of the "Canadian Corps" in the field. (Note that "The Victoria Rifles of Canada" was disbanded in 1965.)
Battle Honour: THE GREAT WAR, 1917

245th Infantry Battalion (Montreal Grenadiers), C.E.F. — MONTREAL, Quebec
The battalion, which is perpetuated by "The Canadian Grenadier Guards (6th Battalion, The Canadian Guards)", was disbanded in the United Kingdom and its' personnel incorporated within a "reserve battalion" for further training prior to their being posted to France as reinforcements for battalions of the "Canadian Corps" in the field.
Battle Honour: THE GREAT WAR, 1917

246th Infantry Battalion (Nova Scotia Highlanders), C.E.F. — HALIFAX, Nova Scotia
The battalion, which is perpetuated by "1st Battalion, The Nova Scotia Highlanders", was disbanded in the United Kingdom and its' personnel incorporated within a "reserve battalion" for further training prior to their being posted to France as reinforcements for battalions of the "Canadian Corps" in the field.
Battle Honour: THE GREAT WAR, 1917

247th (Victoria and Haliburton) Infantry Battalion, C.E.F. — PETERBOROUGH, Ontario
The battalion, which is perpetuated by "The Prince of Wales' Rangers (Peterborough Regiment)", was disbanded in Canada in 1917 and its' personnel incorporated within the "Central Ontario Regiment, C.E.F." for further training prior to their being forwarded to the United Kingdom and subsequent posting to France. (Note that "The Prince of Wales' Rangers (Peterborough Regiment)" was converted in 1946 and re-designated "50 Heavy Anti-Aircraft Regiment (The Prince of Wales' Rangers), R.C.A.".)

248th Infantry Battalion, C.E.F. — OWEN SOUND, Ontario
The battalion, which is perpetuated by "The Grey and Simcoe Foresters", was disbanded in the United Kingdom and its' personnel incorporated within a "reserve battalion" for further training prior to their being posted to France as reinforcements for battalions of the "Canadian Corps" in the field.
Battle Honour: THE GREAT WAR, 1917

249th Infantry Battalion, C.E.F. — REGINA, Saskatchewan
The battalion, which is not perpetuated, was disbanded in the United Kingdom and its' personnel incorporated within a "reserve battalion" for further training prior to their being posted to France as reinforcements for battalions of the "Canadian Corps" in the field.
Battle Honour: THE GREAT WAR, 1918

250th Infantry Battalion, C.E.F. — WINNIPEG, Manitoba
The battalion, which is not perpetuated, was disbanded in Canada in 1917 and its' personnel incorporated within the "Manitoba Regiment, C.E.F." for further training prior to their being forwarded to the United Kingdom and subsequent posting to France.

251st (Good Fellows) Infantry Battalion, C.E.F. — WINNIPEG, Manitoba
The battalion, which is not perpetuated, was disbanded in Canada in 1917 and its' personnel incorporated within the "Manitoba Regiment, C.E.F." for further training prior to their being forwarded to the United Kingdom and subsequent posting to France.

252nd Infantry Battalion, C.E.F. — LINDSAY, Ontario
The battalion, which is perpetuated by "The Victoria and Haliburton Regiment", was disbanded in the United Kingdom and its' personnel incorporated within a "reserve battalion" for further training prior to their being posted to France as reinforcements for battalions of the "Canadian Corps" in the field. (Note that "The Victoria and Haliburton Regiment" was disbanded in 1936 and its' personnel absorbed by "45 Field Battery, R.C.A." which then received the county designation "VICTORIA".)
Battle Honour: THE GREAT WAR, 1917

253rd (Queen's University Highland) Infantry Battalion, C.E.F. — KINGSTON, Ontario
The battalion, which is perpetuated by "The Princess of Wales' Own Regiment", was disbanded in the United Kingdom and its' personnel incorporated within a "reserve battalion" for further training prior to their being posted to France as reinforcements for battalions of the "Canadian Corps" in the field.
Battle Honour: THE GREAT WAR, 1917

254th (Quinte's Own) Infantry Battalion, C.E.F. — BELLEVILLE, Ontario
The battalion, which is perpetuated by "The Hastings and Prince Edward Regiment", was disbanded in the United Kingdom and its' personnel incorporated within a "reserve battalion" for further training prior to their being posted to France as reinforcements for battalions of the "Canadian Corps" in the field.
Battle Honour: THE GREAT WAR, 1917

255th Infantry Battalion (Queen's Own Rifles of Canada), C.E.F. — TORONTO, Ontario
The battalion, which is perpetuated by "The Queen's Own Rifles of Canada", was disbanded in the United Kingdom and its' personnel incorporated within a "reserve battalion" for further training prior to their being posted to France as reinforcements for battalions of the "Canadian Corps" in the field.
Battle Honour: THE GREAT WAR, 1917

256th Infantry Battalion, C.E.F. — TORONTO, Ontario
The battalion, which is perpetuated by "The Algonquin Regiment", was disbanded in Canada in 1917 and its' personnel forwarded to the "Canadian Railway Troops Depot" in the United Kingdom where they were re-organized as the "10th Battalion, Canadian Railway Troops, C.E.F." which fought in France as a unit of the "Canadian Corps".

257th Infantry Battalion, C.E.F. — OTTAWA, Ontario
The battalion, which is not perpetuated, was disbanded in Canada in 1917 and its' personnel forwarded to the "Canadian Railway Troops Depot" in the United Kingdom where they were re-organized as the "7th Battalion, Canadian Railway Troops, C.E.F." which fought in France as a unit of the "Canadian Corps".

258th Infantry Battalion, C.E.F. — QUEBEC CITY
The battalion, which is not perpetuated, was disbanded in the United Kingdom and its' personnel incorporated within a "reserve battalion" for further training prior to their being posted to France as reinforcements for battalions of the "Canadian Corps" in the field.
Battle Honour: THE GREAT WAR, 1917

259th Infantry Battalion, C.S.E.F.
The battalion, which is not perpetuated, served at Vladivostok as a unit of the "Canadian Siberian Expeditionary Force".
Battle Honour: SIBERIA, 1918-1919

260th Infantry Battalion, C.S.E.F.
The battalion, which is not perpetuated, served at Vladivostok as a unit of the "Canadian Siberian Expeditionary Force".
Battle Honour: SIBERIA, 1918-1919

1st Regiment, Canadian Mounted Rifles, C.E.F. — BRANDON, Manitoba
The Regiment, which is perpetuated by "The North Saskatchewan Regiment", fought in France as a unit of the "1st Mounted Rifle Brigade" until 1916 when it was re-designated "1st Canadian Mounted Rifle Battalion, C.E.F." which fought as a unit of the "8th Infantry Brigade".

2nd Regiment, Canadian Mounted Rifles, C.E.F. — VICTORIA, British Columbia
The Regiment, which is perpetuated by "The British Columbia Dragoons", fought in France as a unit of the "1st Mounted Rifle Brigade" until 1916 when it was re-designated "2nd Canadian Mounted Rifle Battalion, C.E.F." which fought as a unit of the "8th Infantry Brigade".

3rd Regiment, Canadian Mounted Rifles, C.E.F. — MEDICINE HAT, Alberta
The Regiment, which is perpetuated by the "19th Alberta Dragoons", fought in France as a unit of the "1st Mounted Rifle Brigade" until 1916 when it was disbanded and its' personnel absorbed by both the "1st" and "2nd" Canadian Mounted Rifle Battalions. (Note that the "19th Alberta Dragoons" was disbanded in 1965.)
Major Battle Honour: FRANCE AND FLANDERS, 1915-1916

4th Regiment, Canadian Mounted Rifles, C.E.F. — TORONTO, Ontario
The Regiment, which is perpetuated by "The Governor-General's Horse Guards", fought in France as a unit of the "2nd Mounted Rifle Brigade" until 1916 when it was re-designated "4th Canadian Mounted Rifle Battalion, C.E.F." which fought as a unit of the "8th Infantry Brigade".

5th Regiment, Canadian Mounted Rifles, C.E.F. — SHERBROOKE, Quebec
The Regiment, which is perpetuated by "The Sherbrooke Hussars", fought in France as a unit of the "2nd Mounted Rifle Brigade" until 1916 when it was redesignated "5th Canadian Mounted Rifle Battalion, C.E.F." which fought as a unit of the "8th Infantry Brigade".

6th Regiment, Canadian Mounted Rifles, C.E.F. — AMHERST, Nova Scotia
The Regiment, which is perpetuated by the "8th Canadian Hussars (Princess Louise's) (Militia)", fought in France as a unit of the "2nd Mounted Rifle Brigade" until 1916 when it was disbanded and its' personnel absorbed by both the "4th" and "5th" Canadian Mounted Rifle Battalions.
Major Battle Honour: FRANCE AND FLANDERS, 1915-1916

7th Regiment, Canadian Mounted Rifles, C.E.F. — LONDON, Ontario
The Regiment, which is perpetuated by "The Governor-General's Horse Guards", was re-organized in the United Kingdom as the "Canadian Mounted Rifles Depot". (Note that "A" Squadron of the Regiment was detached while still in Canada and re-designated "2nd Divisional Cavalry Squadron, C.E.F." which fought in France as a sub-unit of the "Canadian Light Horse".)
Battle Honour: THE GREAT WAR, 1915-1916

8th Regiment, Canadian Mounted Rifles, C.E.F. — OTTAWA, Ontario
The Regiment, which is perpetuated by the "4th Princess Louise Dragoon Guards", was disbanded in the United Kingdom and its' personnel incorporated within a "reserve battalion" for further training prior to their being posted to France as reinforcements for battalions of the "Canadian Corps" in the field.
Battle Honour: THE GREAT WAR, 1915-1916

9th Regiment, Canadian Mounted Rifles, C.E.F. — LLOYDMINSTER, Saskatchewan
The Regiment, which is perpetuated by "The North Saskatchewan Regiment", was disbanded in the United Kingdom and its' personnel incorporated within a "reserve battalion" for further training prior to their being posted to France as reinforcements for battalions of the "Canadian Corps" in the field.
Battle Honour: THE GREAT WAR, 1915-1916

10th Regiment, Canadian Mounted Rifles, C.E.F. — PORTAGE LA PRAIRIE, Manitoba
The Regiment, which is perpetuated by "The North Saskatchewan Regiment", was disbanded in the United Kingdom and its' personnel incorporated within a "reserve battalion" for further training prior to their being posted to France as reinforcements for battalions of the "Canadian Corps" in the field.
Battle Honour: THE GREAT WAR, 1915-1916

11th Regiment, Canadian Mounted Rifles, C.E.F. — VANCOUVER, British Columbia
The Regiment, which is perpetuated by "The British Columbia Dragoons", was disbanded in the United Kingdom and its' personnel incorporated within a "reserve battalion" for further training prior to their being posted to France as reinforcements for battalions of the "Canadian Corps" in the field.
Battle Honour: THE GREAT WAR, 1915-1916

12th Regiment, Canadian Mounted Rifles, C.E.F. — CALGARY, Alberta
The Regiment, which is perpetuated by "The South Alberta Light Horse", was disbanded in the United Kingdom and its' personnel incorporated within a "reserve battalion" for further training prior to their being posted to France as reinforcements for battalions of the "Canadian Corps" in the field.
Battle Honour: THE GREAT WAR, 1915-1916

13th Regiment, Canadian Mounted Rifles, C.E.F. — MEDICINE HAT, Alberta
The Regiment, which is perpetuated by "The South Alberta Light Horse", was disbanded in the United Kingdom and its' personnel incorporated within a "reserve battalion" for further training prior to their being posted to France as reinforcements for battalions of the "Canadian Corps" in the field.
Battle Honour: THE GREAT WAR, 1915-1916

1st Canadian Mounted Rifle Battalion, C.E.F.
The battalion fought in France as a unit of the "8th Infantry Brigade" and is perpetuated by "The North Saskatchewan Regiment".
Major Battle Honours:
VIMY RIDGE —FRANCE AND FLANDERS, 1915-1918

2nd Canadian Mounted Rifle Battalion, C.E.F.
The battalion fought in France as a unit of the "8th Infantry Brigade" and is perpetuated by "The British Columbia Dragoons".
Major Battle Honours:
VIMY RIDGE —FRANCE AND FLANDERS, 1915-1918

4th Canadian Mounted Rifle Battalion, C.E.F.
The battalion fought in France as a unit of the "8th Infantry Brigade" and it perpetuated by "The Governor-General's Horse Guards".
Major Battle Honours:
VIMY RIDGE —FRANCE AND FLANDERS, 1915-1918

5th Canadian Mounted Rifle Battalion, C.E.F.
The battalion fought in France as a unit of the "8th Infantry Brigade" and is perpetuated by "The Sherbrooke Hussars".
Major Battle Honours:
VIMY RIDGE —FRANCE AND FLANDERS, 1915-1918

The "1st Reserve Battalion" received personnel from battalions disbanded in the United Kingdom, in addition to personnel recruited through the "British Columbia Regiment, C.E.F." in Canada, for further training prior to their being posted to France as reinforcements for battalions of the "Canadian Corps" in the field.

The "2nd Reserve Battalion" received personnel from battalions disbanded in the United Kingdom, in addition to personnel recruited through the "2nd Central Ontario Regiment, C.E.F." in Canada, for further training prior to their being posted to France as reinforcements for battalions of the "Canadian Corps" in the field.

The "3rd Reserve Battalion" received personnel from battalions disbanded in the United Kingdom, in addition to personnal recruited through the "1st Central Ontario Regiment, C.E.F." in Canada, for further training prior to their being posted to France as reinforcements for battalions of the "Canadian Corps" in the field.

The "4th Reserve Battalion" received personnel from battalions disbanded in the United Kingdom, in addition to personnel recruited through the "Western Ontario Regiment, C.E.F." in Canada, for further training prior to their being posted to France as reinforcements for battalions of the "Canadian Corps" in the field.

The "5th Reserve Battalion" received personnel from battalions disbanded in the United Kingdom, in addition to personnel recruited through the "1st Central Ontario Regiment, C.E.F." in Canada, for further training prior to their being posted to France as reinforcements for battalions of the "Canadian Corps" in the field.

The "6th Reserve Battalion" received personnel from battalions disbanded in the United Kingdom, in addition to personnel recruited through the "Eastern Ontario Regiment, C.E.F." in Canada, for further training prior to their being posted to France as reinforcements for battalions of the "Canadian Corps" in the field.

The "7th Reserve Battalion" received personnel from battalions disbanded in the United Kingdom, in addition to personnel recruited through the "Eastern Ontario Regiment, C.E.F." in Canada, for further training prior to their being posted to France as reinforcements for battalions of the "Canadian Corps" in the field.

The "8th Reserve Battalion, C.E.F." received personnel from battalions disbanded in the United Kingdom, in addition to personnel recruited through the "2nd Central Ontario Regiment, C.E.F." in Canada, for further training prior to their being posted to France as reinforcements for battalions of the "Canadian Corps" in the field.

The "9th Reserve Battalion" received personnel from battalions disbanded in the United Kingdom, in addition to personnel recruited through the "Alberta Regiment, C.E.F." in Canada, for further training prior to their being posted to France as reinforcements for battalions of the "Canadian Corps" in the field.

The "10th Reserve Battalion" received personnel from battalions disbanded in the United Kingdom, in addition to personnel recruited through the "2nd Quebec Regiment, C.E.F." in Canada, for further training prior to their being posted to France as reinforcements for battalions of the "Canadian Corps" in the field.

The "11th Reserve Battalion" received personnel from battalions disbanded in the United Kingdom, in addition to personnel recruited through the "Manitoba Regiment, C.E.F." in Canada, for further training prior to their being posted to France as reinforcements for battalions of the "Canadian Corps" in the field.

The "12th Reserve Battalion" received personnel from battalions disbanded in the United Kingdom, in addition to personnel recruited through the "1st Central Ontario Regiment, C.E.F." in Canada, for further training prior to their being posted to France as reinforcements for battalions of the "Canadian Corps" in the field.

The "13th Reserve Battalion" received personnel from battalions disbanded in the United Kingdom, in addition to personnel recruited through the "New Brunswick Regiment, C.E.F." in Canada, for further training prior to their being posted to France as reinforcements for battalions of the "Canadian Corps" in the field.

The "14th Reserve Battalion" received personnel from battalions disbanded in the United Kingdom, in addition to personnel recruited through the "Manitoba Regiment, C.E.F." in Canada, for further training prior to their being posted to France as reinforcements for battalions of the "Canadian Corps" in the field.

The "15th Reserve Battalion" received personnel from battalions disbanded in the United Kingdom, in addition to personnel recruited through the "Saskatchewan Regiment, C.E.F." in Canada, for further training prior to their being posted to France as reinforcements for battalions of the "Canadian Corps" in the field.

The "16th Reserve Battalion" received personnel from battalions disbanded in the United Kingdom, in addition to personnel recruited through the "British Columbia Regiment, C.E.F." in Canada, for further training prior to their being posted to France as reinforcements for battalions of the "Canadian Corps" in the field.

The "17th Reserve Battalion" received personnel from battalions disbanded in the United Kingdom, in addition to personnel recruited through the "Nova Scotia Regiment, C.E.F." in Canada, for further training prior to their being posted to France as reinforcements for battalions of the "Canadian Corps" in the field.

The "18th Reserve Battalion" received personnel from battalions disbanded in the United Kingdom, in addition to personnel recruited through the "Manitoba Regiment, C.E.F." in Canada, for further training prior to their being posted to France as reinforcements for battalions of the "Canadian Corps" in the field.

The "19th Reserve Battalion" received personnel from battalions disbanded in the United Kingdom, in addition to personnel recruited through the "Saskatchewan Regiment, C.E.F." in Canada, for further training prior to their being posted to France as reinforcements for battalions of the "Canadian Corps" in the field.

The "20th Reserve Battalion" received personnel from battalions disbanded in the United Kingdom, in addition to personnel recruited through the "1st Quebec Regiment, C.E.F." in Canada, for further training prior to their being posted to France as reinforcements for battalions of the "Canadian Corps" in the field.

The "21st Reserve Battalion" received personnel from battalions disbanded in the United Kingdom, in addition to personnel recruited through the "Alberta Regiment, C.E.F." in Canada, for further training prior to their being posted to France as reinforcements for battalions of the "Canadian Corps" in the field.

The "22nd Reserve Battalion" received personnel from battalions disbanded in the United Kingdom, in addition to personnel recruited through the "1st Quebec Regiment, C.E.F." in Canada, for further training prior to their being posted to France as reinforcements for battalions of the "Canadian Corps" in the field.

The "23rd Reserve Battalion" received personnel from battalions disbanded in the United Kingdom, in addition to personnel recruited through the "1st Quebec Regiment, C.E.F." in Canada, for further training prior to their being posted to France as reinforcements for battalions of the "Canadian Corps" in the field.

The "24th Reserve Battalion" received personnel from battalions disbanded in the United Kingdom, in addition to personnel recruited through the "British Columbia Regiment, C.E.F." in Canada, for further training prior to their being posted to France as reinforcements for battalions of the "Canadian Corps" in the field.

The "25th Reserve Battalion" received personnel from battalions disbanded in the United Kingdom, in addition to personnel recruited through the "Western Ontario Regiment, C.E.F." in Canada, for further training prior to their being posted to France as reinforcements for battalions of the "Canadian Corps" in the field.

The "26th Reserve Battalion" received personnel from battalions disbanded in the United Kingdom, in addition to personnel recruited through the "Nova Scotia Regiment, C.E.F." in Canada, for further training prior to their being posted to France as reinforcements for battalions of the "Canadian Corps" in the field.

The "1st Machine-Gun Company, C.E.F." was incorporated within the "1st Battalion, C.M.G.C., C.E.F." in 1918.

The "2nd Machine-Gun Company, C.E.F." was incorporated within the 1st Battalion, C.M.G.C., C.E.F." in 1918.

The "3rd Machine-Gun Company, C.E.F." was incorporated within the "1st Battalion, C.M.G.C., C.E.F." in 1918.

The "4th Machine-Gun Company, C.E.F." was incorporated within the 2nd Battalion, C.M.G.C., C.E.F." in 1918.

The "5th Machine-Gun Company, C.E.F." was incorporated within the 2nd Battalion, C.M.G.C., C.E.F." in 1918.

The "6th Machine-Gun Company, C.E.F." was incorporated within the 2nd Battalion, C.M.G.C., C.E.F." in 1918.

The "7th Machine-Gun Company, C.E.F." was incorporated within the 3rd Battalion, C.M.G.C., C.E.F." in 1918.

The "8th Machine-Gun Company, C.E.F." was incorporated within the 3rd Battalion, C.M.G.C., C.E.F." in 1918.

The "9th Machine-Gun Company, C.E.F." was incorporated within the 3rd Battalion, C.M.G.C., C.E.F." in 1918.

The "10th Machine-Gun Company, C.E.F." was incorporated within the 4th Battalion, C.M.G.C., C.E.F." in 1918.

The "11th Machine-Gun Company, C.E.F." was incorporated within the 4th Battalion, C.M.G.C., C.E.F." in 1918.

The "12th Machine-Gun Company, C.E.F." was incorporated within the 4th Battalion, C.M.G.C., C.E.F." in 1918.

The "13th Machine-Gun Company, C.E.F." was incorporated within the 1st Battalion, C.M.G.C., C.E.F." in 1918.

The "14th Machine-Gun Company, C.E.F." was incorporated within the 2nd Battalion, C.M.G.C., C.E.F." in 1918.

The "15th Machine-Gun Company, C.E.F." was incorporated within the 3rd Battalion, C.M.G.C., C.E.F." in 1918.

The "16th Machine-Gun Company, C.E.F." was incorporated within the 4th Battalion, C.M.G.C., C.E.F." in 1918.

The "17th Machine-Gun Company, C.E.F." was incorporated within the "2nd Motor Machine-Gun Brigade, C.M.G.C., C.E.F." as "B" Battery.

The "18th Machine-Gun Company, C.E.F." was incorporated within the "1st Motor Machine-Gun Brigade, C.M.G.C., C.E.F." as "D" Battery.

The "19th Machine-Gun Company, C.E.F." was incorporated within the "2nd Motor Machine-Gun Brigade, C.M.G.C., C.E.F." as "D" Battery.

The "20th Machine-Gun Company, C.E.F." served at Vladivostok as a unit of the Canadian Siberian Expeditionary Force (1918-1919).

1st Battalion, Canadian Machine-Gun Corps, C.E.F.
The battalion fought in France as a unit of the "1st Canadian Division" and is perpetuated by "The Irish Regiment of Canada". (Note that "The Irish Regiment of Canada" was disbanded in 1965.)
Major Battle Honours:
PURSUIT TO MONS — FRANCE AND FLANDERS, 1918

2nd Battalion, Canadian Machine-Gun Corps, C.E.F.
The battalion fought in France as a unit of the "2nd Canadian Division" and is perpetuated by "4th Battalion, The Royal Canadian Regiment (London and Oxford Fusiliers) (Militia)".
Major Battle Honours:
PURSUIT TO MONS — FRANCE AND FLANDERS, 1918

3rd Battalion, Canadian Machine-Gun Corps, C.E.F.
The battalion fought in France as a unit of the "3rd Canadian Division" and is perpetuated by "The Argyll and Sutherland Highlanders of Canada".
Major Battle Honours:
PURSUIT TO MONS — FRANCE AND FLANDERS, 1918

4th Battalion, Canadian Machine-Gun Corps, C.E.F.
The battalion fought in France as a unit of the "4th Canadian Division" and is perpetuated by "The Prince of Wales' Rangers (Peterborough Regiment)". (Note that "The Prince of Wales' Rangers (Peterborough Regiment)" was converted in 1946 and re-designated "50 Heavy Anti-Aircraft Regiment (The Prince of Wales' Rangers), R.C.A. (Reserve Force)".)
Major Battle Honours:
PURSUIT TO MONS — FRANCE AND FLANDERS, 1918

The "Automobile Machine-Gun Brigade, C.E.F." fought in France as a unit of the "1st Canadian Division" and was re-organized in 1916 as "A" and "B" Batteries of the "1st Motor Machine-Gun Brigade, C.M.G.C., C.E.F.".

"Borden's Motor Machine-Gun Battery, C.E.F." fought in France as a unit of the "2nd Canadian Division" and was re-organized in 1916 as "C" Battery of the "1st Motor Machine-Gun Brigade, C.M.G.C., C.E.F.".

"Eaton's Motor Machine-Gun Battery, C.E.F." fought in France as a unit of the "3rd Canadian Division" and was re-organized in 1916 as "A" Battery of the "2nd Motor Machine-Gun Brigade, C.M.G.C., C.E.F.".

The Yukon Motor Machine-Gun Battery, C.E.F." fought in France as a unit of the "4th Canadian Division" and was re-organized in 1916 as "C" Battery of the "2nd Motor Machine-Gun Brigade, C.M.G.C., C.E.F.".

1st Motor Machine-Gun Brigade, C.M.G.C., C.E.F.
"A" Battery was formed by the re-organization of "A" Battery of the "Automobile Machine-Gun Brigade, C.E.F.".
"B" Battery was formed by the re-organization of "B" Battery of the "Automobile Machine-Gun Brigade, C.E.F.".
"C" Battery was formed by the re-organization of "Borden's Motor Machine-Gun Battery, C.E.F.".
"D" Battery was formed by the re-organization of the "18th Machine-Gun Company, C.E.F.".
"E" Battery was formed from machine-gun reinforcements.
The Brigade fought in France as a unit of the "Canadian Corps" and is perpetuated by the "1st Armoured Car Regiment (Non-Permanent Active Militia)" which was incorporated within the "6th Duke of Connaught's Royal Canadian Hussars" (now "The Royal Canadian Hussars (Montreal)") in 1936.
Major Battle Honours:
VIMY RIDGE —FRANCE AND FLANDERS, 1915-1918

2nd Motor Machine-Gun Brigade, C.M.G.C., C.E.F.
"A" Battery was formed by the re-organization of "Eaton's Motor Machine-Gun Battery, C.E.F.".
"B" Battery was formed by the re-organization of the "17th Machine-Gun Company, C.E.F.
"C" Battery was formed by the re-organization of the "Yukon Motor Machine-Gun Battery, C.E.F.".
"D" Battery was formed by the re-organization of the "19th Machine-Gun Company, C.E.F.".
"E" Battery was formed from machine-gun reinforcements.
The Brigade fought in France as a unit of the "Canadian Corps" and is perpetuated by the "2nd Armoured Car Regiment (Non-Permanent Active Militia)" which was converted in 1946 and re-designated "Headquarters, 48 Anti-Tank Regiment, R.C.A. (Reserve Force)".
Major Battle Honours:
PURSUIT TO MONS — FRANCE AND FLANDERS, 1918

1st Battalion, Canadian Railway Troops, C.E.F.
The battalion was formed in 1917 by the re-designation of the "1st Railway Construction Battalion, C.E.F." which had been serving in France since the previous year.
Battle Honour: FRANCE AND FLANDERS, 1916-1918

2nd Battalion, Canadian Railway Troops, C.E.F.
The battalion was formed in 1917 by the conversion and re-designation of the "127th Infantry Battalion (York Rangers), C.E.F." which had fought in France since its' arrival that year.
Battle Honour: FRANCE AND FLANDERS, 1917-1918

3rd Battalion, Canadian Railway Troops, C.E.F.
The battalion was formed in Canada in 1917 by the conversion and re-designation of the "239th Infantry Battalion, C.E.F.".
Battle Honour: FRANCE AND FLANDERS, 1917-1918
4th Battalion, Canadian Railway Troops, C.E.F.

4th Battalion, Canadian Railway Troops, C.E.F.
The battalion was formed in 1917 at the "Canadian Railway Troops Depot" in the United Kingdom.
Battle Honour: FRANCE AND FLANDERS, 1917-1918

5th Battalion, Canadian Railway Troops, C.E.F.
The battalion was formed in 1917 at the "Canadian Railway Troops Depot" in the United Kingdom.
Battle Honour: FRANCE AND FLANDERS, 1917-1918

6th Battalion, Canadian Railway Troops, C.E.F.
The battalion was formed in the United Kingdom in 1917 by the conversion and re-designation of the "228th Infantry Battalion (Northern Pioneers), C.E.F.".
Battle Honour: FRANCE AND FLANDERS, 1917-1918

7th Battalion, Canadian Railway Troops, C.E.F.
The battalion was formed in 1917 at the "Canadian Railway Troops Depot" in the United Kingdom from personnel of the "257th Infantry Battalion, C.E.F." which had been disbanded in Canada.
Battle Honour: FRANCE AND FLANDERS, 1917-1918

8th Battalion, Canadian Railway Troops, C.E.F.
The battalion was formed at the "Canadian Railway Troops Depot" in the United Kingdom in 1917 from personnel of the "211th (American) Infantry Battalion, C.E.F." and the "218th (Edmonton Irish) Infantry Battalion, C.E.F." which had both been disbanded in 1917.
Battle Honour: FRANCE AND FLANDERS, 1917-1918

9th Battalion, Canadian Railway Troops, C.E.F.
The battalion was formed in 1917 by the conversion and re-designation of the "1st Pioneer Battalion, C.E.F." which had fought in France since its' arrival in 1916.
Battle Honour: FRANCE AND FLANDERS, 1916-1918

10th Battalion, Canadian Railway Troops, C.E.F.
The battalion was formed in 1917 at the "Canadian Railway Troops Depot" in the United Kingdom from personnel of the "256th Infantry Battalion, C.E.F." which had been disbanded in Canada.
Battle Honour: FRANCE AND FLANDERS, 1917-1918

11th Battalion, Canadian Railway Troops, C.E.F.
The battalion was formed in 1917 by the conversion and re-designation of the "3rd Labour Battalion, C.E.F." which had previously arrived in France.
Battle Honour: FRANCE AND FLANDERS, 1917-1918

12th Battalion, Canadian Railway Troops, C.E.F.
The battalion was formed in 1917 by the conversion and re-designation of the "2nd Labour Battalion, C.E.F." which had previously arrived in France.
Battle Honour: FRANCE AND FLANDERS, 1917-1918

13th Battalion, Canadian Railway Troops, C.E.F.
The battalion was formed in 1918 at the "Canadian Railway Troops Depot" in the United Kingdom.
Battle Honour: FRANCE AND FLANDERS, 1918